The Commons and a New Global Governance

LEUVEN GLOBAL GOVERNANCE

Series Editor: Jan Wouters, *KU Leuven, Belgium*

The Leuven Global Governance series comprises high-quality monographs and edited volumes dedicated to innovative research on global governance. The series covers a wide range of themes, from the EU and global multilateral governance to trade, sustainable development, peace and security, human rights, democracy and rule of law, private standards, and global commons. In full recognition of the complex issues involved, the series favours studies approaching global governance from a multidisciplinary, multi-level and multi-actor perspective.

Titles in the series include:

Global Governance and Democracy
A Multidisciplinary Analysis
Edited by Jan Wouters, Antoon Braeckman, Matthias Lievens and Emilie Bécault

The Contribution of International and Supranational Courts to the Rule of Law
Edited by Geert De Baere and Jan Wouters

Global Governance of Labor Rights
Assessing the Effectiveness of Transnational Public and Private Policy Initiatives
Edited by Axel Marx, Jan Wouters, Glenn Rayp and Laura Beke

Global Governance through Trade
EU Policies and Approaches
Edited by Jan Wouters, Axel Marx, Dylan Geraets and Bregt Natens

Regulating Shale Gas
The Challenge of Coherent Environmental and Energy Regulation
Leonie Reins

Access to Justice and International Organizations
The Case of Individual Victims of Human Rights Violations
Pierre Schmitt

Commercial Uses of Space and Space Tourism
Legal and Policy Aspects
Edited by Jan Wouters, Philip de Man and Rik Hansen

Chinese Perspectives on the International Rule of Law
Law and Politics in the One-Party State
Matthieu Burnay

The Commons and a New Global Governance
Edited by Samuel Cogolati and Jan Wouters

The Commons and a New Global Governance

Edited by

Samuel Cogolati

PhD Fellow of the Research Foundation – Flanders (FWO), Leuven Centre for Global Governance Studies and Institute for International Law, KU Leuven, Belgium

Jan Wouters

Full Professor of International Law and International Organizations, Jean Monnet Chair ad personam *EU and Global Governance, and Director, Leuven Centre for Global Governance Studies and Institute for International Law, KU Leuven, Belgium*

LEUVEN GLOBAL GOVERNANCE

EE Edward Elgar PUBLISHING

Cheltenham, UK • Northampton, MA, USA

Published by
Edward Elgar Publishing Limited
The Lypiatts
15 Lansdown Road
Cheltenham
Glos GL50 2JA
UK

Edward Elgar Publishing, Inc.
William Pratt House
9 Dewey Court
Northampton
Massachusetts 01060
USA

A catalogue record for this book
is available from the British Library

Library of Congress Control Number: 2018946031

This book is available electronically in the **Elgar**online
Law subject collection
DOI 10.4337/9781788118514

ISBN 978 1 78811 850 7 (cased)
ISBN 978 1 78811 851 4 (eBook)

Typeset by Servis Filmsetting Ltd, Stockport, Cheshire

Contents

Figures and tables

FIGURES

TABLE

Contributors

Michel Bauwens is the founder and director of the P2P Foundation and works in collaboration with a global group of researchers in the exploration of commons, peer production, governance, and property. He is also research director of CommonsTransition.org a platform for policy development aimed towards a society of the Commons and a founding member of the Commons Strategies Group, with Silke Helfrich and David Bollier, organizers of major global conferences on the commons and economics. He has (co-)published various books and reports in English, Dutch and French, such as 'Network Society and Future Scenarios for a Collaborative Economy' (with Vasilis Kostakis). Michel currently lives in Chiang Mai, Thailand and last spring, crafted a Commons Transition Plan for the city of Ghent in Belgium, after a similar project for the State of Ecuador in 2014. For the next three years he is also adviser to SMart, a fast growing European labour mutual for autonomous workers.

Maarja Beerkens is Assistant Professor at the Institute of Public Administration at Leiden University. Her research focuses on governance and public policy, with a special interest in the effects of market-based and self-regulatory policy instruments. Recently, she has stumbled on the complexities of globalization in public policy making, which has forced her to study the issues of global policy making, transnational networks, and stakeholder engagement. Currently she is studying the world-wide transition towards open access in science and she examines the interplay between bottom-up community initiatives, (trans)national policies, and the private academic publishing industry. Next to academic work, she has an interest in applied research and policy advising. She has worked for the World Bank and conducted several research projects for the European Commission. She holds a PhD degree in Public Policy Analysis from the University of North Carolina at Chapel Hill, USA.

Christiaan Boonen studied history at Ghent University (MA) and philosophy at Ghent University (BA) and the University of Amsterdam (MA). He is currently writing a PhD on extra-institutional and transnational citizenship practices and is especially interested in the tension between the democratic ideals central to these practices and the logic of citizenship.

In order to tackle these questions, he makes use of authors who work in the tradition of radical democratic theory (Balibar and Tully) and social theory (Marx, Foucault, and their intellectual descendants). This research is funded by a PhD fellowship of the Research Foundation – Flanders (FWO). In addition to his PhD research, he is also junior researcher for the 'Global Governance and Democracy' research programme at the Leuven Centre for Global Governance Studies of KU Leuven. This part of his research is mainly concerned with the role of property in democratic theory and the commonalities and differences between self-governance and cooperation in the commons, on the one hand, and democratic action, on the other.

Nicolás Brando is a junior researcher for the 'Global Governance and Democracy' research programme at the Leuven Centre for Global Governance Studies of KU Leuven. He studied Humanities (with a major in Philosophy) at the Pompeu Fabra University in Barcelona, and at the City University of Hong Kong. He obtained his degree (2013) with a thesis on the cognitive and educational approaches required to teach philosophy to the new young generations. He then entered the MA programme in Political Philosophy at the Pompeu Fabra University, writing his thesis on the global distribution of educational opportunities. He has done research in the field of global justice and natural resources, and has worked as a contributor to the Spanish branch of Academics Stand Against Poverty. He is writing a PhD on global justice and education at the Institute of Philosophy of KU Leuven.

Jutta Brunnée is Professor of Law and Metcalf Chair in Environmental Law, University of Toronto. Her teaching and research interests are in the areas of Public International Law and International Environmental Law. Her recent work has focused on international law and international relations theory, compliance with international law, the inter-state use of force, multilateral environmental agreements, climate change issues and international environmental liability regimes. Jutta Brunnée is co-author of *International Climate Change Law* (Oxford University Press 2017), and of *Legitimacy and Legality in International Law: An Interactional Account* (Cambridge University Press 2010), which was awarded the American Society of International Law's 2011 Certificate of Merit for preeminent contribution to creative scholarship. She has authored numerous articles on topics of international environmental law and international law, and is co-editor of the *Oxford Handbook of International Environmental Law* (Oxford University Press 2007). She is a member of the International Law Association's Committee on Legal Principles relating to Climate Change and of World Conservation Union's (IUCN) Environmental

Law Commission. In 1998–1999, Professor Brunnée was the 'Scholar-in-Residence' at the Legal Bureau of the Canadian Department of Foreign Affairs and International Trade, advising, *inter alia*, on matters under the Biodiversity and Climate Change Conventions. She served on the Board of Editors of the *American Journal of International Law* (2006–2016) and was elected Fellow of the Royal Society of Canada in 2013. She will deliver a course at the Hague Academy of International Law in 2019.

Samuel Cogolati is a PhD Fellow of the Research Foundation – Flanders (FWO) at the Leuven Centre for Global Governance Studies of KU Leuven, where he is writing his PhD thesis on the human rights protection of commons in development projects. He also coordinates the Community of Practice on Human Rights and Development under the World Bank's Global Forum on Law, Justice and Development. He has published articles in journals including the *Cambridge International Law Journal* and *World Bank Legal Review* on global public goods, human rights, and development. He has co-authored a report on the rights of migrants in the Mediterranean for the European Parliament's Subcommittee on Human Rights. Samuel holds an LLM from Harvard Law School, where he was a Fulbright scholar and BAEF Cleary Gottlieb Fellow. He is also a graduate of KU Leuven and King's College London.

Christophe Crombez is a political economist who specializes in EU politics and business–government relations in Europe. His research focuses on EU institutions and their impact on policies, EU institutional reform, lobbying, party politics and parliamentary government. He has been Professor of Political Economy at the Faculty of Economics and Business at KU Leuven since 1994. He is Vice-Chair for Teaching at the Department for Managerial Economics, Strategy and Innovation, and a senior member of the Leuven Centre for Global Governance Studies, LICOS and VIVES. Moreover, Crombez has been Senior Research Scholar at The Europe Center at the Freeman Spogli Institute for International Studies at Stanford University since 1999. Crombez has also held visiting positions at: the Istituto Italiano di Scienze Umane in Florence, Italy; the Department of Political Science at the University of Florence, Italy; the Department of Political Science at the University of Michigan; the Kellogg Graduate School of Management at Northwestern University, Illinois; the Department of Political Science at the University of Illinois at Urbana-Champaign, USA; the European University Institute in Florence, Italy; the University of Antwerp, Belgium; and Leti University in St Petersburg, Russia.

Pierre Dardot is Professor of Philosophy and Associate Researcher at the Sophiapol Laboratory of the University of Paris Ouest Nanterre La

Défense. He is a specialist of Hegel and Marx, has managed the study and research group on Marx since 2004, and has co-written with his colleague Christian Laval a trilogy of books casting a critical look on what they see as the current driving political ideology, neoliberalism: *La Nouvelle Raison du Monde* (La Découverte 2009) and *Marx, prénom: Karl* (Gallimard 2012). In their third landmark volume, *Commun: essai sur la revolution au XXIème siècle* (Common: An Essay on Revolution in the 21st Century) (La Découverte 2014), they claim that the 'common' (in the singular), that implies a collective production of a good that is not up for appropriation, could be an alternative to current international economic policies focused on wealth maximization.

Martin Deleixhe is Assistant Professor at Université Saint-Louis in Brussels. He spent two years at KU Leuven as postdoc researcher and coordinator of the 'Global Governance and Democracy' research programme at the Leuven Centre for Global Governance Studies. Previously, he worked as a fixed-term lecturer at the Université Libre de Bruxelles and as a postdoc researcher at the University of Oxford. His PhD, written under Justine Lacroix's supervision, focused on the conceptual tension arising between the universal norms embodied in the human rights and the principle of self-determination around the issue of border controls. His main research interests lie in migration issues, democratic theories, and cosmopolitanism. In 2014, he published a book titled *Etienne Balibar. L'Illimitation démocratique* (Michalon 2014), and in 2016 another monograph: *Aux bords de la démocratie. Contrôle des frontières et politique de l'hospitalité* (Garnier Classiques 2016). He currently works on the fertile cross-pollination between the literature on the commons and the theories of democracy.

Tine De Moor (PhD; Ghent, Antwerp, and London) is Professor of 'Institutions for Collective Action in Historical Perspective' at the Department for Social and Economic History of Utrecht University. Through an interdisciplinary approach to the study of the long-term evolution of rural commons, De Moor has been able to revise the historical basis of the widely debated metaphor of 'The Tragedy of the Commons', as launched in 1968 by Garrett Hardin. Whereas from a modern-day perspective the flaws in Hardin's theory have been well-documented, the historical deficiencies in his theory were hardly ever studied. De Moor's research, which combines extensive empirical research and analysis with explicit modelling and a strongly developed theoretical framework, has been published in several books and journals. She is also the (co-)founder of the peer-reviewed journal the *International Journal of the Commons*, and she has been member of the Executive Council of the International Association for the Study of the Commons (IASC) since 2008; in 2014, she was elected as President-Elect of the IASC, taking office as President on 15 January 2015. De Moor is currently in charge of or involved in several projects on institutions for collective action, of which one has been awarded a VIDI-Grant by the Netherlands Organisation for Scientific Research (NWO).

Helder De Schutter is Associate Professor of Social and Political Philosophy at KU Leuven and a senior member of the Leuven Centre for Global Governance Studies at KU Leuven. He works on issues of linguistic justice, federalism in multinational states, nationalism and nation-building, migration and citizenship, and the case for non-territorial jurisdictional authority. He also has a strong interest in eighteenth century philosophy of language. He is currently writing a normative theory of language policy. He has held visiting research positions at Princeton University (in 2006, and as a Fung Global Fellow in 2013–2014) and at the University of Oxford, Nuffield College (2008–2009). He is also a guest professor at the Université Catholique de Louvain, where he teaches with Philippe Van Parijs. He supervises nine PhD students and runs a weekly justice seminar for his PhD students in normative political philosophy. In 2014 his co-authored paper 'Mandatory Citizenship for Immigrants' (with Lea Ypi) received the British Academy's Brian Barry Prize.

Olivier De Schutter is Professor at the Université Catholique de Louvain in Belgium and at Sciences Po (Paris), and a Member of the UN Committee on Economic, Social and Cultural Rights since 2015. Between 2008 and 2014 he was the United Nations Special Rapporteur on the right to food. A Visiting Professor at various institutions including, in 2010–2013, Columbia University, he chaired the EU Network of Independent Experts on Fundamental Rights in 2002–2006, and was, in 2004–2008, the General Secretary of the International Federation of Human Rights (FIDH) on the issue of globalization and human rights. His publications are in the area of international human rights and fundamental rights in the EU, with a particular emphasis on economic and social rights and on the relationship between human rights and governance. He is notably the co-editor with Katharina Pistor of a book on common resource management, *Governing Access to Essential Resources* (Columbia University Press 2015).

Thomas R. Eimer is Assistant Professor of International Relations at Radboud University Nijmegen (the Netherlands). His research is at the interface between international political economy, philosophy, international relations, and public policy analysis. Empirically, he is interested in the institutionalization of property rights in various sectors (for example, software, pharmaceuticals, indigenous knowledge, genetic resources, and land rights). Since property governance is embedded in complex multi-level systems, his research encompasses interactions from local to global level. However, he has developed a special focus on international regimes and trade-related relationships between industrialized countries and emerging economies. To discuss property governance in a broader context, he mainly draws on international political economy approaches, but he also uses insights from comparative policy analysis, historical institutionalism, and postcolonial studies.

Maja Groff is a Senior Legal Officer at the Permanent Bureau of the Hague Conference on Private International Law, a global intergovernmental organization for cross-border cooperation in civil and commercial matters. Ms Groff works on Hague Conventions which address the cross-border protection of vulnerable adults (the Hague 2000 Convention) and the cross-border protection of children (the Hague 1980, 1996 and 2007 Conventions), the International Hague Network of Judges, Information Technology solutions to support Hague Children's Conventions, and preliminary work on potential new conventions or international cooperation in the areas of the recognition and enforcement of foreign protection orders and the facilitation of access to foreign legal information. She has conducted liaison work with international professional associations, NGOs and other international organizations (including various UN bodies), and has played a key role in the co-ordination of a range of international conferences and expert groups. She holds degrees from McGill (civil law and common law), Oxford, and Harvard Universities, and is an attorney admitted to practice in the state of New York.

Rutger Hagen is a junior researcher for the 'Global Governance and Democracy' research programme at the Leuven Centre for Global Governance Studies of KU Leuven since October 2014. He received his master's degree with merit in 2006 from Leiden University (the Netherlands) on Public Administration, with a specialization in European Governance. He also completed the one-year Leiden Honours programme on new Institutionalism(s) in politics and public administration in 2005. After his studies, he worked as a scientific employee at the International Politics department of the University of Konstanz (Germany) until he became a senior policy officer for the Dutch labour party (PvdA). Before joining the Centre, Rutger worked in consultancy, focusing mainly on (international) issues concerning plant nurseries (rules and regulations, energy, spatial ordinance). Rutger's main interests include the action of the European Union, political economy and the implementation of policies. He is currently writing a PhD on the relevance of the global public good lens for political economy at the Faculty of Business and Economics of KU Leuven.

Sylvia Karlsson-Vinkhuyzen is Assistant Professor with the Public Administration and Policy Group of Wageningen University, the Netherlands, and Adjunct Professor in global environmental governance at Helsinki University, Finland. Her research tries to understand the key determinants of what makes global governance processes with environmental and social implications exert influence and build legitimacy. In her PhD thesis she applied theories of Elinor Ostrom to analyse multi-level governance of globalized environmental issues and has written on the application of the global public goods concept to a sustainable energy system. She is currently particularly looking at accountability in relation to compliance with international norms (hard and soft law) in the climate change regime and around sustainable development. She is a senior research fellow of the international Earth System Governance Project and a member of the editorial board of the journal *International Environmental Agreements*. Sylvia has a master's degree in biology from Uppsala University and a PhD in political science from Linköping University (both Sweden) and has published in a number of international scientific journals. Sylvia has been a postdoctoral fellow at Yale University and a visiting fellow at the Public International Law department of Leiden University.

Ugo Mattei is Distinguished Professor of Law and Alfred and Hanna Fromm Chair in International and Comparative Law at UC Hastings College of the Law, Professor of Civil Law at the University of Turin, Academic Coordinator of the International University College of Turin and Fellow of Collegio Carlo Alberto. He is also a full member of the International Academy of Comparative Law, a Fellow at the European Law Institute, served as a member of the Executive Editorial Board of the *American Journal of Comparative Law*, is a founding editor of *Global Jurist*, and a general editor to the *Common Core of European Private Law* since its beginning in 1993. He is the Senior Scholar winner of the 2017 international Elinor Ostrom Award on Collective Governance of the Commons.

Pierre Sauvêtre is Assistant Professor in Sociology at the University of Paris Ouest Nanterre La Défense and the New College of Political Studies. He is also a permanent member of the interdisciplinary centre Sophiapol (Paris X). In the light of Michel Foucault's work, he has written his doctoral dissertation on the history of governmentality and his current research focuses on the links between the history of power and the commons. He is the author of a book on Michel Foucault (*Foucault, 'Pas à Pas'*, Paris, Ellipses 2017) and of several articles on the commons and the common, including 'Les politiques du commun dans l'Europe du Sud (Grèce, Italie, Espagne)', *Actuel Marx*, 2016, **1** (59), 123–38.

Jan Wouters is Full Professor of International Law and International Organizations, Jean Monnet Chair *ad personam* EU and Global Governance, and founding Director of the Institute for International Law and of the Leuven Centre for Global Governance Studies at the University of Leuven (KU Leuven), an interdisciplinary research centre with the status of a KU Leuven Centre of Excellence and a Jean Monnet Centre of Excellence. He is also President of the Council for International Policy of KU Leuven. He studied law and philosophy at Antwerp University, obtained an LLM at Yale University and was Visiting Researcher at Harvard University. As Visiting Professor at Sciences Po (Paris), Luiss University (Rome) and the College of Europe (Bruges) he teaches EU external relations law. As Adjunct Professor at Columbia University he teaches comparative EU-US perspectives on international human rights law. He is a Member of the Royal Academy of Belgium for Sciences and Arts and practises law as *Of Counsel* at Linklaters, Brussels. He is Editor of the *International Encyclopedia of Intergovernmental Organizations*, Deputy Director of the *Revue Belge de Droit International*, and an editorial board member in 10 other international journals. He has published widely on international and EU law, international organizations, global governance and financial law, including 65 books, 130 journal articles, and 200 chapters in international books.

Foreword

In his influential book, *The Great Transformation*, Karl Polanyi describes a fundamental *double movement* that has traversed the history of industrial capitalism, which is also referred to as the 'Lib-Lab' pendulum. With the global system understood as a combination of a Capital system, a State system, and an 'Imagined Community', that is, the Nation, Polanyi showed how phases when the market forces prevailed at the cost of increasing ecological and social instability were alternated with periods where the pendulum swung back and social forces mobilized, driving the state to rein in the free market economy.

It seems quite clear that this mechanism no longer functions as it once did. Despite a massive growth of social movements from the right and the left, social and ecological progress remains limited. The impending challenges posed, *inter alia*, by climate change, ecological and resource crises demand new approaches. The reason that the pendulum logic no longer seems applicable is, in all likelihood, that on the one hand, the new neoliberal global system today relies on a financialized transnational capital, coupled with global private platforms, whose global functional governance is threatening the very sovereignty of state actors; and, on the other, that the inter-state system is rather weak, pervaded by rivalries that preclude more united global action.

Part of the solution might be to scale-up the *double movement* to the global level. A vital question then becomes, what kind of processes or institutions might create sufficient countervailing influence, and alternative global governance systems, to rebalance the global system?

This volume seeks to answer just that conundrum, by providing an in-depth analysis of what is likely to drive this rebalancing – the commons. Given the current context, it is vital to start researching this topic at the global level, as well as to revisit previous work on the commons, like that of Elinor Ostrom, who has focused on their local equivalent.

For the last 20 years, we have seen emerging, in particular, global knowledge commons, for example in the form of global open source communities, which are composed of global contributive communities, and usually accompanied by democratic 'FLOSS Foundations' (non-profit foundations involved in open and free software projects). Such communities are operating on a transnational scale, and are often also co-evolving with global entrepreneurial coalitions that operate in the marketplace around these commons. At the local level, we also witness the rise of urban and bioregional material commons, which are reconceiving the major provisioning systems (food, energy, transport, housing), on the basis of new logics such as contributive models of democracy. The city of Ghent in Belgium, for example, has been conducting a pioneering study on the functioning of these urban commons and the necessity for public-commons cooperation and partnerships. Global and shared open design depositories for vital common infrastructures are now on the agenda, perhaps driven by coalitions of such cities. It is, therefore, unsurprising that more and more voices are calling for a reassessment of global resources – for example, natural resource commons – as global commons. For example, the Reporting 3.0 project has created a 'Global Threshold and Allocations Council', which looks at resource availability and sustainability to determine how much of a resource could be used on a global scale without endangering their accessibility for future generations, thereby putting biocapacity accountability on the agenda. Proposals like the Skytrust, suggested by Peter Barnes, which would consider the atmosphere as a commons, have been circulating for more than a decade, proposing 'cap and dividend' schemes for the allocation of these kinds of resources. But how will all this function and interact with the international system, along with powerful global multinational corporate players? Where will we find the social forces to push through these necessary reforms of the global system?

The time has come for researchers and scientists to focus their efforts on potential global governance mechanisms for the commons, existing or to come. This is precisely what has inspired this volume and why it should be considered a significant milestone in the study of the commons at the global level.

Michel Bauwens

Acknowledgements

The present book is the outcome of the efforts of 19 contributors, and the editors would like to express their warmest gratitude to all of them. It is only because of their commitment and trust that this interdisciplinary book has been possible.

In particular, the editors would like to thank Dr Martin Deleixhe, who, as a senior member of the Centre of Excellence Research Programme 'Global Governance and Democratic Government' of our Leuven Centre for Global Governance Studies, paved the way for the conceptual and normative foundations of this volume. Together with the other junior and senior researchers involved in our research programme, Martin initiated this book project in 2016. Among the first authors who contributed to this project from 2016, we would like to thank Professor Dr Pierre Dardot, Professor Dr Maarja Beerkens, Christiaan Boonen, Nicolás Brando, Professor Dr Thomas Eimer, Maja Groff, Rutger Hagen, and Professor Dr Sylvia Karlsson-Vinkhuyzen.

In 2017, as part of the same Centre of Excellence Research Programme, Global Governance Studies organized a high-level Spring Lecture Series 'Interdisciplinary Approaches to Global Commons and Global Public Goods' with distinguished guest speakers who all shared their perspectives on the commons as a new model of global governance. This lecture series drew together leading academic voices on the commons, among whom were Professor Dr Jutta Brunnée, Professor Dr Ugo Mattei, and Dr Pierre Sauvêtre, who each contributed a chapter to this volume afterwards. We also had the honour of welcoming Michel Bauwens and Professor Dr Tine De Moor, to whom we express our deepest gratitude for accepting to write the foreword, resp. afterword to this book and for encouraging us to look further in the direction of the commons as an institutional model of collective action at the global level. We would also like to thank Professor Dr Olivier De Schutter for agreeing to contribute a chapter on international law and the commons based on his experience as a former United Nations Special Rapporteur on the right to food.

This book was made possible within the framework of the Centre of Excellence Research Programme on 'Global Governance and Democratic Government' funded by the KU Leuven Special Research Fund (*Bijzonder*

Onderzoeksfonds, BOF). This programme, conducted jointly by the Leuven Centre for Global Governance Studies and the Centre for Ethics, Social and Political Philosophy at KU Leuven, is aimed at the construction of a new paradigm for democratic global governance. It is managed by an interdisciplinary group of promoters, some of whom have also contributed to this book: Professor Dr Christophe Crombez (political economy), Professor Dr Helder De Schutter (political philosophy), and Professor Dr Jan Wouters (international law). We would like to acknowledge Nils Vanstappen, who, although he did not contribute a chapter, was instrumental in the organization of the aforementioned events and in commenting on various chapters of this volume.

Last but not least, we would like to thank Alex Andrione-Moylan, who reviewed the English language of this edition, which was necessary for a book that brings together prominent authors from non-English countries.

It is especially gratifying to us, editors, to see that our collaborative efforts have been rewarded by the present collection of chapters, which all try to capture, from different academic perspectives, the fascinating potential of the commons as a new model of governance at the global level.

Samuel Cogolati and Jan Wouters
Leuven, 2018

1. Introduction: democratic, institutional and legal implications of the commons for global governance

Samuel Cogolati and Jan Wouters*

> The most important lesson for public policy analysis derived from [my] intellectual journey . . . is that humans have a more complex motivational structure and more capability to solve social dilemmas than posited in earlier rational-choice theory. Designing institutions to force (or nudge) entirely self-interested individuals to achieve better outcomes has been the major goal posited by policy analysts for governments to accomplish for much of the past half century. Extensive empirical research leads me to argue that instead, a core goal of public policy should be to facilitate the development of institutions that bring out the best in humans.
>
> (Ostrom, 2009b: pp. 435–6)

1. BACKGROUND

Since the award of the Nobel Prize in Economic Science in 2009, the pioneering work of Elinor Ostrom on the commons has been given worldwide exposure. Her acceptance speech on that occasion, entitled 'Beyond Markets and States: Polycentric Governance of Complex Economic Systems' (2009), summarized neatly her lifelong effort to unearth the regulating principles and the institutional architecture that accounted for the success of innovative modes of decentralized and bottom-up governance, beyond the much travelled paths of the exclusively public or exclusively private management solutions. Her research, based on extensive fieldworks and relying on three decades spent refining her 'Institutional Analysis and Development' (IAD) framework, looks into the previously underestimated achievements of regimes of self-organization at all levels of governance (Drago Aligica and Boettke, 2009). Her central claim turned conventional wisdom upside down: complex socio-ecological systems (in which goods are subtractable and beneficiaries are hard to exclude) can prove to be sustainable resource domains granted that its stakeholders adopt a polycentric and self-regulated mode of governance. Ostrom's work serves as the background to this book.

Our main endeavour throughout this volume, that builds in part upon an earlier book published in this series (Wouters et al., 2015), will be to assess to what extent this polycentric and self-regulated mode of governance is amenable to new democratic, institutional and legal arrangements at the global level. This book therefore shifts from the traditional focus of the academic literature on small-scale commons and local institutional arrangements. Indeed, the commons used to be, in medieval times, pastures and woodlands that, by custom, could be accessed and jointly managed by a community of villagers. Before Ostrom, the commons were brought back to the attention of the scientific community by the popular article of the American scientist Garrett Hardin: 'The Tragedy of the Commons' (1968). Hardin described an economic model devoid of any empirical evidence but based on rational-choice theory, in which individual actors automatically tend to over-exploit and plunder common-pool resources (CPRs) that are freely available to everyone. Prior to Ostrom's work, it was widely admitted that the twin features of CPRs, namely their difficulty to exclude and the rivalrous nature of the goods they either contained or produced, would lead to a collective action problem akin to the prisoner's dilemma (Olson, 1965). Hardin's prediction of no cooperation is entirely consistent with this inexorable dilemma. Hardin illustrates this with the example of an open-access pasture on which self-interested herders use as much grass as possible to rear their cattle. The commoners, assumed to be rational, incommunicative and selfish agents, are locked into short-term strategies and keep subtracting as much as possible from what Hardin mistakenly termed the 'commons'. The inevitable result is their degradation and depletion. According to Hardin, '[f]reedom in a commons brings ruin to all' (p. 1244). To avoid the unconstrained over-exploitation of natural resources by selfish individuals, Hardin only believes in two possible coercive arrangements: the enclosure of resources through private property, or, failing that, public regulation (p. 1247). Even though he admits that the legal institution of private property is 'unjust', he claims that there is no 'better system': '[t]he alternative of the commons is too horrifying to contemplate' (p. 1247).

As we know, despite the influence up until today of Garrett Hardin's narrative (see Ranganathan, 2016), the story did not stop here. In her landmark book *Governing the Commons* (1990), Elinor Ostrom showed through various case studies how local communities could develop autonomous institutions with their own *ad hoc* rules to govern the resource domains upon which they depend for their subsistence. In her book that quickly became the standard reference in the study of the commons, Ostrom examines the factors that lead self-governance mechanisms to succeed – Swiss Alpine pastures, irrigation systems in Spain, Turkish or Sri Lankan fisheries. Commons have indeed existed over long periods of time and one of the reasons for their long-enduring success is that commoners do not always act as *homines economici.* Commoners are social actors embedded in tight-knit communities that communicate, observe social norms and judge their fellow members on the basis of their reputation. Consequently, commoners are capable of collectively making some binding decisions that supply institutions, refrain their individual consumption and preserve their resource domains in the long run. Despite the wide diversity of local arrangements, Ostrom identifies eight 'design principles' for commons-based institutions that characterize sustainable institutions for collective action in the long term, among which are clearly defined jurisdictional boundaries, clear rules of access and use, conflict-resolution mechanisms that foster mutual trust, and sanctions to deter free-riders (p. 90). In brief, in exploring the empirical realities behind the management of CPRs, Ostrom rebutted Hardin's assumption that commons equate open-access regimes. She proved that it was possible to prevent commons from collapsing through institutions that are neither 'all-private', nor 'all-public', but collectively owned. She convincingly showed that the pessimistic outcome of the prisoner dilemma was misleading.

Since *Governing the Commons* (1990), many researchers have adopted Ostrom's IAD framework to scrutinize the governance of CPRs, be they local and natural, or more ground-breaking such as knowledge or cultural commons. There have been innumerable case studies assessing the robustness of the governance models suggested by Ostrom and refining her findings. Ostrom's design principles have been applied in very different contexts, beyond the sole issue of natural resource management. Her work opened the eyes of many academics to the fact that CPRs were not doomed to a tragic fate unless they were either enclosed and commercialized or turned into public property and administered by the state. Seen in this light, the commons have been burdened by some authors with the responsibility of carving out an autonomous social space independent from both the atomism of capitalist markets and the hierarchical structure of the state. Not only this, but the commons have been embraced by civil society and social activists as a new governance model to rethink the traditional public-private and market-state divides, and to prioritize ecological and human needs of communities (Bollier and Helfrich, 2012; 2015). It is Ostrom's seminal work and the ensuing academic and political debates around the commons, which laid the groundwork for this interdisciplinary book on a new system of global governance.

2. DEFINITIONS

Far from being a monolithic notion, the commons today evoke a wealth of – sometimes contradictory – meanings. This is not different in the various chapters of this book. Whereas some authors focus on well-defined resource domains at the local or global levels, others insist that the commons are primarily about social and political movements against the top-down logic of markets and states. By way of introduction, we attempt to outline below some basic definitions for the notions of the commons (2.1), the common (2.2), global commons (2.3), and global public goods (GPGs) (2.4).

2.1 Commons

To explain the notion of the 'commons', it is usual to resort to the basic economic classification of goods. Contrary to public goods, which are non-rival, CPRs are rival in consumption, and therefore vulnerable for depletion. Yet, today, the commons no longer exclusively refer to tangible CPRs like pastures, seeds, forests or water reserves, but also to intangibles resources such as the Internet, software codes and human genes. Under Ostrom's influence, the commons have become more closely connected with the collective self-governance and participatory mechanisms they imply, than with the strict category of (rivalrous and non-excludable) economic goods they used to refer to. The commons can no longer be abstracted from the social networks which participate in their production and protection: without communities, no commons. This is why we do not simply speak of common 'goods' in this book. Even though it is impossible to apply one single and closed definition, we describe the commons as a social system consisting of three cumulative elements:

1. A common-pool *resource*, be it a tangible, natural resource like pastures, lands, seeds, forests or water reserves, or intangible resources such as traditional knowledge or the Internet (the object);
2. A *community* that has exclusive access to the resource in question and that manages it in common (the subject);
3. The practice of *commoning*: that is the concrete activity of governing a resource through collective action and according to *ad hoc* rules (the practice).

The rules constitutive of the practice of commoning will always be specific to each commons. So it is in this broad and plural sense, as an 'institution for collective action' (De Moor, 2011: p. 424), that the commons are most often understood in this volume. In this sense, the commons represent grassroots institutions developed by communities to share and govern tangible or intangible resources in a horizontal and autonomous fashion. It is this institutional and social element for self-government which makes the commons so different from privately or publicly owned resources.

2.2 The Common

Over the last decade, the commons have also acquired a strong political dimension. Ostrom's work has indeed sparked a new wave of interest for the commons as a 'third way' to overcome the extractive forces of capitalism and the top-down logic of states. In this sense, the commons have evolved into an alternative 'paradigm' to rethink the traditional private-public divide, and prioritize the ecological and human needs of communities over market and state. More and more authors nowadays identify the commons with political strategies of resistance like the commons movement in Italy (the Rodotà Commission that introduced into the Italian Civil Code a third category of *beni communi* beyond the public/private goods, the 2011 Water Constitutional Referendum), the *indignados* in Spain, the water war in Cochabamba (Bolivia), or the Occupy movement in the United States to overcome the extractive force of capitalism and the top-down logic of states (see also De Angelis, 2017: p. 10). They stress that the commons do not exist in a political vacuum of power relations; these are 'social systems' sustained in a competitive struggle against capitalist and state domination. In sum, the commons now serve as a new platform, language, social imaginary that speak to very diverse struggles of self-government against politics of enclosure.

In his landmark book *Commun: Essai sur la révolution au XXIe siècle*, co-written with Christian Laval, Pierre Dardot (who contributes Chapter 2 to this volume) defines the 'Common' as a political principle (Dardot and Laval, 2014). This principle is in line with what Michael Hardt and Antonio Negri wrote earlier in their book '*Commonwealth*': '[t]his notion of the common does not position humanity separate from nature, as either its exploiter or its custodian, but focuses rather on the practices of interaction, care, and cohabitation in a common world, promoting the beneficial and limiting the detrimental forms of the common' (Hardt and Negri, 2009: p. viii). This normative approach to the common is shared by other contributors in the first part of this volume. For them, the common is not a thing limited to marginal areas of natural resource management, but rather a much broader set of practices which represent more direct forms of democracy and resistance against privatization. What these authors regret in Ostrom's work is that it does not sufficiently call into question the capitalist mode of production. In Chapter 5 of this volume, Pierre Sauvêtre even goes as far as to suggest that Ostrom's commons have 'no connection whatsoever with the movements for the common that appear in the 2000s in the context of the wave of state neoliberalization' (p. 80). The denomination of the common in the singular – in parallel with that of the commons – is warranted in this volume.

2.3 Global Commons

If we consider CPRs to be open access and rivalrous goods, we have to acknowledge that several of the resource domains on which we depend are to be found on a global scale. The atmosphere, the high seas, Antarctica, Outer Space, are all vast resource domains whose over-exploitation or misuse could potentially have disastrous consequences for every single individual regardless of his geographical location. Thus, the term 'global commons' has also been used to include these open resources. The United Nations Environment Programme (UNEP) has defined the global commons as 'resource domains or areas that lie outside of the political reach of any one nation State' (2017). More recently, the term has come to include common or global concerns of mankind such as biodiversity conservation and climate change (Ranganathan, 2016: p. 27). Some chapters in this volume also raise democratic, institutional and legal issues regarding such global commons.

However, for global commons, the leap from the local to the global level implies a qualitative change due to the structural absence of a community and of a widely recognized and implemented set of social norms regarding global resource domains. There is a lot of literature on the precise mechanisms that helped commoners to function and to overcome local constraints (Ostrom, 2005; 2009a). One reason why small-scale commons have proven to be sustainable is because they relied on a community whose tight-knit relationships often allowed them to design self-governance schemes and curb egoistic behaviour, notably due to the reiterated nature of the social interactions and the actors' concern for their reputation. In contrast, global commons are not managed by bottom-up institutions tailored by communities. As Tine De Moor already showed, global commons 'lack two important attributes that are characteristic of the commons as they have existed for centuries in Europe and beyond': 'institutionalization and self-governance' (2011: p. 422). This shows that scale matters in these issues (Ostrom et al., 1999; Berkes, 2006). Most global commons lack effective rules of control, management and access to regulate their use. In this sense, global commons seem to come more closely to the notion of common goods ('*res communes*') or open-access resources depicted by Garrett Hardin (1968). A distinction should be made between open access, on the one hand, and self-government by a limited number of users actively involved in the management of the commons, on the other. Global commons and commons should therefore not be confused.

In other words, areas labelled as global commons have little to do with Ostrom's commons and are, in fact, in dire need of a governance framework. Yet, even global collective action issues could possibly be overcome through reiterated interactions, the establishment of mutual trust and an institutional set-up entailing light monitoring and sanctioning mechanisms. The self-organization that is quintessential to the commons model of governance could potentially be found in larger networks of actors, challenging the previously held assumptions that autonomous self-governance should be reserved to small and thick communities. Admittedly, the efforts to coordinate action on the international scene to preserve or develop global commons have had some limited successes (for instance with regard to the mitigation of climate change: see Nordhaus, 1994). They nonetheless generated an exponentially growing literature on how to improve the design of their principles of governance (Stern, 2011). One important question in this volume is therefore whether it is possible to extrapolate the self-governance model of the commons to monitor the sustainability of wider shared resources at the global level.

2.4 Global Public Goods

Finally, some contributors to this volume use the concept of GPGs like climate change mitigation, the eradication of infectious diseases, the fight against corruption, or the protection of the ozone layer. One chapter even defines the rule of international law as a GPG of its own (see Groff and Karlsson-Vinkhuyzen, Chapter 7 in this volume). The notion of GPG is grounded in economic theory. As opposed to a private good, such as a pie or a car, a public good refers to something that is non-rival and non-excludable. Public goods represent a case of market failures – that is, goods and services that cannot be left to the invisible hand of the free market. By virtue of the inherent free-rider problem in the provision of public goods, coercive authority is considered necessary in ensuring, at the very least, a minimal contribution by all. Therefore, at the national level, state intervention is seen as indispensable in the financing and provision of public goods (Samuelson, 1954). In a popular book published by the UNDP Office of Development Studies in 1999, GPGs are defined as 'outcomes (or intermediate products) that tend towards universality in the sense that they benefit all countries, population groups, and generations' (Kaul et al., 1999: p. 16).

This definition means that, in contrast to economic theory, the concept of 'goods', as reconstructed by Kaul et al., covers a very large spectrum of global issues. Under this approach, it should be stressed that there cannot be any fixed list of GPGs and the term 'good' should be understood in the broadest possible sense – not solely as a tangible commodity. GPGs simply point to policy challenges that cannot be adequately resolved at the state level and which, therefore, require collective action at the global level (Cogolati et al., 2016: p. 9). GPGs have gradually become a buzzword in the global policy discourse, evolving from a technical, economic concept to a powerful advocacy tool in favour of increased international cooperation and regulation in today's globalized world (p. 11). In fact, most goods cannot be inherently public: they normally become public through public provision. The choice for (or against) public provision is never a neutral one, as it is generally subject to diverging views. Even goods that are '*de facto* public', on account of their non-excludability and non-rivalry, such as the lighthouse, may, under certain circumstances, be considered unworthy of public provision. For instance, a society could very well decide that, since the lighthouse only benefits foreign ships, it will not bear the cost thereof (p. 14). The authors of the UNDP book acknowledge this basic fact as well: '"[p]ublic" and "private" are in many – perhaps most – cases a matter of policy choice: a social construct' (Kaul and Mendoza, 2003: p. 104).

The authors in this volume agree to draw a strict distinction between the commons and GPGs as models of governance. Pierre Dardot, for example, claims that the common implies a system of bottom-up governance, in contrast to GPGs theory, which is designed to promote more cooperation among existing private and state actors (see Chapter 2 in this volume). Indeed, the power of the commons discourse is to propose an alternative vocabulary and governance paradigm to that of the traditional market-state dichotomy. There are plenty of institutional arrangements which are formed by the communities themselves and which often prove more effective than the typical 'all-public' and 'all-private' solutions in safeguarding shared resources. In contrast, the urgency to produce GPGs seems to justify a turn to old public or private institutions which do not afford to communities the same right to participate and shape their own process of development (see also the Conclusion in this volume). Thus, instead of assimilating commons to GPGs, both governance frameworks should be cautiously distinguished to avoid the powerful alternative force of community-driven initiatives dressing up classic governance models (Cogolati, 2016: p. 18).

3. THE OBJECT AND PURPOSE OF THE BOOK

The main purpose of this book is to understand what the ground-breaking model of cooperation of the commons implies for global governance, especially in relation to the debate on the (non)-democratic nature, institutions and legal underpinnings of global governance. The research on the implications of the commons for our system of global governance is still scarce. As Michel Bauwens writes in his foreword to this volume, '[t]he time has come for researchers and scientists to focus their efforts on potential global governance mechanisms for the commons, existing or to come'. The present book therefore aims to contribute to fill the gap between the study of bottom-up commons and global governance. Global governance, which stands for ways of problem-solving cooperation that take place within global networks of relevant stakeholders, is indeed gradually substituting itself to the democratic deliberation within nation-states and comes to have more of a say over what political projects ought to be prioritized. In an interdependent and globalized world, a fair and representative system of global governance will therefore be critical to protect and promote the commons. Hence, we submit that the commons cannot only be studied at the micro-level, where they often emerge. While it is true that decision-making processes for the commons are generally locally owned, the commons also represent at a more macro-level a 'foundational paradigm of a generative revolution aiming at the construction of a new common sense' (Bailey et al., 2013: p. 19, referring to Bollier and Helfrich, 2012). Following this broader normative interpretation, the commons may also indicate a third way beyond both market and state on a global scale. Given the newly found importance of the commons in the political discourse, it has become necessary to explore the democratic, institutional and legal implications of the commons for global governance today.

In light of this, our principal research questions are:

1. Which democratic qualities and shortcomings in global decision-making processes do the commons reveal? Could global governance be democratized through participatory, decentralized and self-organized communities of 'commoners', and if so, in what form? Could the commons become vehicles for democratization at the global level? If so, what kind of democratic processes should ensure that shared resources be stewarded by communities at the global level?
2. What difference does it make in institutional terms to govern a resource domain as a commons? What kind of institutional cooperation schemes does the concept of the commons imply at the global level? Is it possible to extrapolate the governance of the commons at

the global level for wider shared resources (such as biodiversity or scientific knowledge)?

3. How can the commons be operationalized as a matter of international law? What kind of legal norms and procedures should be devised at the global level to ensure that the commons be protected from enclosure and commodification?

In order to answer these research questions, this book takes a multidisciplinary view across a narrow range of disciplines: political theory, political science, political economy and international law. The commons have indeed been studied through analytical frameworks that can be (and have been) applied to a variety of case studies emanating from multiple scientific disciplines. Respectful of this diversity in the approaches but also in the objects of enquiry, we invited scholars from these four different disciplinary affiliations to contribute to the present volume, thereby assuming that the analytical frameworks associated with the governance of the commons can act as a conceptual bridge between the disciplines and allow for a mutually enriching dialogue across disciplinary boundaries. The themes of the different chapters as well as their authors have been carefully chosen bearing in mind this goal: we bring together scholars to develop a new research agenda surrounding the study of the commons and global governance. We attempt to present a sample of promising researches that lay a special emphasis on the democratic, institutional and legal implications of commons for global governance. Based first on the study of the commons as vehicles for democratization of global governance, then on the assessment of the role played by commons-based institutions in the current global governance system, and finally on a more normative interrogation around how international law *ought* to look to recognize and support the commons, this book will provide its reader with solid foundations to look further into the introduction of 'commoning' practices into global governance. However, the volume will not provide an exhaustive study of all the types and schemes of governance applied to commons; nor does it claim to present a silver bullet to democratize the current model of global governance. Its more humble objective is to illustrate through a handful of carefully chosen examples that the articulation of the commons in global governance constitutes a vast and rich field of research that calls for further study.

4. STRUCTURE

The contributions in this volume can be divided into three parts: those chapters that wrestle with the democratic credentials of the politics of the commons and try to outline how the democracy of the global commons could look (democratic perspectives: 4.1); others that tackle institutional questions related to the provision of GPGs and management of global commons in more specific contexts (institutional perspectives: 4.2); and, finally, chapters on the possible contribution of international law to the protection of the commons (legal perspectives: 4.3).

4.1 Democratic Perspectives

First of all, four chapters look at global governance from the lens of the democratic practices linked to the commons. The democratic dimension was not entirely absent from Ostrom's work. It was rather implicitly present under concepts such as self-governance and participation. However, it was rarely thematized as such and most research conducted on the topic usually lacks a comprehensive account of the ways in which the governance of the commons could integrate some features of democracy. There is certainly no shortage of disagreement on the definition of democracy. Democracy has become the prime example of an 'essentially contested concept' (Gallie, 1956), that is a concept whose importance is denied by none but whose meaning is fiercely debated and regarding which neither eclecticism ('all answers are equally valid') nor dogmatism ('my answer is the exclusive truth') provide an appropriate approach (Garver, 1978: p. 168). It would be impossible to recap, even in broad brushstrokes, the intellectual debate that has surrounded democracy ever since its inception. For the purpose of the present book, we cut this Gordian knot by providing a first and minimal definition of democracy, upon which each contributor has been invited to elaborate further in Part I of the book. Democracy is referred to in this book as the institutional practice through which stakeholders deliberate and/or decide on the regulations that they are submitted to. Regarding the commons more specifically, a group of researchers – led by prominent public intellectuals such as Michael Hardt and Antonio Negri (2009), David Harvey (2011), Naomi Klein (2001) or Ugo Mattei (2011) – has suggested that – since the commons bring the empirical demonstration that self-governance, far from being a utopian ideal, is and long has been a lived reality – the latter could and should be turned into the conceptual matrix of a new account of democracy. The first aim of this volume is to indicate how this new account of democracy based on the commons could also be realized at the global level.

This first part is mostly organized as a dialogue revolving around a chapter submitted by a prominent philosopher in the field, namely Pierre Dardot. In his chapter entitled 'What democracy for the global commons?' (Chapter 2), Dardot suggests that the governance of the commons could be turned into a more general political principle he calls 'the common' in the singular. The common would, in his view, imply to give the kind of collective cooperation quintessential to the governance of the commons a global scope and to export its cooperative strategies to all spheres of social activities. In order to institute the world as a common, he develops the new paradigm of 'cosmodemocracy'. According to Pierre Dardot, this new kind of global democracy based on the common will not come from above, but will emerge from a multiplication of bottom-up and decentralized institutions. The two subsequent chapters discuss critically this claim from two distinct angles. On the one hand, Dardot's suggested institutionalization of the common as an innovative form of multi-layered federalism is challenged by Nicolás Brando and Helder De Schutter. In 'Federal commons' (Chapter 3), they claim that since Dardot refuses to grant any prerogative to a central authority, his ideal model would be best described as 'confederal' or 'treaty-based' and would have to cope with the instability associated with this model of political association. On the other hand, Christiaan Boonen's response, 'A (non-)violent revolution? Strategies of civility for the politics of the common' (Chapter 4), argues that Dardot misjudges the role played by coercion and violence in the governance of the commons and consequently presents a too rosy picture of the type of governance that ought to be widespread into adjacent social spheres. Finally, in 'Forget Ostrom: from the development commons to the common as social sovereignty' (Chapter 5), Pierre Sauvêtre emphasizes the distinction between Ostrom's commons and the common. In a bold and challenging piece, he argues that the movement for the common that appeared in Catalonia (*politica del comú*) or in Bolivia (*lo común*) have in fact nothing to do with Ostrom's developmentalist approach.

4.2 Institutional Perspectives

Second, four other contributions look into the commons-based institutions which shape new collective rules, practices, and spaces in the current global governance system. As Tine De Moor writes in her Afterword, '[t]he topic of global resource governance, central to this book, is probably the most difficult angle to bridge several sides of the debate, but at the same time also the most obvious one: what binds those interested in commons together is a fundamental belief in the capacities in self-governance and collective action by citizens with the purpose of solving current major societal problems'. The objective of this second part is to evaluate to what extent institutional arrangements to govern the commons at the local level can also be applied at the global level for wider resources. Indeed, under Elinor Ostrom's impulse, the commons have been studied as new 'community institutional arrangements' that can operate at multiple scales, including at the global level (Ostrom, 2009a). This is what distinguishes commons from CPRs that are left without any clear access rules and governance mechanisms. As indicated above, much of the literature used the IAD framework developed by Vincent and Elinor Ostrom as a new methodology for investigating commons-based institutions across different contexts and according to bounded variables. This is particularly clear in their polycentric (as opposed to 'monocentric') approach involving the combination of various self-organized centres of decision-making – at the local, regional, national and global levels – that are formally independent of each other but enter into cooperative undertakings (Ostrom et al., 1961; Bauwens and Mertens, 2018). Yet, what is still less known is whether such bottom-up institutional and polycentric arrangements can be extrapolated at the global level for wider and transnational resources like, for example, biodiversity or the academic publishing industry. Under the current political system, strongly relying on both markets and states as basic units, the commons too often operate under the radar of global governance researchers. This book therefore proposes to build on the lessons learned from commons scholarship in order to explore ways for making institutions of global governance more participatory and accountable to communities across the world.

This second part is organized as follows. In 'Governance of the global commons: a question of supply and demand, the answer of polycentricism' (Chapter 6), Rutger Hagen and Christophe Crombez draw lessons from the study of the local commons and apply them to the governance of global commons. They use the economic adage of demand and supply to better understand what kind of collective action problems exist in global governance and how they may be solved. They realize that in smaller settings with fewer participants and increased trust among each other, institutional formation is relatively easy. However, when local commons-based arrangements are transposed to the global level, monitoring and sanction mechanisms become less effective, and uncertainty is higher. Thus, in their view, it is not sufficient to replicate local arrangements at the global level; local initiatives must be linked to regional and global regimes in a multi-layered and polycentric system of governance. In 'The rule of law and accountability: exploring trajectories for democratizing governance of global public goods and global commons' (Chapter 7), Maja Groff and Sylvia Karlsson-Vinkhuyzen advance that international legal cooperation geared towards granting a global scope to the rule of law is instrumental in facilitating the protection of global commons and turning its governance into a democratic endeavour. They describe the international rule of law as a foundational GPG of its own. In addition to institutional change, the authors also plead for 'attitudinal change' in order to strengthen accountability and democracy in global governance. In 'Expropriation by definition? Regime complexes, structural power, and global public goods' (Chapter 8), Thomas R. Eimer looks into the mechanisms that (fail to?) ensure the protection of a specific global commons – in this case, biodiversity – in spite of the huge imbalances in the distribution of power among the various stakeholders. Maarja Beerkens's chapter, 'Knowledge commons and global governance of academic publishing' (Chapter 9), digs deeper into the barriers to a free flow of scientific knowledge raised by the oligopolistic academic publishing industry. Beerkens underscores the different types of efforts that have been undertaken to turn this scientific knowledge into a knowledge commons, and she shows how this shift requires new institutions inspired by self-organization mechanisms beyond market and state hierarchies.

4.3 Legal Perspectives

Third and last, four chapters will question from a normative point of view whether international law as it stands is conducive to the protection of the commons against enclosure and commodification. It is true that the question of legal norms, institutions, and procedures is far from new in the debate on the governance of the commons. In particular, the literature has called for a shift from a traditional system of law based on the protection of individual private property rights, to a new legal order that promotes stewardship of resources by communities. Legal scholars have been invited to rethink the links between communities, shared resources and property rights at the domestic level. Hence, most scholars have focused on shared property regimes (Fennell, 2011; Orsi, 2013), intellectual property regimes to protect knowledge commons (think of the 'Creative Commons License' that protects shared resources) (Frischmann et al., 2014), and public trust doctrines (think of rivers, shorelines and parks protected by the state for future generation) (Wood, 2013). However, what has been overlooked for too long is the role that international law can play in the protection of the commons as institutions of their own. It is true that international legal scholarship has long recognized areas and resources beyond state jurisdiction (like the high seas, the deep seabed, outer space, the Moon and other celestial bodies, as well as Antarctica) as 'global commons'. However, it has given much less attention to commons defined in Ostrom's sense as bottom-up self-governance institutions. Whereas transnational areas and natural resources are now subject to special treaty regimes between states (like the common heritage of mankind), it remains unclear to what extent international law can protect communities from dispossession of their commons. This volume therefore takes a new look at the potential instrumental role of international law in safeguarding the autonomous and collective institutions established by the communities themselves to manage resources in common.

Ugo Mattei, the Senior Scholar winner of the 2017 international Elinor Ostrom Award on Collective Governance of the Commons, accepted to respond to this challenging question based on his latest book *The Ecology of Law: Towards a Legal System in Tune with Nature and Community* (co-written with F. Capra, 2015). In 'The ecology of international law: towards an international legal system in tune with nature and community?' (Chapter 10), Mattei calls for a paradigm shift (an 'ecolegal revolution') in international legal jurisprudence from the materialistic and extractive mentality of the Industrial Age to a new vision of the world as a network based on generative ecological principles. Based on a radical ecological reading of international law, he comes to the conclusion that international law is in itself flawed and incapable of protecting small-scale commons. In 'From eroding to enabling the commons: the dual movement in international law' (Chapter 11), Olivier De Schutter proposes a somewhat more optimistic view of international law. While De Schutter concedes in line with Mattei that international law was at its origins a project aimed at the enclosure of the commons, he shows that a counter-movement is currently emerging from the human rights community to resist the commodification of natural resources. In our own substantive contribution to this volume, 'International law to save the commons' (Chapter 12), we build on the same premise that international law can serve as a potential and additional strategic tool for local communities to reclaim the commons. We show that international and regional human rights instruments can be interpreted in a progressive way so as to protect the commons upon which millions of small-scale farmers, pastoralists, forest-dwellers, artisanal fishers and indigenous peoples depend for their survival around the world and in the Global South specifically. Like Olivier De Schutter, we also point to the project of a UN Declaration of the Rights of Peasants, which provides in its latest draft version a stand-alone obligation 'to recognise and protect the natural commons and their related systems of collective use and management' (United Nations General Assembly, 2017: Article 17(3)). This recent development suggests in our view, for the first time, the existence of a window of opportunity for a new international human right to the commons. Last but not least, in 'Procedure and substance in international environmental law and the protection of the global commons' (Chapter 13), Jutta Brunnée explores the procedural aspects of international environmental law's evolution towards promoting global governance of the global commons. Some global environmental concerns are so complex that she shows that strong procedural obligations can sometimes better serve community interests in the protection of the global commons.

Finally, Martin Deleixhe concludes this volume with this bold question: 'is the governance of the commons a model for a new global governance?' After recalling the proto-democratic, decentralized and bottom-up character of the commons, he argues that the commons indeed put forward an innovative political model to reform global governance. Whereas GPGs require in his view a strong and centralized authority, commons offer a more legitimate polycentric form of federalism which has the potential to democratize global governance.

To sum up, the added value of this volume is that it breaks down the barriers between the studies of commons and wider systems of global governance, and that it connects research agendas that share more theoretical insights than has been traditionally assumed. It elevates the academic debates on the commons by indicating in what ways these bottom-up institutions can also transform the current system of global governance.

NOTE

* The co-editors would like to thank Dr Martin Deleixhe, who contributed to an earlier draft of this introduction and Professor Dr Tine De Moor, who provided very useful comments.

REFERENCES

Bailey, S., Farrell, G. and Mattei, U. (eds) (2013) *Protecting Future Generations through Commons*. Strasbourg, Council of Europe Publishing.

Bauwens, T. and Mertens, S. (2018) Social Economy and Polycentric Governance of Transitions. In: Cassiers, I., Maréchal, K. and Méda, D. (eds) *Post-growth Economics and Society: Exploring the Paths of a Social and Ecological Transition*. Oxon and New York, Routledge, pp. 45–62.

Berkes, F. (2006) From Community-based Resource Management to Complex Systems: The Scale Issue and Marine Commons. *Ecology and Society*, **11** (1), 45.

Bollier, D. and Helfrich, S. (eds) (2012) *The Wealth of the Commons: A World Beyond Market and State*. Amherst, Levellers Press.

Bollier, D. and Helfrich, S. (eds) (2015) *Patterns of Commoning*. Amherst, Levellers Press.

Capra, F. and Mattei, U. (2015) *Toward a Legal System in Tune with Nature and Community*. Oakland, Berrett-Koehler Publishers.

Cogolati, S. (2016) Global Public Goods or Commons as a Lens to Development? A Legal Perspective. Leuven Centre for Global Governance Studies Working Paper No. 179. November 2016. [Online] Available from: https://ghum.kuleuven.be/ggs/publications/working_papers/2016/179cogolati (accessed 25 January 2018).

Cogolati, S., Hamid, L. and Vanstappen, N. (2016) Global Public Goods and Democracy in International Legal Scholarship. *Cambridge Journal of International and Comparative Law*, **5** (1), 4–30.

Dardot, P. and Laval, C. (2014) *Commun: Essai sur la révolution au XXIe siècle*. Paris, La Découverte.

De Angelis, M. (2017) *Omnia Sunt Communia: On the Commons and the Transformation to Postcapitalism*. London, Zed Books.

De Moor, T. (2011) From Common Pastures to Global Commons: A Historical Perspective on Interdisciplinary Approaches to Commons. *Natures Sciences Sociétés*, **19** (4), 422–31.

Dragos Aligica, P. and Boettke, P. (2009) *Challenging Institutional Analysis and Development: The Bloomington School*. London, Routledge.

Fennell, L. A. (2011) Ostrom's Law: Property Rights in the Commons. *International Journal of the Commons*, **5** (1), 9–27.

Frischmann, B. M., Madison, M. J. and Strandburg, K. J. (eds) (2014) *Governing Knowledge Commons*. New York, Oxford University Press.

Gallie, W. B. (1956) Essentially Contested Concepts. *Proceedings of the Aristotelian Society*, **56**, 167–98.

Garver, E. (1978) Rhetoric and Essentially Contested Arguments. *Philosophy and Rhetoric*, **11** (3), 156–72.

Hardin, G. (1968) The Tragedy of the Commons. *Science*, **162** (3859), 1243–8.

Hardt, M. and Negri, A. (2009) *Commonwealth*. Cambridge, Harvard University Press.

Harvey, D. (2011) The Future of the Commons. *Radical History Review*, **109**, 101–7.

Kaul, I. and Mendoza, R. U. (2003) Advancing the Concept of Public Goods. In: Kaul, I., Conceição, P., Le Goulven, K. and Mendoza, R. U. (eds) *Providing Global Public Goods: Managing Globalization*. New York, Oxford University Press, pp. 78–111.

Kaul, I., Grunberg, I. and Stern, M. (1999) Defining Global Public Goods. In: Kaul, I., Grunberg, I. and Stern, M. (eds) *Global Public Goods: International Cooperation in the 21st Century*. New York, Oxford University Press, pp. 2–19.

Klein, N. (2001) Reclaiming the Commons. *New Left Review*, **9**, 81–9.

Mattei, U. (2011) *Beni comuni: Un manifestó*. Roma, Laterza.

Nordhaus, W. D. (1994) *Managing the Global Commons: The Economics of Climate Change*. Cambridge, MIT Press.

Olson, M. (1965) *The Logic of Collective Action: Public Goods and the Theory of Groups*. Cambridge, Harvard University Press.

Orsi, F. (2013) Elinor Ostrom et les faisceaux de droit: l'ouverture d'un nouvel espace pour penser la propriété commune. *Revue de la régulation*, **14**, DOI: 10.4000/regulation.10471.

Ostrom, E. (1990) *Governing the Commons: The Evolution of Institutions for Collective Action*. Cambridge, Cambridge University Press.

Ostrom, E. (2005) *Understanding Institutional Diversity*. Princeton, Princeton University Press.

Ostrom, E. (2009a) A General Framework for Analyzing Sustainability of Social-ecological Systems. *Science*, **325** (5939), 419–22.

Ostrom, E. (2009b) Beyond Markets and States: Polycentric Governance of Complex Economic Systems. Nobel Prize Lecture. 8 December 2009. [Online] Available from: https://www.nobelprize.org/nobel_prizes/economic-sciences/laureates/2009/ostrom_lecture.pdf (accessed 8 January 2018).

Ostrom, V., Tiebout, C. M. and Warren, R. (1961) The Organization of Government in Metropolitan Areas: A Theoretical Inquiry. *American Political Science Review*, **55** (4): 831–42.

Ostrom, E., Burger, J., Field, C. B., Norgaard, R. B. and Policansky, D. (1999) Revisiting the Commons: Local Lessons, Global Challenges. *Science*, **284** (5412), 278–82.

Ranganathan, S. (2016) Global Commons. *European Journal of International Law*, **27** (3), 693–717.

Samuelson, P. (1954) The Pure Theory of Public Expenditure. *The Review of Economics and Statistics*, **36** (4), 387–9.

Stern, P. C. (2011) Design Principles for Global Commons: Natural Resources and Emerging Technologies. *International Journal of the Commons*, **5** (2), 213–32.

United Nations Environment Programme. (2017) Global Commons. [Online] Available from: http://staging.unep.org/delc/GlobalCommons/tabid/54404/Default.aspx (accessed 20 November 2017).

United Nations General Assembly (2017) Promotion and Protection of the Human Rights of Peasants and Other People Working in Rural Areas. Human Rights Council. Thirty-sixth session. 25 September 2017, UN Doc. A/HRC/36/L.29.

Wood, M. C. (2013) *Nature's Trust: Environmental Law for a New Ecological Age*. Cambridge, Cambridge University Press.

Wouters, J., Braeckman, A., Lievens, M. and Bécault, E. (eds) (2015) *Global Governance and Democracy: A Multidisciplinary Analysis*. Cheltenham, UK, and Northampton, MA, USA, Edward Elgar.

PART I

Democratic Perspectives

2. What democracy for the global commons?

Pierre Dardot*

1. INTRODUCTION

This chapter is based on the keynote lecture I gave at the University of Leuven on 23 February 2016 during the International Conference 'Global Commons, Global Public Goods and Global Democracy'. In my latest book co-written with my colleague Christian Laval, and entitled *Commun: Essai sur la révolution au XXIe siècle* (2014), I claim that the 'common', in contrast to global public goods (GPGs) (Kaul et al., 1999), implies a collective production of a good that is not up for appropriation. I suggest that the 'common' could be an alternative to current international economic policies and could have, in that sense, important repercussions on democracy in the global arena. In this chapter, I expand on this premise and try to outline the democracy of the global commons.

In order to clarify my own lexicon, I start by defining different key notions, namely the common, the commons, the common good and common goods (Section 2). Then, I endeavour to justify this way of interrogating the topic – *what democracy for the global commons?* – through an active critique of the current paradigms used to deal with the unlimited cosmocapitalism – that is, the common heritage principle, GPGs and biodiversity (Section 3). Finally, I highlight the positive content of the new paradigm of cosmodemocracy, which I propose in order to address the main question of this chapter (Section 4). Indeed, it seems that global commons require a kind of democracy that is different from that of the local commons. My main argument is that if we wish to have any chance of halting and reversing the logic of cosmocapitalism, we have to institute a global democracy for the global commons.

2. THE COMMON, THE COMMONS, THE COMMON GOOD AND COMMON GOODS

Why speak of the common and 'commons' instead of 'common things', or the 'common good' in a singular or plural sense, since it is more usual to use 'common' as an adjective? Why use this nominalization of the adjective 'common' and what does it mean? And finally, what is *the* 'common' and what is *a* 'common'?

The use of 'common' as an adjective dates back to Roman law, where it designated a certain number of resources as common things (*res communes*): namely, the air, running water, the sea and consequently the shores of the sea. These were considered common by nature – this is to say that they could not be appropriated, the use of which was shared by all. This definition is primarily negative in nature. Common things are excluded from the domain of both state and private ownership. They do not belong to any owner, but rather evade the sphere of ownership given their inherent qualities – in fact, they are supposed to be common.

A second way of conceptualizing what is a common is not directly related to things but instead to the good or to goods. We will, thus, use the term 'common good' to denote what is good in an ethical and political sense. This usage dates back to Aristotle. In fact, it inspired more or less all of Western philosophy. In this sense, the common good is not susceptible to ownership, but instead it represents a norm or rule which unifies a political community. If we speak of 'common goods', it is to better distinguish these types of goods from others within a more general classification system. We will also distinguish 'private goods' from 'public goods' and 'common goods'. This classification was laid out by standard economics, as a result of a certain number of criteria related to rivalry and excludability. Schematically, economic theory defines 'private goods' as rivalrous and excludable; 'public goods' as non-rivalrous and non-excludable; 'club goods' as excludable and non-rivalrous; and a 'common good' as non-excludable and rivalrous.

However, three points within this system of nomenclature remain problematic. The first problem is the *negative* nature of the definition of 'public' or 'collective' goods: these goods cannot be spontaneously produced by the market and are a result of a market failure. Taking into account the consequences of these goods for society ('externalities'), and not just their consumption, does not call into question the primacy of the market. On the contrary, the market is viewed as the best mechanism for the allocation of resources, and it is only in relation to this positive norm that 'public goods' are understood and defined. This is also particularly true for the popular notion of 'GPGs'.

The second point concerns the ambiguity associated with the term 'good' because of this negative character. Indeed, this term can also refer to the useful or advantageous character of something in an ethical or political sense (*agathon* in Greek) rather than what is susceptible to purchase or exchange (*ktèsis* in Greek). Thus the 'common good' in political philosophy identifies with the common advantage, but it is not a good that can be owned and traded. From this perspective, the notion of GPGs becomes somewhat confusing, by encompassing things as diverse as peace, health, justice, financial stability, the ozone layer and so on.

The third point concerns the hybrid nature of 'common goods', which are mixed goods defined by reference to both criteria of rivalry and non-excludability. As such, common goods are always apprehended in economic theory on the basis of their consumption, which prevents us from recognizing the autonomy of the commons.

Using 'commons' as a noun, thus, implies a methodological break with this reification of common things, as well as with the logic underlying the classification of goods in economic theory. A 'commons' is first and foremost an institutional affair and, more specifically, an institutional space defined by collectively developed practical rules. What is most important is the dimension of instituting the activity, and not the technical characteristics of things and goods. Here lies the essential difference between common goods and the common(s). We must specify, therefore, that any commons, insofar as it is instituted as such, is a good in an ethical and political sense. By contrast, any good that is capable of being purchased and sold, is not in itself a commons. This means that a commons is a good only under the condition that it is not a possession or an acquisition. In other words, once it is instituted, a commons is inalienable and inappropriable. It creates a space within which use prevails over ownership. It is, thus, not a resource in itself – even when it is related to one. In this way we understand a commons to be the active link between an object, a place, a natural resource (for example, a waterfall or a forest), or something artificial (for example, a theatre or a square) and the collective activity of those who take charge of it, preserve it, maintain it and take care of it. This activity is not external to the commons, but instead inherent in it.

If we take this to be the definition of every common, then a third implication is that a common, regardless of its specific designation, requires self-government or democratic government. The very act of establishing a common is in and of itself a democratic act. The act of governing a common is nothing more than the continuation of the democratic act; it is thus a sort of continuation of the institution. It consists of reviving this institution by critically assessing its collective rules, whenever the situation demands it. As such, the governance of the common can only proceed from the principle of democracy – the non-democratic governance of a common would threaten, in the short-term, the very existence of this common. I call this the principle *of* the common, this time in the singular form. For that purpose, I refer to the Latin etymology of this word: the common, or '*cum-munus*', is the co-obligation that results from co-participation in the same activity. This co-obligation cannot proceed from the simple fact of belonging. Democracy is, in essence, co-participation in public affairs. The Occupy movement (for example, the anti-austerity movement in Spain, also referred to as the 15-M Movement or the *Indignados*, or the wave of protests in 2013 to contest the urban development plan for Istanbul's Gezi Park) brought with it a strong anti-oligarchic critique of contemporary political representation, advocating for 'real democracy'. Most notable is that this democratic requirement is strongly tied to ecological claims based on preserving the 'commons' (urban spaces in particular) against any sort of private or state enclosure. It then becomes evident that the commons (in the plural) cannot but be established or governed but by the implementation of the principle of the common (in the singular), which is to say, democracy. To sum up, common use requires self-government.

Yet these examples would seem to speak in favour of the establishment of a local democracy, confined within specific geographic limits (for example, a neighbourhood or a city). Aristotle argued for a similar sort of constraint, pointing that beyond a certain number, citizens could no longer know each other. This capacity to mutually engage with one another was, according to him, an important condition for the exercise of democracy. Thus emerges a challenge I will here try to tackle: what sort of democracy is required for commons which are not local, but global in nature – *global commons*? My thesis is that this democracy can only be global. It remains to be seen what this sort of global democracy should look like.

3. CURRENT PARADIGMS TO DEAL WITH THE UNLIMITED COSMOCAPITALISM

With neoliberal capitalism we have come to know a singular historical phenomenon, which I will refer to as '*cosmocapitalism*'. How can this be understood? Cosmocapitalism is not merely a geographical or spatial extension of capitalism, since this extension appeared along with the birth of capitalism. It represents capitalism's tendency to *become universal*. By this, I mean that capital tends to submit all aspects of human existence, even those most intimate and subjective, along with the natural world, to the market's logic, which is nothing more than the logic of competition.

The terms 'world' and 'cosmos' do not describe the planet in a physical sense, or even the global population, but rather the political framework, with its institutional and normative qualities whereby the expansion of the market's logic becomes possible. Max Weber already described the idea of an immense cosmos which imposes its economic activity on the individual caught within the market's grasp (Weber, 2002). Today, this cosmos has grown beyond the single economic sphere to include the social sphere.

3.1 Humanity's Common Heritage Paradigm and the Appropriation of Space

A first example will allow us to highlight this logic of limitlessness by examining the delegation of tasks between the state and private enterprises. On 25 November 2015, just a few days before the opening of the 21st Conference of the Parties (COP) of the Framework Convention on Climate Change in Paris, Barack Obama passed law H.R.2262, which provided authorization for private American companies to use natural resources from outer space (US Congress, 2015).

As we know, the 1967 Outer Space Treaty established the legal status of outer space in the following manner (United Nations, 1967). Article 1 acknowledged that the exploration and use of outer space shall be carried out for the benefit and in the interests of all countries, implying free and equal access without discrimination of any kind. Article 2 established that 'Outer space, including the moon and other celestial bodies, is not subject to national appropriation by claim of sovereignty, by means of use or occupation, or by any other means'. These two conditions, equal access for all and non-ownership, are strictly complementary and both refer to *subjects* recognized by international law, that is to say, the states: 'national appropriation' is state ownership and non-appropriation refers to non-appropriation by states only.

It is precisely from this ambiguity that the law (US Congress, 2015) was cleverly enacted on 25 November 2015. Its name is already quite self-evident: US Commercial Space Launch Competitiveness Act. In a nutshell, the Act gives any United States (US) citizen involved in commercial exploration and exploitation of an asteroid or space resource, the right to own, possess, transport, use, and sell this resource provided it is in accordance with the applicable legislation. This amounts to giving American companies a property right over space resources in due form (Calimaq, 2015). Yet, the law passed by Congress seems to pretend the contrary, as it provides a so-called 'Disclaimer of Extraterritorial Sovereignty' in Section 3 of the Act (US Congress, 2015):

> By the enactment of this Act, the United States–
> Exercises its jurisdiction over United States citizens and vessels, and foreign persons and vessels otherwise subject to its jurisdiction, in the exercise of the high seas freedom to engage in exploration for, and commercial recovery of, hard mineral resources of the deep seabed in accordance with generally accepted principles of international law recognized by the United States; but
> Does not thereby assert sovereignty or sovereign or exclusive rights or jurisdiction over, or the ownership of, any areas or resources in the deep seabed.

We can clearly see how this law circumvents the prohibition of national appropriation articulated by the 1967 Outer Space Treaty: the prohibition forbids states themselves from 'national appropriation by claim of sovereignty', but it does not prevent a private company from exploring or exploiting space resources for commercial purposes. It goes without saying that the enactment of this law was very much applauded by private companies planning to embark on asteroid mining. What is remarkable about this law is that it confirms the international commitment of the US not to assert sovereignty over any space resource, while simultaneously conferring private companies the right to appropriate resources therein without any restriction.

Under the Outer Space Treaty, the legal status of the 'common things' (*res communes*), under which certain resources are known to be common by nature (as in Roman law), is not formally addressed. Under Article I of the Outer Space Treaty, the outer space is not even declared to be the '*common heritage* of mankind', but simply the 'province of all mankind' (United Nations, 1967). The notion of 'common heritage' was only explicitly introduced in 1967 to deal with the legal status of the deep seabed beyond the limits of national jurisdiction (United Nations General Assembly, 1967). Regardless of the ambiguity of this notion, particularly regarding the holder of such heritage, the idea of 'heritage' implies a double duty to both preserve and transmit it. However, international law limits the right of use for states only, as they alone are faced with the prohibition of appropriation. We are, therefore, presented with a way of extrapolating the *res communes* category inherited from Roman law, insofar as non-appropriation and common use are present, but subordinate to the goodwill of the states. Thus, we are faced with a cheap if not unfinished version of a 'common', which is entrusted to states, and limits state sovereignty without even calling it into question.

With the Competitiveness Act (US Congress, 2015), we are faced with an act of state sovereignty that manages to circumvent the prohibition of appropriation by a sovereign state without formally violating it. This represents a sort of 'delegation' under which the state, on the one hand, grants its citizens a legal title that it denies to itself, on the other, it does so in order to better guarantee it to those to whom it has been delegated. The *imperium* (state sovereignty) gives full licence for all candidates to the *dominium*, to privately control and appropriate any resources they are able to seize: statutory law enforces beforehand the power that technology provides. Beyond this collusion between the state and private companies, what emerges here is the powerful homology between state and private ownership: *imperium* and *dominium* appear to be based on two forms of a similar logic of ownership, which affirm one another. The primary challenge facing the heritage of mankind paradigm is that it does not fundamentally break with interstate logic and, as such, leaves leeway for private appropriation.

3.2 The Global Public Goods Paradigm and the Value of Biodiversity

A second example allows us to unveil the same neoliberal capitalist logic at work within the realm of the destruction of the biosphere. At the end of the 1980s, with the momentum of the pollution rights initiated by Reagan, George H. W. Bush encouraged the expansion of the market endorsing the '*No Net Loss*' goal (Feydel and Bonneuil, 2015: p. 45). The seemingly small adjective 'net' carries with it a heavy connotation. It does not mean that we do not have the right to destroy biodiversity but rather, the opposite. Indeed, under the 'No Net Loss' principle, we have the right to destroy biodiversity as long as we replace whatever has been destroyed elsewhere. In other words, damages resulting from human activities must be balanced by at least equivalent gains. For example, we have the right to destroy ten acres of forest in one area, as long as we plant ten acres of trees elsewhere, within the next 30 years, because once the new trees have grown, it will not make any difference. In market lingo, this is referred to as 'biodiversity offsetting'. The neoliberal argument is the same and is now well-established – we have failed to obtain our reduction goals, so we must adapt our strategy by trying new financial mechanisms, which are much more effective than the inefficient laws and regulations. That these so-called 'laws and regulations' have failed because they have bet on the market must be hidden. It is always the same explanation – if we failed, it is not because we conceded to the market, but rather the opposite, because we did not sufficiently take advantage of it.

What is the relationship between this logic of compensation and actual biodiversity, which is made up of the interaction between complex systems, and not of detachable and interchangeable parts? A good example comes from the Brazilian company Vale, which sought to present eucalyptus plantations as a form of reforestation of the Amazon rainforest whose destruction it has actively contributed to. The logic of this compensation can be understood as *equivalency* logic in its most literal sense. That is, it assumes that there is a commensurability between the Amazon rainforest and eucalyptus plantations, which would affirm their *equal value.* This type of reasoning is completely indifferent to the sort of relationship a tree has with the soil: the fact that the eucalyptus, which originated from Australia, actually dries up the Amazonian soil, is not at all taken into consideration (Feydel and Bonneuil, 2015: pp. 94–5).

As Marx so aptly described it in the first Volume of his major book *Capital* (1992), the logic behind market equivalency is at its core a logic of *indifference* to the qualitative differences that exist between different types of work, and the products that stem from each. What is remarkable here is that we are not referring to the products of human work but instead to living ecosystems. Here we have come to a critical point: the marketing of biodiversity requires that *we assign value to something that is not, in fact, a product of work.* This argument was reaffirmed by Pavel Sukhdev, a banker who has directed the Economics of Ecosystems and Biodiversity (TEEB) project launched by the United Nations Environment Programme (UNEP) since 2007: 'We take advantage of nature because it has value. But we lose it because it is free' (Feydel and Bonneuil, 2015: p. 62). Thus, '[t]he economy has become the currency of politics' (sic), we have to learn to understand '[t]he economic value of nature' and express it in a way that is clear to political decision makers. In essence, we must remedy the '[i]nvisible economics of nature' by assigning to it a monetary value or a price. In order to carry out this task we must employ a calculation: in this way, the pollination of trees and flowers by bees constitutes an economically invisible service whose value is estimated at 200 billion dollars, which is almost 8 per cent of the global agricultural production on earth according to Pavel Sukhdev (ibid.: p. 9). The same principle can be applied to pure air or drinking water – the services they render become more and more valuable as they become increasingly rare. Scarcity has always determined value, except that now scarcity represents the services provided by nature.

But what exactly does the notion of an economically assessable 'service' mean? What vision of nature does it propose and is this conceptualization really new? For a long time, biodiversity was conceived of as a group of *resources* comprised of several distinct elements (genes, species, habitats and so on), which were capable of being owned, purchased and sold. This conception prevailed in Rio during the Convention on Biological Diversity (United Nations, 1992). But, at the end of the twentieth century, a more dynamic representation emerged which posited that ecosystems should be recognized as the 'third level of biodiversity', situated above genes and species (Feydel and Bonneuil, 2015: pp. 164–6). Now processes and flows take precedence over individual entities and elements. Although we can measure the intrinsic value of the latter, we can only appreciate the value of process and flow in terms of 'services'. It is, thus, not biodiversity in and of itself which is valuable, but more so the services rendered by the ecosystems that possess value. Hence the notion of 'ecosystem services', consisting of streams of natural capital stock which, when combined with human industrial activities, gives way to human welfare (ibid.: pp. 59 and 165). 'Provisioning services' (related to 'resources': food, wood, grains and so on), 'regulating services' (the climate, rainfall, water quality), and 'cultural services' (spiritual or recreational value of nature) can be counted among such services. Biobanks sell shares to protect species threatened by deforestation to the very companies who carry out such acts (ibid.: p. 154). Many are unwavering in their belief that the biosphere as a whole should be treated as natural capital. In keeping with this line of thought, the following shift occurs: the biosphere should not enter the commercial sphere merely as a *commodity* (the logic underlying the sale of timber and industrial capitalism, marketing 'biological resources' and patented genes, and so on), but also and most importantly as an *asset* (that is, within the context of securities eligible for future revenue based on the logic of annuities) (ibid.: p. 166). Thus, we move from the simple commodification of nature, typical of industrial capitalism, which emphasizes producing goods, to neoliberal capitalist financialization and, simultaneously, from the portrayal of nature as a 'resource' to its representation as capital generating a 'flow of services'.

How does the theory of GPGs (Kaul et al., 1999) allow us to fight against this trend to financialization? Is GPGs theory not designed, on the contrary, to promote governance of private and state actors? As we know, beyond the criteria relative to the beneficiaries of such goods (the *publicum* which turns these goods into global goods), this theory distinguishes between three classes of GPGs: (i) global natural goods (for example, ozone layer, climate stability); (ii) goods that constitute man-made heritage (for example, knowledge, cultural heritage, the Internet); and (iii) goods that result from global politics (for example, peace, health, financial stability). While the first class represents natural goods, the other two result from human activity.

However, the distinction between these three distinct classes becomes blurred in the case of the negative consequences flowing from poorly managed non-renewable energy. As a result of global policies, global natural goods slide into the third category of GPGs. Moreover, an economistic approach in terms of supply requires that these natural goods are reduced to 'stock variables' like the goods of the second category, whereas the goods of the third category are conceived as 'flow variables' since a continued effort is required to ensure their potential. But if natural assets are now part of the third category, should we conclude that they have become 'flow variables'? In any case, the evolution from 'stock' to 'flow' corresponds precisely with the sort of change that accompanies and legitimizes nature's financialization. Finally, and most worryingly, the value attributed to biological diversity is estimated by reference to the costs of protecting it. Thus, biological diversity enters the category of public goods that have an 'intrinsic existence value' 'in an effort to grapple with and ultimately define the intrinsic worth of protecting the [good]' (ibid.: p. 253). We would be better off articulating that this is not intrinsic at all: biodiversity has no value of its own and is not a good in and of itself; instead, its value is derived from the fact that it is the result of subjective appreciation, which amounts to recognizing that this is a good. We see what can result from the ambiguity surrounding the term 'good'. But overall this confirms the rejection of the notion of biodiversity's intrinsic value in favour of the idea that value is assigned by an external party, which expresses in its own way the notion of 'ecosystem services'.

4. COSMODEMOCRACY

Given the logic underlying cosmocapitalism, we must find out a new type of global democracy if we wish to have any chance of halting and reversing it. Such a democracy will be referred to below as *cosmodemocracy*. It is indeed linked to cosmopolitanism; that is, to the idea of global politics and global citizenship.

4.1 Different Types of Cosmopolitanism

4.1.1 Cosmopolitanism as a project

Cosmopolitanism can be defined as the feeling and consciousness of belonging to the same world. It can be expressed in many different ways. It can represent the awareness of living in the same world or sharing the same human condition, the feeling of sharing a common, confined space, and the feeling of being affected by everything that affects another part of humanity. According to Kant's well-known dictum, 'a violation of rights in one place is felt throughout the world' (Kant, 1977). The awareness of belonging to a shared world has been expressed in noteworthy works of philosophy. This is particularly true of stoicism, within which man is seen as belonging to part of a 'Universal' or 'Upper City' and whose political city is just a small image. Individuals are then viewed as a citizens of the world, but this citizenship is not at all political. By virtue of its universalism, Christianity was able to modify and extend its tradition through the 'catholicity' of the Church. The idea that human rights are not limited to any specific country, but are universal in nature, arose from Christian universalism and found support from various scholars and lawyers, including Anacharsis Cloots, author of *Bases constitutionnelles de la République du genre humain* (1793). Yet the framework remains one in which the world is assimilated to the nation: the human race becomes the only ruler so that the Universal Republic must identify with the Republic of Mankind and there is only one nation that corresponds with humanity itself. With Kant's *Perpetual Peace: A Philosophical Essay* (1795), cosmopolitanism begins to take a new meaning. Kant distinguishes between three overlapping components of public law: (i) municipal or civil law (*ius civitatis*), which should be a republican constitution; (ii) international law or the law of nations (*ius gentium*), which provides for the right of states to engage in mutual relations or international law via a federation of free states; and (iii) cosmopolitan law (*ius cosmopoliticum*). However, cosmopolitan law is intended to guarantee the right of 'hospitality' to all individuals – which is a right of access merely to promote trade. In this way, cosmopolitanism restricts the cosmos to the commercial sphere without establishing a genuine political citizenship.

4.1.2 Factual cosmopolitanization

What was once only an idea or ideal has become part of how we now live. Cosmopolitanism has become the new reality, both in an objective and subjective sense, and what Ulrich Beck has called 'banal cosmopolitanism' (2006: p. 26). This factual cosmopolitanization, borne out of the growth of interdependence and transnationalization of ways of life and cultures, should not be confused with transnational political activities and institutional creations, even if the link between these phenomena seems quite obvious. Factual cosmopolitanization is essential to the world's inhabitants, albeit to varying degrees. It became extremely important at the turn of the century. With the rise of global risks, it began to haunt our minds, penetrating the banality of everyday life, for example, with respect to food, altering our aesthetic tastes, and changing our approach to interstate relations by giving preference to human rights over sovereignty. It is no longer a matter of assigning positive value to the world's political organization by imagining what the future might hold. It is rather about establishing and characterizing the multitude of processes that transform everyday life up to the point where they lead to the relativization of national borders. According to Beck, 'reality itself has become cosmopolitan' (ibid.: p. 10). With globalization and resistance to the latter, a new era has emerged – that of 'reflexive modernity'. In order to see, understand, and analyse it, one must abandon the 'national perspective' and 'methodological nationalism', in favour of a 'cosmopolitan perspective' and 'methodological cosmopolitanism'. To see reality as it is, one must have a 'cosmopolitan eye'.

This day-to-day sociological cosmopolitization and banality represents a considerable break from philosophical cosmopolitanism, which, insofar as it was limited to the national experience, was only appealing to a few. This new form of cosmopolitanism bears no resemblance to an active project. It is more part of a factual experience than a conscious choice, and it generates ambivalent attitudes, spanning from a taste for travel and welcoming cultural hybridization, to fear of political dispossession or loss of cultural identity. However, contrary to the claims of Ulrich Beck, the idea that this factual cosmopolitanization is the driver of such overflow from the national state framework, does not date back to the early part of the twenty-first century. It was already Marcel Mauss' argument when he dealt with the notion of 'internation', which comprised, according to him, all the social ties that tended to overflow from the domain of nations, only to end up giving birth to a 'global society', which, as it becomes more and more conscious of itself, could aspire to political self-government (2013). By 'internationalization', an action that unifies nations around the world – 'the opposite of the a-nation' – Mauss includes both the economic and moral interdependencies along with material and ideal phenomena. We can see how cosmopolitization, be it economic, social or cultural, could just as well be described in terms of 'internationalization'.

4.1.3 Normative and institutional cosmopolitanism

What Beck also failed to see is that normative and institutional cosmopolitanism do not flow freely and naturally from factual cosmopolitanization. This is so, firstly, because of the opposition of forces that have no interest in seeing their powers being eroded. Second, and most importantly, because a strictly empirical conceptualization of factual cosmopolitanization runs the risk of overlooking immediately what is generated from internal relations of domination in national and local settings, and what is beyond local level democratic control. Now, because the local and national spheres are losing their 'naturalness', for those who live in those areas, the effects of globalization imply that the normative and institutional issues arise with urgency in a political form that is *antagonistic*. Factual cosmopolitanization is no longer a 'happy globalization', but for many the dispossession of their destiny.

We must give credit to Karl Renner, Austrian Social Democrat and Austro-Marxist, for encouraging the reflection on the switch between a *de facto* internationalism to an institutionalized internationalism (Renner, 1998). This *de facto* internationalism, comprised of economic, social and cultural forms of internationalization, demonstrates how the world's legal fabric extends beyond the mere sum of nations. In the same way that the nation is the product of a historical development which culminates in its legal capacity at the end of the eighteenth century, the 'internation', to use Mauss' term, will inevitably find its legal form from a substrate of facts that is poorly or not at all seen, but as such, represents a legal duty. The term 'international' should not be taken at face value, as it represents much more than international relations between states. Indeed, it involves the way in which the world is constructed, legally and politically, in its post-Westphalian organization. According to Mauss, the enemy is state sovereignty, as it represents an obstacle to real human interests. We are moving towards a world order that will no longer be limited by the coexistence of sovereign nation states, what Renner calls the 'institutional *Oecumene*'. The creation of the League of Nations in 1920 gave way to a new era, as the 'community of nations' was granted legal standing above the states. Renner claims that, as a result of the establishment of the League, a 'supra-State international law' appeared in order to guarantee an infra-state national law, which itself protects minorities. However, as Renner argues, this step remained constrained by the desire to freeze the acquired positions after the First World War. We know that this is also exactly what happened in 1945 with the creation of the United Nations: as demonstrated recently during the COP 21, the most glaring contradiction still exists between the interstate logic of a group of sovereign states, and the need for a global community which undermines the sovereignty of each state in order to respect higher principles which cater to the interests of humanity. Hence Renner's proposal in 1937: delegates representing 'partial international interests' (capital, labour, culture and so on) should be members of the League of Nations Council. It is under this condition that international interests would be taken into account, since the representatives in question would not be able to mandate all issues nationally. The question, then, is how to make this global human community exist as such. We can envision this as Renner did when describing a global parliament or, more specifically, a second chamber of representatives in which the people themselves articulate and make decisions about their economic structure and social values, along with their present grievances and hopes for the future (Renner, 1998: p. 74). Yet it is evident that the creation of a supranational chamber does not respond to the needs of those who represent 'partial international interests'. Indeed, the parliamentary system of representation, with all its inherent vices, is simply replicated on a global scale. In order to overcome the interstate's limitations, we must decide to make the leap from internationalism and cosmopolitanism to cosmo*politics*; that is, to a political organization of humanity.

4.2 Cosmopolitics

The two paradigms discussed above suffer from a crippling limitation – that of humanity's common heritage which subjects the 'common things' to the interstate logic, and that of GPGs, which leave the latter to the governance of private and state actors. Still, progress has been made in the establishment of humankind law. But, even assuming a legal status was assigned to humanity, this would not suffice, and neither would a cosmopolitan consciousness, in reaching cosmopolitan institutions. How do we overcome the double impasse imposed by the interstate and global private law, while paving the way for humanity's common form of political activity; which is to say, a real democracy for humanity? I would like to highlight two points which I feel are complementary. The first relates to the institutional architecture of a global democracy and the second concerns the political activity of world citizens. The first requires, above all, a political imagination, and the second assumes that we extend the observation of collective practices and experimentations already underway.

4.2.1 The dual federation of the commons

In order to introduce the first point, we must return to our discussion of the commons. Early on in this chapter, we established that the commons are institutional matters to the extent that they determine the rules of common use. In this sense, the commons emerge from what we might legally refer to as the 'public', not only in the orthodox economics sense of the collective nature of 'public goods', but also in terms of the public in opposition to the private. It is important to note that this public *sui generis* is *non-state public*. What exactly does this mean? The state's public aims to ensure universal access to services but it does so by allowing state administration to monopolize the management of these services, thereby excluding users reduced to mere consumer status. The non-state public of the commons guarantees universal access via user participation in this management. Note that non-state does not mean anti-state, but rather, autonomous from the state. But what are we to make of the state itself? Under what conditions can it itself become a common? And how can we conceptualize its articulation to what belongs to the infra- and supra-state levels? Moreover, how can the different types of commons be organized among themselves?

The magnitude of these questions led us to imagine a political system, that of *non-centred federalism*, which was inspired by Proudhon (1863). Indeed, he designed a dual federation of social and economic organizations, representing the municipalities as well as the production units and working companies, both of which should be governed by the principle of democracy. In a similar way, we can distinguish, on the one hand, the social-economic commons (common of river, common of forest, seed bank, production unit and so on) independently constituted of territoriality and administrative borders and, on the other hand, political commons formed through the process of increasingly integrating territories (municipalities, regions, states, international groupings of states). Yet, in all of this we are neither statists nor anarchists. We are even reluctant to consider a single global government or a single world state, which would imply a centralized form of authority that is incompatible with the democracy required by the institution of the commons. We are supporters of a *polyarchic* system, which should not be understood as 'government of the many' but instead as 'many governments' democratically coordinated across the world, which naturally implies a systematic intersection of different types of government, state and non-state, politics, and socio-economics.

4.2.2 Global citizenship

These 'demo-cosmopolitan' systems will not come from above and they will not emerge from interstate decisions or contractual agreements between private actors. Historically, the exercise of constructive activist citizenship has been an important precursor to the creation of new political institutions. Today, we observe the elements of an authentic political citizenship, which is diverse, decentred and transnational at the same time. This is exemplified by anti-globalization and social movements, in the missions of non-governmental organizations like Amnesty International, in the commitment of certain ecological associations to the COP 21, and via initiatives supporting public aid for migrants, and so on. This is not a citizenship that is expected to gain legal recognition, status, rights or duties as part of a state, but instead one that is called to act, engaging in transnational actions by those Beck calls 'global public interest entrepreneurs' (2006). We could also refer to them as global commons actors. This non-state and non-statutory citizenship must be thought of in terms of practices aimed at maintaining or acquiring rights rather than formally granting them. Only such transnational citizenship-in-action can give full meaning to the idea of cosmopolitics: politics for the world, as long as the 'world' implies what resonates in the Latin term *mundus*, namely, not the Earth as a planet and not the totality of individuals living on Earth but instead, the living connection between the individuals inhabiting in and the Earth itself. In this sense, the anti-globalization slogan 'the world is not for sale' is more meaningful than it might seem at first sight: the world, in itself, is not a 'thing' that we can own; it must be recognized as inappropriable and instituted as a common.

5. CONCLUSION

To conclude, instituting the world as a common cannot be understood as an extension of the nation-state or city-state models at the global level. The democracy of the global commons is irreducible to a mere change of scale. Instead, it requires a genuine collective political invention, which is based on the multiplication of self-government at all levels. What is at stake here is the confrontation between two diametrically opposed logics: whereas the logic of the commons is fundamentally plural, polymorphic, non-centred in nature, the logic of state sovereignty as it was constructed in the West is intrinsically linked to an indivisible and absolute centre of power. The solution is not for several sovereignties to overlap on the same territory, as this would be incompatible with the very notion of sovereignty, but for several types of self-governments to limit each other's power reciprocally.

NOTE

* This chapter was translated from French to English by Claire Piccinin. It benefited from the reviews of Samuel Cogolati, Martin Deleixhe, Christiaan Boonen and Nicolás Brando.

REFERENCES

Beck, U. (2006) *Qu'est-ce que le cosmopolitisme?* Paris, Flammarion.
Calimaq (2015) Le jour où l'espace a cessé d'être un bien commun . . . [Online] Available from: https://scinfolex.com/2015/11/30/le-jour-ou-lespace-a-cesse-detre-un-bien-commun/ (accessed 24 November 2017).
Cloots, A. (1793) *Bases constitutionnelles de la république du genre humain*. Paris, Imprimerie Nationale.
Feydel, S. and Bonneuil, C. (2015) *Prédation: Nature, le nouvel eldorado de la finance*. Paris, La Découverte.
Kant, I. (1795) *Perpetual Peace: A Philosophical Essay*. London, George Allen and Unwin.
Kant, I. (1977) *Schriften zur Anthropologie, Geschichtsphilosophie, Politik und Pädagogik.* Frankfurt am Main, Surhkamp.
Kaul, I., Grunberg, I. and Stern, M. (1999) *Global Public Goods: International Cooperation in the 21st Century*. New York, Oxford University Press.
Marx, K. (1992) *Capital.* Vol. I. London, Penguin Classics.
Mauss, M. (2013) *La nation*. Paris, Presses Universitaires de France.
Proudhon, P.-J. (1863) *Du principe fédératif et de la nécessité de reconstituer le Parti de la Révolution*. Paris, E. Dentu.
Renner, K. (1998) *La nation, mythe et réalité*. Nancy, Presses Universitaires de Nancy.

United Nations (1967) Treaty on Principles Governing the Activities of States in the Exploration and Use of Outer Space, including the Moon and Other Celestial Bodies. New York, 27 January 1967. United Nations Treaty Series 610 (205).

United Nations (1992) Convention on Biological Diversity. Rio de Janeiro, 5 June 1992. United Nations Treaty Series 1760 (79).

United Nations General Assembly (1967) First Committee Debate. 1 November 1967, UN Docs A/C.1/PV/1515–151.

US Congress (2015) H.R.2262 – US Commercial Space Launch Competitiveness Act. [Online] Available from: https://www.congress.gov/bill/114th-congress/house-bill/2262 (accessed 24 November 2017).

Weber, M. (2002) *The Protestant Ethic and the 'Spirit' of Capitalism*. London, Penguin Classics.

3. Federal commons

Nicolás Brando and Helder De Schutter*

1. INTRODUCTION

Dealing with the commons as both a local and a global concern can raise many issues in an attempt to develop a political structure that can manage these various levels of authority. In this response to Pierre Dardot's proposal (see Chapter 2 in this volume), we focus on his account of how the commons are to be institutionalized in our present world. He presents his proposal as a federal system for managing the commons at both the local and global level. Through the use of the federalist theory literature, we will assess the credentials of his federalist programme, arguing that his refusal to grant salient competences and authority to central institutions makes his proposal more of a confederal or treaty-based argument, rather than a federal system. Based on this assessment, we present three connected concerns with his proposed system of governance of the commons, arguing that it is not fully able to deal with the global problems that it intends to tackle. We consider that solidarity at higher levels is currently not stable enough to protect global commons; that the absence of shared-rule (through state-like authorities) in Dardot's federal proposal cannot fully protect common concerns more broadly than at the local level; and that the exclusive focus on the *practices* of commoning, disregarding seeing commons as *goods*, may enable unsustainable, inefficient, and potentially oppressive practices. We close by recommending a series of amendments to his proposal, in order for it to, first, be a truly federal political system; and, second, to ensure the protection of and access to the commons as both local and global goods.

2. DARDOT'S FEDERAL PROPOSAL

2.1 From Local to Global

Dealing with the commons as both a local and a global issue, can have its difficulties when devising political structures to govern it. On the one hand, we see in Dardot a concern for preserving and empowering the autonomy and self-management of local commons; while, on the other, the aim of dealing with the inevitable globalization of ecological problems. An attempt to deal with the commons in both its local and global dimensions requires devising alternative forms of governance that can, at the same time, ensure the protection and preservation of local communities and their social practices, while effectively tackling the ecological concerns that have a global impact.

Pierre Dardot is aware of this issue: in his work with Christian Laval (2014: pp. 498–519) and in the piece to which this chapter responds (see Chapter 2 in this volume), he proposes instituting a global federation of the commons as a way to deal with the potential dangers of globalization through both local and global initiatives. It may be that, in an ideal world, local communities could be left to their whims, but the forces of globalization demand a shift in perspective that allow us to understand our global common realities and deal with them as such.[1] This requires, according to Dardot, stepping away from the state-centric conception of politics that dominates the current global scene for two reasons: first, as a return to more local forms of politics that promote self-government and autonomy without state intervention (p. 23); and, second, for the promotion of non-state forms of global politics, where local commons are connected across the world through networks built by common interests and concerns (Dardot and Laval, 2014: p. 516).

2.2 From Centralized to Localized

This implies an alternative way of looking at how economic and political concerns are managed, and how people relate to these economic and political structures. By diversifying traditionally state-controlled competences into smaller territorial and non-territorial units, and into larger networks of transnational cooperation, the state loses its role as the central and most relevant source of political and economic authority. Dardot argues that, although the state may be efficient in providing and ensuring access to fundamental services and goods, it does so at the expense of reducing individuals to passive recipients (consumers), unable to have any direct control or participation in this management (Dardot, Chapter 2 in this volume). As a response to the problems that arise from this centralization of authority, a return to communal self-government that is autonomous from the state ensures a more active engagement of society in not only receiving, but also managing the provision of and access to the fundamental services previously controlled by a central authority (Dardot and Laval, 2014: p. 498).

2.3 From Localized to Federalized

Relying solely on communal, small-scaled governance institutions may not be the most efficient way to deal with global problems; there is a need for establishing mechanisms of cooperation and coordination that reach farther than local forms of politics, while respecting the autonomy and self-government fundamental for their survival. Federal principles, in this respect, are the best way to balance global issues, with the sustainment of an active and engaged local democracy.

Building on Proudhon's federal proposal, Dardot and Laval argue for the need to establish mechanisms of governance that can have a wide reach in its scope of action, while maintaining the local institutions that enable autonomy and self-government. The objective is to develop the idea of 'federal contracts' where the contracting parties establish a relationship based on reciprocity and equivalence between what is given to each and what is kept by each. The rationale of such contracts is to foster cooperation between units, while not falling into the dangers of unification of interests, nor of the transformation of cooperative contracts among local commons into communities unified under a common will (Dardot and Laval, 2014: p. 507). In this respect, they are critical of federal approaches such as that of Althusius, where smaller communities cohere with others in a symbiotic manner, transforming the various and diverse practices and interests into a unified community of interests that ends up centralizing the means of economic and political government (Dardot and Laval, 2014: p. 506).

Authority is shared in such federal contracts, but only to the degree that smaller units always keep more rights and liberties than those that they bestow to larger units. Authority of larger units, say Dardot and Laval, 'is specialized and restricted, proportional to its size, it diminishes in number, immediacy and intensity' (2014: p. 507; translation is ours). This process of allocation of competences and authority stems from the smaller possible units (individual persons and their rights), growing in a bottom-up direction to larger units, insofar as the smaller units have agreed to share authority over a given issue with others equal to them. This applies to federal contracts of all sizes; from the smaller contracts within local communities, to transnational federations. There is no exclusive level of authority (as with present day predominance of states as the locus of authority within them and among them); the state is, rather, just another level of authority in an institutional continuum that starts with the smallest commons, and ends in global networks of federal contracts (Dardot and Laval, 2014: p. 508).

2.4 The Double Federation: Dividing the Social from the Political

Concerns with the potential centralization of authority by one unit over many competences, and the objective of maintaining as much as possible the autonomy and self-government of smaller units, presses the boundaries of traditional conceptions of federalism by dividing it into two camps. Still following Proudhon, Dardot and Laval propose separating the authority over the purely *political* domain from the institutions that govern *socio-economic* issues. Unification of political and social concerns, say Dardot and Laval, is a remnant of a statist conception of federalism that assumes the need to centralize the management of these originally diverse camps (Dardot and Laval, 2014: p. 506). In this respect, the federal contracts that concern the purely political (territorial organization of units, diplomatic relations, coordination of smaller units, reciprocal establishment of rights), are separated from those in the socioeconomic sphere (Dardot and Laval, 2014: p. 511). Two forms of federal institution of the commons are, thus, established: (1) *socioeconomic* federal networks, constituted independent of territorial logic, established for exchange, efficient production, and provision of goods. This also includes transnational ecological commons, such as those required for the sustainment of forests or rivers; and (2) the *purely political* networks which follow a logic of increasing integration of territories so as to regulate and coordinate among the socioeconomic commons within these established federal political structures (Dardot and Laval, 2014: p. 514).

This division of federal institutions turns the rationale of a simple vertical dispersion of authority into a 'horizontalization' of authority, where units are not only linked to larger or smaller units in a vertical line, but they relate and contract with each other in a horizontal way, without having to pass through larger units, coordinating on issues that affect them exclusively, thus, pluralizing the *loci* of authority over different issues, in different types and scopes of federal contracts (Dardot and Laval, 2014: pp. 513–14). The sources of democratic involvement are diversified in this respect. Not only are democratic entitlements ensured in the various vertical levels of political participation (from the communal to the global), but they are strongly endorsed and protected in the socioeconomic sphere through the democratization of the workplace, and of the decision-making procedures over the production and provision of various services and goods (Dardot and Laval, 2014: p. 512). This diversified democratic involvement secures the capacity of self-government in the various spheres of human life, protecting from the dangers of bestowing authority over social or economic concerns that are not territorial in nature, thus not apt for political institutions to manage.

3. LOCATING THE INSTITUTION OF THE COMMONS

Our first concern when assessing Dardot's institutionalization of the commons as a federal proposal stems from the use of the idea of 'federalism' as a way to portray his political system. No consensus exists in the literature regarding a specific characteristic that can define federalism as such. However, looking at various relevant characteristics of a political system, and comparing them with the different attributes often ascribed to federations, we can estimate how much that political system relies on federal elements and how much it includes both unitary and confederal/treaty-based mechanisms. Although it may seem a pointless semantic debate, the vagueness in Dardot's use of the term 'federalism' is not without its problems. It allows almost any political system to be labelled as federal, enabling contradictions within the concept to appear as consistent among each other.

Among the various possible characteristics of federations, the following five are characteristic of *most* federal systems, as described in the federalism literature: (1) the diversification of competences (and their salience) at different levels of government; (2) the *Kompetenz-Kompetenz* (the authority to decide over competence allocation) should not be solely decided upon by either the central level or the member units level; (3) the constitutional entrenchment of competences; (4) the ability of both levels to control the constitution(s); and (5) the 'dual' characteristics of the public sphere. We will analyse Dardot's proposal on the basis of these five characteristics, and assess what is the most appropriate way of defining its government system. This will be in keeping with the traditional three-legged typology of unitary/federal/confederal used by most of the federal literature today, in order to define the actual rationale behind Dardot's 'federation of the commons'. We will subdivide and expand this triad into smaller categories when required, following John Law's (2013) more specific typology.

3.1 Diversity and Salience of *Loci* of Authority

The first fundamental characteristic of a federation is the particular distribution of competences in different levels of government. A federal political order, in its most minimalist definition, can be considered as a system where shared-rule and self-rule are combined (Elazar, 1987). Diversification and non-centralization of at least some salient competences, in this respect, is the first fundamental element that defines a federal system (Kelemen, 2003: p. 185; Watts, 1998: p. 124).

At least some salient competences (such as defence, foreign policy, and the judiciary) are governed by the larger, central unit, while at the same time the member units of the federal entity govern (at least some) other salient competences (typically culture, education, and infrastructural matters) that only concern them. This is opposed to both unitary and confederal dynamics: in the first, all or most of the fundamental political (and economic) competences are held by a *central* unit of authority (usually in the hands of a state as it is seen today, but could be imagined as a global system as well); in the second, all or most of the fundamental competences are administered by the smaller units (this could be seen within a domestic society or at a regional/global level). The fundamental difference between the three systems, in this respect, is in the balance between who keeps most of the authority; the scale in the unitary system inclines towards the higher level; the confederal system inclines towards the lower levels; and the federal system intends to achieve a balance between both.

Three features of Dardot's proposal allow us to understand their position regarding the degree of shared-rule of salient governmental competences. First, they emphasize the value and the fundamental role that smaller units have in exercising self-government and autonomy. This is their main concern and their main objective: to maintain and promote as much as possible the capacity of local commons to manage themselves without external impositions. Second, and following from the above, they show high reticence towards any centralization of authority. Their intent to localize government stands against any higher level of governance having any of the salient competences and authority previously held by the smaller communities. Up to this point, it would seem that their proposal would stand on a system of small-scaled self-governed commons that have sole authority over the issues that concern them. This could be imagined as a system similar to that of city-states, or of roman *municipia* (Dardot and Laval, 2014: p. 514). But their concern with larger ecological problems, and the requirements to coordinate and cooperate among larger units in order to sustain production of larger commons, goods, and services, leads them to concede to the need to establish 'contracts' among these local commons. This surely appears to be a move towards a more federal division of competences to deal with issues at different levels of government. But, we argue, the nature of the contracts proposed by Dardot, and the *locus* of most of the salient competences, are not consistent with a federal mechanism. As mentioned above, federal dynamics point towards a balanced diversification of salient competences among the different levels of government, but Dardot's approach is mostly concerned with the conservation of the highest possible degree of authority at the lowest levels of government, restricting and specializing the competences granted to higher levels, and diminishing their intensity and number (Dardot and Laval, 2014: p. 507). It is clear that the objective is not to find a balance between the authority of various levels, as in the case of federal dynamics, but rather to devise a pyramidal structure, more traditional to confederal entities, where most competences stay with local units.

3.2 *Kompetenz-Kompetenz*

This feature looks at which level of government has the authority to allocate competences. This is a fundamental feature that allows to differentiate federal dynamics from other political systems because it defines the final source of authority in a political system. In the case of the federal system, the element of shared-rule plays a fundamental role here as well. Opposite to unitary systems, where this competence to assign competences is held by a central unit (top-down; as in the case of Belgium or Spain); and opposite to confederal dynamics, where the member units are the ones that assign competences to a higher level (bottom-up; as in the European Union (EU)); a federal polity makes use of the institutions at a higher level to assign competences, but does so through a deliberation by and among the smaller units. In this sense, it seems that the competence is at the central level, but acquired through a decision-making procedure controlled by the smaller units. The *kompetenz-kompetenz* in federal systems can be considered not to rely, thus, in one sole level of government, but rather transcends these levels by adjudicating this authority to the *citizens* themselves (see Law, 2013: pp. 101–2) or by involving both levels of government. In this respect, a fundamental difference between the three systems is how the *kompetenz-kompetenz* deals with the subordination of one level of government to another. In unitary systems, the final source of authority is the larger central level, thus subordinating smaller levels to it; in confederal systems, higher levels are subordinated to the mandates and allocation of competences by the member units; and federal dynamics aim at achieving an 'equality of status' among the various levels by not assigning this basic authority to either side (Law, 2013: p. 105).

Regarding the allocation of competences, Dardot's proposal seems clearly to rely on confederal dynamics, where the sole authority that can decide on granting competences to other levels of government is the smaller unit. Their objective is to promote a system of grass-roots democracies that have the final authority to bequeath competences to higher levels if it is in their interest. Their concern with centralization of authority and with top-down approaches to global governance shows that neither the unitary nor the federal allocation of competences is sufficient.

3.3 Entrenchment of Competences

The existence of an insured and protected entrenchment of competences at different levels is another relevant characteristic of a federal system (King, 1982). Unitary systems may devolve competences to smaller units, and a confederal system usually assigns competences to larger entities, but it is a federal characteristic to ensure that the competences allocated to smaller and larger units are entrenched (usually through the use of constitutions). The equal standing of the various levels of government is sustained in federal systems by ensuring that no level can withdraw competences from another without common accord. In this respect, salient competences are: first, allocated at diverse levels of government; second, this allocation is specified by joint mechanisms; and, third, they are constitutionally defined in order to protect the competences of member units, and ensure the stability of the federation through the entrenchment of competences at the higher levels. This achieves two of the fundamental aims of a federal system: on the one hand, ensure the autonomy and self-government of smaller units; and, on the other, protect the stability of the federation by constitutionally defining the role that the central polity plays (Watts, 1996: pp. 6–7; 1998: p. 124). Contrary to this equilibrium achieved between stability (of the larger polity) and autonomy (of the member units), confederal dynamics focus especially on the second element, protecting the liberties and identities of member units. This allows for greater self-government, but restricts the capacity of the system to maintain stable and long-enduring relations (Downs, 2011).

Defining Dardot's proposal regarding the entrenchment of competences is more complicated due to the lack of an explicit explanation for how the stability of larger units is to be sustained in their institutionalization of the commons. Regarding smaller units, Dardot's proposal is very clear as to how a political constitution establishes the fundamental principles, rights, and authority that local commons have (Dardot and Laval, 2014: p. 514). But the protection and assurance of these competences at higher levels is less clear. It relies on Proudhon's idea of 'mutuality' as a way to secure that reciprocity and equality in social and economic relations is sustained (Dardot and Laval, 2014: p. 340). This is a complicated concept because it is not clear in what way it is institutionalized. They mention the idea of a 'social constitution' where the reciprocity and equality of social and economic relations is secured across various commons, and at different levels of government (Dardot and Laval, 2014: p. 340).

This would seem to be an entrenchment of the competences and rights of smaller units at a higher level, but two characteristics make this statement difficult to sustain: first, the fact that this 'social constitution' affects only social and economic relations but not political relations (due to their separation of competences into two different federal camps) leaves the stability of political competences on a thin rope. It could be argued, even more, that this is precisely one of the objectives that they have in mind. Their concern with centralization leads them not to entrench competences on the political arena so that potentially coercive or problematic authorities are unable to keep smaller units under their control against their will. Second, even within the sphere of social and economic relations where the social constitution is in place, it is unclear what enforcement mechanisms would secure the existence of this constitution in cases of violation. There is no account of how this constitution is institutionally enforced, thus allowing one to assume that its entrenchment relies on the willingness of the units to comply by its directives. This could lead to a declaration that the entrenchment of competences follows, once again, a confederal dynamic: it is just established at the lower levels of government, making the contracts at higher levels seem more like present day international treaties, which do not have strong enforcement mechanisms, do not necessarily include stakeholders, and which can be broken at any moment.

Of course, Dardot might decide to add measures to ensure some form of strong entrenchment of the higher level's competences, bringing the proposal closer to a federal order. Nothing in the proposal explicitly makes such a move inconsistent. Yet, if our reasoning above is correct, the gist of their theory appears to go against tying the hands of the lower levels by committing to entrenchment of powers at a higher level.

3.4 Legislative and Constitutive Diversity

Another feature of federal structures is the existence of legislative capacities (especially constitutive) at the different unit levels, with a significant degree of autonomy for smaller units to develop a constitution and legislation. This is contrary to unitary systems, where legislative (and constitutive) powers lie solely with the central unit; and contrary to confederal treaties, where only the member units have legislative (and constitutive) authority, with no enforcement mechanisms at the higher level. Federal systems maintain significant autonomy over legislative procedures, with smaller units having their own constitution and legislation which the larger unit cannot contest or overrule, except in cases of major violations or major discrepancies between legislatures. But, just as there are spheres where self-government of smaller units is sustained, a characteristic of federal systems is the existence of binding legislation and enforcement mechanisms at the higher levels of government which affect member units directly (Law, 2013). This aims at ensuring that the interests of all member units are protected in equal terms by the central government.

It seems that the same problems that arose with the previous feature arise here as well. It is clear that the unitary dynamic is out of the picture, but the indeterminacy in the explanation of the capacity to enforce legislation at higher levels of government makes it difficult to assess whether their proposal stands closer to a federal or to a confederal dynamic. Dardot's focus on constitutive and legislative elements at the lower levels seems to point towards a confederal strategy. But the fact that the proposal acknowledges the existence of constitutions (both political and social) at the higher levels of government, even if their enforcement mechanisms remain in the power of smaller units, makes it incline towards a more federal legislative and constitutive structure (Dardot and Laval, 2014: pp. 342–4, 514). To fully assess the proposal as far as this issue is concerned, we would need more information on the nature of the constitutional existence that Dardot intends to give to the wider constitution, and the degree of inclusiveness and formality this constitution can have. Perhaps it is reasonable, therefore, to locate the proposal in a middle point between federal and confederal as far as this issue is concerned, due to the fact that its account of constitutional variety does seem to drink from both sources.

3.5 The Public Sphere

The public sphere is a fundamental element of a democratic political community.[2] An assessment of the general outlines of the type of public sphere emphasizes the variation between the different political systems. Unitary systems tend to have a sole public sphere at the higher level where all political activity is carried out, leading to a conception of the individuals within this system as one unified community; on the other hand, confederal dynamics tend to have public spheres within the member units, while only indirect political involvement at the higher level. This approach emphasizes the distinction between various communities and groups within the system, giving a more prominent role to this diversity, rather than to the unifying interests of the whole political system. As argued previously, the peculiar characteristic of a federal system is the diversity of levels where a public sphere exists. Not only do smaller units have their own spaces where political activity develops (sometimes in different languages, and through different means), but they also have a stable sphere of political activity at the higher levels of government. In this respect, citizens in a federation are not only citizens of the larger polity, nor exclusively part of their own local communities; rather they are simultaneously part of both public spheres, as citizens of their own local groups *and* of the larger polity (De Schutter, 2011: p. 168). What this entails is that the population needs to be involved both with their local political arenas, and with the issues that affect the federation as a whole. The relevance of the public sphere for the assessment of the federation relies in that it looks, not only at the purely institutional mechanisms that make a federation, but also at the spaces and interests that society has in being involved with the decision-making procedures at different levels of the polity.

This is another difficult feature to deal with, not because of the lack of an explicit statement in Dardot's proposal, but rather because its (very explicit) conception of the public sphere, and of how the *demos* is constituted, does not fit clearly within any of the traditional categories of political systems. In his chapter in this volume, as in his work with Laval, Dardot argues for the need of plural demo-cosmopolitan systems that are not institutionalized in any way (Dardot, Chapter 2 in this volume: p. 34; Dardot and Laval, 2014: pp. 459–64, 515–16). They are, rather, 'insurgent citizenships' that arise outside of the traditional arenas of politics, in a bottom-up direction, with a scope of action that can arrive to the higher levels of government. Their conception of the *demos* and the public sphere is that of plural, decentralized, and non-institutionalized arenas of activism, where both socioeconomic and political issues are discussed, ranging from activism within local commons, to global ecological concerns. From this account, it seems that the overall objective put forward by Dardot is to decentralize as much as possible the *loci* of political engagement and activism, as a way to counter the reifying effects of institutionalized public spheres and *demos*. Although his account cannot be clearly assessed within the categories used in this chapter, it is clear that it does not follow some of the requirements of a federal public sphere due to the absence of a unified political arena. Opposite to Dardot's reluctance to give space to a common identity among citizens of the federation, a cornerstone of a federal system is its capacity to sustain and foster the differing identities and public spheres of the various units, while having the unifying power to generate a common identity, and a sense of 'togetherness' among them (De Schutter, 2011: p. 177; Jewkes, 2015). Without this sense of community that includes the whole citizenry of the polity, there does not seem to be much of a federal dynamic.

This section has sought to show that it is terminologically possible, though not evident, to label Dardot's proposal 'federalist' in nature. Seen in the light of contemporary federal and confederal theory, the proposal is closer to the confederal or even international treaty category than to federalism as commonly understood. This in itself leads to a number of normative concerns. These concerns originate in the normative consequences of the very reason for Dardot's *confederal* proposal: its emphasis on local forms of politics that are primarily concerned with autonomy and self-government of smaller units are unable to deal with the issues and conflicts *among* local units that federal structures intend to solve.

4. GOVERNMENT OF THE COMMONS OR SELF-GOVERNMENT?

As we just discussed, it is not evident to classify Dardot's proposal as federal; instead it could be more properly described as exhibiting a confederal logic. This brings to mind two typical problems that confederal settings give rise to: lack of solidarity among the member units, and lack of coercive capacities at the level of the confederation. But before discussing these in Sections 5 and 6 respectively, we want to discuss the nature of the sites of self-government that Dardot envisions. A first task for any theory that combines different levels of government – be they federal, confederal or still otherwise in nature – is to identify the relevant units of self-government, and to identify principles for allocating competences to each of them. What are the relevant sites at which democratic self-government will be exercised?

Here it appears to us that Dardot romanticizes the social practices of the commons by presenting an idea of human cooperative behaviour (within and between the commons) that, as we shall argue, can lead to problematic results if institutionalized as a result of the confederal focus on the local sites of self-government. In particular, the self-government and autonomy of each currently existing common *as a social practice* does not ensure the fair sustainment of the commons *as fundamental goods* in need of steering and/or preservation. We cannot simply assume that the commons as current social practices will ensure the protection of common goods, or the access to fundamental common resources or services to all those who depend on them. By granting a 'confederal' priority to existing local sites of self-government, Dardot's programme risks neglecting the fundamental goods nature of the commons at higher levels.

In fact, we argue, positively, that democratic practices should track commons as goods: we should have democratic practices where we find the need for a certain commons to be collectively governed. Dardot's proposal seems to work with the opposite model: to organize democracy around existing sites of self-government. His model is decidedly bottom-up, focusing on respect for local units of communal self-government whose autonomy is crucial. Yet, existing sites of local self-government can clash with those sites where the commons (as fundamental goods) reside and where, therefore, self-government ought to be organized.

In our view, a political philosophy of the commons ought not to protect current sites of self-government, but instead current sites of the commons. This intuition, we think, is close to some central understandings of democracy. Take the all-affected principle, now often discussed in the political theory literature on transnational or global democracy. The all-affected principle states that whoever is (relevantly or significantly) affected by a public decision should have a right to inclusion in the democratic process that produces that decision (see, for instance, Cavallero, 2010). The argument is deployed in the current literature on global democracy to justify the expansion of democracy beyond national boundaries. This expansion is desirable, so the defenders of this principle argue, where decisions made within domestic polities significantly affect others living outside those units, for example in cases such as river management, nuclear plant location, or global warming. Similarly, Dardot's local sites of self-government are likely to make such decisions that affect others living outside those sites, given the fact that the commons as fundamental goods are likely to have a wider geographical ambit than local self-governing units have. So the all-affected principle calls for identifying the units that are to decide on certain decisions based on those who are likely to be affected by the decisions taken by a unit. Where such other-affecting decisions are made, it goes radically against limiting democracy to existing sites of self-government.

Or take Jeremy Waldron's principle of proximity, which states that political communities ought to consist of those people who are territorially close to each other, especially if they are likely to have conflicts among themselves (Waldron, 2011). On Waldron's view, it is around territorially based conflicts that the zone of self-government ought to be organized, because those are the zones over which we want democratic control. These zones should thus explicitly not be limited to existing sites of self-government, but should transcend them. The result is a situation in which the zone where we want democratic control determines the site of self-government, rather than the other way around.

We mention the principles of all-affectedness and proximity here not to defend specifically these principles, but to point to a more general aspect about democracy, which is its problem-solving focus. Democracy does not exist for its own sake: it is a manner of deciding over the solution to problems or collective choices, be they local or global. Democrats want the decision-making over fundamental questions, such as the governance of global commons, to occur in such a way that it involves the people themselves. But the people that are to be involved are not the people of existing sites of self-government, but instead those who are significantly affected or who need to solve the problem together. In the typical case of a river that streams from unit A to unit B, whereby B needs the clean water from the river, we ideally need to take the control over the river management out of the hands of solely the upstream group, so that the downstream community can co-decide over, for example, the dumping of waste in the river. And it should not be up to the upstream group whether they want to participate in this joint or communal management. Because the river is a common good to both communities, it ought to be governed together. In short, democracy should be organized where shared commons exist, not where it traditionally was exercised. And because the governance of shared commons is likely to include people who are not part of those traditional sites of self-government, the units of self-government must often be widened.

5. SOLIDARITY AND SHARED-RULE

It is not enough for the sites to be widened though. Ideally, the widened sites of self-government must decide in a manner that allows for sufficient solidarity to emerge between the people who are to decide over the commons. A related concern with Dardot's proposal that stems from its 'confederal inclination', is, in our view, its meagre capacity to cultivate solidarity among the co-governing constituent units. The strong emphasis on self-rule, and the lack of mechanisms of shared-rule, present an outlook of units being highly concerned only for themselves. There seems to be no attempts to build a *demos* across units, or to engender federal forms of identity that transcend self-interest and foster the emergence of common interests and goals. The protection of self-government authority of the constituent units is not the sole objective of a federal system; generating a sense of unity and togetherness is as important as maintaining authority at local levels (De Schutter, 2011: p. 168). The solidarity promoted by federal dynamics points towards the establishment of strong ties among the various groups which transcend self-interest and can actually achieve the mutuality that Dardot intends to build through his Proudhonian contracts.

Solidarity among the horizontal and vertical relations of political units requires strong assurance of how mutual cooperation and reciprocity are to be achieved. Although Dardot (and Laval) clearly defend that 'federal contracts' are to be promoted with the objective of mutuality (reciprocity and equity), it seems that the instability of these contracts makes them prone to falling apart. Their institution of the common seems to use federalism as an unwanted but inevitable *modus vivendi* founded on the self-interest of the various groups, rather than on the search for commonalities. This fosters an existing 'what's in it for me' view, which local actors employ when they look with suspicion at higher forms of democratic decision-making. But issues and endeavours that require stable and on-going cooperation among various groups, such as those that affect the global commons and ecological sustainment of the planet, demand more than coordinated self-interest; as Wayne Norman argues, there is a need for a *moral* commitment among the various parties, in order for the political system to be stable and effective (Norman, 1994: p. 87). Self-interested contracts established as a *modus vivendi*, as Dardot seems to defend, may be a first step towards the creation of a federal system, but a shared political identity is required in order to ensure the stability of the political system and the protection of the global interests that are involved in this endeavour (Weinstock, 2001).

Dardot and Laval's proposal assumes a very high degree of cooperative behaviour in individuals and groups, where there is no need for an enforcement mechanism that can ensure that this cooperative behaviour is actually sustained. We consider that if there is no sense of solidarity and some degree of unified will, then stability cannot be achieved. Mutuality, opposite to solidarity, seems to be too focused on the self-interest of groups and individuals; making contracts dependent on the willingness of local units to cooperate (in fair terms) among them. Solidarity, on the contrary, emphasizes the idea that self-interest has to be transcended in order for larger projects (such as sustaining global commons) to be properly carried out; a conception of an 'us', of a community (which Dardot is extremely reluctant to build), is the best way of approaching common issues and problems.

It is important to note that Dardot's account of global networks of insurgent citizenship is intended as a source of unification of interests at levels higher than the local. But the excessive focus on these being constructed through the shared self-interest of the parties makes it difficult for those who would not receive benefits from these contracts to do their part in supporting the others' plea. We can imagine an ideally formed network of forest communities establishing federal contracts to protect their environment. But, as long as non-forest communities are not bound by this contract, the externalities generated by their production processes may counter the efforts made by the forest networks. We can imagine as well a network of commons united in the equitable use of a river, but what is there to gain for the upstream units in sharing its benefits with those farther downstream? There seems to be no assurance that those at the source would willingly stop polluting the river for those at the mouth. Unless solidarity is fostered, and unless a central protection of the interests of more vulnerable communities is ensured, a political system would be unable to cultivate the 'mutuality' that Dardot intends to secure among various peoples.

6. THE ROLE OF COERCIVE, STATE-LIKE INSTITUTIONS

As we just discussed, existing levels of solidarity may not suffice in order for distinct groups to meaningfully work together in a setting that can never be more than a *modus vivendi*, to be broken up whenever power dynamics, or solidarity tendencies, change. This is not just problematic from the point of view of the lack of a common we-feeling and overarching identity. It can also perpetuate and exacerbate relevant inequalities in power and wealth among units. Dardot's conception of federal contracts is based on mutuality (reciprocity and equality) and consent. This may, however, allow wealthier and more powerful units to seize control in the decision-making procedures (such as in cases of 'equal and reciprocal' treaties among states of the world; or in the EU). It also enables wealthier units to opt out of contracts that may require them to distribute part of their benefits to other less-wealthy units. With no obligatory distributive mechanisms, inequalities would rise.

This leads us to our final concern: the lack of central authorities. As mentioned before, solidarity is a fundamental objective of systems that intend to tackle large issues, and due to the lack of assurance that self-interested groups will respect mutuality, solidarity has to be built through some degree of unification of interests, and through a common source for the protection of the rights of smaller groups. In our view, the global layer(s) of the federal entity that is to preserve global or near-global commons should also have coercive power. Some degree of centralization of competences, and some coercion over their exercise, is fundamental for the equitable and reciprocal protection of interests. As mentioned above, relying solely on the willingness of groups to cooperate fairly with others is too much of an ideal assumption of human behaviour. Although efforts to prove the sustainability of commons and equitable relations among local groups without the need of a state or a central authority have been thoroughly researched with outstanding outcomes (Ostrom, 1990), the likelihood is slim that this can be achieved on a great scale without the role of central agencies at higher levels, such as those able to enforce some measure of cooperation in dealing with global commons.

So, if we cannot have pure solidarity ensuring cooperation, then a form of coercion must be installed, for two purposes: in order to enforce cooperation where it does not exist; and to foster a common identity, or federal 'peoplehood', in order to make uncovered, spontaneous cooperation more likely. This latter understanding of federal identity is in fact similar to identity structures in existing federal states: such are, and are encouraged to see themselves as, members of two peoples: one people ruling over local manners, and one, state-wide people, ruling over state-wide manners.

Take, for instance, Dardot's example of the Obama administration's decision to authorize American companies to use natural resources from outer space. As Dardot persuasively argues (see Dardot, Chapter 2 in this volume: p. 24), this decision effectively circumvents the prohibition on appropriation by a sovereign state of what is considered *res communis* by the Outer Space Treaty. The decision does not establish collective American property rights or sovereignty over resources in outer space, but it grants companies usage rights. Dardot concludes that this vision does not break with the inter-state logic, and leaves room for private appropriation.

We agree with Dardot that the appropriation of space resources by the United States is problematic. But it does not occur to us that the problem would dramatically change or improve if instead existing sites of self-government were to make decisions over natural resources from outer space. The same inter-unit logic would then apply: in the absence of global solidarity, one such unit might decide to appropriate what it desires or what serves its interest, to its own benefit, and the solution might be as pernicious as the current one. We agree that the current content of the decision that is made is problematic, but we do not agree that the solution is to take the matter out of the hands of state-like power. In our view, the central problem here is that the decision is made by only one of the parties of a global community that should instead decide. It is the lack of globality that is the real problem here. This kind of decision emanating from a single level of American authority, over a veritably universal commons, should be made by the global community, in a global site of self-government.

This argument is not compatible with Dardot's federal proposal as it currently stands. Dardot is reluctant about centralizing common concerns of various local commons into larger unified entities. He argues that the various commons should not turn into a sole community because this would transform the diverse identities and practices of smaller units into the common will of the whole, thus, reducing self-determination and autonomy.

However, we would like to stress that this overarching objection to community building is relevant especially in the context of strongly unified and centralized polities, but not necessarily with respect to less centralized types of states, including federal state systems that accommodate the demands of self-government of smaller units, while, at the same time, protecting common interests of the larger polity through central institutions that can ensure more efficient and egalitarian outcomes. The kind of federal global entity that could decide over global commons, create solidarity in governing them, and also enforce cooperation where solidarity fails, would structurally be very different from a unitary state. It would exhibit all the properly federal features that we discussed above. Competences should be diversified over different levels of government, ensuring local autonomy. This autonomy must be constitutionally entrenched. Changes to the constitution should not be possible solely by one of the levels: every transfer of power upwards or downwards needs the involvement of both (or multiple) vertical levels. And efforts must be undertaken to ensure a public sphere (and corresponding identities) at both levels. A structure characterized as federal in these ways, with 'state-like enforcement power', we argue, would allow for a fair and sustainable management of global commons, that would in some cases certainly curtail, but in no way jeopardize the autonomy of the local management of local commons.

7. CONCLUSION

In this chapter, we analysed and evaluated the federal credentials of Dardot's theory of the common. Based on a comparison of his theory of the common with federal political theory, we argued that, while the concept of federalism is polysemic enough to warrant many interpretations, the conception of federalism that Dardot puts forward comes closer to confederalism than federalism as typically understood. The main reason for this is the priority Dardot grants to local self-governing communities. We then proceeded to a normative critique of this 'confederal' position, based on three grounds. Firstly, his theory shows a lack of capacity to organize democratic self-government around the commons as fundamental goods, as a result of the empirical and normative primacy granted to local sites of self-government. Secondly, the democratic government of the commons that it does allow for is unlikely to engender sufficient supra-local or global solidarity. And finally, the lack of coercive state-like institutions at the global level is unable to enforce cooperation in the sharing of burdens and benefits of governing global commons, in those cases where solidarity indeed is lacking. Finally, we argued therefore, for a friendly amendment to Dardot's theory, pushing it in a more federal direction, where some measure of balance and power-sharing exists between the global (and other supra-local) levels and the local level, not granting full sovereignty to the local units over questions of the management of locality-transcending commons, and not making the authority of the global level depend solely on the consent of the local sites. To be a member of a federation is to be a member of two or more self-governing units which are in a position of parity vis-à-vis one another: the local and the global, and possibly other levels in between.

NOTES

* This research was supported by the KU Leuven Research Council (Grant PF10/001). The authors would like to thank Christiaan Boonen, Samuel Cogolati, Martin Deleixhe, Rutger Hagen, and Nils Vanstappen for their comments.
1. Single pages without date reference Dardot, Chapter 2 in this volume.
2. We follow Jürgen Habermas's definition of 'the public sphere', understood as a deliberative space in which 'private people come together as a public' (1989: p. 27) to engage in critical debate over their socioeconomic and political governing mechanisms, open to all in a free and equal manner.

REFERENCES

Cavallero, E. (2010) Federative Global Democracy. In: Tinnevelt, R. and De Schutter, H. (eds) *Global Democracy and Exclusion*. Oxford, Wiley-Blackwell, pp. 55–77.

Dardot, P. and Laval, C. (2014) *Commun: Essai sur la révolution au XXIe siècle*. Paris, La Découverte.

De Schutter, H. (2011) Federalism as Fairness. *Journal of Political Philosophy*, **19** (2), 167–89.

Downs, W. M. (2011) Comparative Federalism, Confederalism, Unitary Systems. In: Ishiyama, J. and Breuning, M. (eds) *Twenty-first Century Political Science: A Reference Handbook*, Vol. I. Los Angeles, Sage, pp. 168–76.

Elazar, D. (1987) *Exploring Federalism*. Tuscaloosa, University of Alabama Press.

Habermas, J. (1989). *The Structural Transformation of the Public Sphere: An Inquiry into a Category of Bourgeois Society*. Cambridge, MIT Press.

Jewkes, M. (2015) Theorising Federal Togetherness in Multinational States. *Ethnicities*, **15** (3), 323–40.

Kelemen, R. D. (2003) The Structure and Dynamics of EU Federalism. *Comparative Political Studies*, **36** (1–2), 184–208.

King, P. (1982) *Federalism and Federation*. London, Croom Helm.

Law, J. (2013) How Can We Define Federalism? *Perspectives on Federalism*, **5** (3), 88–120.

Norman, W. J. (1994) Towards a Philosophy of Federalism. In: Baker, J. (ed.) *Group Rights*. Toronto, University of Toronto Press, pp. 79–100.

Ostrom, E. (1990) *Governing the Commons: The Evolution of Institutions for Collective Action*. New York, Cambridge University Press.

Waldron, J. (2011) The Principle of Proximity. Public Law Research Paper No. 11-08. NYU School of Law.

Watts, R. (1996) *Comparing Federal Systems in the 1990s*. Montreal, McGill-Queen's University Press.
Watts, R. (1998) Federalism, Federal Political Systems, and Federations. *Annual Review of Political Science*, **1**, 117–37.
Weinstock, D. (2001) Towards a Normative Theory of Federalism. *International Social Science Journal*, **53**, 75–83.

4. A (non-)violent revolution? Strategies of civility for the politics of the common

Christiaan Boonen*

1. INTRODUCTION

In an attempt to make sense of our current political conjuncture – showing both signs of crisis and political invention – many are starting to pay attention to the ascendance of political practices echoing those of the 1871 Paris Commune: the occupation of public spaces, the adoption of direct democratic forms, attempts to organize social life according to principles of association and cooperation, resistance to centralized government and a refusal to renounce an internationalist horizon (Ross, 2015: pp. 1–9). Every now and then, it seems, political actors recover the 'lost treasure' of the revolutionary tradition. These are the new forms of government that emerge during the course of all great revolutions – popular organs that, as a result of the concerted action of citizens, constitute spaces of freedom beyond the purview of the nation state (Arendt, 2016 [1963]: pp. 215–81).

The recent work of Pierre Dardot (Chapter 2 in this volume) and Christian Laval relates to this context. As the subtitle of their latest book *Commun: Essai sur la révolution au XXIe siècle* reveals, they are engaged in a fundamental reassessment of the theory and practice of revolution (Dardot and Laval, 2014). Yet, they are equally suspicious of the grand schemes typical of nineteenth- and twentieth-century revolutionary thought, which tended to obscure or suppress the *actual* political and social revolutions taking place in the name of a 'greater' revolution-to-come. Following an incisive analysis of our current predicament that traces the extension of neoliberal reason to the different spheres of human existence, they set upon developing a political answer (Dardot and Laval, 2009). Central to this book entitled *La nouvelle raison du monde* is the assertion that the neoliberal project is a 'constructivist project'.[1] Whereas classical liberalism works under the assumption that the propensity to truck and barter is inherent to human nature, neoliberalism recognizes that economic rationality cannot be assumed as a natural given. Consequently, neoliberalism should not be seen as a politics that removes the obstacles to our natural inclination to truck and barter, but as a political project that stimulates market competition through permanent intervention. What Dardot and Laval are looking for, then, is a rival project that can counteract this neoliberal form of rationality. They are in search of an alternative to a rationality that reduces every issue of valuation to the simple question: does it enhance market competition or does it weaken it? This alternative reason they call *the reason of the common* (Dardot and Laval, 2009: pp. 457–81). To neoliberalism's depoliticization of all spheres of society, they oppose a project for the democratization of all the important spheres of society (work, nature, culture and so on). To an individualist and competitive neoliberal subjectivity, they oppose a form of collectivity and solidarity. And, perhaps most importantly, to neoliberalism's celebration of private property, they oppose a project of making the important spheres of human life non-appropriable. In the end, this is the baseline identified in *Commun*: what is important to human flourishing should never become a form of property.

It is important to emphasize that this new guiding principle should be *political* in nature. This means that they position themselves in opposition to two sets of literature. On the one hand, they counter the literature on the enclosure of the commons (for example, David Bollier and James Boyle) and common-pool resources (CPRs) (for example, Elinor Ostrom). On the other, they engage critically with a radical left literature on the common (for example, Michael Hardt and Antonio Negri). As opposed to the first set of literature, they maintain that it is more fruitful to speak of the principle of the common than of common*s* in the plural. The principle of the common, they argue, is expansive: generally speaking you can make any sphere of society operate according to the principle of the common. In contrast to this view, the literature on the enclosure of commons and CPRs assumes that commons are specific economic entities that either have to be defended against market and state, or live in harmony with market and state. In both cases the implications are potentially conservative: commons have a specific place in the socio-economic sphere and the borders with other economic or social entities should be maintained (Dardot and Laval, 2014: pp. 95–187). *Pace* their radical leftist colleagues, they do not believe that political change will come forth from a specific social place or will be initiated by an already existing 'universal' class (Dardot et al., 2007). It might be the case that certain evolutions in the make-up of our economies are already realizing the principle of the common. We see it, for instance, in the way that Wikipedia makes encyclopaedic knowledge into a common.

However, economic tendencies, they argue, do not automatically translate into political projects. Hence, a collective political subject will have to be constructed and this requires political practices and institution-building. To be more precise, 'common acting' (*agir commun*) produces a collective subject, and not the other way around (Dardot and Laval, 2014: pp. 49–51, 281–2).

This brings us to the issue at hand: the revolutionary change they envisage does not involve a violent conquest of the state. This old revolutionary recipe only ended up reproducing the forms of domination that it was supposed to abolish. In contrast, Dardot and Laval imagine an 'auto-institution of society' as practices of commoning more or less spontaneously proliferate *in spite of and autonomously from* the state, which, at some point, is transformed as a consequence of this expansion (Dardot and Laval, 2014: p. 575).[2] However, this raises the question of what will happen when either state or capital see their authority or interests endangered. As Ramond Geuss argues, revolutions – as opposed to reforms – always imply a form of extra-legality. Sometimes revolutions are merely extra-constitutional or take place in a grey area of the law. But more structural transformations of society are often illegal – in which case they can be non-violent or violent (Geuss, 2006: p. 111).

Either way, every political project envisioning a fundamental transformation of society (even those willing to adopt the principle of non-violence) will at some point have to reflect on the relation between transformational politics and violence. Reflections on violence are a constant presence in Dardot and Laval's *Commun*, which addresses the violence of primitive accumulation, statist domination and the systemic violence of the capitalist economic system. Nonetheless, a more systematic reflection on the relation between revolutionary politics and violence, we argue, is missing. To be more precise, we do not criticize them for proposing a non-violent revolution, but for not specifying why non-violence, as a revolutionary strategy, is preferable to violent ones.

This chapter will be structured as follows: in the first section (Section 2) we will determine which concept of politics is present in the revolutionary politics of Dardot and Laval and show that they cannot account for the relation between politics and violence. In particular, we will construct a brief genealogy of the concept of political power inherent to the concept of the common. This is done in order to show how this concept of power makes the violence/non-violence dilemma disappear before it can rear its head. In the second section (Section 3) we sketch the dynamics of power and violence that result from a conflict between the state and the politics of the common. We do this in order to show that political violence is a problem that should be accounted for in the commons literature. In the final section (Section 4), we explore the role violence can play and, more importantly, should not play in a revolutionary situation.

2. THREE CONCEPTS OF POLITICS: EMANCIPATION, TRANSFORMATION AND CIVILITY

In order to grasp Dardot and Laval's concept of revolution we have to determine which concept of politics – or, rather, political change – is implicit in their work. For ages political theorists have been bickering about the 'what' and 'how' of revolutionary political change and often the debate revolves around the question of which concept of politics to prioritize. Do we prioritize the struggle for rights? Or is it rather the recurrent attempt to seize the means of (re)production that moves history forward? Or maybe we should focus less on the ends of politics and more on the ways in which we relate to political *means* such as violence and coercion?

When we think about radical political change[3] – Étienne Balibar writes – we cannot get by without at least three distinct concepts of politics: the politics of emancipation, the politics of transformation and the politics of civility (Balibar, 2002: p. 1). It is an open question whether this list is exhaustive, but at any rate one cannot study radical political change without having at least a notion of these three and their reciprocal interactions.

2.1 The Politics of Emancipation and the Politics of Transformation

The first concept of politics is that of the *politics of emancipation*, which is concerned with the expansion of human rights and the building of civic institutions. The idea that all men are 'free and equal in rights' resides at its core: any situation in which restrictions are imposed on liberty or equality (for example, when civil liberties are based on discrimination) is illegitimate (Balibar, 2002: p. 3). Hence, the main task of emancipatory politics is to build civic institutions that guarantee this equal liberty and give an institutional form to the idea that 'all men are born free and equal'. However, as equal liberty is rarely ceded by those in power, conflict remains a decisive factor. That is, it is the 'history of . . . the real struggle to enjoy rights which have already been declared' or 'the battle against the denial of citizenship' that is the vital heart of the politics of emancipation (p. 6).

The *politics of transformation*, on the other hand, challenges one core assumption of the politics of emancipation: namely, that politics is a wholly autonomous activity. Fundamentally, politics takes place in 'non-political' conditions that (over)determine it or, at the least, limit it. The boundaries separating the sphere of politics from other societal subsystems are, to a certain extent, artificial. This explains why they can always be contested and why the 'non-political' conditions of political institutions are eminently political (p. 11). Accepting that oppression or inequality cannot always be sublated by the state, law or the rights of man, critical theorists such as Marx and Foucault have sought to show how important forms of political change often take place in the social, economic and cultural contextual conditions of politics (Balibar, 2015a: p. 10).

Dardot and Laval position their revolutionary politics on a terrain comprising these two concepts of politics. To be more precise, they present the politics of the common as a form of politics encompassing transformational politics *and* the politics of emancipation.[4] The politics of the common, they argue, is 'transversal to instituted separations' (Dardot and Laval, 2014: p. 460). The political logic of democratic self-governance cannot be limited to the field of state politics or even the political sphere at large, but should also be extended to the social and economic sphere. This is why they argue that a revolution cannot be restricted to – yet should include – political institutions (in the form of 'more rights', or a 'greater inclusivity'), but should also transform the conditions in which politics takes place (p. 572). They envisage this revolutionary movement as 'moment of acceleration, intensification and collectivization of [the] instituting praxis [of "common acting"] in certain important areas of society' (p. 575). As more and more areas of social life are made non-appropriable (*inappropriable*) through practices of commoning, a qualitative change takes place as state and market, public and private property, are finally subordinated to the principle of the common (p. 582).

As a result, they find themselves at odds with political thinkers who narrowly circumscribe the sphere of politics in order to remove all social and economic questions from its domain. The problem with this reasoning, Dardot and Laval argue, is that it assumes that the sphere of the political is a given even though in a lot of cases social questions *are* political questions (p. 577). The governance of a natural resource, a workplace or a theatre all merit recognition as *public* affairs (pp. 463–5).

2.2 The Commons, Power and Violence

A third way to look at the problem of political change is to pay attention to political *means* such as force and violence, as opposed to the ends and objects of change. This particular point of view involves asking questions such as: can we force or coerce those not willing to participate in the revolution? And: can we use violence in order to initiate the revolution or safeguard some of its achievements? In other words, it involves asking questions about the nature of (political) action, power and their relation to violence. These questions are central to the politics of civility (see infra).

If we consider the politico-theoretical tradition in a schematic way, we can delineate at least two influential positions on the nature of political power and its relation to violence. On the one hand, we have thinkers like Thomas Hobbes and Max Weber, who conceive of power as *power-over*, that is, the ability of one person or group of persons to make others perform a specific action (whether or not this action is against the interest of the latter). In the words of Max Weber: power is 'the probability that one actor within a social relationship will be in a position to carry out his own will despite resistance, regardless of the basis on which this probability rests' (Weber, 1978: p. 53). Consequently, violence, domination and coercion are treated as modalities of political action.[5]

On the other hand, we have another view, famously defended by Hannah Arendt which involves an understanding of power as *power-with*. Power comes into being only when people act in concert or when they engage in cooperation (Saar, 2010: pp. 9–12). Here, power is not something that a certain actor 'has' and exercises over others, but exists 'in between' people. In other words, power is relational as opposed to unilateral (Penta, 1996: p. 212). According to this conception of the political, violence appears as the opposite of power and politics. And this applies irrespective of whether violence manifests itself in the form of legitimate or illegitimate domination, structural or subjective violence, revolutionary or counter-revolutionary violence. In short, violence appears as a form of anti-politics (Arendt, 1969; Frazer, 2014: p. 158).[6]

We argue that their quarrels with Arendt's positions notwithstanding,[7] Dardot and Laval share her understanding of political action in this particular respect. First of all, they emphasize that a commons revolution would not be violent (Dardot and Laval, 2014: p. 575). Furthermore, significant parts of their book, *Commun*, are dedicated to analyses of the internal workings of the politics of the common, all of which end up stressing their cooperative and deliberative aspects (for example, Dardot and Laval, 2014: pp. 280–83, 445, 578–82). Violence, on the other hand, is something that is *done to* the commons. They were captured by socialist states and subjected to the structural violence of bureaucracies (pp. 79–85); they were enclosed in violent episodes of primitive accumulation (pp. 120–24); and, increasingly, we are seeing the echoes of these different forms of violence (pp. 98–119), while new forms of dispossession attest to the structural violence that is inherent in the workings of globalized financial markets (pp. 127–31).

This view, we would add, is not entirely accidental. In the different intellectual origins of their concept of the common, we see a similar understanding of the nature of power.[8] Take, for instance, the work of Elinor Ostrom. If we look at her writings, it quickly becomes apparent that she is partisan to the notion of 'power-with'. Her research on CPRs, she argues, challenges 'the Hobbesian conclusion that the constitution of order is only possible by creating sovereigns who then must govern by being above subjects, monitoring them, and by imposing sanctions on all who would otherwise not comply' (Ostrom et al., 1992: p. 414). In other words, people can cooperate and keep credible commitments without there being an external enforcer. This means that, in commons, power does not rest in an external institution or a centralized authority with the ability to impose and enforce rules of action (Ostrom, 2000). It exists in between people in a horizontal contract they conclude among themselves and keep alive through communication and their shared action.

Although this brief outline already shows how coercion and violence are unassimilable to Ostrom's concept of power in commons, we do have to acknowledge that political and social revolutions were never one of her concerns. It is important, then, to point out that the same applies to Dardot and Laval's more radical and explicitly anticapitalistic influences – a tradition of theorizing worker's self-management that has its roots in the work of Pierre-Joseph Proudhon and was further developed in the writings of Marcel Mauss (Dardot and Laval, 2014: pp. 367–403). Proudhon is equally critical of the concept of 'power-over'. To be more precise, Proudhon opposes something he calls collective force to political power. In his own words, '[t]he problem consists, then, for the working classes, not in capturing, but in defeating both power and monopoly' (cited in Allen, 1952: p. 5). The concept of political power refers to every form or instrument of domination – the state, police, workplace hierarchies and so on. It can, in other words, be equated with all forms of 'power-over'. On the other hand, Proudhon's own concept of the institution of collective force can, perhaps somewhat confusingly, be seen as a form of 'power-with'. It is a form of collective, shared power that is immanent to workers' self-organization. Taken together this adds up to a specific concept of revolution: a revolution takes place as these practices of self-organization spread, realizing a form of social justice in more and more parts of society. As this form of 'power-with' is extended, it will prevail over a state that has become useless (Dardot and Laval, 2014: p. 367). Put differently, as practices of workers' self-organization spread, all forms and instruments of domination, having become obsolete, will wither away. This revolution, consequently, takes place without force or violence being exercised (Solari, 2012: p. 229). Proudhon's revolution was to be non-violent: a survey of his positions during the 1848 revolutions shows that he opposed violence and force against the government at every point (Allen, 1952: pp. 3–9).

To be clear, this view on the nature of power has its merits (see: Bernstein, 2013: pp. 78–104). It remains the task of every emancipatory political project to challenge those political imaginaries that unreflexively equate politics with force and violence. However, its particular take on the relation (or, rather, non-relation) between political change and violence is problematic. For instance, it is not very clear whether the oppositions that are established in such a view – between dialogical cooperation and mute violence, or being-with-others and the domination of others – can always be upheld.[9] This is especially the case in revolutionary situations as temporal pressures and the opposition of fellow citizens work together to undermine cooperative politics (Breen, 2012: pp. 144–50). The problem with this position, however, is not that it presents a non-violent version of radical political change. What is problematic is the implicit assumption that political change and non-violent change are identical. Non-violence is no longer a *strategy*, but is simply inherent to the nature of the political.

We do not believe, however, that this is a tenable position. It is not possible to strictly separate politics and violence. This brings us into the realm of Balibar's third concept of politics: the politics of civility. All forms of radical politics, as he argues, face a tragic dilemma: we 'need to politically transform the existing state of things – characterized by structural and circumstantial violence – though we can renounce neither the struggle for emancipation nor resistance (interior or exterior) to the nihilism of violence' (Balibar, 2009: p. 11). There is always a risk that, in the face of oppression, a revolt or a revolution turns into destructive or self-destructive counter-violence (p. 29). The tragic character of political action consists in the fact that it can never completely divest itself of the different forms of violence, but once this violence gets out of control (that is, turns into extreme violence or cruelty) politics is made impossible as the shared political space collapses under the weight of hostilities. Once this happens, the conditions for political action to occur disappear and – perhaps more significant for a politics of transformation – so does the possibility of a truly political conflict (Balibar, 2015b: p. 47).

This involves an important perspectival shift: instead of opposing politics to violence in general, it opposes politics to a *type* of violence – namely, cruelty. Cruelty is that kind of violence that can never be converted into a form of *political* change. Cruelty is an extreme form of violence that severs all relations – of communication as well as conflict – between opposing political groups. But political violence is not reducible to cruelty and as a consequence political violence is not to be condemned a priori. Instead what is opened up is a realm of political action in which an active choice has to be made between different political strategies, some of which involve violence and others of which adhere to non-violence. These are what Balibar calls *strategies of civility*: they intervene in the politics of emancipation and transformation in order to prevent them from slipping into anti-politics (or cruelty) (Balibar, 2015a: p. 51). In this particular respect, Balibar's thought is deeply Weberian: it is not impossible that the limited exercise of violence might prevent a far worse violence. Consequently, resistant actors need to develop a *political ethic* that is appropriate to this tragic nature of political action. They have to cultivate a political sensibility appropriate to a world that often is violent, meaning that they have to learn when to avoid violence, but also – if necessary – when to resort to violence (Balibar, 2009: pp. 28–9).

We argue that *Commun* is lacking such a perspective precisely because it (a) analytically separates the concept of political action from that of violence and (b) overemphasizes the cooperative nature of the politics of the common.[10] What is missing in this account is an appraisal of the different ways in which resistance to forms of violence – for example, in the form of a confrontation between the politics of the common and the authority of state – inserts the politics of the common into a dynamic of violence that it can neither evade nor control. In the following section we will sketch this dynamic of violence between state and the politics of the common. We do this in order to show why the problem of civility is *a concrete problem* for the politics of the common.

3. AS THE COMMON CONFRONTS THE STATE: THREE POSSIBLE SCENARIOS

The politics of the common presents a challenge to state authority in many ways, but the mutual exclusivity of modern constitutionalism and the 'law of the commons'[11] is probably the clearest manifestation of such a challenge (see also Part III of this volume). The modern, Western tradition of law ascribes a fundamental importance to state sovereignty, public property and private property, and is therefore fundamentally irreconcilable with the law of the common (Dardot and Laval, 2014: p. 467; Bailey and Marcucci, 2013: p. 973; Broumas, 2015: p. 14) (see also Mattei, Chapter 10 in this volume). For instance, whereas the law of the common refuses to appoint a proprietor of the common (the common is inappropriable and, thus, cannot belong to anyone), the Western tradition cannot conceive of a common without an owner (Dardot and Laval, 2014: p. 470; Broumas, 2015: p. 18).[12]

Should these legal orders clash at some point, different scenarios are conceivable. First, we could witness an illegalization of practices of commoning. States have an interest in preventing these new ways of organizing common life from stabilizing into new institutions, so they could prohibit them. They are, for instance, already doing this by tightening anti-squatting laws (Vishmidt, 2014).[13] A continuation of these practices in the face of their illegalization could have the effect of reinforcing state authority. As Hans Lindahl notes, even though illegal behaviour 'breaches legal order, its qualification as illegal has a "positive" normative significance: illegality counts as the privative manifestation of legal order, hence as its reaffirmation' (Lindahl, 2013: p. 28). As long as these confrontations between commoners and the state are relatively rare and the community of citizens recognizes the illegality of the commoners' acts, the state is 'justified' if it responds to resistance with violence.

A second, contrasting scenario would see the incorporation of practices of commoning into the legal order of the state. One example is the occupation of the Teatro Valle in Rome – demanding that culture be recognized as a common good – and its subsequent legalization. Whereas the initial occupation of the Teatro was illegal, the occupants managed to get legal recognition for the occupation through the employment of a private law tool (Bailey and Marcucci, 2013: p. 399). The problem with this strategy, however, is that it only works insofar as state authority is not fundamentally threatened. Once the state notices that legal(ized) practices of commoning threaten its authority, it might impose additional legal measures. For instance, new legal demands were imposed on the Teatro Valle threatening to hinder its operation (Vishmidt, 2014; Dardot and Laval, 2014: p. 479).

A third scenario, we argue, coincides with what Dardot and Laval call the auto-institution of society: in this case practices of commoning would be so widespread and normatively pertinent that they actually challenge the distinction between legality and illegality. They would constitute what Hans Lindhal calls, a form of *a-legal* behaviour 'that deplete[s] the normativity of a legal order' as it reveals how this same legal order closes down on the possibility of acting in ways that 'claim a normative force of their own' (Lindahl, 2013: p. 36). For example: commoners might breach property laws, but at the same time their practices of sharing claim a normative force of their own. Accordingly, they compel us to question certain normative distinctions inherent to the regulation of property as codified in the legal order.

In the end, most revolutions end up re-enacting scenes of all three scenarios: the fragile beginnings that are in danger of being suppressed, the recurring risk of co-optation, but also the possibility of becoming a true event that – if only for a moment – upends our conceptions of what is and is not politically feasible. The challenge for commoners exists in getting from scenario one – the fragile beginnings – to scenario three – the start of a revolutionary transition – without succumbing to state violence. As some theorists have already noted, it is naïve to think that practices that challenge the state as a unity of power (even in cases where this challenge is not explicit) will not elicit a violent response. The fact that states are nowadays increasingly losing power due to processes of globalization and decentralization does not curb this tendency. On the contrary, in order to maintain the illusion of the unity of power they resort to visible supplements to whatever power they still have, and state violence seemingly provides such a supplement (Balibar, 2015b: pp. 38–42; Jameson, 2016: p. 4).

Another factor to take into account is that state violence – as Johanna Oksala argues – is inherent to neoliberal governmentality. As we already argued in the introduction, neoliberalism is a constructivist project – it is a project that recognizes its own artificiality. Market competition is never taken as a natural given, but is something that has to be brought into existence through 'permanent vigilance, activity and intervention' (Oksala, 2012: p. 140). State violence is one of the means through which market competition is created and secured. This explains why practices of commoning that are not co-optable are met with violence. As Oksala notes, '[t]he violent suppression of such activism in Western democratic states must be seen not only as an attempt to protect private property – effective policing of the economic game – but also as an attempt to close off possibilities for opting out of it' (p. 141). In these cases violence is not merely restrictive, but also productive of subjectivity (p. 105). That is to say, state violence does not only protect private property, but also guards the boundaries of political and social reality: it establishes which ways of living are acceptable, and which ones are not.[14]

In this context, resistance to a state – whether it presents itself as insubordination, revolution or subversion – might initiate a cycle of violence. The political problem that this dynamic poses, forces resistant or revolutionary actors to develop strategies that would allow them to further their resistance or revolution while – at the same time – resisting the logic of the escalation of violence.

4. THE COMMON(S) AND STRATEGIES OF CIVILITY

In this last section, we will explore the role that violence could play in the revolutionary politics of the common.[15] The problem that we should tackle, then, is that violence and democracy, which is central to the definition of the common, are generally seen to be opposites. Violence, or 'the use of considerable force or destroying force against people or things'

(Honderich, 1980: p. 153), is deemed to be incompatible with uncoerced, egalitarian and autonomous democratic decision-making.[16] This same argument would also be relevant for Dardot and Laval. Democracy, as Dardot defines it, can be characterized as 'co-participation in public affairs' and 'self-government' (see Dardot, Chapter 2 in this volume). Violence seemingly does not fit into this picture.

Nonetheless, political violence could enter the scene in roughly two kinds of situations: either, when the logic of the common is *extended through the strategic or non-strategic use of violence*, or, when practices of commoning have to be *defended against hostile actors*.

4.1 Extending the Logic of the Common through Violence

Regarding the first kind of situation, we would adhere to Dardot and Laval's reluctance towards the strategic use of violence in pursuit of long-term political and economic goals (for example, Dardot and Laval, 2014: pp. 84, 451). The instrumentalization of violence is not an appropriate strategy for a democratic commons revolution. For one, as Howard Caygill points out, there is a tension between 'the political control of violence, and the inherent tendency of violence to escalate beyond such control' (Caygill, 2013: p. 81). Violence is nothing like an instrument. It is part of a complex set of dynamics that cannot be controlled by its perpetrators. Although violence might help to achieve certain short-term goals, its unpredictable consequences tend to overwhelm long-term goals (Frazer and Hutchings, 2008: p. 103).

More importantly, violence is not only too unpredictable to be instrumentalized, it also has a bearing on the subjectivity of those that exercise it. The dynamics of violence, once unleashed, do not only play out in the physical realm, but also in the realm of imaginary representations. Images of enmity, destruction or conspiracy capture the subjectivity of political actors and consequently introduce forms of cruelty in what was once a political conflict (Balibar, 2015a: pp. 105–6). Of course, one could – as Georges Sorel does – celebrate violence's function as an accelerator of social divisions (Sorel, 1961 [1908]). In order to understand Sorel's perception of revolutionary violence, we have to comprehend his political voluntarism. Orthodox Marxists believe class antagonism derives automatically from an objective conflict in social reality – the conflict of interests between the proletariat and the capitalist class. Sorel, on the other hand, recognizes that this objective conflict does not translate mechanically into a subjective conflict. Class consciousness is not produced by the objective existence of classes, but has to be created politically and ideologically (Ciccariello-Maher, 2017: pp. 28–33). Violence, then, plays a role in the creation and delimitation of class consciousness. To be clear, Sorel does not believe that violence has a purely instrumental function: it should not be put to use in order to implement utopian plans. On the contrary, Sorel despises the figure of the Jacobin: the revolutionary who claims to have uncovered a moral truth or the laws of history and intends to implement this truth through the use of force and violence (ibid.: pp. 26, 36). Instead, violence has the function of unifying the working class, on the one hand, and the bourgeoisie, on the other. Violence polarizes and, as a result, clarifies the lines of conflict. Moreover, it provokes the state in the hope of revealing its true face as its repressive function becomes apparent. Consequently, violence neither has a *strategical* function, it is not put to use as a means to achieve long-term goals, nor does it necessarily have a *tactical* function, it is not used to break the enemy's will in a specific situation. Violence, rather, has a *theatrical* function: it provides the proletariat with a narrative that motivates and orientates (Finlay, 2009: p. 32).

Would this form of violence, drastically stripped of the illusion of its controllability, be more appropriate to a commons revolution? As Ernesto Laclau and Chantal Mouffe argue, Sorel's thinking provides a welcome antidote to a form of economic determinism that completely eliminates the factor of political will (Laclau and Mouffe, 2014 [1985]: pp. 30–36). In this sense, it fits nicely with Dardot and Laval's project of breaking with the determinist tendencies present in some theories of the common (see Section 1). On the other hand, however, we believe this approach to violence would be problematic for two interrelated reasons. For one, it puts the horse before the cart. Sorel was, of course, rightfully critical of revolutionaries that put violence in service of a political project. However, in turn, he made the opposite mistake of assuming that, once violence performed its polarizing function, the contours of a proletarian political project would materialize. As Elisabeth Frazer and Kimberly Hutchings argue, Sorel upholds 'an ethic of struggle in which fighting well is more important than being able definitively to articulate the substance of what you are fighting for' (Frazer and Hutchings, 2009: p. 57). This seems like a problematic stance to say the least. Although antagonism plays an important part in any revolution, the real basis of its power is its creative energy – the fact that a political experiment is taking place. While this does not mean that one has to have a political blueprint at hand, eventually a political project – the substance of what you are fighting for – should emerge from these revolutionary practices and the debates surrounding it.

A second problem, as Sorel's own discourse already shows, is that this position involves a shift from political action to acts of war (Sorel, 1961 [1908]: 115). Sorel essentially depoliticizes both violence and revolution: violence is meant to sever *all* political and ethical relations between the proletariat and the capitalist class (Laclau and Mouffe, 2014 [1985]: p. 33; Frazer and Hutchings, 2009). As Balibar points out, this is the paradox that any attempt to equate class struggle to civil war produces: on the one hand, civil war appears as *the condition of possibility* of politics: without it a radically new form of politics can never emerge. But on the other hand, it becomes *a condition of impossibility* of politics as the political space, where communication and conflict between opponents can emerge, collapses (Balibar, 2017: p. 164). Hence, also in this respect the Sorelian account of violence falls short of the politics of the common. As Dardot and Laval stress at multiple points in their argument, the politics of the common always require a self-alteration of the political actors involved. Commoners change themselves as they change the world around them. They develop certain habits, patterns of action and a form of self-understanding appropriate to democratic acting-in-common (Dardot and Laval, 2014: pp. 436–45). However, this also applies to *violent* political action. The problem then is that violence could negatively affect the actors' subjectivity. Violence, as John Kean succinctly puts it, 'kills off the potential democrat in both the violator and violated' (Kean, 2004: p. 156). A form of extreme, antagonistic violence would, eventually, form an obstacle to the universalization of the logic of the common as political relations are dissolved into absolute divisions between warring factions.

4.2 Defending the Logic of the Common through Violence

Whether this aversion towards political violence can be upheld in situations where democratic commons have to be defended, however, remains in question. When it comes to this matter, Dardot and Laval's position is not entirely clear. As we already noted, their main focus lies on socialist cooperative practices (*associations* in French) – their democratic nature, practices of sharing, the institution of rules of cooperation and their pedagogical function (Dardot and Laval, 2014: pp. 391–403, 497–505). Be that as it may, their discourse on the defence of these associations is couched in terms that suggest conflict (for example, the language of struggles or resistance (pp. 484, 501)), but do not confront the question of violence head-on. However, practices of commoning often (if not always) find themselves in situations defined by particular forms of violence they cannot simply subtract themselves from. We will thus have to find a way to navigate the paradox of civil violence, which consists in the fact that there are 'times and circumstances . . . when violence functions as a basic, if highly paradoxical, precondition of the pursuit or preservation of a civil democracy' (Kean, 2004: p. 139).

Applied to the specific subject at hand, this might mean that in order to distance themselves from the state, networks of commons will have to find ways to undermine its monopoly of violence. For instance, there may be specific cases in which political violence is warranted to the extent that it helps 'defend the spaces . . . opened up for non-violent political action from the forces trying to suppress or destroy them' (Finlay, 2009: p. 37). Throughout the history of cooperative practices we can find multiple instances of this phenomenon. Take, for instance, the Paris Commune of 1871: as Martin Breaugh confirms, the living heart of the Commune were the clubs and societies that operated according to the principle of association and constituted a veritable alternative to state power (Breaugh, 2007: pp. 364–74). Still, violence was not entirely missing from this picture. While physical violence may have been rare and was seldom gratuitously employed, verbal and symbolic violence were less so. These different forms of violence and the potential threat of physical violence created an atmosphere in which opponents of the Commune were more wary of intervening (pp. 296–7). Still, we all know what happened to the Commune: it ended up being violently repressed.

This is why it is worth considering a more contemporary example, which Dardot and Laval refer to as well (Bauwens, 2016): Rojava, also known as the Democratic Federation of Northern Syria. Rojava is an autonomous region in the northern part of Syria that consists of three self-governing cantons: Afrin, Jazira and Kobani. What makes this political entity so extraordinary is the fact that it approximates – although imperfectly – what we take to be a federation of commons. It is organized according to the principles of direct democracy, democratic confederalism, economic and social life are democratized, and ecological principles are central to the organization of their society. Last, but certainly not least, it organizes society in a way that continuously defends 'itself against the emergence of centralized power and state-ness' (Üstündağ, 2016: p. 199). In other words, it consciously subverts the process of nation state formation.

This radical experiment, however, takes place in circumstances that are hostile to say the least. On the one hand, Rojava has to deal with a Turkish state, which is determined to suppress Kurdish autonomy. On the other hand, it is constantly on the defence against Islamist organizations such as al-Nuzra and ISIS seeking to extend their territory (pp. 197 and 205). This implies that Rojava is confronted with the paradox that we outlined above, having to defend their achievements against hostile forces, without abandoning their principles. The practical solution that the Rojavans developed in response is fascinating. Instead of organizing their resistance in response to the violence/non-violence dilemma, they posed the problem as a choice between the monopolization of violence, on the one hand, and the democratization of violence, on the other. If the choice between violence and non-violence is not an option, then the organization of a defence against reactionary violence should be democratic to its core. Nazan Üstündağ describes how this plays out in the day-to-day reality of Rojava: '[the] self-defence of women requires', she writes, 'that women and men participate equally in all formations, institutions, economies, and leadership positions'. In addition, all institutions must give women and youth the right to veto any decision affecting them so that they can defend themselves against the corruption of the men and the elderly (pp. 199–200). In other words, there are mechanisms in place that prevent the monopolization of violence in the hands of the few.

What is admirable about the Rojava case is that it proves new, democratic forms of life can be built *despite* the context of an armed struggle. Hence, we should not succumb to the allure of military heroism. As Michael Hardt and Toni Negri forcefully argue, the only proper way to judge the efficacy of the weapons of self-defence is to judge them 'first and foremost for how they serve the constructive struggle [of] creating and maintaining . . . new forms of life' (Hardt and Negri, 2017: p. 271). Moreover, different contexts require different weapons. Strategies of guerrilla warfare are out of place in our Western, liberal democracies. In this context, violence might be more limited and geared towards protecting people from police violence or the violence of far-right movements. The main lesson that Rojava teaches, then, is that while violence might play a role in the defence of what are sometimes fragile, new forms of life, it should not overtake them. This intricate balancing act should be at the centre of a democratic revolution of the common.

5. CONCLUSION

In order to restate our argument, let us return to what are ultimately the stakes of the revolution of the common: proposing an alternative to a dominant neoliberal governmentality. Leaving its devastating effects to the side for a moment, what is so problematic about this neoliberal rationality is that it presents serious obstacles to resistant and revolutionary actors. Neoliberal forms of subjectification, for instance, isolate citizens from each other as competition becomes the organizing principle of society. Isolation and competition, in turn, prevent forms of solidarity from emerging. In the striking formulation of Alex Williams, we are living in a time of *negative solidarity*: not merely the absence of solidarity, but an active resentment towards those willing to act collectively in order to demand a form of justice. If I truly believe that better living conditions or better working conditions should be the result of *personal* achievement, then collective action can only be seen as spoiling the party. And if I am willing to endure hardship because I know that one day *I* will succeed, then others must do so too (instead of wanting to change the rules of the game through collective action) (Williams, 2010). In this sense, Dardot and Laval's principle of the common responds to the root of the problem: if competition between isolated actors is the organizing principle of society, then *learning* to act in common is the first and foremost task of a revolutionary politics. Commoning is not only an alternative way of organizing economic and social life, it is also a pedagogic project that teaches people how to resist neoliberal subjectivity.

We believe this context partly explains Dardot and Laval's theoretical positions. If we have to overcome a rationality that opposes people to each other as competitors and does not have a concept of the common good, then cooperating to reach a common goal becomes a form of resistance in itself. Moreover, if we do not want to repeat the mistakes of past revolutionary movements that ended up in authoritarian regimes, we have to develop an alternative conception of power. This is why Dardot and Laval reach back to a leftist tradition of cooperative, non-authoritarian political and social thinking. We agree with Dardot and Laval that the insights of this tradition are absolutely indispensable. However, as our short genealogy of the concept of power in this tradition shows, the unintended result is that questions of revolutionary violence and force stop being posed. As a result, an alternative leftist tradition that sees politics in terms of radical antagonism and division is left to the side.[17]

However, resistance to our contemporary neoliberal states will eventually impose exactly these kinds of questions. History has shown that states do not take kindly to movements that challenge their authority and neoliberal states will likewise respond with violence. Resistance and revolutions unfold in situations that ask of political actors to consider different strategies of civility, some of which are violent and some of which are not. And as we maintained in the last section, while non-violence might be a valid strategy, so are certain forms of defensive violence. At times these forms of self-defence might be the only way in which a radical political experiment can be sustained.

NOTES

* The research for this paper was funded by an FWO research grant. The author would like to thank Antoon Braeckman, Nicolás Brando, Samuel Cogolati, Martin Deleixhe, Rutger Hagen, Pierre Saûvetre and Nils Vanstappen for their comments.

1. As Wendy Brown, who coined the idea, explains: 'Neoliberalism is a constructivist project: it does not presume the ontological givenness of a thoroughgoing economic rationality for all domains of society but rather takes as its task the development, dissemination, and institutionalization of such a rationality' (Brown, 2005: pp. 40–41). These ideas essentially go back to the work of Michel Foucault (Burchell et al., 2008).
2. Since this chapter is mainly focused on the relation between practices of commoning and the state, it might give the impression that the revolution of the common should be restricted to the *national* level. We would like to make clear that this is definitely not the case. First, Dardot and Laval themselves emphasize that the revolution of the common will be a global and 'cosmopolitical' revolution (Dardot and Laval, 2014; also see Chapter 2 in this volume). Second, global governance is a necessary component of neoliberal governmentality. It is impossible to clearly separate neoliberal governmentality on a national level and neoliberal governmentality on the transnational and global levels. (I would like to thank Samuel Cogolati for highlighting this crucial point.) However, we do believe that there are good reasons to focus on the relation between the common and the nation state. The most important one being that this is a chapter about violence and, as of now, nation states still have a monopoly on the legitimate exercise of violence. It is possible that nation states will at some point lose this monopoly, or that this monopoly will be transformed. However, we believe that this will ultimately not affect our argument.
3. We leave the definition of 'radical political change' relatively open. The adjective 'radical' merely expresses a difference with political change that takes place within the confines of the status quo (for example, a change of government or a new law being passed).
4. This accentuation of the importance of the *social* revolution and a critical attitude towards a specific take on political revolutions (defined as attempts to 'seize power') is typical of most commons literature (see, for example, De Angelis, 2014).
5. The very fact that they are seen as *modalities* of political action, does not imply that violence and coercion are always *legitimate* forms of political action.
6. Another way to look at the commons literature in relation to the question of power is to work with the pairings 'power-to' and 'power-over', on the one hand, and '*potential*' and '*potesta*', on the other (Van de Sande, 2017). However, this leads to slightly different stakes: here, the question of violence gives way to the question of the ontological relation between the common and the social and political structures it struggles against. The question then becomes: are commons internal to these structures or are they, or do they become, external to them?
7. Dardot and Laval are influenced by Arendt's work on the council system, but disapprove of her strict separation between the political and the social. For Arendt the council system is a purely political innovation, whereas for Dardot and Laval its novelty consists in the merging of the political and the social (Dardot and Laval, 2014: p. 401).
8. We do have to add that Dardot and Laval appropriate these influences in a *critical* way. In the case of Elinor Ostrom they build on her institutional analysis, but take her to task for restricting the logic of the common to a specific place in society. That is to say, they criticize her because Ostrom – as an economic pluralist – thinks that the commons could live peacefully beside the state and the market (as opposed to becoming a rival logic) (Dardot and Laval, 2014: pp. 155–7). In the case of Proudhon, they point out that he insists too much on the social and apolitical logic of workers' self-organization. In contrast, Dardot and Laval contend that these forms of self-organization are political through and through (something which the later Proudhon came to accept as well) (p. 382).
9. There exists, for instance, a literature exploring the relation between non-violence and authoritarianism. A strict adherence to non-violence can lead to the emergence of hierarchies where some come to occupy a place of moral authority that allows them to police the behaviour of others (Frazer, 2016: pp. 5–6).
10. There is, as Martin Deleixhe has argued, also an internal aspect to this assertion: that is, underlining the cooperative aspect of the politics of the common also distracts from

the internal conflicts that either already exist or may arise. As a result, different forms of domination in commons (for example, women bearing the brunt of the labour in commons) disappear from view (Deleixhe, 2018).

11. There is a clear tendency in the literature on the commons to emphasize the need for a new paradigm of legality. The assumption being that there are some elements in the tradition of modern constitutionalism (for example, the importance of property rights, the legal enshrinement of a particular form of representative democracy and so on) that conflict with the principles that inhere in practices of commoning. That is why most of these thinkers develop some version of an alternative law of or for the common(s).
12. However, this does not mean that we should reduce this conflict to its strictly legal terms. A legal order is always more than a set of rules: it entails specific forms of subjectivity and norms that shape the practices of those subject to them.
13. It should be noted that not all forms of squatting are automatically acts of commoning. Squatting becomes an act of commoning when the right of use – in the form of a right to have a roof over one's head – is opposed to the right to property. Another important factor is that the squatters/commoners autonomously and democratically develop rules that regulate this right of usage.
14. And this is still leaving out the factor of race, a question about which Dardot and Laval – focused on a more traditional, white labouring class – have little to say. Should the logic of the common become universal, it will have to develop a more expansive concept of the working class. Hence, it will have to include a population that, often due to the factor of race, lives on the borders between the proletarian condition and that of the lumpenproletariat. However, this surplus population, as became evident in the twentieth- and twenty-first-century race riots, is more intensely caught up in a relation with state violence (see: Clover, 2016: pp. 130–92). A proper consideration of the relation between the common(s) and race, however, would take more space than this chapter can offer. For two important takes on the subject see: Harney and Moten, 2013; and Mezzadra and Neilson, 2013: pp. 277–312.
15. Of course, as we argued above, the set of strategies of civility also includes non-violent strategies. However, within the limits of this chapter it is not possible to cover both violent and non-violent strategies in depth. Since non-violent strategies have been at the centre of the commons literature, it seemed more appropriate to shed some light on a topic that is less written about in relation to the common(s).
16. Even, as John Medearis notes, in its more radical and oppositional forms (Medearis, 2015: p.148).
17. This is not to suggest that there can be no overlap between these two traditions. The most interesting political positions are the ones that balance the two traditions.

REFERENCES

Allen, M. B. (1952) P.J. Proudhon in the Revolution of 1848. *The Journal of Modern History*, **24** (1), 1–14.

Arendt, H. (1969) *On Violence.* San Diego, Harcourt.

Arendt, H. (2016 [1963]) *On Revolution*. London, Faber and Faber.

Bailey, S. and Marcucci, M. E. (2013) Legalizing the Occupation: The Teatro Valle as a Cultural Commons. *The South Atlantic Quarterly*, **112** (2), 396–405.

Balibar, É. (2002) *Politics and the Other Scene*. London, Verso Books.

Balibar, É. (2009) Violence and Civility: On the Limits of Political Anthropology. *Differences: A Journal of Feminist Cultural Studies*, **20** (2/3), 9–35.

Balibar, É. (2015a) *Violence and Civility: On the Limits of Political Philosophy*. New York, Columbia University Press.

Balibar, É. (2015b) Violence, politique, civilité. In: Caloz-Tschopp, Marie-Claire (ed.) *Violence, civilité, révolution*. Paris, La Dispute, pp. 15–50.

Balibar, É. (2017 [1993]) *The Philosophy of Marx*. London, Verso Books.

Bauwens, M. (2015) Interview with Pierre Dardot and Christian Laval on the Politics of the Common. *P2P Foundation*. Available from: https://blog.p2pfoundation.net/interview-with-pierre-dardot-and-christian-laval-on-the-politics-of-the-common/2015/07/24 (accessed 11 July 2018).

Bernstein, R. J. (2013) *Violence: Thinking without Banisters*. London, Polity.

Breaugh, M. (2007) *L'expérience plébéienne: Une histoire discontinue de la liberté politique*. Paris, Éditions Payot et Rivages.

Breen, K. (2012) *Under Weber's Shadow: Modernity, Subjectivity and Politics in Habermas, Arendt and Macintyre*. Surrey, Ashgate.

Broumas, A. (2015) Movements, Constitutability, Commons: Towards a *Ius Communis*. *Law and Critique*, **26**, 11–26.

Brown, W. (2005) *Edgework: Critical Essays on Knowledge and Politics*. Princeton, Princeton University Press.

Burchell, G., Davidson, A. and Foucault, M. (2008) *The Birth of Biopolitics: Lectures at the Collège de France 1978–1979*. London, Palgrave Macmillan.

Caygill, H. (2013) *On Resistance: A Philosophy of Defiance*. London, Bloomsbury.

Ciccariello-Maher, G. (2017) *Decolonizing Dialectics*. Durham, Duke University Press.

Clover, J. (2016) *Riot. Strike. Riot.* London, Verso Books.

Dardot, P. and Laval, C. (2009) *La nouvelle raison du monde: Essai sur la société néolibérale*. Paris, La Découverte.

Dardot, P. and Laval, C. (2014) *Commun: Essai sur la révolution au XXIe siècle*. Paris, La Découverte.

Dardot, P., Laval, C. and El Mouhoub, M. (2007) *Sauver Marx? Empire, multitude, travail immatériel*. Paris, La Découverte.

De Angelis, M. (2014) Social Revolution and the Commons. *South Atlantic Quarterly*, Spring, 299–311.

Deleixhe, M. (2018) Conflicts in (the) Common(s)? Radical Democracy and the Governance of the Commons. *Thesis Eleven*, **144** (1), 59–79.

Finlay, C. J. (2009) Hannah Arendt's Critique of Violence. *Thesis Eleven*, May, 26–45.

Frazer, E. (2014) Power and Violence. In: Hayden, P. (ed.) *Hannah Arendt: Key Concepts*. Durham, Acumen, pp. 155–66.

Frazer, E. (2016) The Diversity of Tactics: Anarchism and Political Power. *European Journal of Political Theory*, Advance Publication.

Frazer, E. and Hutchings, K. (2008) On Politics and Violence: Arendt Contra Fanon. *Contemporary Political Theory*, **7**, 90–108.

Frazer, E. and Hutchings, K. (2009) Politics, Violence and Revolutionary Virtue: Reflections on Locke and Sorel. *Thesis Eleven*, May, 46–63.

Geuss, R. (2006) Dialectics and the Revolutionary Impulse. In: Rush, F. (ed.) *The Cambridge Companion to Critical Theory*. Cambridge, Cambridge University Press, pp. 103–38.

Hardt, M. and Negri, T. (2017) *Assembly*. Oxford, Oxford University Press.

Harney, S. and Moten, F. (2013) *The Undercommons: Fugitive Planning and Black Study*. New York, Minor Compositions.

Honderich, T. (1980) *Violence for Equality: Inquiries in Political Philosophy*. Harmondsworth, Penguin Books.

Jameson, F. (2016) An American Utopia. In: Žižek, S. (ed.) *An American Utopia: Dual Power and the Universal Army*. London, Verso Books, pp. 1–96.
Kean, J. (2004) *Violence and Democracy*. Cambridge, Cambridge University Press.
Laclau, E. and Mouffe, C. (2014 [1985]) *Hegemony and Socialist Strategy: Towards a Radical Democratic Politics*. 2nd edn, London, Verso Books.
Lindahl, H. (2013) *Fault Lines of Globalization: Legal Order and the Politics of A-legality*. Oxford, Oxford University Press.
Medearis, J. (2015) *Why Democracy is Oppositional*. Cambridge, Harvard University Press.
Mezzadra, S. and Neilson, B. (2013) *Border as Method, Or the Multiplication of Labor*. London, Duke University Press.
Oksala, J. (2012) *Foucault, Politics and Violence*. Evanston, Northwestern University Press.
Ostrom, E. (2000) Collective Action and the Evolution of Social Norms. *Journal of Economic Perspectives*, **14** (3), 137–58.
Ostrom, E., Walker, J. and Gardner, R. (1992) Covenants With and Without a Sword: Self-governance is Possible. *American Political Science Review*, **86** (2), 404–17.
Penta, L. (1996) Hannah Arendt: On Power. *The Journal of Speculative Philosophy*, **X** (3), 210–29.
Ross, K. (2015) *Communal Luxury: The Political Imaginary of the Paris Commune*. London, Verso Books.
Saar, M. (2010) Power and Critique. *Journal of Power*, **3** (1), 7–20.
Solari, S. (2012) The 'Practical Reason' of Reformers: Proudhon vs. Institutionalism. *Journal of Economic Issues*, **46** (1), 227–40.
Sorel, G. (1961 [1908]) *Reflections on Violence*. Toronto, Collier Books.
Üstündağ, N. (2016) Self-defense as a Revolutionary Practice in Rojava, or How to Unmake the State. *The South Atlantic Quarterly*, **115** (1), 197–210.
Van de Sande, M. (2017) The Prefigurative Power of the Commons. In: Ruivenkamp, G. and Hilton, A. (eds) *Perspectives on Commoning: Autonomist Principles and Practices*. London, Zed Books, pp. 25–63.
Vishmidt, M. (2014) All Shall Be Unicorns: About Commons, Aesthetics, and Time. *Open*. [Online] Available from: www.onlineopen.org/download.php?id=128 (accessed 12 June 2016).
Weber, M. (1978) *Economy and Society*, Vol. I. Oakland, University of California Press.
Williams, A. (2010) On Negative Solidarity and Post-Fordist Plasticity. *Splintering Bone Ashes*. [Online] Available from: http://splinteringboneashes.blogspot.be/2010/01/negative-solidarity-and-post-fordist.html (accessed 30 October 2017).

5. Forget Ostrom: from the development commons to the common as social sovereignty

Pierre Sauvêtre*

1. INTRODUCTION

From the 1990s onwards, and particularly since the early 2010s, a body of theoretical works and practical (social, economic, legal, political) experiences brought to the fore a demand that was formulated either as the recovery of 'common goods' (Mattei, 2012; Parance and De Saint Victor, 2014), as the development of 'commons' (Bollier and Helfrich, 2013; Bollier, 2014; Linebaugh, 2014; Coriat, 2015) or as the institution of 'the common' (Hardt and Negri, 2011; Dardot and Laval, 2014). This has led to significant ambiguity as each of these three notions, while pretending to be the most relevant approach, does not cease to find affinities and to communicate with the other two. There is, thus, a tendency to strongly condemn in theory what is accepted in practice in order to avoid factionalization.

How can we escape such ambiguity? A first possibility might be to say that all these notions refer to the same thing, that is, that we could use any of the three indifferently. However, this position is not tenable: the notion of common goods designates resources that are inherently accessible to everyone, while commons or the common suggest, instead, that institutions and forms of governance are required to turn resources that are not common per se, into common things. The second possibility would be to make these notions compatible with each other. Among the several options, one solution would be to classify common goods as referring to law, commons as part of the economy, and the common as belonging to philosophy. However, this cannot be fully justified, as common goods can be related to the economy and commons to law, whereas concrete political experiences, such as the *indignados* and anti-austerity movement in Spain, are conducted on behalf of the common. Another solution could be to argue for a fruitful plurality so as to foster public debate, but this contradicts the tendency of each side to refute the others. A last option would seek to consider these notions as distinct yet non-exclusive aspects of a same reality, viewing common goods as common resources, commons as the self-governing institutions for the management of these resources, and the common as the underlying political principle of those institutions, but this would not work better. Garret Hardin, for example, used the term ‘commons’ to refer to open access resources (Hardin, 1968), while the Italian *beni comuni* movement undoubtedly includes self-governing institutions (see Giardini et al., 2012).

A further clarification seems necessary. So far, the respective critiques that each side has addressed to the others have been mostly theoretical: the analysis of the inherent limitations of one notion justifies the use of another, yet no empirical analysis proves capable of ascertaining the intrinsic factual value of any such concept. In other words, no sociological critique of these notions has been truly undertaken from the vantage point of social totality. Yet, each of these was elaborated in specific historical contexts, framing concrete experiences and producing identifiable effects. Historical and sociological insights, thus, would allow for useful distinctions.

The aim of this chapter is to lay the groundwork for this critique by establishing a distinction between Ostrom’s commons and the common. Such divergence can be drawn from a comparison between distinctive ‘pro common(s) (goods) politics’, such as the Ostromian developmentalist policy of the commons, on the one hand, and the Water War in Bolivia, the Italian *beni comuni* movement, or the Catalonian *politica del comú*, on the other. By ‘pro common(s) (goods) politics’, we refer to practical and theoretical ensembles produced by the mutual constitution between theoretical research on common(s) (goods) and the discursive or non-discursive practices of actors (social movements, political organizations, institutional actors) who claim to follow these principles, and that have taken the form of organized movements aiming at the implementation of the common(s) (goods). At first glance, these ensembles share similar characteristics that warrant comparison: a lexicon of the common (common goods, commons or the common), the preference for a third way distinct from the market and the state, as well as self-governing and self-organizing practices. Moreover, what justifies the interest in these cases is that, as organized movements, they have reached a critical threshold, which makes them something more than a mere experiment restricted to a group of insiders.

The two main parts of this chapter compare the Ostromian developmentalist policy of the commons with the mobilization for *lo común* (the common) in the context of the Water War in Bolivia. It is not possible, given the limits of this chapter, to carry out a detailed analysis of the Italian movement of *beni comuni* or the Catalonian *politica del comú* (see, however, Sauvêtre, 2016; 2018). Nevertheless, we will argue that the latter pro common(s) (goods) politics share close links and common features with the mobilization for *lo común* in Bolivia.

This chapter contends that, despite a seemingly shared historical background, the studies stemming since the 1980s from Ostrom's work on the commons and their inscription within international development policies, have no connection whatsoever with the movements for the common that appear in the 2000s in the context of the wave of state neoliberalization. On the one hand, historical and sociological analysis shows that the commons refer to an intervention aimed at structuring the community-based management of resources in the Global South, and are intended as a shift away from public intervention by the state and towards a deepening of the market economy. On the other hand, such analysis also indicates that the common constitutes a social fact, an original practice developed by certain social groups, in states that favoured market players and ceased serving the public interest, based upon the exercise of a 'social sovereignty' within a non-state public space.

2. OSTROM AND THE DEVELOPMENTALIST POLICY OF THE COMMONS

Understanding the political significance of Elinor Ostrom's perspective on the commons is decisive, all the more so since a vast majority of scholars have taken up her conceptual categories to analyse all kinds of objects, which – according to them – allegedly become commons as soon as they fulfil the eight design principles for sustainable governance that she has outlined, even if she was herself more careful in outlining these principles as mere 'similarities' (Ostrom, 1990: pp. 88–102).[1] However, this endorsement of the Ostromian model is mostly made in an uncritical and ahistorical manner. It is largely based on the symbolic authority Ostrom has gained by winning the Nobel Prize in Economics, without awareness of the specific background in which these categories were developed and the political effects they may have produced. No mention of this specific historical context is ever made in the literature in French devoted to the presentation of Ostrom's theoretical framework (see, for example, Coriat, 2013; Weinstein, in Cornu et al., 2017: pp. 861–6; and Ingold, in Cornu et al., 2017: pp. 866–71), but this is also the case for the overwhelming majority of the commons literature in English (Cole and McGinnis, 2017; Sebatti and Castiglione, 2016; Agilica, 2014).

It is therefore essential to show firstly that Ostrom's work was very closely linked to American development aid policy, secondly that her scientific background made her the ideal candidate to provide the theoretical framework for these policies, and finally that the implementation of these policies have produced identifiable effects. The point is not, then, to question Ostrom's research as a unified theory but to situate her work on the commons within a developmentalist policy of the commons, for the purpose of which it was used.

2.1 The Formation of Development Commons

Fabien Locher has carefully retraced the historical context that led to the writing of *Governing the Commons* (1990), the reference book for the scientific literature on the commons (Locher, 2016). The historical roots of the commons paradigm and common-pool resources (CPR) analysis are inseparable from a change in United States (US) development policies and doctrine, with the replacement, during the 1970s and 1980s, of a state-centred development model with a model combining markets with forms of community governance. According to Locher, a number of developments in the 1970s, such as the global ecological crisis evidenced in the situation of the Sahel, the critique of the imported Western model of agricultural cooperatives as a means of development, the peasants' revolt against imperialist states, and an emerging generation of anthropologists advocating for traditional and community-based natural resources management, were all contextual elements that drew development actors towards common property resource management systems. Michael Horowitz, an anthropologist funded and tasked by the US Agency for International Development (USAID) to recommend solutions to the Sahelian crisis, was one of the first to stress the responsibilities of governments and emphasize the positive effects of traditional community practices and indigenous institutions on the sustainability of resource management systems, at a time in which most interpretations identified peasant mismanagement as the culprit.

Disputing evolutionist arguments about the necessarily primitive and non-rational character of collective property and its historical replacement by systems of private property, a new conception of the peasant emerged with the works of anthropologists like James Scott and Robert Netting, or economic historians like Donald McCloskey (Scott, 1976; Netting, 1976; and McCloskey, 1983; all cited in Locher, 2016). The peasant came to be seen as operating a symbiosis between the heritage of a traditional culture, and the attitude of a rational individual agent capable of adapting to his changing environment and making optimal choices to ensure his subsistence in a context of scarce resources. It was no longer necessary to pit tradition against economic development goals. In the early 1980s, in an attempt to resolve the Sahel crisis, USAID ultimately sought to combine agricultural modernization with the promotion of traditional community systems, in order 'to reconcile development, conservation of ecosystems and involvement of local people' (Locher, 2016: p. 323).

It was under these circumstances that in 1984 USAID, while cooperating with the Board on Science and Technology for International Development (BOSTID), started promoting and financing the creation of an international academic research network on the collective management of resources, the Common Property Resource Network (CPR Network). Ostrom became a member. The network was founded at the Annapolis Conference in 1985, and Ostrom was made responsible for drafting its final report. With 1,100 members by June 1987, it led two years later to the formation of the International Association for the Study of Common Property (IASCP), of which Ostrom was first elected president (Hess, 1999). Ostrom also obtained funds from USAID to compile a set of case studies on collective resource management, and this led her to undertake one of the CPR Network objectives: to build a general analytical framework capable of modelling case studies and measuring their respective performance, in order to draw up a list of successful criteria for institutional sustainability that could be used in development policy. This resulted most notably in the publication of *Governing the Commons* and its famous eight institutional design principles, among many others articles and papers.

This close connection between US development policy and Ostrom's work follows from one specific goal, as Locher also points out: the conjunction, under the Reagan administration, between the delegitimization of the modernizing, technocratic and state-centred development model stemming from the New Deal, and the promotion of a new, alternative model favouring a convergence between the market and the customary practices of local communities called upon to adapt to the latter. This programme eventually included two main components of the neoliberal project: a critique of public intervention by the state and the empowerment of individuals and communities through their acculturation to the economic rationality of the market. As for this second aspect, it presupposes an endorsement of the 'rational choice' theory and its assimilation by the members of the community:

> The decisions and actions of CPR appropriators to appropriate from and provide a CPR are those of broadly rational individuals who find themselves in complex and uncertain situations. An individual's choice of behavior in any particular situation will depend on how the individual learns about, views and weighs the benefits and costs of actions and their perceived linkage to outcomes that also involve a mixture of benefits and costs. (Ostrom, 1990: p. 33)

What are the commons according to Ostrom? She considers them through the prism of the interests of individuals within community management systems, which are based on a cost–benefit analysis. It is the efficiency of the commons in terms of costs and benefits that determines their legitimacy. Commons are both *community-based* resource management systems, because they rely on local communities, and *efficient* economic solutions within the framework of a market economy that can serve as benchmarks for rural community development policies. Ostrom's contribution is not only to have made traditional communal property rights systems fashionable again, but also to have modelled the economic rationalization of traditional commons. She invented *efficient commons*, as opposed to the classical approach to historical commons, which was based, as Karl Polanyi pointed out, on the antinomy between those institutions that ensured 'the welfare of the community', and the 'economic improvement' that 'upse[t] the social order', ruined the country and 'decimat[ed] its population' (Polanyi, 2001 [1944]: pp. 35–6).

2.2 Ostrom and 'Public Choice' Theory

In order to understand why Ostrom was the perfect candidate to accomplish both parts of this programme – the delegitimization of government action and the subjectivation of members of traditional communities into '*homines economici*' – it is worth examining Ostrom's relationship with Public Choice theory. Vincent and Elinor Ostrom were both founding members of the Public Choice Society, initiated by James Buchanan in 1963, and they both chaired it from 1967 to 1969 and from 1982 to 1984 respectively (Wall, 2014). Ostrom acknowledged her intellectual debt to the flagship textbook of 'Public Choice' theory – Buchanan and Tullock's *The Calculus of Consent* (1962) – as well as the influence it exerted throughout the course of her academic career, from her work in the 1960s on urban policy up to her CPR case studies in the 1980s (Ostrom, 2011).

Three defining features of 'Public Choice' theory – its conception of the failures of central government, its assumption of economic rationality to comprehend every problem of political organization, and its nature as a 'science of government' – are reflected in the Ostromian approach.

This current of Public Choice, as defined by Buchanan and Tullock in their seminal work of 1962, is based on the idea that it is too simplistic to redress market failures by means of state interventions, since failures also abound in the public action of any government. Those failures of bureaucratic government are particularly apparent when it comes to the provision of public goods and services, which should be its primary objective, according to Public Choice theorists. They do pose in this way the problem of choosing institutional frameworks or rule systems that are the most effective in the production of public goods, which amounts to questioning the performance of the state from a cost–benefit perspective. Evaluating the ratio of costs to benefits can therefore be applied to public administrations and public officials to introduce reforms meant to improve efficiency and accountability. Budget cuts and constraints, privatization and competition in public services, introduction of user fees, separation of provision from production in the procurement of public goods, outsourcing and decentralization, are all reform tools inspired by Public Choice theory that directly contributed to the ascendancy of New Public Management (Gruening, 2001).

In the wake of *The Calculus of Consent*, Ostrom claimed to have always pleaded for decentralization and institutional diversity in accordance with what was for her the 'fundamental lesson' of the book (Ostrom, 2011: p. 370). With their 'Workshop in Political and Policy Analysis' set up in 1973 at the University of Indiana, whose objective was to develop a theory readily capable of producing policy recommendations, Vincent and Elinor Ostrom also converged with the 'science of government' posture adopted by Buchanan and Tullock. Like Mancur Olson[2] in his famous 1965 book, *The Logic of Collective Action* (Olson, 1965), Ostrom's theoretical approach was, thus, to apply Public Choice theory to collective action. However, she drew a conclusion opposite to his: Olson had concluded, on the basis of individual economic rationality that justifies the existence of free riders taking advantage of collective benefits without assuming individual costs, that collective action could not be attained without external constraints. Ostrom argued, to the contrary, that a self-organized action that achieves collective benefits is possible through the ability of individuals to implement new rules, as well as monitoring and sanctioning mechanisms that prevent the possibility of free riding. From this point of view, the neo-institutionalism of Vincent and Elinor Ostrom, with at its heart the concepts of 'institutional diversity' and 'polycentric government', can be seen as an original extension of the 'Public Choice' theory. Such approach consists in overcoming the limitations of bureaucratic government through the development of various modes of governance, decision-making, rule-making and institutions (see Aligica and Boettke, 2009; Aligica, 2014; Cole and McGinnis, 2017), rather than by means of a generalized logic of privatization. Ostrom, therefore, frequently emphasized the civic dimension of collective self-organization in the tradition of American local democracy and referred in this spirit to Hamilton, Madison or Tocqueville (Ostrom, 2006).

Yet, it remains no less true that these references coexist with others (see Buchanan, Coase, North, Sheple, Williamson) (Ostrom, 1990: p. 216, n. 22, p. 244) and that every problem of collective action is explained and analysed by the individual economic evaluation of the ratio between costs incurred and profits obtained. Collective action is thus, understood as a result of 'coordinated strategies', as an aggregation of individual preferences in 'order to obtain joint benefits or reduce common damages' (ibid.: p. 39). Institutional choices, such as sticking to collective ownership, rather than moving to private property, are likewise explained by transaction cost analysis and Coase's theorem: 'If the transaction cost involved in managing communal property had been excessive, compared with private property institutions, the villagers would have had many opportunities to devise land tenure arrangements for the mountain commons' (ibid.: p. 61). In other words, private property may still be a preferable choice, if the cost of communal property proves excessive.

Whatever the democratic potential of some of Ostrom's proposals, the fact remains that the manner in which her work combined the criticism of bureaucratic government, the insistence on citizen autonomy and the generalization of economic rationality to all spheres of action, made it perfectly suitable to support the political project that took shape during the 1980s with regard to development policy: that of abandoning forms of bureaucratic regulation and shifting the responsibility for financial costs onto individuals and communities.

2.3 The Commons and the Governance of Subaltern Populations

In addition to the original historical context of commons theory and the intellectual trajectory of Elinor Ostrom, this critique of the developmentalist policy of the commons would not be complete without an analysis of its real effects on the communities where it has been applied.

Pierre-Marie Aubert is one of those who empirically established, in the case of forest management, the link between Ostromian CPR analysis, development policies, and their effects on targeted populations. Defining the literature on commons as an 'epistemic community' (Haas, 1992) – that is, a group of researchers whose work provided the expertise for the decisions of development actors[3] – he notes that the acceleration of land reforms aiming at entrusting ownership or at least management of many forests to local communities in the early 1990s, coincided with the rise of CPR analysis. In this regard, he points out that the circumscribed location of these reforms in the Global South countries – and their absence in the North – is due to the fact that the former had been forced to accept them because of their dependence on the assistance provided by international organizations (Aubert, 2010, pp. 125–31).

Aubert demonstrates that researchers from the CPR Network were directly involved in an effort to push international development organizations to adopt its views. James T. Thomson, a founding member of the IASCP and close collaborator to Ostrom, wrote several reports and a handbook for the Food and Agriculture Organization of the United Nations (FAO) (Thomson, 1992; Thomson and Coulibaly, 1995; Thomson and Freudenberger, 1997). As for the World Bank, it directly launched two key initiatives. Firstly, it created, in 1995, the IASCP-affiliated World Bank Common Property Resource Management Network (CPR Net), to connect research experts, World Bank staff and actors on the ground (Scharl, 2004). Secondly, it organized in 1998 the seminar of the International Community Based Natural Resource Management (CBNRM), to which Ostrom was invited to deliver a lecture on 'self-governance and forest resources' (Ostrom, 1999).

As Aubert remarks, the conclusion of this seminar indicates its universalist claim that 'the CBNRM approach [is] of universal relevance, across geographical, political and administrative boundaries, across cultural and ethnic boundaries, and across disciplines' (World Bank, 1999, cited in Aubert, 2010: p. 129). To be sure, more moderate, even critical, proposals were also submitted by CBNRM members to other international organizations, including those that Melissa Leach and Tim Forsyth made to the United Nations Development Programme (UNDP), which focused more on the fight against poverty, but there were fewer such proposals. The key ideas of the CPR Network were also promoted through the creation of specialized agencies, such as the International Forest Resources and Institutions (IFRI), through partnerships with organizations such as the Center for International Forestry Research (CIFOR), or by being adopted by associations like the World Wide Fund for Nature (WWF), or smaller structures like the Community-based Natural Resource Management Learning Institute in Cambodia.

Pierre-Marie Aubert and Bruno Romagny (2012) also analysed, in the field of water management, various cases of development policies supported by the World Bank and inspired by community-based natural resource management models. In the case of a rural hydraulic development project set up between 2002 and 2006 in the Ait Bougmez valley in Morocco, they first noted that as part of a national policy of Participatory Irrigation Management that dated back to the beginning of the 1980s, the project was intended both to strengthen the integration of farmers in the management of hydro-agricultural infrastructures, and as a way to make them financially responsible for infrastructure maintenance in the context of structural adjustment policies. This policy required irrigators to join together in Agricultural Water User Associations, which led to the creation of new inter-village governance structures that destabilized traditional forms of irrigation.[4] In the case of Burkina Faso, in a context also marked by structural adjustment policies and a rolling back of the state, the introduction of community-based natural resource management forms entailed the top-down establishment of formal water management committees controlled by local authorities, at odds with ostensibly bottom-up intentions. Another consequence was the introduction of fees for the water service, required by the creation of an infrastructure maintenance fund, whereas water had been free of charge under the previous public water distribution system. Lastly, this change in management resulted in the delegation of water services to private operators, involved in the financing, rehabilitation, management and maintenance of water systems, with water user associations merely confined to monitoring and evaluation activities. However, such power shifts and their impact on the populations, which are supposed to benefit from the community-based management models, are precisely what the CPR analysis, by referring only to isolated and local self-regulating management systems, is unable to explain.

In the case of forestry management in Nepal, Mauve Létang has also shown how the integration and application of the CPR analysis by the Nepalese government since 1982, enabled the liberalization of community forest management. The setting up of an agency funded by USAID (ACAP – Annapurna Conservation Area Project) to officialize the transfer of management to local communities has led to delegitimizing their traditional knowledge and redistributing power within communities in favour of young educated people with economic expertise who are supported by NGOs (Létang, 2017; forthcoming).

In sum, if Ostrom was able to highlight the long term sustainability of certain traditional forms of community management, the use of her theory as a tool for development policy induces a performative contradiction in the action of international organizations, as they impose foreign frameworks upon traditional and *already self-organized* natural resource management systems. In the context of structural adjustment plans for the Global South countries, these policies have no other effects than enabling control over the populations' behaviour, thus placed in a subaltern position, in the sense that their capacities for self-organization, far from being encouraged, are bridled.

To conclude this first part, it becomes clear that not only the developmentalist context of its formation, but also the very theoretical content that Ostrom's intellectual trajectory gives to it, as well as its socio-political effects on local populations, confer to the concept of commons a very specific scope. This makes its use, at the very least, problematic, and certainly not generalizable, despite the uncritical self-evidence with which the great majority of researchers working on these issues take it on board.

3. THE COMMON AS AN EXERCISE OF SOCIAL SOVEREIGNTY: THE CASE OF THE WATER WAR IN BOLIVIA

With the pro common(s) (goods) politics of Cochabamba's Water War that broke out at the end of 1999 in Bolivia, *lo común* (the common) takes on a whole new meaning. Even though the Water War followed only by a couple of decades the moment when Ostrom began her research on the commons, these two contexts have nothing to do with each other. Whereas Ostrom's commons were, under the Reagan administration, introduced willy-nilly in the neoliberal programme aiming to undermine the public-state basis of development policy in the South, the Water War in Bolivia, conversely, marked the first victorious struggle, in a southern country, against government authorities supporting the neoliberal privatization of public goods and services. Above all, what the term common(s) designates is significantly different in the two instances. While the commons refer to an *economic framework* for community-based resource management, the common refers to a *social fact*, which consists in an innovative social practice to collectively deliberate and decide on the use of resources.

3.1 Water War in Bolivia: From *Usos y Custombres* to *lo Común*

In September 1999, under the pressure of structural adjustment policies recommended by the World Bank and the International Monetary Fund, the Bolivian parliament passed law 2029, allowing the privatization of the municipal water utility in Cochabamba, the third largest city in Bolivia, via a 40-year concession granted to *Aguas del Tunari*, a consortium of companies registered in the Cayman Islands, of which the US-based multinational Bechtel was the major shareholder. The concession agreement between the Bolivian government and *Aguas del Tunari* provided for an increase in water tariffs and stipulated that an access fee would also be charged to every community water management system in the metropolitan area that was not connected to the public water and sanitation company (*Servicio Municipal de Agua Potable y Alcantarillado* (SEMAPA)). This measure directly affected the peasant irrigators who had had access for a long time to water sources that they managed through traditional methods, as well as the inhabitants of Cochabamba's southern districts, where residents, being unconnected to the public water system, had dug their own wells and built their own community water management systems (Dwinell and Olivera, 2014; Bresnihan, forthcoming). As for the cooperatives, which until then had been granted a public concession to administer part of the water service, they were now liable to prosecution by *Aguas del Tunari* and threatened with expropriation at the company's behest.

The first to mobilize against this measure were the peasant irrigators organized in the Cochabamba Department Federation of Irrigators Organizations (*Federación Departamental Cochabambina de Organizaciones de Regantes* (FEDECOR)), who established contacts and found support with the Departmental Federation of Factory Workers of Cochabamba (*Federación Departamental de Trabajadores Fabriles de Cochabamba* (FDTFC), also known as 'Fabriles'). Their union resulted in the formation, on 12 November 1999, of the *Coordinadora por la Defensa del Agua y la Vida* (Coordination for the Defence of Water and Life (*La Coordinadora*)), which led the protest against the Bolivian authorities between December 1999 and April 2000. This organization, thus, managed to bring together rural and urban groups. After several months of mobilization, sometimes violent confrontations with the army and difficult negotiations with governmental authorities, it obtained the expulsion of the private company and the return to the public water system managed by SEMAPA. The Water War was the first 'victorious' struggle of Bolivian social movements after fifteen years of failures in the face of neoliberal reforms (Assies, 2003).

However, this conflict cannot be truly understood through the mere opposition between the public and the private, because it also entailed the protection of community water management systems. Peasant irrigators had for a long time developed community-based forms of water management and governance based on the notion of *usos y costumbres* ('habits and customs'). Tom Perreault defines them as customary practices characterized by three basic features:

> 1. They are practices that are repeated, habitual, and regular; 2. They are based on a thorough and intimate knowledge of the social and environmental context in which irrigation takes place; 3. They are voluntary, mutually agreed on, and accepted within a given social context (e.g., the members of the irrigation system), and not imposed by an external actor. '*Usos y costumbres*' are, then, the mutually understood rules that govern rights to and management of water within a given irrigation system: when irrigation occurs, how much water each irrigator is entitled to, the order in which individual fields are to be irrigated, the labor or monetary contributions each irrigator is to make to the maintenance of the canal system, and the penalties for water theft or the shrinking of responsibilities. (Perreault, 2008: p. 839)

While some relate this model of habits and customs to a tradition that can be traced back to the Incas (Olivera, 2015), it is much more a symbolism built over time, in order to preserve peasant autonomy in the management and access to water, against development projects or public attempts to take ownership. Such was the case during the 'war of the wells' (*guerra de pozos*) in 1995 that opposed peasant irrigators and the SEMAPA, which threatened to dig deeper wells to capture their water sources. Furthermore, poor urban dwellers in the southern neighbourhoods of the city had developed their own modes of collective decision-making, organization of labour, and allocation of resources outside state and market institutions. Their self-managed water systems covered a variety of realities in terms of decision-making processes and organizational structures. As Patrick Bresnihan (forthcoming) points out, water cooperatives, which have a president and a board of regularly elected representatives, are more formal than water committees. These are structured around weekly and mandatory meetings and assemblies, while in larger cooperatives there may only be two meetings a year. Yet, all these self-managed systems collectively share the costs and work needed to build and maintain water infrastructures (pipes, wells, pumps), and decisions are made in assemblies where all members are allowed to participate.

Within this context, the situation preceding the Water War in Cochabamba was characterized by tensions and social differentiations between community water management systems, on the one hand, and market and public-state institutions, on the other. Consequently, if the mobilization of the *Coordinadora* sought, with the repeal of law 2029, a return to the public water management by the SEMAPA, it was only to the extent that the *status quo ante* for community-based and autonomous water management systems would also be maintained.

3.2 The Emergence of *lo Común* in the Course of the Conflict

Nevertheless, it is not possible to truly understand what is at stake with the common(s) (goods) in the Bolivian context by only analysing the management forms of aquifer resources. It is crucial, on the contrary, to examine thoroughly the role and the specific meaning of the lexicon of common(s) (goods) in the course of the Water War through the practices of the *Coordinadora*,[5] given that this lexicon *has not been* specifically used for the defence of autonomous water management systems. It is, then, not so much a question of analysing social relations within the resource management systems, but rather the new political socialization produced by the *Coordinadora*.

The first phase of the mobilization (December 1999–15 January 2000) ended with the Bolivian government promising to cancel the concession granted to *Aguas del Tunari* and to change Law 2029 according to the interests of self-managed water systems. On 20 October 1999, the various social forces that were soon to merge into the *Coordinadora* had agreed on these two objectives of the cancellation of the contract and the modification of the law (Olivera et al., 2008: p. 143). The major events that took place during this first phase, that is, the demonstration of 23 December against the rise in the price of water, followed by the blockade of motorways on 11 January, were mostly framed as a defence of immediate popular interests.

The government's refusal to lower water tariffs, however, provoked a second phase of mobilization, with the *Coordinadora* deepening and broadening its role. Thanks to its horizontal and democratic approach to decision-making – inspired by the customary forms of deliberation and decision-making within irrigators associations, water committees and cooperatives – more than a mere convergence of various social interests, it became a 'confluence' (Gutiérrez Aguilar, 2008: p. 85) instrument enabling its different members to speak with one voice, freely and regardless of political parties. The *Coordinadora* put forward its own criticisms, denouncing the link between the privative appropriation of natural resources and the confiscation of political decision-making, claiming 'the reappropriation of decisions' (Gutiérrez Aguilar, in Olivera et al., 2008: p. 60) and raising the political problem of the right to decide on basic resources and its legitimacy. The slogan 'Water is ours', which marked the mobilization until the end, was an answer to that problem:

> The Bolivian government prefers to comply with what the World Bank tells it rather than to take into account what the population considers to be its needs. Such is the fundamental problem: who decides about the present and the future condition of the people, the resources, the work and the living conditions? As far as water is concerned, we want to decide for ourselves: and this we call democracy. (Communication from the *Coordinadora*, 28 January 2000, in Notes from Nowhere, 2003)

From that moment on, the *Coordinadora* raised the stakes of the conflict by questioning the very nature of sovereignty as the legitimate basis of the right to decide, whose direct exercise by the people is the only possible meaning of democracy:

> For us, working people of the city and the countryside, this is the true meaning of democracy: we decide and we do, we discuss and we execute. We risk our lives to accomplish what we propose, what we believe is right. Democracy is the sovereignty of the people, and that is what we have achieved. (Communication from the *Coordinadora*, 6 February 2000, in Olivera et al., 2008: p. 171)

It is precisely in this phase of the mobilization, linking up the assembly as a political practice, in the context of a conflict on the definition of democracy and on the legitimacy of power, popular sovereignty over natural resources and the contestation of how the state regulates them, that the lexicon of the common (*lo común*) and the common good and use (*bien y uso común*) emerged within society – not around the comparative economic interest of such and such resources management formula:

> The people of Cochabamba, in their struggles of 4 and 5 February, claimed that 'water is ours', as a right, as a fundamental good for common use, and not as a commodity, as a business object, and for this reason, it demanded the revision and the discussion of the contract and of the law on drinking water and sanitation. (Communication from the *Coordinadora*, 24 February 2000, in Olivera et al., 2008: p. 174)

With the political construction of the *Coordinadora*, a shift in the goals of the mobilization was reflected in the distinction between the notion of *usos y costumbres* and that of *bien y uso común*: whereas the first notion aims for the defence of popular interests, the second makes the exercise of the right to decide the condition itself of the right to access the resource.

3.3 A New Politics of the Common?

The *Coordinadora* and all the actors of the mobilization did not use the notion of commons, but only those of *bien común* (common good) and *lo común* (the common). Raquel Guttiérez Aguilar, a member the *Coordinadora* and a Mexican intellectual, emphasized how *lo común* (the common) had been constituted by the *Coordinadora* as a political horizon going well beyond the return to the state as guarantor of the public interest. After the expulsion of *Aguas del Tunari* and the effective return to public municipal water management in April 2000, the *Coordinadora* raised the issue of a 'social appropriation' of the SEMAPA by Cochabamba's workers and water users. Leveraging a favourable balance of power, it acted for the transformation of the public municipal company into a 'self-managed social company', through the introduction of 'self-management, decision-making, participation and social control' (Gutiérrez Aguilar in Olivera et al., 2008: pp. 67–8). The *Coordinadora*'s plan was to organize neighbourhood committees around water and sanitation concerns, bringing together residents and workers to develop and communicate solutions and to cooperate with those in the company who had technical skills. It focused its efforts, thus, on the creation of water committees in every city district, with the aim of converting the 'political style of assembly' characteristic of the mobilization, into the institutionalization of 'democratic practices and participatory public spaces' (Gutiérrez Aguilar in Olivera and Lewis, 2004: pp. 55–8), albeit not without encountering strong governmental resistance.

In the wake of this attempt and with the difficulties it had to face, the association ASICA-SUR (Association of Community Water Systems of the South) was created in 2004 to coordinate the work of the water committees of Cochabamba South. It soon established a partnership with the SEMAPA, in which the company served as a functional medium to consolidate the self-managed water systems of the inhabitants, and to achieve a co-management within what became a 'public-communal' model of water system (Sánchez-Gomez and Terhorst, 2005). However, this cooperation fizzled out when, following the election of Evo Morales, his government, which initially supported the water committees, ended up seeing them as a threat to its post-neoliberal policy of reaffirming the legitimacy of the state. Patrick Bresnihan showed, accordingly, how, particularly since 2011, constant tensions have opposed the water policy of the Bolivian state and the repeated efforts of water committees and cooperatives to self-manage water resources and infrastructures.[6] Moreover, Bresnihan highlights the diverging logics of the common, the private and the public in the new Bolivian context. He explains how, after the municipality had granted land to private owners, they connected illegally to the water sources of the self-managed systems, and then used the 'right to water' guaranteed by the new Bolivian Constitution in order to claim the legality of their connection. However, it is the Bolivian state that ultimately determines who has rights to which water sources (Bresnihan, forthcoming). The existence of this right to water guaranteed by the state is, therefore, responsible for a conflict between the logic of the common and the logic of the public, in the sense of ownership by the state.

Given the conditions of the Water War and its consequences, *lo común* (the common), unlike *usos y costumbres*, cannot be reduced to a resource management modality in Ostrom's sense, since it is a way of exercising sovereignty that raises the question of power and its legitimacy. Furthermore, because it is also a means of transforming the public enterprise, *lo común* cannot be simply considered as an object to be defended against privatizations, as the enclosure paradigm would suggest. In the immediate wake of the Water War in 2000, Raquel Guttiérez Aguilar, Álvaro García Linera and Luis Tapia fully explained the meaning of *lo común*:

> The proposal of the Coordinadora of a self-managed enterprise demolished the fallacious dualism between privatism and statism that had hitherto structured the contemporary political proposals. Just as politics was exercised as an issue managed by all, from assemblies to councils, collective goods such as water must receive the same treatment, said the assembly of the Coordinadora: they must be managed by those who are in need of them and use them, they must be self-managed by the citizens themselves. A *new sense of social sovereignty previously deposited in the State* has arisen in this way. The common, the collective

> is no longer in the State that has proven to be a form of private property of government officials. The common, the general is not an 'illusory community' of bureaucrats; it is the management regulated by all, it is an ethical sense of responsibility and of the techniques relevant to each situation, assembly, council, rotation in office, fiscalization of social policy. (Gutiérrez Aguilar et al., 2000: p. 177)[7]

The practice of the common, as it was built in the Bolivian experience of the Water War, combines three elements: a *politics of public assembly*, a form of *social sovereignty* based on the power of the users, and an *autonomous norm* that conflicts with both the state and the market. These three elements are articulated and inseparable from each other: it is to the extent that the *Coordinadora* has adopted the form of a public assembly capable of making its own decisions that it could reclaim decision-making and engage in a practice of social sovereignty. The latter does not correspond to a specific and limited scale of sovereignty according to the principle of subsidiarity, but is in itself a normative challenge to both the state's bureaucratic sovereignty and to the sovereignty of the capitalist command.

One of the most remarkable features of the Bolivian experience is that the practice of the common through the public assembly politics of the *Coordinadora* disrupted the traditional political framework, through both criticism of the political parties accused of corruption and of monopolizing political decisions, and the renewal of collective and labour union action that traditionally mobilized either against certain government proposals, or to obtain the satisfaction of some demands. With the *Coordinadora*, Cochabamba workers' unions, by putting their own practices into question, have developed a democratic organ of the civil society itself, thus enabling irrigators, farmers, urban workers and precarious populations to deliberate beyond their immediate sectional interests, to make decisions and execute them by controlling their representatives and, eventually, by dismissing them. The *Coordinadora*, thus, sought to extend this new way of doing politics with the proposal of a 'constituent assembly' that would act as a space of expression, participation, deliberation and public decision for all Bolivians, with the aim of building a political organization of the citizens, independent from political parties, and with the objective of a global transformation of political institutions. Such 'constituent assembly' should not be confused with what is usually understood by this term, that is, the appointment of a group of representatives to reform the Constitution of the state; it is rather a sovereign assembly of civil society, which makes concrete proposals for organizing the country and transforming the political system (Gutiérrez Aguilar, in Olivera et al., 2008: pp. 71–6). This proposal was nevertheless buried by the official Constituent Assembly that began its work after the election of Morales.

In any case, the common appears here as a new, non-partisan way of doing politics that goes hand in hand with a new definition of the 'public': a civic rather than statist definition of the public, understood as that which is accessible to all thanks to the action of all citizens. It follows that a politics of the common is not so much a policy that should promote the establishment of common goods or even of commons, but rather a new way of doing politics in common, characterized by an equal share in power and decision-making. This way of doing politics is both 'performative' (Butler, 2015) and transformative, because its aim is to transform the dominant representative political system into a space for exercising the common, in essence, to change it into a common. To quote Rebecca Hollender's excellent formula, the issue is less that of a 'politics of the commons' than of 'commoning the political' (Hollender, 2016).

What is the common at the end of this analysis? The common is a social fact, a set of real relations and rules immanent to the specific social practices of certain groups that can only be understood from the point of view of social totality. More precisely, it arises in societies marked by an alignment of the state with the interests of market actors, and beyond this, by the inability of states, political parties and representative political systems to satisfy the social interests of the majority. It is the socio-historical capacity, for certain social groups and by means of autonomous deliberation and decision-making mechanisms, to set the rules of economic, social or political life. The common is, finally, an autonomous practice of the popular classes, an exercise of social sovereignty that contributes to the building of civic, non-state, public institutions (for a very similar definition of the common, see Dardot, Chapter 2 in this volume).

4. CONCLUSION

This chapter sought to establish a comparative sociological analysis of the developmentalist policy of the Ostromian commons politics and the mobilization for *lo común* in the context of the Bolivian Water War. The outcome of this socio-historical analysis is that the commons and the common are two completely different realities. Forged in the context of a transformation of American international development policy, derived from the Public Choice theory and its critique of bureaucratic government, the Ostromian commons perspective was remarkably well-suited to be enlisted in a joint operation to weaken the southern states, and to transfer financial responsibility to local communities, under the guise of empowerment. In the radically different context of a critique of the neoliberal policy of states' alignment with the interests of market players, *lo común* of the Bolivian Water War presents itself as a social fact that goes beyond a customary mode of resource management, that is, as a social movement aimed to collectively deliberate and decide on the rules of resource management, and as an alternative to both the market and the state. Leaning on a politics of public assembly, the practice of the common is an exercise of social sovereignty that comes into conflict with state and capitalist sovereignties and opens the prospect of civic, non-state, public institutions.

While it is not possible, of course, to demonstrate it here, we have emphasized elsewhere that the Italian *beni comuni* movement or the Catalonian *politica del comú* (Sauvêtre, 2016; 2018) also share the three characteristics of the common that we have just distinguished: public assembly politics, social sovereignty and the elaboration of an autonomous norm conflicting with those of the state and the market. A historical analysis of social totality would show that these different mobilizations developed similar criticisms against the neoliberal policies of public services privatization and the ensuing incapacity of the state to respond to the most essential needs of the population. Moreover, a study of the circulation of practices would provide convincing clues that they also inspired one another and shared the same goals. The Italian *beni comuni* movement, like the Bolivian Water War, was launched following a decree that privatized public water services. The Italian mobilization for a referendum on the privatization programme was explicitly referred to and inspired by the Bolivian movement (Yaku, 2011). Like in Cochabamba, an attempt was made in Naples to institutionalize the 'social property' of the municipal water management company (Lucarelli, 2014). As for Barcelona *en comú*, the citizen organization that promotes a politics of the common (*politica del comú*), its name was adopted in direct reference to the Italian *beni comuni* movement (Russo Spena and Forti, 2016: p. 63).

Lastly, it should be pointed out that the social sovereignty of the common as a regime of power, distinct from the market and the state, has materialized in each of these movements at two levels: at the level of the social activities that link an object (a water source, a theatre, a square and so on) to those who take charge of it (for example water management at the level of a water committee self-governed by the inhabitants) and at the level of the municipality, in the form of a popular assembly or neighbourhood assemblies (like in Cochabamba or Barcelona in the period after the anti-austerity movement called the '15-M'). These experiences, therefore, fit into the institution of a 'municipalism of the commons' (Blanco and Gomà, 2016; Sauvêtre, 2018) that could interlink these two levels of social sovereignty.[8] At the global level, the political horizon that has been opened at recent summits gathering Latin American and European Cities in Barcelona ('Fearless Cities – Internationalist Municipalist Summit',

9–11 June 2017) and Naples ('Commons and Cities', 17–19 November 2017), is a transnational municipalism consisting of municipal confederations able to create 'a fundamental *duality of power* in which increasingly independent and confederated municipalities emerge in flat opposition to the centralized nation-state' (Bookchin, 1992: p. 10).

NOTES

* The author would like to thank Jean-François Bissonnette who has revised the English language of this chapter.

1. Ostrom (1990: p. 90) clearly states that 'these design principles are necessary conditions for achieving institutional robustness in CPR settings', and that 'further theoretical and empirical work is needed before a strong assertion of necessity can be made'.
2. He was also president of the Public Choice Society from 1972 to 1974.
3. More precisely, it is a group of researchers sharing common values, with a more or less unified theoretical corpus, whose work could have been used at different stages in framing the decisions of development actors and preventing the emergence of other alternatives.
4. That is unlike what happened in the neighbouring Aït Boulli Valley, where the creation of Agricultural Water User Associations under a similar World Bank programme was based on pre-existing and endogenous forms of resource appropriation.
5. For a detailed analysis of the conflict, see Sauvêtre (2013).
6. At the national level, Jeffery Webber showed that the TIPNIS conflict was a turning point. From 2011, alternative development and governance opportunities were foreclosed in favour of the establishment of a strong and centralized state built around a model of an extractivist economy (Webber, 2011).
7. Emphasis added.
8. See Dardot, Chapter 2 in this volume on 'the dual federation of the commons'.

REFERENCES

Aligica, P. D. (2014) *Institutional Diversity and Political Economy: The Ostroms and Beyond*. Oxford, Oxford University Press.

Aligica, P. D. and Boettke, P. (2009) *Challenging Institutional Analysis and Development: The Bloomington School.* London and New York, Routledge.

Assies, W. (2003) David versus Goliath in Cochabamba: Water Rights, Neoliberalism, and the Revival of Social Protest in Bolivia. *Latin American Perspectives*, **130** (30), 14–36.

Aubert, P.-M. (2010) *Action publique et société rurale dans la gestion des forêts marocaines: changement social et efficacité environnementale*. Thèse de doctorat en sociologie, Paris, AgroParisTech.

Aubert, P-M. and Romagny, B. (2012) De l'économie néoinstitutionnelle et patrimoniale à la sociologie de l'action organisée. In: Auclair, L. and Alifriqui, M. (eds) *Patrimoine écosociologique de l'Atlas marocain*. Marrakech-Marseille, IRCAM-IRD, pp. 245–81.

Blanco, I. and Gomà, R. (2016) *El municipalisme del bé comú*. Barcelona, Icària.

Bollier, D. (2014) *Think like a Commoner: A Short Introduction to the Life of the Commons*. Gabriola Island, New Society Publishers.

Bollier, D. and Helfrich, S. (eds) (2013) *The Wealth of the Commons*. Amherst, Levellers Press.
Bookchin, M. (1992) *From Urbanization to Cities: Toward a New Politics of Citizenship*. New York, Cassell.
Bresnihan, P. (forthcoming) Re-staging the Water Wars: What Does It Mean to Win? In: Cortesi, L. and Joy, K. J. (eds) *Split Waters: Examining Conflicts Related to Water and their Narration*. Forum for Policy Dialogue, India.
Buchanan, J. and Tullock, G. (1962) *The Calculus of Consent: Logical Foundations of Constitutional Democracy*. Ann Arbor, University of Michigan Press.
Butler, J. (2015) *Notes toward a Performative Theory of Assembly*. Cambridge, Harvard University Press.
Cole, D. and McGinnis, M. (eds) (2017) *Elinor Ostrom and the Bloomington School of Political Economy: A Framework for Policy Analysis*. Lanham, Lexington Books.
Coriat, B. (2013) Le retour des communs. *Revue de la régulation*, **14** (2). [Online] Available from: http://journals.openedition.org/regulation/10463 (accessed 20 November 2017).
Coriat, B. (ed.) (2015) *Le retour des communs: La crise de l'idéologie propriétaire*. Paris, Les liens qui libèrent.
Cornu, M., Orsi, F. and Rochfeld, J. (eds) (2017) *Dictionnaire des biens communs*. Paris, Presses Universitaires de France.
Dardot, P. and Laval, C. (2014) *Commun: Essai sur la révolution au XXIè siècle*. Paris, La Découverte.
Dwinell, A. and Olivera M. (2014) The Water Is Ours Damn It! Water Commoning in Bolivia. *Community Development Journal*, **49** (1), 44–52.
Giardini, F., Mattei, U. and Spregelburd, R. (2012) *Teatro Valle Occupato: La rivolta culturale dei beni comuni*. Roma, Derive Approdi.
Gruening, G. (2001) Origin and Theoretical Basis of New Public Management. *International Public Management Journal*, **4** (1), 1–25.
Gutiérrez Aguilar, R. (2008) *Los ritmos del Pachakuti: Movilización y levantamiento indígena-popular en Bolivia (2000-2005)*. Buenos Aires, Tinta Lemón.
Gutiérrez Aguilar, R., García, Á., Tapia, L. and Prada, R. (2000) *El retorno de la Bolivia plebeya*. La Paz, Comuna.
Hardin, G. (1968) The Tragedy of the Commons. *Science*, **162** (3859), 1243–8.
Hardt, M. and Negri, A. (2011) *Commonwealth*. Cambridge, Harvard University Press.
Haas, P. (1992) Epistemic Communities and International Policy Coordination. *International Organization*, **46** (1), 1–35.
Hess, C. (1999) Tracking the IASCP. Crafting an Organization: The Early History of IASCP and the Workshop Connection. *Polycentric Circles*, **VI**/1, 1–2.
Hollender, R. (2016) Politics of the Commons or Commoning the Political? Distinct Possibilities for Post-capitalist Transformation. *Spectra*, **5** (1). [Online] Available from: https://spectrajournal.org/SPECTRA/article/view/351/229 (accessed 20 December 2017).
Létang, M. (2017) Du bien commun au commun: nouvelles pratiques de gouvernement des terres collectives et circulation des inégalités dans l'Himalaya indien. *Tracés*, **33**, 127–44.
Létang, M. (forthcoming) L'alternative du commun dans les Suds: cartographie d'une géopolitique locale de l'Himalaya. In: Laval, C., Sauvêtre, P. and Taylan F. (eds) *L'alternative du commun*. Paris, Hermann.

Linebaugh, P. (2014) *Stop, Thief! The Commons, Enclosures and Resistance*. Oakland, PM Press.

Locher, F. (2016) Third World Pastures: The Historical Roots of the Commons Paradigm (1965–1990). *Quaderni Storici*, 2016 (1), 303–33.

Lucarelli, A. (2014) Biens communs et fonction sociale de la propriété: Entretien avec Jacqueline Morand-Deville. *Journal du Mauss*. [Online] Available from: http://www.journaldumauss.net/?Biens-communs-et-fonction-sociale-1118 (accessed 20 December 2017).

Mattei, U. (2012) *Beni comuni: Un manifesto*. Bari, Laterza.

McCloskey, D. (1983), The Rhetoric of Economics. *Journal of Economic Literature*, **XXXI**/2, 482–504.

Netting, R. (1976), What Alpine Peasants Have in Common: Observations on Communal Tenure in a Swiss Village. *Human Ecology*, **IV**/2, 135–46.

Notes from Nowhere (ed.) (2003) *We are Everywhere: The Irresistible Rise of Global Anticapitalism*. London and New York, Verso.

Olivera, M. (2015) Water Beyond the State. In: Bollier, D. and Helfrich, S. (eds) *Patterns of Commoning*. Amherst, the Commons Strategies Group, pp. 86–91.

Olivera, O. and Lewis, T. (2004) *¡Cochabamba! Water War in Bolivia*. Cambridge, South End Press.

Olivera, O., Gutiérrez Aguilar, R. and others (2008) *Nosotros somos la Coordinadora*. Cochabamba, Fundación Abril.

Olson, M. (1965) *The Logic of Collective Action: Public Goods and the Theory of Groups*. Cambridge, Harvard University Press.

Ostrom, E. (1990) *Governing the Commons: The Evolution of Institutions for Collective Action*. New York, Cambridge University Press.

Ostrom, E. (1999) Self-governance and Forest Resources, Plenary Presentation, International CBNRM Workshop Washington, DC, USA, 10–14 May 1998. [Online] Available from: http://citeseerx.ist.psu.edu/viewdoc/download?doi=10.1.1.334.5152&rep=rep1&type=pdf (accessed 20 December 2017).

Ostrom, E. (2006) A Frequently Overlooked Precondition of Democracy: Citizens Knowledgeable About and Engaged in Collective Action. In: Brennan, G. (ed.) *Preconditions of Democracy*. The Tampere Club Series, 2. Tampere, Tampere University Press, pp. 75–89.

Ostrom, E. (2011) Honoring James Buchanan. *Journal of Economic Behavior and Organization*, **80** (2), 370–73.

Perreault, T. (2008) Custom and Contradiction: Rural Water Governance and the Politics of Usos y Costumbres in Bolivia's Irrigators' Movement. *Annals of the Association of American Geographers*, **98** (4), 834–54.

Polanyi, K. (2001 [1944]) *The Great Transformation: The Political and Economic Origins of Our Time*. Boston, Beacon Press.

Parance, B. and De Saint Victor, J. (2014) *Repenser les biens communs*, Paris, CNRS éditions.

Russo Spena, G. and Forti, S. (2016) *Ada Colau, la città in comune: Da occupante di case a sindica di Barcelona*. Roma, Alegre.

Sánchez Gomez, L. and Terhorst, P. (2005) Cochabamba, Bolivia: Public-collective Partnership after the Water War. In: Balanyá, B. (ed.) *Reclaiming Public Water: Achievements, Struggles, and Visions from around the World*. Porto Alegre, Transnational Institute and Corporate, pp. 121–30.

Sauvêtre, P. (2013) Crises de gouvernementalité et généalogie de l'Etat aux XXème et XXIème siècles. Thèse pour le doctorat de science politique. Paris, IEP de Paris.

Sauvêtre, P. (2016) Les politiques du commun en Europe du Sud (Italie, Grèce, Espagne): pratiques citoyennes et restructuration du champ politique. *Actuel Marx*, 2016 (1), 123–38.

Sauvêtre, P. (2018) Le nouveau paradigme politique du commun à Barcelone et en Catalogne: un municipalisme des communs. In: Alix, N., Bancel, J.-L., Coriat, B., and Sultan, F. (eds) *Vers une République des biens communs?* Paris, Les liens qui libèrent, pp. 185–94.

Scharl, A. (2004) *Environmental Online Communication*. London, Springer.

Scott, J. (1976) *The Moral Economy of the Peasant: Rebellion and Subsistence in Southeast Asia*. New Haven/London, Yale University Press.

Sebatti, F. and Castiglione, D. (2016) *Institutional Diversity in Self-governing Societies: The Bloomington School and Beyond*. Lanham, Lexington Books.

Thomson, J. (1992) *A Framework for Analysing Institutional Incentives in Community Forestry*. Community Forestry Note 10. Roma, FAO.

Thomson, J. and Coulibaly, C. (1995) Common Property Forest Management Systems in Mali: Resistance and Vitality under Pressure. *Unasylva* (FAO), **46** (180), 16–22.

Thomson, J. and Freudenberger, K. (1997) *Crafting Institutional Arrangements for Community Forestry*. Community Forestry Field Manual, Vol. 7. Roma, FAO.

Wall, D. (2014) *The Sustainable Economics of Elinor Ostrom: Commons, Contestation and Craft*. London and New York, Routledge.

Webber, J. (2011) *From Rebellion to Reform in Bolivia: Class Struggle, Indigenous Liberation, and the Politics of Evo Morales*. Chicago, Haymarket Books.

Yaku (2011) (ed.) *La visione dell'acqua: Un viaggio dalla cosmogonia andia all'Italia dei beni comuni*. Roma, Nova Delphi Libri.

PART II

Institutional Perspectives

6. Governance of the global commons: a question of supply and demand, the answer of polycentricism

Rutger Hagen and Christophe Crombez

1. INTRODUCTION

Global commons refer to resource domains or areas that lie outside the physical or political reach of any one nation state, such as the Atmosphere or the High Seas. With a growing world population and the related challenges of pollution, food shortages and political tensions, these global commons are under pressure. Resources can also be harvested on a scale larger than ever before as a result of technological advancements. This makes many global commons vulnerable to over-consumption and degradation. Global collective action problems need to be tackled to avoid catastrophes. But what does (and should) such global governance look like? We will try to answer this question by regarding actors involved in such governance regimes, ranging from indigenous tribes to international organizations, as actors with a bounded rationality, vying to achieve results that reflect their preferences. Using rational choice theory we assume that these actors have their preferences in what global governance must supply, which in turn determines their demand of certain governance regimes. We underline that these preferences are not, necessarily, economically driven. An actor strives to maximize its preferences, but these preferences are not only about wealth and power but can encompass many other aspects, such as improving the quality of life or the environment. This expansion of a primarily economic concept builds further on the work of Elinor Ostrom (1999), in which she recognized the rationality of involved actors but was critical of thin models of rational choice and the supposed inability of actors to govern a commons collectively. Such collective governance can create a system that is able to protect the resources in a commons, enabling participants to create higher pay-offs than when individuals do not organize. In his famous article 'The Tragedy of the Commons', Garrett Hardin (1968), building on the work of Coase (1960), did not believe rational actors could move beyond their short-term interests. In his view, individuals would seek to maximize their short-term profits even if it would lead to the degradation of a commons. Actors would display such behaviour since the individual would assume the other users would follow the same rationale and exhibiting self-restraint would have no substantial effect on the well-being of the commons. This would lead to a tragedy of collective overuse. We distance ourselves from that pessimistic view and believe that the forming and workings of governance of global commons can be explained with a bounded rational choice approach. Actors are influenced by their past experiences and norms and trust, reputation and reciprocity when we allow for actors to have longer time-horizons. Communication and information sharing are crucial in understanding how collective action is achieved on a global level. In this chapter, we will look deeper into the dynamics that may give rational actors incentive to pursue long-term strategies and try to explain their political behaviour. We do this by laying bare social mechanisms that occur in strategic interactions, thus building a behavioural foundation for collective action on global governance for global commons.

The puzzle of what global governance exactly is and how it functions has intrigued many scholars. A vast literature exists on international cooperation, but much of it is fragmented and focused only on specific arrangements. In this chapter we will try to link together many of the insights of these studies, while focusing on global commons governance. This focus is motivated by our observation of the deepening common action problems global commons encounter. Unlike international governance systems such as the European Union (EU) or North Atlantic Treaty Organization (NATO) that can give direct benefits to its participants (Abbott and Snidal, 2000; Koenig-Archibugi, 2004), the direct benefits of good global commons governance are less obvious. One reason for this is that global commons are large (world-spanning) and complicated to monitor. The participants of global commons governance regimes and the actors who have direct interests in these commons are very diverse and not necessarily the same, which can result in severe collective action problems. According to many scholars, there is also a large discrepancy between, on the one hand, the vital ingredients of successful governance, such as monitoring and sanctioning, and on the other, current international global commons governance regimes where those elements appear absent. In this chapter we will expose the challenges global commons governance encounters and present the reader with the prerequisites we believe are needed to achieve successful management of the global commons. We take the next step, and move on from understanding governance regimes as separate independent entities and approach the governance of global commons as linked to many other governance regimes in a polycentric setting. The linkage between these regimes provides us with a convincing explanation on how collective action problems on a global scale can be overcome.

We start this chapter by reviewing the lessons learned in the study of local commons and their applicability to global commons governance. With these lessons in mind, the central part of this chapter (Sections 3 and 4) is divided into two sections: demand and supply. There we will discuss how and by whom the demand for global governance and institution formation can be voiced. We continue by discussing the products a successful global governance system must supply. To achieve and maintain a governance system is costly for its members. Participating in such a system does not come for free and, thus, the perceived benefits of participation must outweigh the perceived costs. Otherwise, the demand and support for the system will dissipate and a governance system is not viable. When demand and supply of governance is matched in a satisfying fashion, global commons can be successfully managed and protected from degradation. We mirror our arguments using the micro-economic model of supply and demand. In such a model the demand for a particular good will equal the supply, resulting in an equilibrium (Coston, 1998). We argue that governance and, in particular, the governance of a commons, can be seen as a public good, and in the case of global commons as a global public good (GPG). The defining characteristics of a public good are that it is non-excludable and non-rival (Samuelson, 1954). In other words, no one can be excluded from it and the good does not diminish when it is used. A public good is, thus, a term for a broad range of goods and services that can have an effect on everyone. Since a governance regime applies to all subjects and actors under its jurisdiction, it makes it non-excludable since no actor can be barred from it. It is also, to a large degree, non-rival since the governance system and the products it provides, such as courts or monitoring systems, do not diminish when an extra actor uses/consumes it (see Figure 6.1 for a representation of the classic distinction of goods based on the characteristics of excludability and rivalry or subtractability).

In our final section we bring the demand and supply side together and discuss institutional arrangements needed in doing so. We argue that interconnectedness and overlapping of several governance regimes can be a solution for the observed collective action problems. We disagree that polycentricism is solely problematic as it can lead to inefficient, opaque and undemocratic governance (Buchanan and Keohane, 2006). Interconnectedness of regimes also enables us to create a setting whereby actors can be given a fair representation and where sufficient monitoring

		Rivalry/Subtractability	
		Low	High
Excludability	Low	Public goods	Common pool resources/ Open access goods
	High	Club goods/ Toll goods	Private goods

Figure 6.1 Classic economical representation of different types of goods

and sanctioning systems are in place, when this is not possible in a single global all-encompassing arrangement.

2. FROM LOCAL TO GLOBAL COMMONS

In this section, we revisit the lessons learned in some of the fundamental literature on the (local) commons. We then attempt to apply these lessons on global governance systems and consider how global governance can incorporate them. As we will see, global commons share some characteristics with commons on a local level, but differ from them in some crucial aspects. Determining the differences and similarities helps us in establishing the characteristics of the supply and demand for governance of commons on a global scale.

The first studies on commons focused on physical areas producing common pool resources (CPRs). This concept of collectively owned goods stems from economic theory, most notably from the works of Samuelson (1954), Buchanan (1965) and Olson (1965). They were the first to distinguish specific goods, based on characteristics of rivalry and excludability. When a good has non-excludable and rivalrous characteristics, it is labelled a CPR. An individual unit of a CPR can only be appropriated by an individual user, making the system sustainable if the rate of replenishment is higher or equal to the rate of withdrawal. When withdrawal exceeds the replenishment rate, the CPR declines and the commons deteriorates. These characteristics lead to collective action problems described by Hardin (1968). In his seminal article entitled 'The Tragedy of the Commons', he outlined a bleak future for the commons where these CPRs can be found. Although in his article he does not distinguish between open access and communal property (Ciriacy-Wantrup and Bishop, 1975), his 'Tragedy of the Commons' is still a good starting point to explain over-exploitation in a commonly owned territory on a local, but also on a global, level.

In Hardin's view, economically rational users of a commons do not take the negative externalities of their actions into account, but will solely try to increase their own utility. Such users make demands on a resource until the expected benefits of his or her actions equal his or her expected costs, and because each user ignores costs imposed on others, individual decisions cumulate to a tragic overuse and the potential destruction of an open-access commons. Hardin partly based his article on the concept of maximum sustainable yield, developed by Gordon and Schaefer in the 1950s (Gordon, 1954). They managed to calculate the maximum yield point after which resources will decline. Hardin's proposed solution of preventing this over-consumption was either instating public regulation or privatization of free enterprise. In his view, rational users do not have a demand for a governance scheme because they are not willing to let an authority curb their own exploitation of it. Users of a commons, in that view, are trapped in a situation they cannot change themselves. External authorities are then the only way out. But this disregards the fact that both government ownership and privatization are themselves subject to failure as well, in part because the direct link between demand for governance and governance itself is lost.

One of the strongest critics of Hardin's theorem was Elinor Ostrom (1990; 1996; 1999), who received the Nobel Prize in Economics in 2009 for her work on the analysis of economic governance of the commons. Ostrom (1990) proved that when communities manage CPRs themselves, a commons can thrive. When a community takes control, the demand and supply for governance are directly linked and this helps to overcome Hardin's disempowering and pessimistic vision of the human prospect. The recognition of her work stimulated many more researchers to study the underlying mechanisms that shape the governance of CPRs. Research has shown that even as early as in the Middle Ages, plots of land or pastures were commonly owned and had communal institutions supplying rules and regulations to its users. These commons were able to be extensively cultivated while remaining common property (Zückert, 2003; De Moor, 2011). However, while local commons have a history of being able to function well, the broadening of the governance principles from these local commons to a global scale has, as we will see later, proven dissatisfactory.

Overcoming collective action problems is germane to governing any commons successfully. Global commons, however, differ widely from local commons because they are domains that have cultural and/or natural resources on an international, supranational or global scale and can also be degraded on a large scale affecting millions (or even billions) of actors.

There is much debate on what intrinsically distinguishes a commons from other property regimes, since it can encompass anything that is commonly owned (De Moor, 2011). Dardot and Laval (2014) argue that a common can be virtually anything; not bound by intrinsic features, but is defined based upon the mode of governance administered (see Dardot, Chapter 2 in this volume). Historically, from a juridical viewpoint there are only a couple of commons on a global scale: the High Seas, the Atmosphere, Antarctica and Outer Space. The conception of these areas have been guided by the principle of the common heritage of humankind – the open access doctrine or the *mare liberum* (free sea for all). That these areas were historically designated as global commons is no coincidence, as the resources found there were, at least at the time of their establishment, either especially hard to appropriate, or so abundant that restricting access or striving for exclusive control was not economically justified (Wijkman, 1982). Next to these four classic global commons, other domains can also be considered as global commons, even under international law. This can be the case when an area is viewed as of global concern. These areas are usually not under an international regime but are subject to national jurisdictions. Examples are rainforests or national waters (Costanza, 1999). The Internet (or cyberspace) can be considered a global commons and has a complicated multi-layered governance system (Hess and Ostrom, 2003; 2007). Global commons are thus widely diverse in nature and can supply goods behaving as CPRs or even public goods (De Moor, 2011: p. 430).

While research on local commons focused on CPRs, global commons can have very different characteristics. The Internet, for example, does not behave as a commons in Hardin's Tragedy because, even though it is hard to exclude people from using it, the resources it produces (knowledge) are not reduced when consumed. It can even be argued that in consumption, the resource grows since information can actually be added by its users, as Figure 6.2 illustrates. It is clear that commons that have a low degree of rivalry do not need to be protected from over-exploitation. In these cases, the resources in the commons do not exhibit the characteristics of a CPR but that of a public good and the main problem associated with public goods is under-provision. And this is indeed what we witness in these commons that have resources that are non-subtractable. Many users access, use and share information at the same time, leading to the existence of a shared resource or a knowledge commons. The demand for information is extremely high but information can be restricted due to reasons such as limited access, bandwidth limitations or copyright issues. In a commons that produces such non-subtractable (or public) goods, a certain governance regime is also demanded by its users, but the prerequisites and set up would be very different to that of a commons producing CPRs. It is

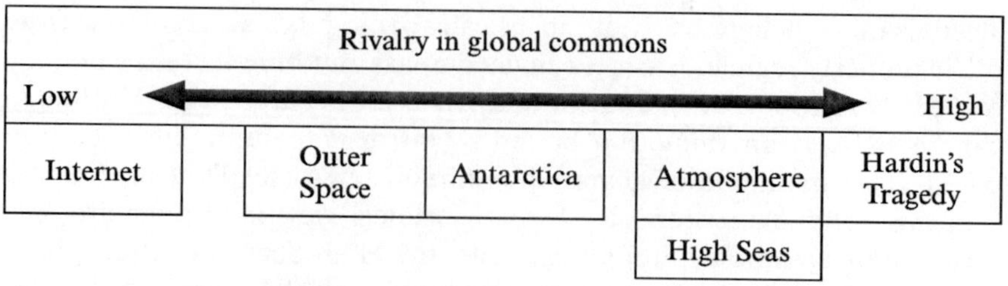

Figure 6.2 Typological positioning of global commons on an indicatory rivalry scale

clear that the traditional framework of maximum sustainable yields is not well applicable for such an instance, and we are in need of a new paradigm.

Global commons, however diverse their nature, are intrinsically difficult to manage. They transcend the scale of a town, region or even a single country and some of these resources can only become effectively depleted or made available in an international context. Resources in such vast areas are also more difficult to measure and monitor or require measurement with advanced and costly technology. Some global commons, such as the global climate, are largely self-healing in response to a broad range of human actions, until these actions exceed a certain threshold (Broecker, 1997: p. 1582) making it hard to predict the eventual outcome of a certain level of use. The enormous scale of global commons, and the complications that this entails, makes it impossible for small, relatively unorganized societies to efficiently manage these resources and match demand and supply for governance. A governance system must be formed by a cooperation of the appropriate international, national and local institutions. Ostrom et al. (1999) sum up the six main challenges in creating these global governance structures:

- '*Scaling up problems*': When many participants are involved in managing a CPR, it is increasingly difficult for the members to organize and to reach agreements on rules and their enforcement.
- '*Culture diversity challenge*': Finding shared interests and understandings can become more difficult when there is a wide cultural diversity of participants.
- '*Complications of interlinked CPRs*': Since the world is getting more and more interconnected and interdependent it will become increasingly difficult to manage resources in an adherent fashion.
- '*Accelerating rates of change*': Population growth, economic development, capital and labour mobility, together with technological change pose new challenges on our learning ability.

- '*Requirement of unanimous agreement as a collective-choice rule*': Since most governance schemes concerning global resources are negotiated treaties with a voluntary assent, governments can hold out for special privileges before they join. This strongly affects the policies that can be adopted.
- '*We have only one globe with which to experiment*': With a local commons, it is possible to move on to better pastures when a tragedy occurs, but with global commons there is no such escape clause.

The challenges identified are indeed problematic in creating successful global governance structures. Basic premises, such as face-to-face communication, which helps to increase joint gains and improve defection rates (Ostrom et al., 1992; 1994), are much harder, or even impossible, to accomplish on a global scale, but still remain important alongside autonomy to establish rules duties and an allocation of rights (Walker, 2000). Global commons with more heterogeneous sets of participants are more difficult to govern and have a greater tendency to deteriorate (Keohane and Ostrom, 1994). It is far more challenging to develop trust among participants that do not share common understandings. It is also more problematic to reach agreements and to monitor and impose sanctions (Choucri, 1993). On a global scale, the heterogeneity of interests grows exponentially with different political ideologies, culture and economies that pose challenges that must be taken into account. A governance regime should overcome the existing heterogeneity through good institutional design (Varughese and Ostrom, 2001). However, because of the large and complicated interconnectivity of our actions, it is hard to recognize their exact consequences. This ambiguity shrouds the true interests and intentions of actors even from themselves, since the outcome resulting from actions taken is, to a high degree, unknown and uncertain. Consumers, for instance, cannot observe the degradation that is occurring because of their purchases. Since they are not aware of the true consequences of their behaviour their pay-offs are unknown and they will not have an incentive to change their behaviour. Corporations, while they can observe the degradation, have little to no incentive to inform their clientele. Such actors have a strong incentive to focus on short-term interests and disregard the ecological degradation (Stern, 2011). Creating governance regimes that can protect these resources is, as we have discussed, very difficult. But aside from facing organizational difficulties, these processes are also under time pressure. The timeframe for achieving good governance systems is limited. For many natural global commons the resources are non-renewable in a human lifetime. Carbon dioxide emissions for instance can affect the global climate for the next 1,000 years (Weber and Stern, 2011) – meaning that in many cases action has to be undertaken now to prevent catastrophe in the near and not so near future.

It is difficult for individual actors to comprehend the significance of global commons and what the actual need for cooperation and governance is. Yet, understanding of these aspects is crucial for resources to be managed successfully. The true demand for governance on a global level is extremely hard to unravel and this complicates assessing whether the supply of governance is just – even more so because of the interactions between global commons and the complexity of existing governance schemes. The following section will focus on the actors who are considered to be the owners of a global commons and who can find themselves voicing demands for its governance. We will look into the underlying demand for governance and try to determine how demand can manifest itself, leading to the formation of new institutions.

3. DEMAND FOR GLOBAL COMMONS GOVERNANCE

When resources are commonly owned, collective action problems typically emerge. Under-investment in maintenance and overuse, for example, can damage the resources, depleting benefits for other users. CPRs are also susceptible to free riders, which can be seen as the most typical example of a collective action problem. Free riders shirk costs of maintenance and access, leaving others to bear them. Free riding occurs particularly when a resource is widely available to a large population (Russett and Sullivan, 1971). Since rational individual actors would prefer not to fall under a restrictive governance regime themselves (so they can continue to free ride), the demand for such a regime is not straightforward. Yet, authoritative structures capable of supplying sufficient investment in the maintenance of common resources, as well as supplying or restricting equal access to users, are needed to prevent the deterioration of a (global) commons (Dietz et al., 2003). Users of a commons will, thus, have to step over their own restrictive personal rationale and be prepared to work with the other users, in order to reach a self-sustaining commons and so increase the collective pay-off. This, however, remains difficult.

As mentioned, collective action problems arise when 'personal interest' of a user, or player, is not aligned with 'group interest'. This leads to outcomes with inefficient Pareto Nash equilibria (Kollock, 1998). The prisoner's dilemma, assurance and playing chicken, are all basic games that can be applied to the governing of global commons (Ward, 1993). These 2×2 games show some of the fundamental dilemmas when dealing with collective action, as when collaboration is absent, an inefficient equilibrium is achieved instead of a Pareto-optimal one. In these games, alternative outcomes, whereby the pay-off for the entire collective is higher, without reducing the pay-offs of the other players, are possible. But that outcome cannot be reached because there is no cooperation due to the actions of the players who act solely egocentrically. A certain incentive is needed to move beyond this self-defeating behaviour and governance can be the vehicle that supplies the players with this.

We have already argued that a governance regime for a global commons can be seen as non-excludable and, to a degree, non-rivalrous, so it can be viewed as a GPG. The amount of protection that is provided by a governance regime can be enjoyed by all. This non-excludability can lead to under-provision because actors will want to lower their own contributions for such a regime and so will be unwilling to show their true demand. The costs for a governance system must be borne by the participants, while non-participants will receive the benefits as well. It is therefore attractive for actors not to participate but let others pay for the protection. The true demand for the good will, thus, be higher than is visible (Hirshleifer, 1983).

When actors have a self-interest to deviate from actions that serve the common interest, it is shown that repeated games help conformance to the rules (for example, Axelrod and Hamilton, 1981). In a single game, it is not possible to be punished later on, so self-interest prevails. When the same game is being played over and over, the players can adapt their strategy to each other, making deviation from the common interest unattractive. Defectors can then be punished in later stages. These interactions enable those who use reciprocity to gain a reputation for trustworthiness, and others in turn will be willing to cooperate with them (Nowak and Sigmund, 1992).

Reciprocity and trust are, thus, very important to rule confirmation and the development of norms. Modern technology, such as the Internet and the media, enable large groups to monitor one another's behaviour and coordinate activities in order to solve collective action problems. Although evolved norms are not always sufficient to prevent deterioration of a commons, they play a crucial part when constructed by the participants themselves (Ostrom, 1999). These rules must then be monitored and enforced. These rules define, for example, who can enter a commons, use it and, if so, how much.

The production of any good is only viable if actors are indeed willing to bear the costs of producing it. They will only do so if the perceived benefits (direct and/or indirect) are at least equal to the perceived costs. Establishing and maintaining a governance system is costly and includes costs of negotiating, monitoring and enforcement of the rules. Coasian theory suggests that when these costs are too high, the creation of an efficient regime that can govern the resources is unlikely (Coase, 1960). When the resource is large and complex, users will also lack a common understanding of the dynamics of the resource (Ostrom et al., 1999). Such a caveat makes the perceived benefits hard to observe, while the costs are much more certain. This will make potential participants of a governance regime more hesitant in joining.

In our next section we will examine who the governance demanding parties, or the users and managers of a global commons, might be. The subsequent step is to discuss how these parties might be able to overcome collective action problems and form a new institution to govern the global commons.

3.1 Participants of a Governance Regime

A demand for a governance system must typically come from the managers, or users, of a commons. Although a global commons would typically be owned by all, it is beneficial here to define ownership more closely. The concept of ownership in relation to the commons has puzzled many scholars. This is for a large part the case because for a long time it was assumed that when a person did not have the right to sell the property (alienation rights), such individual would not have any property rights at all (Alchian and Demsetz, 1973). Since a commons typically cannot be sold by anyone, this led to the unsatisfactory concept of commons being a place with resources without any ownership at all. Schlager and Ostrom (1992) moved away from seeing ownership as a single undividable concept and built further on the work of John Rogers Commons (1924), who defined ownership as a bundle of rights that are divisible, separable and alienable.

The bundle of rights as defined by Schlager and Ostrom (1992) consists of the right to:

- have access to the resource;
- appropriate the resource;
- manage the resource;
- exclude others from using the resource and how that right might be transferred;
- sell the management and exclusion rights.

These property regimes are independent and can be combined in multiple ways so the diverse nature of a commons is correctly displayed – although many theorists discarded the possibility of efficient management of resources without the right of alienation. Schlager and Ostrom (ibid.)

criticize this by showing that efficient management is possible when the four other rights are well defined.

It is hard to apply these rights directly to global commons. Not only because we cannot truly speak of ownership of a global commons, since when it is subject to the common heritage principle they cannot be appropriated or be subject to sovereignty claims. But also because the actors with property rights are found across the globe, and are therefore often unable (or unwilling) to come and participate in accomplishing a shared governance system. This is true for the natural, but also for the knowledge commons. The Internet, for instance, is subject to diverse national laws and legislations that differ widely from country to country. Another important difference with local commons is the absence of a clear community. In international relations, individual people are not the main participating actors. They are (for a large part) represented by governments, intergovernmental organizations, corporations and non-governmental organizations (NGOs) (Stern, 2011). Because not all users and managers of a global commons can be included in its governance, the costs will be shared disproportionally. The actors that do participate must bear all costs, which in turn makes the reaching of the break-even-point (the moment where the costs equal the benefits) more difficult, thus leading to increased under-provision.

Our assessment that most users and managers of a global commons cannot execute their bundle of ownership rights directly by participating in a governance system may seem pessimistic and discouraging. It is, however, the first indication that a governance scheme of a global commons cannot be truly understood when it is studied as existing in a presumed vacuum without links to other (more local) governance systems. A governance system that governs (part) of a global commons is, in fact, in connection with many other governance schemes. This interconnectedness ensures that owners of a global commons that are not well represented in a certain governance scheme can still have influence (albeit indirectly) when they are represented in another. Such polycentric governance can not only give us a way out of the representation dilemma, it can also help us in solving many collective action problems, an aspect we will now turn to.

3.2 Institution Formation

We have showed that the formation of a governance system for a global commons is not straightforward. These difficulties are primarily caused by the fact that global commons deal, and are 'owned' by, a multitude of actors. The number of actors alone can pose a challenge in institution formation, but so can their size and diversity. Actors involved in global commons range from individuals to international organizations and everything in between. This poses extra challenges, but also opportunities, for efficient and effective governance. Many authors do not include this premise in their analysis but implicitly accept the constrictive framework set by Hardin (1968), where a central authority is necessary to effectively manage collective resources (Stern, 2011). This is a major departure of Ostrom's contribution in promoting collective self-governance and institutional design. A central authority on a global scale is also not in accordance with what we observe in contemporary global governance. In many instances, multiple governments have worked together in protecting the global commons (Haas et al., 1993; Tietenberg, 2002; Young, 2002). Also international NGOs play a major part in these governance regimes (Prakash and Potoski, 2006). Such regimes are thus very complex, and can differ widely from one instance to another. Due to the size and complexity of global commons, it is apparent that their governance should be able to deal with changing circumstances. Dietz et al. (2003) present us with some requirements for adaptive governance systems. Next to a trustworthy provision of information on resource stocks, flows and processes, and in addition to interactions with the environment and a system that deals with solving conflicts that arise between actors and the inducement of compliance to rules through formal and informal mechanisms, they find that a physical and technological institutional infrastructure, which is adaptive, is necessary to handle complex systems.

To arrange the infrastructure for an adaptive governance regime is costly, and its costs must be borne by the participants. We have already argued why participants would prefer to free ride while others form the institution. If all actors would behave this way, a governance regime would not be formed. Such a formation can be seen as a second-order free-rider problem and applies to any mechanism that solves the first-order free-rider problem, of actors not following rules. Theoretical and empirical analyses indicate that institution formation can, even so, be an important and effective solution in social dilemma situations (Kosfeld et al., 2009).

Despite the second-order free-rider problem, the institution formation process can be structured in such a manner that the implementation of a sanctioning organization is supported by a Nash equilibrium. When each player earns a higher pay-off than in the status quo equilibrium (where no players contribute to the public good), an organization can be implemented by only a subset of players. This subset takes for granted free riders that do not contribute. Experimental results of Kosfeld (ibid.), however, show the crucial role of fairness in such an institution formation process. Individuals are very reluctant to comply with a sanctioning system that governs only a subset of individuals. This is true even if the subset of individuals can earn a higher material pay-off than in the status quo with no sanctioning system, thus making the implementation of the system optimal, at least from a material standpoint. Buchanan and Congleton (1998) use this argument to propose the so-called generality principle as a normative guideline for political action. The principle asserts that political choices should be general in nature, that is, non-discriminatory and based on equal treatment of all individuals. They, thus, impose upon it yet another hurdle in achieving successful governance regimes for global commons.

We have argued that actors have an incentive to hide their true preferences, in order to free ride on the efforts of others. This premise suggests that the level of protection or management of global commons, whether they produce CPRs or public goods (such as knowledge), will be lower than the true aggregated demand, which can lead to degradation of a commons. Establishing a governance regime is made more difficult because of the lack of transparency and the complexity that global commons inherently entail. Governance regimes that are established will not be able to accommodate all the owners of a global commons because of the sheer numbers of actors who can claim partial ownership. Studies have also shown, however, that individuals are less likely to implement a system when it only applies to a subset, as opposed to the entire collective. These observations all reinforce our main argument that a successful global governance regime must be linked to others, in order to achieve a more universal coverage with more information about the individual actors and the status of the global commons. On a smaller scale, for instance within local communities, institution formation can be achieved more easily. When these systems work together, a global commons might be managed successfully. But what is successful governance exactly; what must it supply? This is something we will discuss in the following section.

4. SUPPLY OF GOVERNANCE FOR GLOBAL COMMONS

The puzzle of how to achieve collective action lies at the core of the challenges global commons face. When collective action fails, a commons deteriorates. As we discussed, global commons have widely different characteristics. Some produce resources that are highly rivalrous in nature, such as fish in the oceans, while others do not produce any goods at all. Antarctica is the prime example here. While it does harbour natural resources, the harsh environmental conditions make almost any economic activity unviable, at least at the time the agreement came into force in 1961. Governance schemes in place focus instead on protecting the area from any negative externalities that can harm the environment or endanger peace, such as military and economic activities in its direct vicinity (Wijkman, 1982). This governance regime, thus, restricts access. Knowledge commons, such as the Internet, require different governance schemes, since the knowledge they produce does not diminish when consumed and so shares commonalities with a public good. Successful governance schemes here should supply measures that ensure the accessibility of the commons and limit negative externalities that emanate from this. Examples of such negative externalities are the usage of the Internet to facilitate illegal activities such as terrorism or child abuse. We will first discuss the main ingredients a governance regime can supply us with – transparency, monitoring and sanctioning – after which we will look at more concrete measures a governance regime for a global commons can take.

4.1 Transparency, Monitoring and Sanctioning

Governance can only function if there is a certain degree of transparency. The actions of an actor must be known, to a certain degree, to others. If one cannot observe the actions of other actors and ascertain when a rule is breached, it is also not possible to sanction or punish the defector. This makes monitoring and sanctioning the two key concepts a governance system must supply. How this should be achieved in governing commons has been discussed by Weissing and Ostrom (1991). They argue that monitoring should not be directly carried out by the actors themselves, since there is always a temptation to deviate from rules and obligations, and this does not exclude monitoring activities. Special independent monitoring actors can sufficiently restrain the participants. A regime should, thus, be able to function relatively independently from its users if it is to supply adequate governance. Only with such independence is it possible to reach an equilibrium without perfect cooperation.

Next to monitoring, a successful governance regime should also be able to issue sanctions. Formal and informal sanctions include: fines, restrictions, peer pressure, gossip and social ostracism. All these instruments are an encouragement for actors to exhibit group-oriented behaviour (Blau, 1964). Experiments indicate that a formal sanctioning system can increase contributions (Fehr and Gächter, 2000). Masclet et al. (2003) also show that, in addition to a formal system of monetary fines, the sanctioning system is a vehicle to express disapproval of decisions by others and, thus, functions as an informal system as well. Punishment can be a powerful form of communication because it serves as a warning that in the future the player will have a lower pay-off if things do not change. It has also been shown that direct punishment of non-co-operators can cause a rise in the level of the average contribution to the system and co-operators are even prepared to pay a cost for punishing ('altruistic punishment') (Milinski et al., 2002).

Many CPR regimes around the world rely on sanctions, and there is almost unanimous agreement in the literature that an effective sanctioning system is a major determinant of the success of such regimes (see, for instance, Baland and Platteau, 1996; Ostrom, 1999). Examples in the international arena are the EU Stability and Growth Pact (Buti et al., 2003), which was created to enforce budgetary discipline among EU member states, or the World Trade Organization (WTO), which regulates international trade by implementing legally binding agreements (Barton et al., 2008). These institutional arrangements are not imposed from without, by an external actor, but are formed from within in the sense that, at some point in time, a set of agents voluntarily agreed to implement this kind of arrangement. In this situation, two different types of subgame perfect Nash equilibria exist: a so-called organizational equilibrium, where players successfully implement an organization, and a so-called status quo equilibrium, where no organization is implemented. A sanctioning system in itself is often not enough to ensure that participants fully conform to the rules. In the Stability and Growth Pact, large countries such as Germany and France managed to escape fines on multiple occasions, and the financial crisis of 2008 has highlighted that the monitoring system implemented was inadequate in finding discrepancies in the Greek financial reports. In many instances, it becomes apparent that the eventual sanctioning system in place is not adequate and cannot produce the desired results. In some cases, it is lacking all together (Börzel and Risse, 2005). Empirical studies also find that monitoring and sanctioning are not central in international negotiations. This is remarkable, since if a sanctioning system were important, the negotiating parties would put a lot of emphasis on it (Kennan and Wilson, 1989). Apparently the demand or need for these instruments is not as prevalent as one would expect. An explanation for this absence is given by Coleman (1990), who states that shared behaviour is vital when members of a group have individual incentives to take actions that reduce the overall welfare of the group. Nevertheless, most authors do assume that norms should be backed up by implicit or explicit sanctions that penalize deviations from acceptable behaviour (Homans, 1961).

4.2 Measures and Barriers

We have taken a closer look into the scientific discourse on governance and the roles transparency, monitoring and sanctioning play. We then discussed the difficulties in achieving these elements in realizing a governance regime for something as large and complex as a global commons. We will now consider actions a governance regime of a global commons can take to protect it from degradation. For natural global commons harbouring CPRs, trade barriers of any kind need to be implemented and enforced. Otherwise the users of such a commons will extract more resources than can be replenished (Gordon, 1954). These barriers can either help to reduce the demand for the goods in a commons, or make it less attractive or impossible to (over)exploit them. Conventional trade barriers are tariffs and quotas and they are regularly used in protecting (global) commons. An environmental tariff on imports or exports can be used to increase the costs of purchasing a product. This higher cost will lower the demand for these items. These measures can be instated when resource extraction or the production process causes natural degradation. These external costs are then borne by the consumers. This can be used to fight eco-dumping and prevent an ecological race to the bottom. Non-tariff measures (NTMs) are all policies affecting trade, other than tariffs, and can prove to be very effective to curb natural common degradation. They often reduce welfare and distort trade flows; however, since we do not have a perfect market without externalities and information asymmetries, the instruments are highly valuable in a non-perfect market (Van Tongeren and Marette, 2009). The prime example of NTMs are quotas. Quotas put a direct limit on the amount of resources available to consumers and are used in areas such as fisheries and the emission of greenhouse gases. The advantage of using a quota in comparison to a tariff is that it is clear from the start how many resources exactly can be extracted from a commons (Kraus, 2013). For a quota system to be incentive-feasible it must be implementable by a Perfect Bayesian equilibrium, meaning that players need to have conditional beliefs about the other players at every information set and define a strategy accordingly to maximize their pay-off. In the case of a global commons, each country (or other manager of the resource), after updating its beliefs by observing the resource consumption over the previous period, chooses its own rate of consumption for the following period. Since the destruction of a global commons would be disastrous for all, participants would be able to agree on a punishment system. In such an equilibrium the quota system can be dynamically self-enforcing (Haurie et al., 2008; Harrison and Lagunoff, 2017). Such a system would require a certain degree of transparency and enforceability. We have already established that due to the size and complexity of global commons, they are very vulnerable to externalities and information asymmetry, making effective monitoring difficult.

NTMs were traditionally applied for protectionist purposes but are now also being introduced by policy makers to address market imperfections and so help facilitate trade. In order to strengthen assurances of safety and quality, for instance, standards and regulations can be implemented. Certification is helpful to signal to consumers whether they are acquiring sustainable products. Forest certification has proven to lower demand for unsustainable wood, and is therefore a good incentive for corporations to engage in sound environmental practices (McDermott and Cashore, 2009). NTMs can, thus, facilitate trade since reputation and certification increases trust, while quality standards help reputation (Blind et al., 2013). Also transparency provisions can facilitate regulated trade flows (Lejárraga et al., 2013). Such measures, nonetheless, receive their fair share of criticism. Because it is expensive to meet such standards, more so for foreign suppliers than for domestic, it can reduce market access for foreign producers. This is contentious especially in North-South trade (Jaffee and Henson, 2005).

Global commons with CPRs thus need protection from over-exploitation. Knowledge commons, however, must be governed quite differently, since their resources are non-rival. Instead of limiting access, governance systems here must focus on combating under-provision. Although, as stated above, information is in essence non-rival, the existence of copyrights and patents enables actors to invoke exclusivity. Governance regimes must balance this exclusivity of private information with promotion of access to information because:

> Properly linked, private property can enhance the value and importance of the commons, and vice-versa. Thus there is – or should be – an important place for both commons and property in Internet governance, and it is unwise to emphasize one to the exclusion of the other. Indeed, the very structure of the Internet, which combines exclusive, private network facilities and services with open, nonproprietary standards, is a prime example of this interdependence. (Mueller, 2007: p. 24)

Private property can range from patents to personal pictures or information on web browsing behaviour. This information should not be considered public. A governance system must, thus, be able to protect these personal interests because otherwise the commons will degrade, while, on the other hand, open access should be stimulated so public information can be exchanged more freely.

The measures a global commons governance system must supply differ. Executing tariffs, quotas and quality standards can suffice to protect natural global CPR commons. However, often economic interests prevail when governing bodies must choose between them or combating, for instance, pollution (Birdsall and Wheeler, 1993). And the adverse results of climate change are felt more with each passing year. Promoting the sharing of information, while combating negative externalities that occur when private or illegal information is accessible by limiting and restricting access to those types can make information commons thrive. While Internet laws are now in place, their execution is hampered by physical barriers and legislative frontiers. Hacking and identity theft are becoming more prevalent (Taylor et al., 2014). Thus on the one hand, governance regimes do not supply us with enough restrictive measures so the exploitation of our physical natural resources can be lowered to acceptable levels. While on the other, the protection of information is lacking and criminal organizations or malicious governments seem to be able to regularly obtain and misuse private information. More restrictions on information are not the sole answer, however. Over-protection of information can cause problems, since it can lead to underuse of scientific resources when intellectual property rights are too strict (Heller, 1998). The classical solution to these problems, that is, the instalment (Hardin, 1968) of a single all-encompassing governance regime that can weigh all interests and has universal applicability, is not only unfeasible given the very diverse interests of the many actors involved in the creation of such an institution; it is also no true solution, since global commons are too large and complex to be managed by a single behemoth-regulator. We believe polycentricism is the solution for this conundrum, since it can be inclusive, diverse and adaptive to handle large complex systems. We will discuss polycentric governance in more detail in the following section.

5. POLYCENTRIC ORGANIZATION OF A SUCCESSFUL GOVERNANCE REGIME

Collective action problems were typically presented as simple 2×2 games. We argue that this classical approach, which prevails throughout the literature, starting with Stein (1982) and Snidal (1985), is unable to capture the complicated reality of global commons governance and that a new paradigm has to be developed that links governance regimes to one another.

A governance system of a global commons must have a functioning monitoring system of the resources it contains. In this respect, it is not important whether the resources are rivalrous (such as fish or mineral deposits) or non-rivalrous (such as knowledge). Governance must also supply us with rules and regulations to avoid degradation of the global commons. The system must monitor the actors that use the resources of the commons and must be able to punish defectors of the rules. McGinnis and Ostrom (1996) made an overview of institutional arrangements that, in theory, could be used in international regimes that govern commons.

This classification includes governmental, intergovernmental, corporate and NGO-actors. These actors can either be monitoring the resource or sanctioning the defectors. This can happen in different configurations. A government can, for instance, fine a corporation when it is observed that it violated a law. NGOs can play a significant role in monitoring corporations and governments. Defecting governments can then be punished by fellow governments. McGinnis and Ostrom recognize that there are no powerful external authorities that can enforce agreements. The absence of an external authority means that voluntary assent by countries to negotiated treaties is the standard collective-choice rule for global resource management (Wiener, 1999). This voluntary assent allows some national governments to insist upon special privileges before they join the governance system, thus strongly affecting the kinds of resource management policies that can be adopted at this level, as they lack universal coverage. In local commons, this is not really an issue, since there is always the state and the rule of law that can help keep violators in check. Although international law of course exists (see Brunnée, Chapter 13 in this volume), there is no true active enforcement regime (Koh, 1997). Sanctioning must, therefore, come from the participants themselves, since the participants of the regime in principle will want to do so. Otherwise they would not have agreed that a global commons is worth protecting. They may, however, be tempted to act as free riders and try to break the rules themselves. Participants will also be hesitant to pay for monitoring and punishment.

When sanctioning only applies to members of the institution, non-members remain free in their choices and, hence, following public good logic, are given a strong incentive to free ride (Kosfeld et al., 2009). Everyone, thus, profits if an institution is formed, but each individual profits more if others form, and bear the costs for, that institution. If all participants followed that logic no institution at all would be formed, and everyone would be worse off. This is what can be termed a 'dilemma of endogenous institution formation'. A possible solution is proposed by Haas (1980), who advocates the linkage of issue-areas, so players can adapt their behaviour in one arena based on what happens in another policy area. This can help coerce players to conform to the set rules, because even if it is not possible to sanction someone in one governance scheme it might be possible in another. Since most research focuses on only one governance regime, the influence of linkage has been mostly disregarded (Contandriopoulos et al., 2010). We argue that the concept of linkage is crucial in understanding global governance and how monitoring and sanctioning can truly be supplied. Considering only single governance arrangements has led to many false assumptions on how sanctions and monitoring are not important because they are not instated on a sufficient level or fail to be executed properly. As discussed, global commons are so large and complicated that monitoring is difficult. We also discussed the diffuse users and managers of a global commons. It cannot be said that countries are the only managers and/or users of a global commons but that they share this with a plethora of other actors such as indigenous communities, NGOs or even ordinary citizens. Instead of creating a Gordian knot that cannot be unravelled, we believe the combination of a complex problem with complex management can be a solution for our governance conundrum. We argue that a good mix of actors in a global commons governance regime can ensure a better estimation of the demand for governance and can also provide a successful monitoring and sanctioning system. Actors will only be willing to invest in monitoring when the (perceived) benefits outweigh the costs. These benefits are, on a global scale, uncertain – but on a local scale much more apparent. For instance, indigenous communities, or NGOs that are active on the ground, witness climate degradation on a daily basis. Their costs for monitoring are low, while possible benefits for well-executed governance are very apparent. It is key that they are able to communicate (and convince) other owners of the need for governance measures. When other global actors can be made aware of the degradation, their involvement can lead to successful governance. Informed citizens all over the world can then punish polluters themselves (by boycotting products from certain companies or countries) or by inducing their governments to do so (by voting for certain parties or demonstrating for policy change). When citizens demand action, costs for punishment by country governments can be compensated by electoral support.

When local actors and global communities interact, they can create a powerful mix. Such a governance regime will not be monocentric. Local actors can only be involved in a small piece of the puzzle. But these pieces are interconnected, enabling the linkage between different regimes. Linkage also makes rule conformance possible when this might not be likely in isolated instances. Because countries and other actors in global governance participate in several social games simultaneously, the interaction or linkage of these games provides a sophisticated way by which trust is gained and collective action problems can be overcome. In global governance indirect reciprocity, that is, 'give and you shall receive', is built on reputation that can be gained in the multiple international policy arenas. Indirect reputation can sustain a high level of cooperation. The need to maintain reputation for indirect reciprocity can help ensure cooperation at a surprisingly high level (Milinski et al., 2002).

Linkage helps us to understand why punishment regimes in a single governance scheme may seem to be inadequate. The more complex a commons is, the more challenging it is to craft a well-tailored set of institutional arrangements that can protect a global commons from degradation. Through polycentric governance, or in other words multiple governing authorities operating on different scales, the complexities can be matched and rules and regulations can become more flexible (Nagendra and Ostrom, 2012). It also enables punishment regimes to become more effective. Actors will be hesitant to break a rule when they may be punished in any number of other policy arenas, or are hampered in their actions on the world stage because they no longer enjoy the trust of the other participants. This line of reasoning implies that actors who participate in many policy arenas at once and who are, thus, vulnerable to sanctions on multiple levels, will be more inclined to follow the rules, while actors who are fairly isolationist can disregard more easily international sanctions for the governance regimes of which they are a part. Also the size of actors matters. Large and economically strong actors are able to withstand the backlash they receive from breaking the rules or as a result of their unwillingness to participate in a certain governance scheme. Strong actors are also able to compensate participants for the damages or coerce them and so hamper the monitor and sanction functions. The results that are found in diverse theoretical models (see, for instance, Nordhaus and Yang, 1996; Baliga and Maskin, 2003; Dutta and Radner, 2006; 2009; Harrison and Lagunoff, 2017) point towards polycentric governance, whereby different types of actors shape the monitoring and sanctioning system, as being most effective in governing global commons. A mix of organizations is important, since exclusive monitoring responsibility provides a strong incentive for bribery and corruption. Collusion must also be avoided since it would likely result in poor rule enforcement (McGinnis and Ostrom, 1996). Large power imbalances can also severely obstruct governance regimes from successfully protecting global commons. These imbalances may be countered when such groups can keep each other in check, as consumers versus multinationals, voters versus governments, or multinationals versus cyber-terrorists. A further complication is that the effective implementation of formal polycentricism must rely on clear boundaries, but global commons sometimes require approaches that are not always geographically or legally coterminous (Andereis and Janssen, 2013). This has as its result that a polycentric system in a global commons setting will have to remain informal and, to some degree, ambiguous. Nonetheless, polycentric governance with linked governance regimes gives us a convincing explanation of how a successful global commons governance is formed. When diverse interests are accommodated these are able to better estimate the demand for governance. At the same time, monitoring and sanctioning is facilitated because of the increased number of countries and organizations involved that are able to execute them. It is a comforting thought that, although our global commons are under increasing strain, our modern ways of communication make the world smaller, allowing us to link demand and supply for governance on a global scale more effectively than ever before.

6. CONCLUSION

We have assumed that actors involved in global commons are participants with a bounded rationality striving to maximize their preferences. The size and complexity of global commons prevent actors from achieving successful collective action in single, world-spanning, governance systems. In this chapter, we have approached the governance of global commons as a GPG, because governance supplies us with non-excludable rules and regulations, while being non-rivalrous in nature. Looking through a public good lens, we can use the economic adage of demand and supply to better understand what kind of collective action problems exist in global governance and how they may be solved. It becomes intuitively apparent that global governance is at risk of being under-provided, which can lead to the degradation of global commons. A successful governance regime must lead to a perceived benefit for the participating actors that is higher than the perceived costs. But governance on such a level is costly and inefficient while the direct benefits to the participants are unclear.

Monitoring and sanctioning devices are crucial for any governance system to succeed, but they are difficult to construct when actors on a global level typically can choose whether to participate or not. In smaller settings with fewer participants or a limited policy scope, institution formation is easier. When actors know each other better, trust between them is improved and monitoring and sanctioning are more effective. With a small policy scope, uncertainty is low and transparency high. When these local arrangements are transposed to the global level many of these virtues are lost. We believe that the solution for successful global governance lies not in simply copying local arrangements but in linking local initiatives to governance regimes on regional and global levels. Such polycentric governance regimes can best handle the complexities of a global commons. Linkage of governance regimes enables the reputation of actors to cross over and so act as a deterrent for free-rider behaviour, since rule breaking in one policy arena can lead to repercussions in many other arenas. By harnessing the knowledge of local actors, the true demand for governance can be better estimated while the costs for monitoring a global commons can decrease since there are local observers. But local actors cannot achieve a successful global commons governance regime by themselves. The involvement of global actors can, next to the execution of coordinative activities, help divide costs between many actors, thus reducing the risks of participation. Paradoxically, while some modern developments put our global commons under pressure, our modern communication methods can help generate polycentric governance systems to protect them.

We have provided the reader with some of the building blocks for creating and developing successful governance regimes for global commons. Empirical research on polycentricism and linkages between governance regimes on an international level is still far behind on what we have learned already on a local level. Our hope is that the theoretical framework we have presented can lead to a better understanding of what our common responsibilities are and how we can protect on a global scale the shared resources we hold dear.

REFERENCES

Abbott, K. W. and Snidal, D. (2000) Hard and Soft Law in International Governance. *International Organization*, **54** (3), 421–56.

Alchian, A. and Demsetz, H. (1973) The Property Right Paradigm. *The Journal of Economic History*, **33** (1), 16–27.

Anderies, J. M. and Janssen, M. A. (2013) Robustness of Social-ecological Systems: Implications for Public Policy. *Policy Studies Journal*, **41** (3), 513–36.

Axelrod, R. and Hamilton, W. D. (1981) The Evolution of Cooperation. *Science*, **211** (4489), 1390–96.

Baland, J. M. and Platteau, J. P. (1996) *Halting Degradation of Natural Resources: Is There a Role for Rural Communities?* Rome, Food and Agriculture Organization of the United Nations.

Baliga, S. and Maskin, E. (2003) Mechanism Design for the Environment. In: Mäler, K. G. and Vincent, J. (eds) *Handbook of Environmental Economics*. Vol. 1, Amsterdam, North-Holland, pp. 305–24.

Barton, J. H., Goldstein, J. L. and Josling, T. E. (2008) *The Evolution of the Trade Regime: Politics, Law, and Economics of the GATT and the WTO*. Princeton, Princeton University Press.

Birdsall, N. and Wheeler, D. (1993) Trade Policy and Industrial Pollution in Latin America: Where are the Pollution Havens? *The Journal of Environment and Development*, **2** (1), 137–49.

Blau, P. M. (1964) *Exchange and Power in Social Life*. New York, John Wiley & Sons, Inc.

Blind, K., Mangelsdorf, A. and Wilson, J. S. (2013) Mutual Recognition of Accreditation: Does It Matter to Trade? Evidence from the Food, Beverage, and Tobacco Industry. In: Beghin, J. C. (ed.) *Nontariff Measures with Market Imperfections: Trade and Welfare Implications*. Frontiers of Economics and Globalization, Vol. 12. Bingley, Emerald Group Publishing, pp. 291–310.

Börzel, T. A. and Risse, T. (2005) Public–private Partnerships: Effective and Legitimate Tools of International Governance. In: Grande, E. and Pauly, L. W. (eds) *Reconstituting Political Authority: Complex Sovereignty and the Foundations of Global Governance*. Toronto, University of Toronto Press, pp. 195–216.

Broecker, W. S. (1997) Thermohaline Circulation, the Achilles Heel of our Climate System: Will Man-made CO_2 Upset the Current Balance? *Science*, **278**, 1582–8.
Buchanan, A. and Keohane, R. O. (2006) The Legitimacy of Global Governance Institutions. *Ethics and International Affairs*, **20** (4), 405–37.
Buchanan, J. M. (1965) An Economic Theory of Clubs. *Economica*, **32** (125), 1–14.
Buchanan, J. M. and Congleton, R. D. (1998) *Politics by Principle, not Interest: Towards Nondiscriminatory Democracy*. Cambridge and New York, Cambridge University Press.
Buti, M., Eijffinger, S. C. and Franco, D. (2003) Revisiting the Stability and Growth Pact: Grand Design or Internal Adjustment? CEPR Discussion Paper No. 3692.
Choucri, N. (1993) Multinational Corporations and the Global Environment. In: Choucri, N. (ed.) *Global Accord: Environmental Challenges and International Responses*. Cambridge, MIT Press.
Ciriacy-Wantrup, S. V. and Bishop R. C. (1975) Common Property as a Concept in Natural Resources Policy. *Natural Resources Journal*, **15** (4), 713–27.
Coase, R. H. (1960) The Problem of Social Cost. *Journal of Law and Economics*, **3**, 1–44.
Coleman, J. S. (1990) Commentary: Social Institutions and Social Theory. *American Sociological Review*, **55** (3), 333–9.
Commons, J. R. (1924) *Legal Foundations of Capitalism*. New Brunswick, Transaction Publishers.
Contandriopoulos, D., Lemire, M., Denis, J. L. and Tremblay, É. (2010) Knowledge Exchange Processes in Organizations and Policy Arenas: A Narrative Systematic Review of the Literature. *The Milbank Quarterly*, **88** (4), 444–83.
Costanza, R. (1999) The Ecological, Economic, and Social Importance of the Oceans. *Ecological Economics*, **31** (2), 199–213.
Coston, J. M. (1998) Administrative Avenues to Democratic Governance: The Balance of Supply and Demand. *Public Administration and Development*, **18** (5), 479–93.
Dardot, P. and Laval, C. (2014) *Commun: Essai sur la révolution au XXie siècle*. Paris: La Découverte.
De Moor, T. (2011) From Common Pastures to Global Commons: A Historical Perspective on Interdisciplinary Approaches to Commons. *Natures Sciences Sociétés*, **19** (4), 422–31.
Dietz, T., Ostrom, E. and Stern P. C. (2003) The Struggle to Govern the Commons. *Science*, **302**, 1907–12.
Dutta, P. and Radner R. (2006) A Game-theoretic Approach to Global Warming. *Advances in Mathematical Economics*, **8**, 135–53.
Dutta, P. and Radner R. (2009) A Strategic Analysis of Global Warming: Theory and Some Numbers. *Journal of Economic Behavior and Organization*, **71**, 187–209.
Fehr, E., and Gächter, S. (2000) Fairness and Retaliation: The Economics of Reciprocity. *Research in Economics*, **40**, 159–81.
Gordon, H. (1954) The Economic Theory of a Common-property Resource: The Fishery. *Journal of Political Economy*, **62** (2), 124–42.
Haas, E. B. (1980) Why Collaborate? Issue-linkage and International Regimes. *World Politics*, **32** (3), 357–405.
Haas, P. M., Keohane R. O. and Levy M. A. (1993) *Institutions for the Earth: Sources of Effective International Environmental Protection*. Cambridge, MIT Press.

Hardin, G. (1968) The Tragedy of the Commons. *Science*, **162**, 1243–8.
Harrison, R. and Lagunoff, R. (2017). Dynamic Mechanism Design for a Global Commons. *International Economic Review*, **58** (3), 751–82.
Haurie, A., Drouet, L., Vielle, V., Vial, J. P., Bosetti, V., Yeung, D. and Zhang, C. (2008) A Dynamic Game Model of Strategic RDD Cooperation and GHG Emission Mitigation (No. REME-Workingpaper–2009–006). [Online] Available from: https://infoscience.epfl.ch/record/134205/files/wp51.pdf (accessed 20 November 2017).
Heller, M. A. (1998) The Tragedy of the Anticommons: Property in the Transition from Marx to Markets. *Harvard Law Review*, **111**, 621–88.
Hess, C. and Ostrom, E. (2003) Ideas, Artifacts, and Facilities: Information as a Common-pool Resource. *Law and Contemporary Problems*, **66**, 111–46.
Hess, C. and Ostrom, E. (2007) *Understanding Knowledge as a Commons: From Theory to Practice*. Cambridge, MIT Press.
Hirshleifer, J. (1983) From Weakest-link to Best-shot: The Voluntary Provision of Public Goods. *Public Choice*, **41** (3), 371–86.
Homans, G. C. (1961) *Social Behavior: Its Elementary Forms*. New York, Harcourt Brace.
Jaffee, S. and Henson S. (2005) Agro-food Exports from Developing Countries: The Challenges Posed by Standards. In: Aksoy, M. A. and Beghin, J. C. (eds) *Global Agricultural Trade and Developing Countries*. Washington, DC, The World Bank.
Kennan, J. and Wilson, R. (1989) Strategic Bargaining Models and Interpretation of Strike Data. *Journal of Applied Econometrics*, **4** (S1), S87–S130.
Keohane, R. O. and Ostrom, E. (1994) Local Commons and Global Interdependence: Heterogeneity and Cooperation in 2 Domains. *Journal of Theoretical Politics*, **6** (4), 403–28.
Koenig-Archibugi, M. (2004) International Governance as New Raison d'État? The Case of the EU Common Foreign and Security Policy. *European Journal of International Relations*, **10**, 147–88.
Koh, H. H. (1997) Why Do Nations Obey International Law? *Yale Law Journal*, **106** (8), 2599–659.
Kollock, P. (1998) Social Dilemmas: The Anatomy of Cooperation. *Annual Review of Sociology*, **24** (1), 183–214.
Kosfeld, M., Okada, A. and Riedl, A. (2009) Institution Formation in Public Goods Games. *American Economic Review*, **99** (4), 1335–55.
Kraus, C. (2013) *Import Tariffs as Environmental Policy Instruments*. Dordrecht, Springer Science and Business Media.
Lejárraga, I., Shepherd B. and Van Tongeren F. (2013) Transparency in Nontariff Measures: Effects on Agricultural Trade. In: Beghin, J. C. (ed.) *Nontariff Measures with Market Imperfections: Trade and Welfare Implications*. Frontiers of Economics and Globalization, Vol. 12. Bingley, Emerald Group Publishing, pp. 99–125.
Masclet, D., Noussair, C., Tucker, S. and Villeval, M. C. (2003) Monetary and Nonmonetary Punishment in the Voluntary Contributions Mechanism. *American Economic Review*, **93** (1), 366–80.
McDermott, C. and Cashore, B. (2009) Forestry Driver, Mapping Project: Global and US Trade Report. Yale University, School of Forestry and Environmental Studies, GISF Research Report 012. [Online] Available from: https://www.cabdirect.org/cabdirect/abstract/20133400145 (accessed 20 November 2017).

McGinnis, M. and Ostrom, E. (1996) Design Principles for Local and Global Commons. In: Young, O. R. (ed.) *The International Political Economy and International Institutions*. Vol. 2, Cheltenham, UK, and Northampton, MA, USA, Edward Elgar, pp. 465–93.

Milinski, M., Semmann, D. and Krambeck, H.-J. (2002) Reputation Helps Solve the 'Tragedy of the Commons'. *Nature*, **415** (6870), 424–6.

Mueller, M. (2007) Property and Commons in Internet Governance. *SSRN Electronic Journal*. [Online] Available from: https://papers.ssrn.com/sol3/papers.cfm?abstract_id=1828102 (accessed 20 November 2017).

Nagendra, H. and Ostrom, E. (2012) Polycentric Governance of Multifunctional Forested Landscapes. *International Journal of the Commons*, **6** (2), 104–33.

Nordhaus, W. D. and Yang, Z. (1996) A Regional Dynamic General-equilibrium Model of Alternative Climate-change Strategies. *American Economic Review*, **86** (4), 741–65.

Nowak, M. A. and Sigmund, K. (1992) Tit for Tat in Heterogeneous Populations. *Nature*, **355** (6357), 250–53.

Olson, M. (1965) *Logic of Collective Action: Public Goods and the Theory of Groups*. Cambridge, Harvard University Press.

Ostrom, E. (1990) *Governing the Commons: The Evolution of Institutions for Collective Action*. Cambridge, Cambridge University Press.

Ostrom, E. (1996) Crossing the Great Divide: Coproduction, Synergy, and Development. *World Development*, **24** (6), 1073–87.

Ostrom, E. (1999) Coping with Tragedies of the Commons. *Annual Review of Political Science*, **2** (1), 493–535.

Ostrom, E., Walker, J. and Gardner, R. (1992) Covenants With and Without a Sword: Self-governance is Possible. *American Political Science Review*, **86** (2), 404–17.

Ostrom, E., Gardner, R. and Walker, J. (1994) *Rules, Games, and Common-pool Resources*. Ann Arbor, University of Michigan Press.

Ostrom, E., Burger, J., Field, C. B., Norgaard, R. B. and Policansky, D. (1999) Revisiting the Commons: Local Lessons, Global Challenges. *Science*, **284** (5412), 278–82.

Prakash, A. and Potoski, M. (2006) Racing to the Bottom? Trade, Environmental Governance, and ISO 14001. *American Journal of Political Science*, **50** (2), 350–64.

Russett, B. M. and Sullivan, J. D. (1971) Collective Goods and International Organization. *International Organization*, **25** (4), 845.

Samuelson, P. A. (1954) The Pure Theory of Public Expenditure. *Review of Economics and Statistics*, **36** (4), 387–9.

Schlager, E. and Ostrom, E. (1992) Property Rights Regimes and Natural Resources: A Conceptual Analysis. *Land Economics*, **68**, 249–62.

Snidal, D. (1985) Coordination versus Prisoner's Dilemma: Implications for International Cooperation and Regimes. *American Political Science Review*, **79**, 23–42.

Stein. A. (1982) Coordination and Collaboration: Regimes in an Anarchic World. *International Organization*, **36**, 299–324.

Stern, P. C. (2011) Design Principles for Global Commons: Natural Resources and Emerging Technologies. *International Journal of the Commons*, **5** (2), 213–32.

Taylor, R. W., Fritsch, E. J. and Liederbach, J. (2014) *Digital Crime and Digital Terrorism*. Upper Saddle River, Prentice Hall Press.

Tietenberg, T. (2002) The Tradable Permits Approach to Protecting the Commons: What Have We Learned? *SSRN Electronic Journal*. [Online] Available from: https://papers.ssrn.com/sol3/papers.cfm?abstract_id=315500 (accessed 20 November 2017).

Van Tongeren, F. J. C. B. and Marette, S. (2009) A Cost–benefit Framework for the Assessment of Non-tariff Measures in Agro-food Trade. *OECD Food, Agriculture and Fisheries Working Papers*, 21, OECD Publishing. [Online] Available from: http://dx.doi.org/10.1787/220613725148 (accessed 20 November 2017).

Varughese, G. and Ostrom, E. (2001) The Contested Role of Heterogeneity in Collective Action: Some Evidence from Community Forestry in Nepal. *World Development*, **29** (5), 747–65.

Walker, N. (2000) *Policing in a Changing Constitutional Order*. London, Sweet and Maxwell.

Ward, H. (1993) Game Theory and the Politics of the Global Commons. *Journal of Conflict Resolution*, **37** (2), 203–35.

Weber, E. U. and Stern, P. C. (2011) Public Understanding of Climate Change in the United States. *The American Psychologist*, **66** (4), 315–28.

Weissing, F. J. and Ostrom, E. (1991) Irrigation Institutions and the Games Irrigators Play: Rule Enforcement Without Guards. In: Selten, R. (ed.) *Game Equilibrium Models II: Methods, Morals, and Markets*. Heidelberg, Springer, pp. 188–262.

Wiener, J. B. (1999) Global Environmental Regulation: Instrument Choice in Legal Context. *The Yale Law Journal*, **108** (4), 677–800.

Wijkman, P. M. (1982) Managing the Global Commons. *International Organization*, **36** (3), 511–36.

Young, O. R. (2002) Institutional Interplay: The Environmental Consequences of Cross-scale Interactions. In: Ostrom, E., Dietz, T., Dolšak, N., Stern, P. C., Stonich, S. and Weber, E. U. (eds) *The Drama of the Commons*. Washington, National Academy Press, pp. 263–91.

Zückert, H. (2003) *Allmende und Allmendaufhebung: Vergleichende Studien zum Spätmittelalter bis zu den Agrarreformen des 18./19. Jahrhunderts*. Stuttgart, Lucius and Lucius.

7. The rule of law and accountability: exploring trajectories for democratizing governance of global public goods and global commons

Maja Groff* and Sylvia Karlsson-Vinkhuyzen

1. INTRODUCTION: GLOBAL PUBLIC GOODS AND THE RULE OF LAW

Defining the practice of the 'rule of international law' as a global public good (GPG) is, with some exceptions, surprisingly scarce in the GPG literature.[1] Or perhaps it is not surprising as the roots of GPG concepts and theory are firmly in the economic sciences. In Kaul et al.'s (2003) seminal work, international law was only described as one of the contexts for global governance. In a paper 10 years later, however, Kaul (2013: p. 12) stresses that governments are the actors in the best position to provide 'the most essential global public good: an institutional architecture that allows the currently messy process to take on a more organized, focused and, thereby effective shape'. While not mentioning norms or law as such, a regime of binding and enforceable rules would very likely be considered an essential part of such an institutional framework. Adam Smith, in fact, considered the establishment and maintenance of an effective justice system as a vital public good which represented one of three core 'duties' of a national government (Ver Eecke, 2013; Kaul, Grunberg and Stern, 1999). Indeed, an effective 'rule of law' at the international level may be considered a 'meta' or 'core' GPG, and as an equally fundamental part of global society as it is currently in domestic, democratic societies. Furthermore, international rule of law is not only a key GPG in itself; it would also support both the provision of 'classical' GPGs and the preservation/management of global commons, and the very process of achieving it would be a common good, a good of the community 'which comes into being in and through that enterprise' (Deneulin and Townsend, 2007: p. 25), demarcating a certain type of responsible international political community or *civitas*.

There is something disturbing about a governance system in which core actors (that is, states) on the one hand can year after year adopt a range of new international norms and goals encased in those norms (for example, binding multilateral treaties, as well as 'soft law' statements such as most United Nations (UN) General Assembly Resolutions, 'Action Programmes' for UN Decades and so on), in what might be considered as a manifestation of unity of thought and purpose in global undertakings, yet on the other hand, year after year, allow those core actors to escape (in large part) any formal accountability mechanisms for what they have *not* done to implement those norms and achieve those goals. Such a circumstance is antithetical to well-accepted governance norms which link legitimate governmental authority, normally associated with democratic forms of government, with the operation of the rule of law and the accountability of subjects to the law (Waldron, 2016: p. 2).[2]

This chapter will first elaborate definitions, in part based on statements made in UN fora on the subject, to provide an anatomy of components of the rule of (international) law, including perspectives on conceiving of the rule of law as a core GPG. It will then discuss two suggested accountability trajectories associated with building a meaningful global rule of law – 'input' and 'output' accountability – between states and other relevant actors, identifying some of the associated challenges and proposing various pathways to address them. We suggest that strengthening such accountability trajectories would signal a further 'democratization' of the international order.

2. EVOLVING UN DEFINITIONS OF (INTERNATIONAL) RULE OF LAW

A range of international statements emanating from UN bodies, in particular within the last 20 to 25 years, testify to a preoccupation of the international community with the concept of the rule of law as fundamental to establishing a coherent international order. These official statements provide a normative foundation for future movement on strengthening the international rule of law, whether catalysed by governmental or non-governmental actors.[3] A host of recent UN initiatives, institutions and thematic subject-matter areas interweave with the notion of the rule of law, clearly articulating that it is considered interdependent with and a necessary ingredient for achieving a range of significant global policy goals.[4]

The UN General Assembly notably deliberated on the notion of 'the rule of law' in 1993 at the Vienna World Conference on Human Rights

(United Nations, 2016).[5] This was followed by the establishment of the Office of the High Commissioner of Human Rights (OHCHR) and the adoption of annual resolutions by the Third Committee of the General Assembly on 'strengthening the rule of law' from 1993 until 2002, which expressed, for example, a conviction that 'the rule of law is an essential factor in the protection of human rights, as stressed in the [Universal] Declaration [of Human Rights], and should continue to attract the attention of the international community' (United Nations General Assembly, 2002).

Another watershed moment in the evolution of UN rule of law discourse (linking the notion to 'democratic' governance) occurred in 2005 when world leaders came together at the UN World Summit to produce an Outcome document, adopted by the General Assembly (United Nations General Assembly, 2005b). In its statement of 'Values and Principles', the 2005 World Summit Outcome document affirmed that the rule of law is one of four core areas to address, in order to push forward efforts to 'create a more peaceful, prosperous and democratic world' (United Nations General Assembly, 2005b: p. 3),[6] also acknowledging 'that good governance and the rule of law at the national and international levels are essential for sustained economic growth, sustainable development and the eradication of poverty and hunger' (United Nations General Assembly, 2005b: principle no.11). A dedicated section on the rule of law in the 2005 document underlined the need for 'universal adherence to and implementation of the rule of law at both the national and international levels' and reaffirmed states' commitment to 'an international order based on the rule of law and international law' (United Nations General Assembly, 2005b: p. 29, para. 134).

'The Rule of Law at the National and International Levels' was subsequently introduced onto the agenda of the Sixth Committee (Legal) of the General Assembly, catalysing a new series of General Assembly resolutions on the rule of law from 2006 to 2014, as well as annual reports on the topic by the Secretary-General.[7]

As noted in the brief passages quoted above, the rule of law has in these UN fora been framed as a concept with strong interlinkages with democracy and the protection of fundamental human rights across various policy areas, including sustainability and peace and security. Notable Declarations of the Human Rights Council underscore this triangular linkage, stressing that 'human rights, democracy and the rule of law are interdependent and mutually reinforcing', and referencing a report of the Secretary-General which 'addressed the ways and means of developing further the linkages between the rule of law and the three main pillars of the United Nations: peace and security, human rights and development'

(United Nations General Assembly, 2015b: p. 2, citing the UN Secretary-General: United Nations General Assembly, 2014).

The range of disparate topics in which the concept of the rule of law has played a central role in UN documents or initiatives include transitional justice in conflict and post-conflict situations, the peaceful settlement of international disputes, legal empowerment of the poor, peacekeeping and peacebuilding, the 'Responsibility to Protect' (R2P), counter-terrorism, national reconciliation, gender equality, international criminal law, preventing and combating national and transnational crime, among a host of other matters (United Nations, 2016).

Despite these modern statements that have seemed to gather momentum since 1993 and 2005 in particular, a connection should also properly be made with the UN Charter and early instruments in the post-World War II environment, including, as indicated above, with the 1948 Universal Declaration of Human Rights (UDHR). The Declaration gives striking prominence to the rule of law, stating in its preamble that 'it is essential, if man is not to be compelled to have recourse, as a last resort, to rebellion against tyranny and oppression, that human rights should be protected by the rule of law' (United Nations, 1948).

In hopes of a future rule-based international order, the UN Charter provides for the progressive development and codification of international law, in particular under Article 13(1)(a) (United Nations, 1945) leading, *inter alia*, to significant studies and work by the International Law Commission.[8] The Charter's preamble affirms an overarching goal of the UN is to 'establish conditions under which justice and respect for the obligations arising from treaties and other sources of international law can be maintained'. Article 1(1) additionally states that one of the purposes of the UN is 'to bring about by peaceful means, and in conformity with the principles of justice and international law, adjustment or settlement of international disputes or situations which might lead to a breach of the peace'.

Lastly, the recently adopted Sustainable Development Goals (SDGs) incorporate a range of references to rule of law issues, in particular under Goal 16, to '[p]romote peaceful and inclusive societies for sustainable development, provide access to justice and build effective, accountable and inclusive institutions at all levels', which includes a specific target to '[p]romote the rule of law at the national and international levels and ensure equal access to justice for all' (United Nations General Assembly, 2015a). As with the above-noted trends, the notion of the rule of law and related concepts of integrity of justice systems and good governance are interwoven with a range of important policy goals in the targets. The policy objectives under Goal 16 relate to, for example, reducing forms of violence, reducing illicit financial and arms flows, strengthening the recovery and return of stolen assets, combating all forms of organized crime, and reducing corruption and bribery. Other policy goals in the SDGs refer to protecting global commons such as biodiversity and the oceans, or providing 'classical' GPGs such as a stable climate system.

In analysing the range of modern UN statements on the rule of law, and in particular the General Assembly Resolutions and Secretary-General reports since 2006, it is important to note that rule of law at the national and international levels are considered as interdependent. This follows observations made in the analysis of the provision of GPGs that national communities, in their policy-making, must make awareness of such interdependence of the national and international integral and instinctive, rather than positioning the latter as anomalous and part of a detached 'foreign policy' domain (Kaul et al., 1999). National rule of law matters for the international community and vice versa.

3. THE RULE OF LAW AND DEMOCRACY: LINKAGES AND DEFINITIONS

As might be deduced by the multitude of UN statements on the topic, promotion of the 'rule of law' is today common among national and international governmental bodies and officials, seeming to reflect a 'consent that adherence to rule of law is an accepted measure of government legitimacy' (Bedner and Vel, 2010), presumably including legitimacy of governance at the international level. Indeed, the 2012 Declaration of a High-level Meeting on the Rule of Law at the National and International Levels of the General Assembly at its 67th Session sounded this keynote of governance 'legitimacy' in relation to the rule of law at the international level, recognizing:

> that the rule of law applies to all States equally, and to international organizations, including the United Nations and its principal organs, and that respect for and promotion of the rule of law and justice should guide all of their activities and accord predictability and legitimacy to their actions. We also recognize that all persons, institutions and entities, public and private, including the State itself, are accountable to just, fair and equitable laws and are entitled without any discrimination to equal protection of the law. (United Nations General Assembly, 2012, para. 2)

Despite the common usage of 'rule of law' terminology (some might say 'rhetoric')[9] in the discourse of public officials, it is noted that there is no one agreed upon academic definition of the concept. In its most basic

Table 7.1 Tamanaha's alternative rule of law formulations

Number of requirements	Formal versions	Substantive versions
Few = 'thin'	Rule by law: law as instrument of government action	Individual rights: property, contract Privacy, autonomy
More = 'thicker'	Formal legality: + general, prospective, clear, certain for all citizens	+ Rights of dignity and justice
Many = 'thick'	Democracy and legality: + Consent determines content of law	+ Social welfare: substantive equality, welfare, preservation of cultural rights

Source: Bedner and Vel (2010), drawing on the work of Tamanaha (2004).

formula, one could simply state that '[t]he rule of law means literally what it says: the rule of laws. Taken in its broadest sense this means that people should obey the law and be ruled by it' (Raz, 1979). However, there is an observed tendency for theorists to associate the notion of the rule of law with systems of governance that privilege human liberty and dignity, as well as finding it a 'substantive dimension' of democracy (Waldron, 2016: p. 10).

Some have set out to frame various definitions of the rule of law on a continuum of concepts or attributes, proposing a 'thin' to 'thick' axis and 'formal' versus 'substantive' understandings (see Table 7.1). The two axes intend to show (normally) cumulative attributes of the various notions of rule of law, from more simple/reductionist understandings, to the more complex and multifaceted. For example, a formal definition of the rule of law would include certain minimum requirements, including that laws 'must be set forth in advance (be prospective), be made public, be general, be stable and certain, and be applied to everyone according to its terms' (Bedner and Vel, 2010: n. 17). The orientation in formal theories would be centred on sources of law, procedures and the form of legality, while substantive definitions venture into fundamental rights and the content of laws (Bedner and Vel, 2010). The 'thin' to 'thick' axis graduates from a rudimentary rule by law system to a democratic/evolved social contract approach as intrinsic to a system of rule by law.

In the UN context, the Secretary-General has offered a definition of the rule of law as:

> a principle of governance in which all persons, institutions and entities, public and private, including the State itself, are accountable to laws that are publicly promulgated, equally enforced and independently adjudicated, and which are consistent with international human rights norms and standards. It requires, as well, measures to ensure adherence to the principles of supremacy of law, equality before the law, accountability to the law, fairness in the application of the law, separation of powers, participation in decision-making, legal certainty, avoidance of arbitrariness and procedural and legal transparency. (United Nations Security Council, 2004: p. 4, para. 6)

It would seem in this UN definition that the more complex and cumulative definitions of rule of law are presented: that is, those that include substantive rights, and give attention to participation in decision-making, thereby embodying types of democratic engagement. We would agree that, in the modern international legal order, it is reasonable to include substantive and 'thicker' versions of a definition of the international rule of law, in consonance with, for example, the contemporary international human rights *acquis* (which include social and economic rights), UN statements or work on democracy and democratization processes, as well as international civil society involvement or consultation processes (however imperfect) that are by now well established within many UN bodies and working methods. Moreover, scholars have rightly noted, and history has shown, the dangers which are inherent in subscribing to 'thin' versions of a definition of rule of law; for example, infamous examples of rule by law under an apartheid system (Tamanaha, 2007: pp. 17–18). Indeed, one can observe that around the world, national human rights violations are often objected to, for example, in civil society advocacy discourse, on the grounds that they are a violation of international law, as if the latter represent higher principles of natural justice (and/or, practically speaking, the hope of a higher level of appeal beyond national systems). The founding of the UN indeed presented a crossroads as to whether to embrace a human rights mandate within the Charter and UN agencies as part of the modern international order. As history has affirmed, this 'thicker' rule of law mandate, which included a range of substantive human rights, was incorporated from the inception of the UN.[10]

And indeed, to make tighter the close theoretical relationship between substantive human rights entitlements, the rule of law and democracy, Article 21 of the UDHR and the Article 25 of the International Covenant on Civil and Political Rights affirm a right of individuals to take part in their governments, either 'directly or through freely chosen representatives', and a right to genuine periodic elections with 'universal and equal suffrage' and voting procedures by secret ballot or similar methods. UN Secretary-General Boutros Boutros-Ghali went so far as to seek to affirm an international customary norm of a right to democracy, and also that part of the UN's fundamental mission should be to promote and support democratization processes founded in 'grassroots' needs and aspirations (see Wouters et al., 2004; Boutros-Ghali, 1996). While periodic elections of a certain standard are considered to be a distinguishing feature of democracies, notions and practices (ideal and real) also include, of course, such operational values as liberty, equality, accountability of state organs (see *infra*, Section 6), social protection and participation/deliberation (for example, see four main theories of democracy – libertarian, pluralist, social democratic and deliberative – identified by Moravcsik (2004)).

Importantly, we would also draw attention to the crucial component of access to justice; that is, the entitlement of the *individual* (a 'justice seeker' (Bedner and Vel, 2010)) to meaningful remedies under a system of rule by law, which should likely constitute an important criterion in assessing the performance of the international legal system:

> While there is considerable disagreement about rule of law definitions, and whether one prefers a formal or a substantive version, virtually everyone agrees on the two functions the rule of law serves. The first one is to curb arbitrary and unjust use of state power. The rule of law can then be understood as an umbrella concept for a number of legal and institutional instruments to protect citizens against the power of the state. The rule of law's second function is to protect citizens' property and lives from infringements or assaults by fellow citizens. In fact, both objectives seem to correspond with the justice 'access to justice' seeks to bring into citizens' reach. (Bedner and Vel, 2010: p. 21)

Such an expectation and reality of access to justice at the international level by the individual – for example, reasonably swift remedies for the violation of international human rights entitlements or the ability to ensure that a government implements international environmental agreements (IEAs) – would signal that there is both genuine respect for the citizen's individual dignity (that is, within a global *demos*) and that the citizen benefits from a contractual relationship of accountability with his or her government.

4. THE INTERFACE BETWEEN (INTERNATIONAL) RULE OF LAW AND GLOBAL PUBLIC GOODS

The GPG denomination is seen by its proponents as a way to make national governments as a whole, not just the foreign or development aid ministries, engaged and responsible for their provision (International Task Force on Global Public Goods, 2006). An effective international rule of law – one in which enforcement of and compliance with international (legal) norms by states and other implicated actors is both expected and common – would enable significant progress in the delivery of all GPGs and the management of global commons, for which there are currently international treaties in place to ensure their adequate provision or protection. To take just one area of international law, the degree of compliance with IEAs is patchy (Mitchell, 2003). At the same time as such IEAs have ambitious overall objectives, the specific obligations that countries consider as legally binding often fall far short of ensuring adequate provision of the GPG in question (for example, in the United Nations Framework Convention on Climate Change, the Kyoto Protocol and the Paris Agreement on Climate Change). It is therefore also necessary to consider the international rule of law not only in a narrow legalistic sense but as encompassing a fundamental commitment to undertake best efforts to comply not only with the letter but also with the spirit of associated international norms and the goals, including those which are legally binding or those considered as 'soft law'/ aspirational, and everything in between.[11]

Recent important examples that illustrate the need to go beyond international norms considered to be legally binding include the Paris Agreement on climate change and the SDGs, both adopted in 2015. The Paris Agreement provides a number of legal obligations for most countries, including submitting nationally determined contributions for emission reductions every five years (United Nations, 2015). The content of those contributions, however, are not part of the legal agreement and the total sum of the contributions offered until 2025/2030 do not enable reaching the objective of keeping the global climate system stable by limiting temperature increase to well below 2 (or ideally 1.5) degrees. The SDGs formulate the aspirations of national governments worldwide in a broad number of areas, many of which relate to GPGs. They fall in the category of UN General Assembly Resolutions that would be considered in the category of a non-binding norm (that is, considered to be of a 'recommendatory' nature) unless they lead to changed dominant state practice over the years, and thus (arguably) contributing to customary international law.

Our argument is that to approach the international rule of law as a GPG can have the same benefit as that of the GPG discourse more broadly – that is, it makes more visible to various (governmental) actors how much all policy domains in all countries have to gain from the international rule of law, thereby increasing the motivation to invest in its provision and to create ambitious new projects with clear objectives in this respect.[12] While many non-state actors have a role to play in the provision of GPGs and the management of global commons, the GPG approach does assign a special role to states. Yet these states still only provide support for the provisioning of GPGs 'haphazardly, mainly in response to major crises' (Kaul, 2013: p. 11).

The benefits of providing a better international rule of law would accrue 'non-rival' and 'non-excludable' effects.[13] Effective practice of this GPG would not exhaust the possibility of its provision to others, but rather, the opposite effect would be expected, as clear legal precedents are set and fair procedures affirmed as a matter of practice/culture.[14] This corresponds to the character that Deneulin and Townsend (2007) and Kaul et al. (2003) give common goods – that their supply can increase when they are consumed more.[15] Nor would it be possible to exclude non-participating states from the range of benefits.[16] For example, effective and rule-based collective security and human rights regimes ensuring the maintenance of peace at the international level would produce positive externalities likely for all or most states. The rule of international law would be (as we take the position it does not yet exist) a system characteristic of the global order just as other system characteristics have been defined as GPGs; for example, a stable climate system, international peace and security, a stable international financial system (Kaul et al., 2003) or a sustainable global energy system (Karlsson-Vinkhuyzen et al., 2012).

5. RULE OF LAW AS A 'CORE'/'META' GLOBAL PUBLIC GOOD AND ITS RELEVANCE IN FACILITATING DEMOCRATIC CULTURES

The rule of law (and a commitment to the same), we argue, is somehow at the heart of the delivery of key international public goods, including peace at various levels of society (local, national, regional and global). In support of a quintessential connection between rule of law and (global) peace, see, for example, Hans Kelsen: '[l]aw is, essentially, an order for the promotion of peace. Its purpose is to assure the peaceful living together of a group of individuals in such a way that they settle their inevitable conflicts in a peaceful manner; that is, without the use of force, in conformity with an order valid for all. This order is the law' (Kelsen, 1942: p. 1). Moreover, in connecting the concept of rule of law with recent GPG theories, one useful theoretical approach could employ various strains and philosophical iterations of social contract theory, which have been a dominant basis of modern notions of political legitimacy and democratic governance in the Western tradition. As seen in the various approaches/definitions of the rule of law discussed above, most or all have a notion of a 'pact' or reciprocal understanding between state and citizen, and a conceived role of the state as entity that mediates among the rights and freedoms of equal individuals. For example, '[t]he rule of law, at its core, requires that government officials and citizens are bound by and act consistent with the law' (Bedner and Vel, 2010). The law serves as itself a contract or common commitment among citizens and those in government. As expressed by Martha Nussbaum: 'social contract theory . . . sees principles of justice as the outcome of a contract people make, for mutual advantage, to leave the state of nature and govern themselves by law' (Nussbaum, 2004). See also Habermas (2012: p. 340), describing the characteristics of a democratic community where 'governmental authority is programmed through the democratic process and channelled in the grammar of general laws in such a way that the citizens can exercise their authority through legislative, executive and judicial bodies', and thus accept/are subject to law which they consider to be legitimate.

Influential early modern social contract thinkers, such as Hugo Grotius, Thomas Hobbes and John Locke, proposed new theories of political legitimacy, 'grounded in the idea that naturally free and equal human beings have no right to exercise power over one another, except in accordance with the principle of mutual consent' (Neidleman, 2012: p. 1). They proposed versions of the social contract as the basis of legitimate government, founded upon the explicit or implied consent of citizens. While diverging on important points and theoretical implications of Rousseau's theory of 'general will', more recent social contract theorist John Rawls elaborated upon the notion of 'general will' ('where associates reach consensus by privileging their collective interest over their particular interests'), by proposing the devices of 'original position' and the 'veil of ignorance' ('behind which associates derive principles of justice without any knowledge of the social, political, or economic status they may hold in the society they are envisioning') (Neidleman, 2012: p. 2). Rawls and Rousseau prescribed such an (ethically grounded) approach to reasoning about the design of the collective social and political space in order to transcend narrow individualist thinking and to reach outcomes based on maximal fairness for all individuals and collective well-being.

The thinking proposed by Rawls, Rousseau and other social contract theorists is, in fact, the type of rational thought process, predicated upon an 'enlightened self-interest', required to provide GPGs. GPGs are creatures of collective action (for example, requiring the engagement of multiple actors at both the national and international levels), which provide for distinctively public goods for common benefit. The pursuit and construction of a workable (global) social order and an understanding of the value of GPGs should be enhanced by drawing from the philosophical resources presented in variations of social contract theory.

In relation to the international plane, a number of social contract thinkers have extrapolated their theories, originally focused principally on national governance systems, to the international sphere. Immanuel Kant and John Rawls proposed a transposition where states, at the international level, would replace individual citizens at the national level (Neidleman, 2012: p. 3). One can see the strength of such reasoning, where individual nations, afflicted by a 'state of nature' of endless and precarious international conflagrations and wars (where they must, for example, constantly be concerned about the balance of power architectures, strategic alliances and pre-emptive armament), choose to cede their traditional notions of sovereign prerogative in favour of a rule-based international order. However, Nussbaum (2004) has in particular criticized Rawls for the focus on the state as the dominant or key actor in a conception of a just international social contract, and has rather proposed a focus on the individual and 'a set of basic human entitlements, similar to human rights [as] a minimum of what justice requires for all' (p. 4). Nussbaum's critique is in fact consonant with modern developments in international law, which one might say evidence a further democratization of the international sphere, where the individual person has become increasingly an actor in the international legal domain, at times possessing international legal personality, among other things (Parlett, 2011).

Thus in this powerful philosophical tradition there should lie a repository of helpful notions that can assist in rethinking our current global governance framework in a way that strengthens its democratic character, and in shaping appropriate expectations of the fulfilment of commitments by the international community and individual states. Attention to GPGs rests on the assumption that there are certain human problems that are in need of *global* cooperation – they can only be addressed and resolved at the global level and binding law/obligations would seem imperative to do so. Having agreed norms upon which both nations and individuals can rely is at the heart of a workable international society, as it is of a national society. Indeed the preamble of the UN Charter itself gives the impression that it is some 'Great Charter',[17] and an international social contract whose inherent potential for global society has yet to be realized: 'We the peoples', the Charter begins, implying a contract between national governments in assembly, individuals globally and the UN as an international organization. The UDHR sets out similarly comprehensive ambitions (that is, with respect to recognizing the individual and allotting to him or her what might be seen as position within a global social contract), affirming the 'inherent dignity and of the equal and inalienable rights *of all members of the human family*' (United Nations, 1948, emphasis added).[18]

6. STRENGTHENING RULE OF LAW AND INTERNATIONAL DEMOCRATIC PRACTICE THROUGH ACCOUNTABILITY

The international community is increasingly adept at identifying issues of common concern and negotiating international norms, both legal and non-legal, to address them (see Brunnée, Chapter 13 in this volume). As mentioned above, this prominently applies to the field of providing GPGs and protecting and managing global commons. What the international community is less proficient at is ensuring that states do their very best to act in accordance with those norms. The rule of international law is often weak, at best, which is partly manifested by the very lenient or absent accountability mechanisms following the adoption of many international norms or instruments. But there is potential to strengthen accountability in various ways, thereby improving international democratic practice and thus the legitimacy of global governance, in particular for those who find the democratic deficit in such governance problematic and at least partially linked to accountability deficits. Perceptions of legitimacy in turn can influence the inclination to comply with international norms – and therefore strengthen the rule of international law even beyond what is expected in accountability mechanisms.

'Accountability' has become a popular concept 'that no one can be against' as it 'conveys an image of transparency and trustworthiness' (Bovens, 2007: p. 448). The concept as a catchphrase is elusive, as it relates to a number of other concepts – for example, transparency, equity, democracy, efficiency, responsiveness, responsibility, integrity, liability, controllability. While it is difficult to translate – many languages do not distinguish the concept from 'responsibility' (Bovens, 2007) – its association with 'good governance', democracy, and indeed, a 'social contract' between the governed and those governing, is strong. Accountability implies a social relation where trustworthiness is expected and there are formal and informal mechanisms in place to ensure it is also realized. Mashaw (2006: p. 118) characterizes an 'accountability regime' through answering the questions 'to whom, about what, through what processes, by what standards, and with what effect' is an actor held answerable? These questions can be answered empirically, thereby forming a picture of what accountability mechanisms and their impact look like: Wolfe (2015) provides an example of such a study in a global governance context. The questions can also be answered normatively by exploring links to principles within various strains of democratic theory, for example, those identified by Moravcsik (2004), considering who should hold whom to account, how, by what standards and with what effects. In this chapter we give several examples in order to partially answer the question empirically, but focus on exploring some normative scenarios for what accountability could look like if the GPG international rule of law is to be strengthened in ways that also strengthen the democratic character of existing global governance/the world order.

In the particular context of global governance it has been argued that the rapid growth of international institutions and governance initiatives has created a democratic deficit which for some (for example, Goodhart, 2011) is closely linked to insufficient accountability relationships. Such arguments are linked to viewing accountability as necessary in order to control those with power and to protect their subjects from abuse of that power (Goodhart, 2011). In response there has been growing attention to accountability dilemmas associated with emerging actors and arenas of power in global governance, such as accountability of new transnational (non-state) governance actors (Bäckstrand, 2006; Black, 2008; Harlow and Rawlings, 2007; Papadopoulos, 2007; Slaughter, 2004) and towards diverse intergovernmental organizations (Blagescu et al., 2005; Borowiak, 2012; Grant and Keohane, 2005; Keohane, 2006). More relevant for our argument here – as we focus on the lack of supra-national power in the field of rule of law – are those scholars who consider the general low level (or lack of) accountability of *states* in global governance as a major contribution to the democratic deficit of such governance, as states remain key actors in such governance (Goodhart, 2011; Held, 2004; Keohane, 2006). From this perspective, global governance lacks authority as norms generally cannot be enforced in a reliable and systematic fashion. Goodin (2010) argues that one cannot democratize central institutions of authority until they have attained de facto authority and, drawing on the example of the history of the United Kingdom, argues that accountability is a way leading towards democracy and that in global governance 'the circle of those to whom the powerful are accountable almost inevitably expands over time'. While we do not argue that strong accountability is sufficient to remedy the democratic deficit of global governance, it is an important component. Furthermore, strong accountability of states is properly associated with expectations of more effective international regimes, concretely strengthening compliance with international norms and thereby the rule of international law (Black, 2008; Goodhart, 2011; Karlsson-Vinkhuyzen and McGee, 2013; Karlsson-Vinkhuyzen and Vihma, 2009; Zürn, 2004).

With states and their relationship to international law as an analytical focus, accountability can be approached along two trajectories, 'input' and 'output' accountability, described in turn below. Input accountability is particularly relevant for increasing democratic practice in global governance while output accountability is particularly relevant for strengthening the rule of law.

6.1 Input Accountability

What we refer to as 'input' accountability relates to the possibilities for various actors who may have rightful expectations – drawn from democratic/social contract theories – to inform and hold states to account for the positions they take in developing the content of international treaties and other types of norms, and thus the normative 'content' of global governance. Of particular relevance for strengthening the democratic aspect of governance is related to citizen engagement in this activity. Steffek (2010: p. 53) defines democracy as 'an institutional arrangement that enables citizens to govern themselves' and looks at the process of negotiating collectively binding rules as the *ex-ante* process for citizens to voice their views, directly or indirectly through representation. Citizens' indirect participation through representation can be achieved through, for example, parliaments, civil society organizations, formalized consultative processes and so on.

National parliaments are the route of citizen engagement that links most directly to traditional democratic ideas of representation, and those adhering to the 'statist' ideas of how to achieve more democracy in global governance argue that when the international community is composed of sovereign democracies this will be sufficient to ensure democratic input accountability (Scholte, 2014). It is also a route that builds on established and accepted accountability relationships, and is potentially highly influential. Parliaments, however, have only provided loose oversight of their state's involvement in global governance (Scholte, 2002). The concept of 'executive multilateralism' amply illustrates this, referring to how the power over foreign policy is largely residing within the executive arm of governments (Zürn, 2004). An additional constraint for parliaments to have influence on and hold their governments to account for their negotiating positions is the fact that such negotiations are often conducted through coalitions of countries, such as the European Union or the Group of 77 and China (Vihma et al., 2011). This means that states within the coalition first negotiate a joint position and parliaments may only have had an opportunity to express their views on a state's initial position. But much will happen during the course of negotiations that takes parliaments, and even more so citizens, far from being able to express their views on the matters on the table.

Strengthening input accountability through parliaments would entail more thorough deliberation on issues of global governance domestically, giving the governments that negotiate a stronger democratic mandate

(Dingwerth, 2014). This could partly be achieved through institutional changes, requiring consultation by way of various procedures, but it would also require a substantive interest among parliamentarians, and the public, in global affairs – a shift falling in the realm of attitudinal change.

There have been efforts to solicit the views directly from people from around the world in global governance processes, thus making participation more direct and not dependent on representation. One example is the Brazilian government's organization of Sustainable Development Dialogues during the 2012 UN Conference on Sustainable Development ('Rio+20'). These took place first through a digital platform for the express reason of providing the 'wider public with a democratic space for discussion'. In most cases, however, intergovernmental negotiations are too complex for individual citizens to engage with and it is non-governmental organizations (NGOs) that are often the actors having 'the potential to act as a discursive interface between international organizations and a global citizenry' (Nanz and Steffek, 2004: p. 315). It is indeed NGOs that we find crowding the hallways of those negotiations where they are welcomed as observers, NGOs who organize side-events to inject ideas, strike up conversations with negotiators, and who write commentaries in blogs and tweets to share with those outside the negotiation halls. At times they are invited to take the floor to give a short statement in plenary, at other times they have had a few seats in roundtables or multi-stakeholder dialogues with diplomats, ministers or even heads of state. For the negotiation process of Rio+20, the organizing Bureau also allowed anyone to send submissions before they released the initial zero draft text – they received 6,000 comments (Powers, 2012). NGOs, or the broader notion of global civil society, play a strong role in proposals to democratize global governance along the cosmopolitan route (Dryzek, 2012).

One way to strengthen the pathway of accountability through NGOs is the rise of so-called 'citizen diplomacy' (Williams and Goose, 2008) and 'smart coalitions' (Commission on Global Security, 2015: p. 105), where, typically, civil society coalitions form alliances with like-minded states (usually considered 'middle powers'[19]) in order to advance a human rights or an international legal reform agenda and create binding international legal instruments. Notable success stories by smart coalitions include the creation of the International Criminal Court (ICC) with the Rome Statute of 1998 and the conclusion of the Land Mine Treaty in 1999. The creation of the ICC is a striking development in the international institutional and legal architecture, arguably the most significant since 1945. Instrumental in its creation was the Coalition for the International Criminal Court (CICC), established in 1995 initially as a group of only 25 civil society organizations (Coalition for the International Criminal Court, 2016).

There are currently 162 states parties to the 1999 Land Mine Treaty,[20] which would not exist but for the civil society coalition working under the banner of the International Campaign to Ban Landmines (Williams and Goose, 2008). Moreover, the participation of landmine survivors in the campaign to realize core provisions of the treaty was significant: '[w]ithout the strong leadership and participation of landmine survivors . . . there would be no treaty obligation for governments to "do their utmost for the care, rehabilitation and social and economic integration of mine victims"' (White and Young, 2008: p. 241). A similar broad civil society engagement, including the very active contributions of those directly affected by the subject matter of the treaty, is also noted in relation to the development of the most recent UN thematic human rights treaty, the 2006 UN Convention on the Rights of Persons with Disabilities (CRPD) (White and Young, 2008: p. 241). Indeed, it has been proposed that the disability rights movement and its role in the creation of the UN CRPD may have 'raised the bar with respect to increased participation and inclusion of civil society in future UN negotiations and multilateral diplomacy', and established new precedents of participation and inclusion which are emerging legal obligations, rather than simply 'principled guidelines' (White and Young, 2008: pp. 242, 254). The value of civil society engagement in the CRPD negotiations in terms of enhancing government accountability is described as follows: '[the] grassroots presence globally was enormously helpful to build public awareness and political credibility and clout. Governments knew from experience they would hear directly from disability organizations back home in their capitals' (White and Young, 2008: p. 255).

Many proposals on how to strengthen the democratic character and practice of global governance through civil society engagement focus on institutional or structural changes. The former concerns rules for access to information, to the negotiation arenas and to decision-makers. The latter highlights the need for reducing inequalities including within civil society with respect to resources and skills to contribute to global governance processes. Dingwerth (2014), for example, argues that there is less a need for institutional reform but rather a greater need to build capacity among civil society actors to encourage their use of all relevant opportunities for participation through, for example, education, as education is a key determining factor in political participation. While we see the need to pursue both these avenues of institutional and structural change we would also argue that substantive change will depend on the ability of those NGO 'representatives' of various populations (as well as state representatives) to adopt an open, listening and learning attitude, and, in the words of Scholte (2014), to express humility instead of immediately assuming the superiority of a given position when engaging in transcultural communications and global deliberation processes.[21] This will also likely require a re-conceptualization of 'representation', as traditional notions where actors are expected to represent a particular constituency and discourse may stand in the way of true deliberation (des Bouvrie et al., n.d.).

Each of these various routes for strengthening democratic practice in the development of international norms, including those which are legally binding, has considerable limitations – but they represent options which currently seem to be the most readily available. And, it is also plausible that greater participation by, for example, parliaments and civil society organizations in the development of those norms will strengthen the 'buy in' of those actors, thereby exerting greater pressure for meaningful enforcement.

6.2 Output Accountability

When we speak of 'output' accountability it relates to theories of democracy and the important strains of political philosophy mentioned above, which imply that citizens should have a reasonable expectation that laws duly adopted or promulgated are enforced and carry with them the promise of effective access to justice. This concept thus refers to what happens after states have adopted international norms and looks at state behaviour *ex post*. It can be seen as part of what Steffek (2010: p. 54) considers as one of the contestatory dimensions of democracy, where citizens are able to challenge political decisions both 'individually and collectively'. This in turn is linked to the fundamental acknowledgement that 'all decision-makers, even the democratically legitimated ones, are fallible' (Steffek, 2010: p. 54). According to Klabbers (2013), drawing on an argument from Austin in the 1830s, international law provides statesmen and others with 'a vocabulary for voicing approval and disapproval of acts of public power', which shows the instrumental role it can indeed play for strengthening accountability. The most common approach to analysing how states are/can be held to account for implementing international norms (that is, according to the rule of law) is to look at how nations hold each other to account through formal reporting, review or compliance mechanisms in a given global regime (Duyck, 2014; Treves et al., 2009). However, states rarely accept strong mutual accountability with regard to their individual obligations under international norms, although there are exceptions in, for example, areas of trade and security. The recently adopted SDGs and Paris Agreement on climate change are unlikely to move much beyond the history of weak review and compliance mechanisms in global governance (United Nations, 2015; United Nations General Assembly, 2015a). Such a narrow analysis of state accountability can thus paint a rather gloomy picture.

However, a full picture of the (potential) accountability regimes for states vis-á-vis international norms needs a much broader perspective. There are at least three additional 'pathways' (which do not necessarily rely upon the strengthening of supra-national mechanisms) through which accountability relationships can be enacted – national institutions, publics and the state itself (Karlsson-Vinkhuyzen et al., 2018).

States (in the form of their executive governments) may be held to account with respect to international norms by national institutions such as parliaments, audit agencies, or judicial bodies, depending on the characteristics of each state's legal and political system (Karlsson-Vinkhuyzen et al., 2018). International legal norms often require formal domestic ratification and thus can involve parliaments in various ways (van Dijk and Tahzib, 1994). For non-binding international norms – such as the national goals countries have adopted (or are expected to adopt) as their contribution to the SDGs and the Paris Agreement – parliaments may have no formal role but there are very few studies, especially comparative ones, of how such norms are addressed by national institutions.

Individuals and collectives (for example, civil society organizations) may also directly hold governments to account. In some cases 'representatives' of the public may appropriate or be assigned roles in formal state-to-state accountability mechanisms (Duyck, 2014). For example, the High-Level Political Forum includes civil society in the review process of the SDGs (United Nations General Assembly, 2013). However, in general, international and national civil society organizations do not wait to be formally invited as 'accountholders'. They use various means to make countries answerable. They, for example, monitor actions, sponsor their own research, publish reports, organize seminars, share views on traditional and social media, and organize demonstrations. At the national level, civil society actors may also directly engage formal institutions by, for example, taking governments to court for lack of ambition or implementation. Such efforts by civil society to enforce compliance have been largely unsuccessful. One exception is the recent case in which the Dutch government was ordered by a national court to reduce national emissions by a minimum 25 per cent over five years in accordance with international commitments (BBC News, 2015). The effectiveness of this public pathway to strengthen the international rule of law through higher output accountability depends much on the public interest on which they rest and governments' sensitivity to public opinion (McHarg, 2011). Like all pathways it is also enabled by a high degree of transparency of what the organs of the state are doing (or not doing).

The way that states, through the machinery of the executive government, hold themselves directly to account for their international commitments will differ depending on the traditions and administrative cultures of each state and the legal form of those commitments. Procedures for monitoring and evaluation that apply to various aspects of government policy may also be enacted for 'domesticated' international commitments. While internal accountability mechanisms should have potential for high impact, this pathway is quite vulnerable to shifts in national public opinion (McHarg, 2011) and most likely therefore also subject to changes when the government changes, particularly in relation to non-legal norms (see ibid.).

There is no comparative research on which of these pathways is more effective in pushing reluctant governments to do more to honour their international commitments, or how they interact and possibly reinforce each other. Clearly, there are many institutional and structural changes that would strengthen either of these pathways and thereby the exercise of authority in global governance. We discuss several directions at the global level below. However, we also suggest that such changes would need to be preceded and accompanied by attitudinal changes. For example, the exercise of holding-to-account by members of the public requires the manifestation of a kind of civic virtue to evaluate those with public power and to correct them if necessary (Klabbers, 2013). Equally pertinent would be the exercise of virtues such as humility, trustworthiness and perseverance, enthusiasm and creativity among public servants charged with the task of steering the implementation of international norms (ibid.).

Addressing output accountability on the international plane itself (that is, focusing on the existing international architecture of key supranational institutions dating from the adoption of the UN Charter and subsequently), theoretically speaking there is a great deal of 'low hanging fruit' in relation to establishing a governance system with a better rule of international law. However, as noted, despite the perceived need, there are common and persistent resistances to reform of the existing order (Commission on Global Security, 2015). Intransigent path dependencies exist with respect to existing international institutions, in particular when it comes to the enforcement and implementation of international law. One antidote – in an effort to make 'aspirational' rule of law language more grounded in the concrete – would be to employ, as a basis of reform, analogical reasoning to compare the attributes of mature national legal systems that have established a measure of the rule of law to requirements at the global level to establish a more credible international rule of law.

A first case in point is the International Court of Justice (ICJ), which is intended to be the 'principal judicial organ of the United Nations' (United Nations, 1945, Article 92). However, to date, more than 70 years after the Court's creation, only 72 UN Members states have accepted the compulsory jurisdiction of the Court, representing less than 40 per cent of

UN membership.[22] UN statements dealing with the rule of law regularly mention the ICJ, and states are encouraged to accept the compulsory jurisdiction of the Court. However, such admonishments are generally framed in tentative language, for example, suggesting that states 'consider' accepting the jurisdiction of the ICJ (United Nations General Assembly, 2005a: para. 134f). At the national level, it would be incongruous to think that any individual (or other entity with legal personality) would only be called before a court of law at their own pleasure and that being held to account by a court of law was in effect optional. Yet this is the current state of affairs with respect to the ICJ; the principal actors in the international legal system, states, are not subject to a basic accountability mechanism that would be taken for granted in a national system predicated on the rule of law.[23] There are a range of other reforms to the ICJ that have been suggested in order to strengthen its adjudicatory and enforcement functions, along the lines of making the Court closer to what would be considered at the national level to be a true, impartial tribunal with requisite powers and prerogatives.[24]

A second general case is the issue of the enforcement of binding human rights obligations owed by states to individuals, under the range of human rights treaties negotiated under the auspices of the UN.[25] Some progress has been made in recent years to improve the UN human rights treaty body system and to diagnose its weaknesses,[26] but again, key features which would be considered indicative of a genuine system of rule of law remain largely absent. In the past approximately 15 years, more states have become party to the various 'core' international human rights instruments, and – importantly – a number of new individual complaint mechanisms have been established or activated under the various UN human rights treaties or their protocols (Pillay, 2012: p. 17). But these individual complaint mechanisms inevitably involve delay (normally accessible only after all domestic remedies are exhausted) and any decisions are non-binding on states – although it is laudable that these procedures exist, they are still far from the effective remedies one would hope for the individual 'justice seeker' (OHCHR, 2013: pp. 8, 11).

Moreover, systemic problems exist in relation to state engagement with the treaty bodies, with, for example, accounts of only 16 per cent of states fulfilling their reporting obligations under various human rights treaties on time (Pillay, 2012: p. 9). Additionally, the former UN High Commissioner for Human Rights, Navi Pillay, has noted that 'even though human rights is one of the UN's three pillars, it remains so poorly funded, receiving only around 3% of the overall UN budget' (The Global Justice Monitor, 2014). She has also highlighted the vicious circle produced by low expectations:

> by resigning ourselves to the inevitability of noncompliance and inadequate resources, the system was left to suffer a long history of benign neglect to the point where, today, it stands on the verge of drowning in its growing workload, even when leaving aside the shocking fact that on average 23 per cent of States parties to one treaty have never engaged in the review procedure of that treaty. (Pillay, 2012: p. 94)

The various pathways outlined above to strengthening output accountability of states in relation to their international (legal) commitments are all within reach for at least incremental change – but with such change heavily dependent on public and political support for compliance with specific international norms, which aim, for example, to provide specific GPGs or protect global commons. The two examples of the ICJ and the human rights regime alone show how existing international institutions or systems, if strengthened, could very significantly contribute to the integrity of the international legal system and provide the GPG of international access to justice/rule of law (and accountability) in relation to two primary actors in the global order: states and individuals, as framed in the UN Charter and the UDHR. However, there is a notable absence of coordinated actors who work for the strengthening of the international rule of law itself – across issue areas.

7. DISCUSSION AND CONCLUSION

Classical public international law has – to this day – retained an intransigent deference to the (narrowly conceived) sovereignty concerns of nation states (see Mattei, Chapter 10 in this volume) and studies of compliance with, for example, multilateral environmental treaties (see Brunnée, Chapter 13 in this volume) and international human rights treaties, show a poor record of very weak mechanisms for monitoring, review and indeed enforcement, almost across the board. International obligations are more often than not treated in a casual way in the international community and are still not taken with the seriousness that one would normally ascribe to legally binding norms at the national level possessing the 'force of law' (Bourdieu, 1987). The approach to the whole body of non-legally binding norms (soft law) is even more casual. If GPGs are critical for the well-being of global societies (which are interdependent), then a better international rule of law must be concretely addressed.[27] However, reaching a state of international rule of law would amount to nothing less than a cultural transition.[28] Believing that it is possible to reach such a state lies within each person's worldview: 'our perceptions of how the world works and what is possible' (Beddoe et al., 2009, p. 2484).

By describing an effective international rule of law as a GPG – and indeed a very fundamental one – we hope to make a small contribution to '[t]ransform[ing] the dimensions of the debate and elevat[ing] the concept to a new and urgent plane of importance' (Speth, 1999: p. xii). Also, if a truly effective international rule of law were to be considered a foundational GPG, national governments and international organizations should be further enabled and motivated, in a more pressing and concrete way, to: (1) engage in developing better enforcement devices for international norms as a default requirement (rather than as an exceptional measure), against a narrative backdrop focusing on what is gained at the international level by such an approach, rather than focusing on narratives of what is lost at the national level (for example, based on impoverished understandings of individual state sovereignty); and (2) contemplate and develop concrete and workable financing for the provision of such a fundamental GPG (as Adam Smith noted, '[t]he administration of justice . . . may, no doubt, be considered as laid out for the benefit of the whole society . . . [t]here is no impropriety, therefore, in its being defrayed by the general contribution of the whole society' (Smith, 1937: p. 767)).

We have elaborated above some strategies as to how to strengthen, within the current international system, the various pathways to maximize input and output accountability of states vis-á-vis international law/norms. In most cases our analysis indeed shows that strategies depend on attitudinal change in addition to or as a condition precedent to institutional change. Discussion on strengthening accountability and democracy in global governance has mostly argued for institutional changes (Borowiak, 2012), or in the case of Dingwerth (2014), for changes in the structural preconditions for formal democratic institutions to function adequately. However, Klabbers (2013: p. 320), for example, also argues for the implementation of a 'positive morality' in relation to international legal norms, noting that 'it appears inescapable to pay attention not just to what the rules say, but also to the character traits of those making and applying the rules'. Such an approach speaks to former UN High Commissioner for Human Rights Navi Pillay's plea that the international community not resign itself to low expectations; our aims should be set much higher. Fundamental institution-building and constitutional efforts at the international level are likely required, based upon the wishes of the international community to be bound by a rational, rule-based order, which seeks the collective well-being of all.

NOTES

* The views expressed in this chapter are those of the author alone and do not reflect the views of the Permanent Bureau or the Hague Conference on Private International Law.

1. Some exceptions include, for example, proposing human rights protection as a global public good, focusing on two international human rights instruments (Brydensholt and Yigen, 2007).
2. Waldron notes that '[t]he Rule of Law is one ideal in an array of values that dominates liberal political morality: others include democracy, human rights, social justice and economic freedom'. The 'moral and political commitment' to the rule of law also typically figures as an enshrined element in theories of constitutionalism (Waluchow, 2014: p. 6). On the international plane, as of the 1990s, an emerging 'consensus' has been observed that (market-based) democratic societies may be the 'sole feasible social structure' (Wouters et al., 2004: p. 4). Falk (2014b: p. 125), has noted that despite the enthusiasm/consensus on democracy by Western nations in particular, there has been 'surprisingly little spill over with respect to world politics', with 'most liberal democracies . . . quite comfortable with the lack of popular participation, transparency, accountability, even the rule of law, when it came to the procedures and decisions of international institutions'.
3. Shared understandings by the international community of the notion of the rule of law – as exemplified by official statements emanating from various UN bodies – are as important, if not more important, than those definitions put forward by academics (see below for a discussion of various academic definitions/approaches). International definitions which have been endorsed politically by governments around the world can become a basis for collective action and concrete global policy development.
4. See an historical synopsis of UN work in the area of rule of law (United Nations, 2016).
5. This progressive attention to the notion of rule of law in UN discourse, as foreshadowed above (*supra*, note 2), would seem to be linked to broader international political shifts after the Cold War, which brought a de-escalation of certain 'ideological tensions' and a growing consensus of 'a democratic polity founded on the rule of law' as a widely accepted governance model (Wouters et al., 2004: p. 4).
6. The four areas identified are: development; peace and collective security; human rights and the rule of law; and strengthening of the United Nations.
7. The reports and other key documents are available at: https://www.un.org/ruleoflaw/key-documents/ (Accessed 3 July 2018).
8. Article 13(1)(a) provides that: 'The General Assembly shall initiate studies and make recommendations for the purpose of: . . . promoting international co-operation in the political field and encouraging the progressive development of international law and its codification.'
9. May (2014: p. 75), for example, warns that 'rule of law' terminology and practices currently employed by various (international) political actors are by no means neutral, and are largely deployed to support a neoliberal economic agenda while aspects of the rule of law related to non-economic 'political values' such as human rights and democracy are downplayed.
10. See a summary description of this transitional moment in the foundation of the United Nations in Sears, 2008: pp. 4–5.
11. The diversity in 'legality' of international norms has been captured in the concept of 'legalization' that ranges from hard to soft law, where the degree of hardness is determined by how high the norms score on indices of obligation, precision and delegation (Abbott et al., 2000; Abbott and Snidal, 2000). For an overview of how to compare hard and soft law see Karlsson-Vinkhuyzen, 2011.
12. The emphasis here is on theory. While there are examples of countries in which the GPGs have had political traction, such as the Netherlands where it has been explored as a way to approach development aid, many countries, particularly in the Global South are very skeptical about the concept.

13. It is rightly noted, however, that 'at this point in time' the (global) rule of law, at the national and international levels, could be characterized as 'an exclusive club good' due to its very inadequate and irregular provision (Brydensholt and Yigen, 2007: p. 237).
14. Indeed, it has been observed that, based upon experiences of the international community, buy-in of elites/local populations are crucial to (re-)establishing the rule of law: '[t]he rule of law's technical elements (procedures) are dependent on a normative acceptance of the wisdom of adopting this mode of ordering in the first place' (May, 2014: p. 73). Therefore aspects of normative culture – and aspirations of relevant actors – are extremely important, and precede the broader acceptance and implementation of rule of law techniques.
15. Indeed Deneulin and Townsend (2007) distinguish GPGs from common goods with the notion that common goods cease to exist when people do not participate in them. Of course it is possible to argue that international law is thus more akin to a common good in their definition than a GPG.
16. We do agree, however, with those who stress that these two characteristics do not alone predict 'publicness', which is often a matter of political choice.
17. Indeed, when adopted in 1948 the UDHR was hailed as an international Magna Carta for all humankind by Eleanor Roosevelt. See elaboration of this theme in Klug, 2015.
18. Falk has called for a 'just new constitutionalism' and a new form of 'humane global governance', based, for example, on 'the aspirations of Articles 25 and 28 of the Universal Declaration of Human Rights' (Falk, 2014a: p. 312).
19. Which would thus presumably be most interested in developing a rule-based international system, as middle powers without 'super-power' attributes.
20. The 1997 Ottawa Convention on the Prohibition of the Use, Stockpiling, Production and Transfer of Anti-Personnel Mines and on their Destruction.
21. However, there are indeed many concerns raised around the ability of NGOs to 'represent' constituencies they claim to work for, the need to scrutinize their own accountability relationships, or that the NGO category is so broad that it also covers organizations that support private rather than public interests. We, however, do not elaborate on these legitimate concerns here.
22. Under Article 36(2) of the Statute of the International Court of Justice (United Nations, 1946).
23. The former President of the ICJ, HE Judge Rosalyn Higgins, has indeed commented that fundamental principles of domestic rule of law models 'do not fit easily within the international framework', noting, among others, the lack of compulsory jurisdiction of the ICJ and enforcement of international law, and a lack of clear hierarchy among international courts (Higgins, 2007).
24. See, for example, the range of reforms suggested by Palmer (1998). See also suggestions in Commission on Global Security, 2015: p. 90.
25. See the United Nations Treaty Collection, Chapter IV: Human Rights: https://treaties.un.org/pages/Treaties.aspx?id=4&subid=A&lang=en (accessed 3 July 2018).
26. See, for example, comprehensive suggestions for improvement in Pillay (2012).
27. As Barrett (Barrett, 2007: p. 190) notes: '[w]hen the world succeeds in supplying global public goods, people everywhere benefit. Our international institutions, however, are clumsily suited to this task [as] they lack the coercive powers that every state uses to supply national public goods'.
28. 'The rule of law presupposes the coming together of commitment to common values (which are marked, at the level of custom, by the presence of spontaneous and collective sanctions such as moral disapproval) and of the existence of explicit rules and sanctions and normalized procedures' (Bourdieu, 1987: p. 844).

REFERENCES

Abbott, K. W. and Snidal, D. (2000) Hard and Soft Law in International Governance. *International Organization*, **54** (3), 421–56.

Abbott, K. W., Keohane, R. O., Moravcsik, A., Slaughter, A.-M. and Snidal, D. (2000) The Concept of Legalization. *International Organization*, **54** (3), 401–19.

Bäckstrand, K. (2006) Multi-stakeholder Partnerships for Sustainable Development: Rethinking Legitimacy, Accountability and Effectiveness. *European Environment*, **16** (5), 290–306.

Barrett, S. (2007) *Why Cooperate? The Incentive to Supply Global Public Goods*. Oxford, Oxford University Press.

BBC News (2015) Netherlands Ordered to Cut Greenhouse Gas Emissions. [Online] Available from: http://www.bbc.com/news/world-europe-33253772 (accessed July 12, 2016).

Beddoe, R., Constanza, R., Farley, J., Garza, E., Kent, J., Kubiszewski, I., Martinez, L., McCowen, T., Murphy, K., Myers, N., Ogden, Z., Stapleton, K. and Woodward, J. (2009) Overcoming Systemic Roadblocks to Sustainability: The Evolutionary Redesign of Worldviews, Institutions, and Technologies. *Proceedings of the National Academy of Sciences*, **106** (8), 2483–9.

Bedner, A. and Vel, J. (2010) An Analytic Framework for Empirical Research on Access to Justice. *Law, Social Justice and Global Development*, **15** (1), 2–29.

Black, J. (2008) Constructing and Contesting Legitimacy and Accountability in Polycentric Regulatory Regimes. *Regulation and Governance*, **2** (2), 137–64.

Blagescu, M., de Las Casas, L. and Lloyd, R. (2005) *Pathways to Accountability: The GAP Framework*. London, One World Trust.

Borowiak, C. T. (2012) *Accountability and Democracy: The Pitfalls and Promise of Popular Control*. New York, Oxford University Press.

Bourdieu, P. (1987) The Force of Law: Toward a Sociology of the Juridical Field. *The Hastings Law Journal*, **38** (July), 805–53.

Boutros-Ghali, B. (1996) *An Agenda for Democratization*. New York, United Nations.

Bovens, M. (2007) Analysing and Assessing Accountability: A Conceptual Framework. *European Law Journal*, **13** (4), 447–68.

Brydensholt, H. H. and Yigen, K. (2007) Legal Protection and the Rule of Law as a Global Public Good. In: Andersen, E. A. and Lindsnaes, B. (eds) *Towards New Global Strategies: Public Goods and Human Rights*. Leiden, Martinus Nijhoff Publishers, pp. 237–54.

Coalition for the International Criminal Court (2016) About the Coalition. [Online] Available from: http://www.coalitionfortheicc.org/?mod=coalition (accessed July 12, 2016).

Commission on Global Security, Justice and Governance (2015) *Confronting the Crisis of Global Governance*. The Hague, The Hague Institute for Global Justice and the Stimson Center.

Deneulin, S. and Townsend, N. (2007) Public Goods, Global Public Goods and the Common Good. *International Journal of Social Economics*, **34** (1/2), 19–36.

des Bouvrie, N., Karlsson-Vinkhuyzen, S. and Hemmati, M. (n.d.) Multi-stakeholder Participation in the United Nations: Challenges for Representation and Legitimacy, manuscript.

Dingwerth, K. (2014) Global Democracy and the Democratic Minimum: Why

a Procedural Account Alone is Insufficient. *European Journal of International Relations*, **20** (4), 1124–47.
Dryzek, J. S. (2012) Global Civil Society: The Progress of Post-Westphalian Politics. *Annual Review of Political Science*, **15**, 101–19.
Duyck, S. (2014) MRV in the 2015 Climate Agreement: Promoting Compliance through Transparency and the Participation of NGOs. *Carbon and Climate Law Review*, **3**, 175–87.
Falk, R. (2014a) New Constitutionalism and Geopolitics: Notes on Legality and Legitimacy and Prospects for a Just New Constitutionalism. In: Gill, S. and Cutler, A. C. (eds) *New Constitutionalism and World Order*. Cambridge, Cambridge University Press, pp. 295–312.
Falk, R. (2014b) *(Re)Imagining Humane Global Governance*. Abingdon, Routledge.
Goodhart, M. (2011) Democratic Accountability in Global Politics: Norms, Not Agents. *The Journal of Politics*, **73** (1), 45–60.
Goodin, R. E. (2010) Global Democracy: In the Beginning. *International Theory*, **2** (2), 175–209.
Grant, R. W. and Keohane, R. O. (2005) Accountability and Abuses of Power in World Politics. *The American Political Science Review*, **99** (1), 29–43.
Habermas, J. (2012) The Crisis of the European Union in the Light of a Constitutionalization of International Law. *The European Journal of International Law*, **23** (2), 335–48.
Harlow, C. and Rawlings, R. (2007) Promoting Accountability in Multilevel Governance: A Network Approach. *European Law Journal*, **13** (4), 542–62.
Held, D. (2004) Democratic Accountability and Political Effectiveness from a Cosmopolitan Perspective. *Government and Opposition*, **39** (2), 364–91.
Higgins, R. (2007) The Rule of Law: Some Skeptical Thoughts. Lecture at the British Institute for International and Comparative Law. Annual Grotius Lecture. London. 16 October 2007.
International Task Force on Global Public Goods (2006) *Meeting Global Challenges: International Cooperation in the National Interest*. Final Report. Stockholm, International Task Force on Global Public Goods.
Karlsson-Vinkhuyzen, S. (2011) Global Regulation through a Diversity of Norms: Comparing Hard and Soft Law. In: Levi-Faur, D. (ed.) *Handbook on the Politics of Regulation*. Cheltenham and Northampton, MA, USA, Edward Elgar, pp. 604–14.
Karlsson-Vinkhuyzen, S. and McGee, J. (2013) Legitimacy in an Era of Fragmentation: The Case of Global Climate Governance. *Global Environmental Politics*, **13** (3), 56–78.
Karlsson-Vinkhuyzen, S. and Vihma, A. (2009) Comparing the Legitimacy and Effectiveness of Global Hard and Soft Law: An Analytical Framework. *Regulation and Governance*, **3** (4), 400–420.
Karlsson-Vinkhuyzen, S., Jollands, N. and Staudt, L. (2012) Global Governance for Sustainable Energy: The Contribution of a Global Public Goods Approach. *Ecological Economics*, **83**, 11–18.
Karlsson-Vinkhuyzen, S., Groff, M., Tamás, P. A., Dahl, A. L., Harder, M. and Hassall, G. (2018) Entry into Force and Then? The Paris Agreement and State Accountability. *Climate Policy*, **18** (5), 593–9.
Kaul, I. (2013) Global Public Policy: A Policy in the Making. Paper presented at the First International Conference on Public Policy, Grenoble.
Kaul, I., Grunberg, I. and Stern, M. A. (eds) (1999) *Global Public Goods:*

International Cooperation in the 21st Century. New York, Oxford University Press.

Kaul, I., Conceição, P., Le Goulven, K. and Mendoza, R. U. (eds) (2003) *Providing Global Public Goods: Managing Globalization*. Oxford, Oxford University Press.

Kelsen, H. (1942) *Law and Peace in International Relations*. Cambridge, Harvard University Press.

Keohane, R. O. (2006) Accountability in World Politics. *Scandinavian Political Studies*, **29** (2), 75–87.

Klabbers, J. (2013) Law, Ethics and Global Governance: Accountability in Perspective. *New Zealand Journal of Public and International Law*, **11**, 309–21.

Klug, F. (2015) *A Magna Carta for All Humanity: Homing in on Human Rights*. London, Routledge.

Mashaw, J. L. (2006) Accountability and Institutional Design: Some Thoughts on the Grammar of Governance. In: Dowdle, M. (ed.) *Public Accountability: Designs, Dilemmas and Experiences*. Cambridge, Cambridge University Press, pp. 115–56.

May, C. (2014) The Rule of Law as the Grundnorm of the New Constitutionalism. In: Gill, S. and Cutler, A. C. (eds) *New Constitutionalism and World Order*. Cambridge, Cambridge University Press, pp. 63–75.

McHarg, A. (2011) Climate Change Constitutionalism? Lessons from the United Kingdom. *Climate Law*, **2**, 469–84.

Mitchell, R. B. (2003) International Environmental Agreements. A Survey of their Features, Formation, and Effects. *Annual Review of Environmental Resources*, **28**, 429–61.

Moravcsik, A. (2004) Is there a 'Democratic Deficit' in World Politics? A Framework for Analysis. *Government and Opposition*, **39** (2), 336–63.

Nanz, P. and Steffek, J. (2004) Global Governance, Participation and the Public Sphere. *Government and Opposition*, **39** (2), 314–35.

Neidleman, J. (2012) The Social Contract Theory in a Global Context. *E-International Relations Publishing*. [Online] Available from: http://www.e-ir.info/2012/10/09/the-social-contract-theory-in-a-global-context/ (accessed November 30 2017).

Nussbaum, M. C. (2004) Beyond the Social Contract: Capabilities and Global Justice. *Oxford Development Studies*, **32** (1).

OHCHR (2013) Individual Complaint Procedures under the United Nations Human Rights Treaties. New York and Geneva Fact Sheet No. 7/Rev. 2.

Palmer, G. (1998) International Law and the Reform of the International Court of Justice. In: Anghie, A. and Sturgess, G. (eds) *Legal Visions of the 21st Century: Essays in Honour of Judge Christopher Weeramantry*. The Hague, Kluwer Law International, pp. 579–600.

Papadopoulos, Y. (2007) Problems of Democratic Accountability in Network and Multilevel Governance. *European Law Journal*, **13** (4), 469–86.

Parlett, K. (2011) *The Individual in the International Legal System: Continuity and Change in International Law*. Cambridge, Cambridge University Press.

Pillay, N. (2012) Strengthening the United Nations Human Rights Treaty Body System. A Report by the United Nations High Commissioner for Human Rights. *United Nations Human Rights Office of the High Commissioner*. [Online] Available from: http://www2.ohchr.org/english/bodies/HRTD/docs/HCReportTBStrengthening.pdf (accessed 30 November 2017).

Powers, A. (2012) The Rio+20 Process: Forward Movement for the Environment? *Transnational Environmental Law*, **1** (2), 403–12.
Raz, J. (1979) *The Authority of Law: Essays on Law and Morality*. Oxford, Clarendon Press.
Scholte, J. A. (2002) Civil Society and Democracy in Global Governance. *Global Governance*, **8**, 281–304.
Scholte, J. A. (2014) Reinventing Global Democracy. *European Journal of International Relations*, **20** (1), 3–28.
Sears, J. F. (2008) *Eleanor Roosevelt and the Universal Declaration of Human Rights*. Lausanne, The Task Force – Celebrating Eleanor Roosevelt Leader in Human Rights.
Slaughter, A.-M. (2004) Disaggregated Sovereignty: Towards the Public Accountability of Global Government Networks. *Government and Opposition*, **39** (2), 159–90.
Smith, A. (1937) *The Wealth of Nations*. New York, The Modern Library.
Speth, J. (1999) Foreword. In: Kaul, I., Grunberg, I. and Stern, M. A. (eds) *Global Public Goods: International Cooperation in the 21st Century*. New York, Oxford University Press, pp. xii–xiv.
Steffek, J. (2010) Public Accountability and the Public Sphere of International Governance. *Ethics and International Affairs*, **24** (1), 45–68.
Tamanaha, B. (2004) *On the Rule of Law: History, Theory, Politics*. Cambridge, Cambridge University Press.
Tamanaha, B. (2007) A Concise Guide to the Rule of Law. St. John's Legal Studies Research Paper No. 07-0082.
The Global Justice Monitor (2014) Interview with Navi Pillay: 'Africa has Benefited Most from the ICC'. *Journal of the Coalition for the International Criminal Court*, **46**, 18–19.
Treves, T., Pineschi, L., Tanzi, A., Pitea, C., Ragni, C. and Romanin, F. (eds) (2009) *Non-compliance Procedures and Mechanisms and the Effectiveness of International Environmental Agreements*. The Hague, T.M.C. Asser Press.
United Nations (1945) Charter of the United Nations. San Francisco, 26 June 1945. United Nations Treaty Series, 1 (XVI).
United Nations (1946) Statute of the International Court of Justice. San Francisco, 18 April 1946, United Nations Treaty Series, 33 (933).
United Nations (1948) Universal Declaration of Human Rights. 10 December 1948. UN Doc. A/RES/3/217.
United Nations (2015) The Paris Agreement. Paris, 12 December 2015, UN Doc. FCCC/CP/2015/L.9.
United Nations (2016) The Rule of Law in the UN's Intergovernmental Work. [Online] Available from: https://www.un.org/ruleoflaw/what-is-the-rule-of-law/the-rule-of-law-in-un-work/ (accessed 30 November 2017).
United Nations General Assembly (2002) Strengthening the Rule of Law, 27 February 2003, UN Doc. A/RES/57/221.
United Nations General Assembly (2005a) 2005 World Summit Outcome, 24 October 2005, UN Doc. A/RES/60/1.
United Nations General Assembly (2005b) Implementation of Agenda 21, the Programme for the Further Implementation of Agenda 21 and the Outcomes of the World Summit on Sustainable Development, 7 November 2005, UN Doc. A/C.2/60.L.20.
United Nations General Assembly (2012) Declaration of the High-level Meeting

of the General Assembly on the Rule of Law at the National and International Levels, 20 November 2012, UN Doc. A/RES/67/1.
United Nations General Assembly (2013) Format and Organizational Aspects of the High-level Political Forum on Sustainable Development, 12 July 2013, UN Doc. A/RES/67/290.
United Nations General Assembly (2014) Strengthening and Coordinating United Nations Rule of Law Activities. Report of the Secretary-General, 24 July 2014, UN Doc. A/69/181.
United Nations General Assembly (2015a) Transforming Our World: The 2030 Agenda for Sustainable Development, 25 September 2015, UN Doc. A/RES/70/1.
United Nations General Assembly (2015b) Human Rights, Democracy and the Rule Of Law. Resolution adopted by the Human Rights Council, 23 March 2015, UN Doc. A/HRC/28/L.24.
United Nations Security Council (2004) The Rule of Law and Transitional Justice in Conflict and Post-conflict Societies. Report of the Secretary-General, 23 August 2004, UN Doc. S/2004/616.
van Dijk, P. and Tahzib, B. (1994) *Parliamentary Participation in the Making and Operation of Treaties: A Comparative Study.* The Hague, Martinus Nijhoff.
Ver Eecke, W. (2013) *Ethical Reflections on the Financial Crisis 2007/2008: Making Use of Smith, Musgrave and Rajan*. London, Springer.
Vihma, A., Mulugetta, Y. and Karlsson-Vinkhuyzen, S. I. (2011) Negotiating Solidarity? The G77 through the Prism of Climate Change Negotiations. *Global Change, Peace and Security*, **23** (3), 315–34.
Waldron, J. (2016) The Rule of Law. In: Zalta, E. N. (ed.) *The Stanford Encyclopedia of Philosophy*. [Online] Available from: https://plato.stanford.edu/entries/rule-of-law/ (accessed 30 November 2017).
Waluchow, W. (2014) Constitutionalism. In: Zalta, E. N. (ed.) *The Stanford Encyclopedia of Philosophy*. [Online] Available from: https://plato.stanford.edu/entries/constitutionalism/ (accessed 30 November 2017).
White, J. and Young, K. (2008) Nothing About Us Without Us: Securing the Disability Rights Convention. In: Williams, J., Goose, S. D. and Wareham, M. (eds) *Banning Landmines: Disarmament, Citizen Diplomacy, and Human Security*. Lanham, Rowman and Littlefield, pp. 241–62.
Williams, J. and Goose, S. D. (2008) Citizen Diplomacy and the Ottawa Process: A Lasting Model? In: Williams, J., Goose, S. D. and Wareham, M. (eds) *Banning Landmines: Disarmament, Citizen Diplomacy, and Human Security*. Lanham, Rowman and Littlefield, pp. 181–96.
Wolfe, R. (2015) An Anatomy of Accountability at the WTO. *Global Policy*, **6** (1), 13–23.
Wouters, J., De Meester, B. and Ryngaert, C. (2004) Democracy and International Law. Leuven Interdisciplinary Research Group on International Agreements and Development (LIRGIAD). Working Paper No 5. [Online] Available from: https://www.law.kuleuven.be/iir/nl/onderzoek/working-papers/WPLirg5.pdf (accessed 30 November 2017).
Zürn, M. (2004). Global Governance and Legitimacy Problems. *Government and Opposition*, **39** (2), 260–87.

8. Expropriation by definition? Regime complexes, structural power, and global public goods

Thomas R. Eimer*

Denn die Verhältnisse, die sind nicht so.

(Bertolt Brecht)

1. INTRODUCTION

Does complexity facilitate comprehensiveness? Since the early 2000s at the latest, scholars of international cooperation tend to answer this question in the affirmative. Given that the cross-cutting nature of the world's most pressing challenges exceeds the problem-solving capacities even of the most powerful nation states (Held, 2003; Castells, 2008), it is assumed that a densely institutionalized collaboration of public and private actors on an international level may lead to an inclusive definition of global public goods (GPGs) in many fields such as economic development, environment, and human rights (Abbott, 2014; Keohane et al., 2009).

Most particularly, the literature on regime complexes argues that 'partially overlapping and non-hierarchical institutions governing a particular issue-area' (Raustiala and Victor, 2004: pp. 279–80) provide adequate solutions to intrinsically interrelated problems on a global scale. Global governance scholars assume that the inclusiveness of the decision-making procedures opens a space for 'systemic deliberation' (Kuyper, 2014: p. 6), while the malleability of the institutional structure provides a sufficient degree of flexibility for an effective implementation of commonly agreed decisions. Scholars of regime complexity are well aware that the reconciliation of diverging interests is subject to opportunistic behavior and depends on political clout (Morin and Orsini, 2013). But they expect that the loose coupling of various international organizations, low entry costs for recalcitrant states (Keohane and Victor, 2011), and the inclusion of transnational actors (Orsini et al., 2013) help to spread new normative orientations and to enhance the legitimacy of international cooperation. In the end, the institutionalized structure of global commons will facilitate the production of 'complex public goods' (Abbott, 2014: p. 57), whose 'benefits are quasi universal' (Kaul et al., 1999: pp. 2–3).

This chapter challenges the analytical and normative optimism of the global governance literature and its functionalist underpinnings. It does not deny that sophisticated institutional structures may indeed at least partially compensate for *relational* power imbalances. However, it is argued that the search for common solutions remains embedded in a context of *structural* power relationships, which 'shape and determine' the negotiation context and hereby define the policy space even in the absence of outspoken pressure politics (Strange, 1988: pp. 24–5). Under these conditions, international cooperation may perpetuate and even reinforce the already existing power differentials both among and within states (Terhalle, 2016; Cohen and Cutler, 2013). By this, regime complexes may effectively expropriate less powerful actors and deprive them of their already scarce resources. Eventually, attempts to create GPGs may only produce globalized 'club goods' (Sandler, 1999) which entail the dispossession of those who are structurally excluded from their definition.

To substantiate this claim, the chapter empirically draws on the regime complex on biodiversity (RCB), one of the most advanced international institutional frameworks to reconcile the sustainable use of natural resources, economic as well as scientific progress, and human (indigenous) rights (Morin and Orsini, 2011). Given its thorough institutionalization, its broad, yet flexible membership, and its outstandingly participatory decision-making procedures, this regime complex can be regarded as a least likely case (Odell, 2001: pp.165–6) for the critical argument of this chapter. If already the RCB is characterized by structural power imbalances and exploitative tendencies, it can be assumed that less institutionalized and inclusive regime complexes will entail even more dispossessing mechanisms and consequences.

The chapter is organized as follows. It first connects the debate on GPGs to the literature on regime complexes (Section 2). The third section (3) shows that the academic debate tends to disregard the implications of structural power imbalances both among and within states. In the fourth section (4), this critique is illustrated by an analysis of the RCB. The chapter concludes with a short summary and some recommendations for further research.

2. THE FUNCTIONALIST PROMISE: REGIME COMPLEXES AND GLOBAL PUBLIC GOODS

This section shows that the definition of GPGs is often discussed as a result of internationally institutionalized forms of cooperation in a dense network of states, international organizations, states, and transnational actors. At least in the global governance literature, it is assumed that the pooling of problem-solving capacities within regime complexes helps to overcome collective action problems on a potentially global scale and will eventually produce 'complex public goods' (Abbott, 2014: p. 57). Global governance scholars hereby draw on the literature on transaction cost economics which defines public goods as to be inclusively usable by all interested parties while remaining non-rival in consumption, which means that they do not decrease in quantity or quality if they are used by a multiplicity of actors (see Kaul et al., 1999: pp. 3–5).

As early as during the 1970s and 1980s, many commentators observed that the increased exchange of goods and services, as well as the liberalized flow of capital within the triad of industrialized countries, was associated with 'negative externalities' (for example, temporarily high unemployment rates, currency crises, environmental degradation), which could no longer be absorbed by the national states alone (Beck, 1986). At the same time, the United States (US), which had successfully stabilized the (capitalist) world order in the aftermath of the Second World War, appeared increasingly incapable, or at least unwilling, to continue its role of a 'benevolent hegemon' (Verbeek, 2000a). The US defeat in the Vietnam war (Katzenstein, 1978: p. 9), the collapse of the Bretton Woods system in the 1970s, and the increased emphasis on US competitiveness since the early 1980s (Sell, 2000: p. 95) illustrated that industrialized states could no longer rely on the US as a unilateral provider of GPGs such as security, financial stability, and economic growth (Gilpin, 2001: p. 342 ff.), let alone the more 'postmodern issues' such as environmental pollution and the decimation of natural species. At the same moment, the recently decolonized countries started to claim for a 'new economic world order', but they made it clear from the outset that they would not renounce any chances of domestic economic growth for the sake of globally desirable (for example, environmental) goals (Bernstein, 2000: pp. 468–9).

Despite substantial geopolitical, socio-economic, and ideological cleavages, liberal scholars assumed that an institutionalization of interactions between states would (and should) entail a large potential for cooperation and commonly agreed solutions even in the absence of US hegemony. Based on the insights of institutional economics (Coase, 1960) and the literature on collective action (Olson, 1968), they argued that self-sustaining cooperation might still be possible if the institutional design would imply a net benefit for the participating member states. Stephen Krasner famously introduced the notion of international regimes as 'principles, norms, rules and decision-making procedures around which actor expectations converge in a given issue-area' (Krasner, 1983: p. 1). His seminal article spurred an intensive research on international cooperation in various policy fields.

The first wave of scholars put particular emphasis on the prevention of free-riding as a precondition for in-depth cooperation. In this logic, regimes were mainly interpreted as an institutional device against defection from previously agreed commitments (Stein, 1982), and compliance was understood as the result of anticipated reciprocity among rationally self-interested states (Krasner, 1983; Grieco, 1988). In the beginning, the regime literature focused on 'negative integration' (Scharpf, 1993), that is, the abstention from collectively harmful behavior and the avoidance of 'public bads'.[1] Since the 1990s, however, scholars have increasingly redirected their attention to the production of GPGs ('positive integration') in the context of internationally institutionalized cooperation (Young, 1999). Especially since the end of the Cold War, previously rather neglected issue areas like human rights and environmental protection have experienced more attention in the regime literature and its offshoots (for example, Young, 1999; Keck and Sikkink, 1998). When compared to the initial regime literature, three extensions appear particularly noteworthy – regime complexity, relevant actors, and rationales for cooperation.

To begin with the first, the current academic debate recognizes that regimes do not exist in an institutional void. Instead, it has become commonplace to acknowledge that new forms of international coordination are strongly influenced by pre-existing institutional structures (Levy et al., 1995: pp. 317–18). Linkages between already established and new regimes can be intentionally devised, but they also result from the functional interrelatedness of the addressed policy issues. The constellation of varying regimes can be hierarchically organized ('nested regimes') or display a rather ambiguous relationship of mutual interdependence ('overlapping regimes') with competing and potentially contradictory rules and procedures (Alter and Meunier, 2006). Empirically, however, a clear distinction is difficult to maintain. That is why Raustiala and Victor introduce the overarching notion of 'regime complexes', by which they mean 'an array of partially overlapping and non-hierarchical institutions governing a particular issue-area' (Raustiala and Victor, 2004: pp. 279–80).

While the production and maintenances of substantial consistency are often perceived as the Achilles' heel of regime complexes (Morin and Orsini, 2014), liberal scholars assume that the particularities of their structure also imply centripetal counter-mechanisms (for example, mutual adaptation) which prevent regime complexes from breaking apart (Oberthür and Pożarowska, 2013). In this view, the internal stability of regime complexes is increased by the inclusion of non-state actors as constitutive elements of international cooperation. Most prominently, international organizations are regarded as an important cornerstone. The current literature on regime complexity interprets them as (albeit limited) actors in their own right. Their practical knowledge, executive competencies, and normative reputation enable them to assert their own policy preferences at least in specific sectors of 'transnational new governance' (Abbott and Snidal, 2010: p. 325).

The cooperation between states and international organizations is frequently reinforced by the inclusion of societal actors. Beginning with the notion of epistemic communities (Haas, 1992), many scholars have shown that experts, civil society actors, and business representatives play an important role for international institutionalization (Young, 1999: pp. 263–8). Since the late 1990s, the regime literature has departed from the previously prevailing conceptualization of regime formation as a result of a 'two-level game' in which societal actors only contribute to the preference formulation on the domestic level (Putnam, 1973). Instead, it is argued that societal actors directly address the international level of negotiations (Levy et al., 1995: p. 279). Acting as lobbyists, campaigners, or experts in a particular field, they significantly contribute to the emerging 'spheres of authority' beyond the nation state (Rosenau, 1997).

Drawing on neo-functionalist explanations of European integration, it is assumed that the secretariats of international organizations proactively use the support of societal actors to legitimize their own claims against the preferences of states (Martin and Simmons, 1998: p. 735). At the same time, transnationally operating scientists, civil societal groups, and corporate actors are interpreted as a means to facilitate the implementation of internationally agreed regimes on the domestic level. Their transnational activities make it possible to transmit internationally agreed norms to the domestic level and to report back on the (lack of) compliance in the context of international meetings and international court proceedings (Keck and Sikkink, 1998; Chayes and Chayes, 1993). But their role as 'transmission belts' is not limited to the vertical axis of regime implementation. Perhaps even more important, they are also assumed to facilitate horizontal policy transfers among the involved international institutions (Haas, 2004).

The increased attention to non-state actors has also inspired scholars to amend the initially rationalist interpretation by the insights of social constructivism. Most notably, the literature assumes that international organizations as well as societal actors are able to enhance the policy-specific expertise in their fields of action (Haas, 2004; Kennedy, 2007; Barnett and Finnemore, 1999). At least for civil society actors, it is expected that their core function is to facilitate 'production, exchange, and strategic use of information' (Keck and Sikkink, 1998: p. x). The delivery of 'usable knowledge' makes it possible for decision-makers to conceptualize efficient and effective policy tools (Haas, 2004). That is why expertise enhances the chances of comparably weaker actors to be considered as relevant participants and contributors to the deliberations in a 'global agora' (Stone, 2008).

The inclusion of a broader range of actors also facilitates an increased attention to the normative dimension of policy-making. Civil society groups are particularly important in this regard, because it is their self-acclaimed 'raison d'être' to contribute to the (moral) betterment of the world. Human rights organizations and environmental groups are frequently cited in this context (Ruggie, 2014; Abbott, 2014), because they are able to propose a norm-based reinterpretation of political problems and conflicts. This also changes the negotiation culture to the extent that a mere interest-based bargaining behavior becomes less acceptable. Instead, negotiations are (at least partially) transformed into deliberations. This makes it possible for less resourceful actors (for example, civil society groups) to emphasize general public interest considerations, which significantly strengthens the democratic quality of global governance (Nanz and Steffek, 2004).

Scholars of regime complexity are generally confident that the cooperation between states, international organizations, and societal actors may lead to the institutionalization of global commons governance (Ostrom, 1999), which facilitates the enhancement of GPGs. In essence, they still depart from the basic assumption of the classical regime literature that institutionalized collaboration is based on the self-interests of states and creates mutual expectations of reciprocity which in turn furthers even more far-reaching and ambitious cooperation in various and increasingly interconnected fields – 'cooperation induces further cooperation' (Morin and Orsini, 2014: p. 306). At the same time, the complexity of the institutional arrangement opens a discursive space for a global 'public sphere' which advances the deliberative nature of global ordering (Castells, 2008: pp. 78–9).

3. STRUCTURAL POWER – THE CRITICAL CAVEAT

This section summarizes the major theoretical critique on regime complexity, which is essentially centered on the literature's neglect of international power imbalances. It describes how liberal scholars have successfully shown that regime complexes can mitigate the consequences of *relational* power differentials, whereas the impact of *structural* power imbalances has remained disregarded for the time being.

Since its early beginnings, the regime literature has been confronted with strong criticism both from mercantilist scholars and structuralist authors (for example, Robert Gilpin, Susan Strange). Both camps fundamentally question the procedural inclusiveness of regimes as well as their ability to create GPGs (Keeley, 1990; Drezner, 2005). Most of the criticism refers to the direct and intentional influence of powerful states and their companies. Three arguments are crucial. First, it is assumed that powerful states can decide by themselves whether to join or to abstain from a given regime complex, whereas weaker states are subject to their pressure politics (Strange, 1982; Drezner, 2009). Second, it is expected that powerful states have sufficient resources to steer the direction of an already established institutional structure by shifting their attention towards particular elements of the complex ('regime-shifting', Helfer, 2004; Sell, 2010; Betts, 2009). Third and finally, powerful states can force weaker countries to comply with the rules they deem to be essential, whereas they themselves remain free to opt for an 'implementation à la carte'. In the end, regime complexity leads to a 'world of plastic rules' (Drezner, 2009: p. 67) whose enforceability depends on the relative power position of the participating states.

While liberal scholars do not deny the impact of relational power differentials, they assume that the institutional structure of regime complexes may at least mitigate the worst forms of muscle flexing. Their argumentation connects rational choice (interest) based assumptions to the insights of social constructivism. They affirm that domestic cost–benefit analyses are crucial for the decision of powerful states to initiate or to take part in internally institutionalized cooperation (Raustiala and Victor, 2004: pp. 280–81). It is nevertheless assumed that the relative low degree of bindingness and enforceability may motivate powerful states to participate in international cooperation even if this is not fully in line with their material interests (Kersbergen and Verbeek, 2007). Reputational considerations, for example, can make it attractive to formally adhere to a regime complex with apparently low entry costs (Keohane and Victor, 2011). However, once they have pledged their support for international cooperation, even the most powerful states get rhetorically entrapped. Since any attempt to withdraw at a later moment can be criticized by civil society actors, the reputational costs of such a maneuver may outweigh the price of adherence (Abbott, 2014: p. 68).

Moreover, most global governance scholars agree with their critics on the risk of regime-shifting. However, they argue the overarching interests of powerful states will often deter them from endangering the functionality of the regime complex as a whole (Oberthür and Pożarowska, 2013: p. 105). They also assume that regime-shifting is not necessarily a privilege of the most powerful states. Weaker countries can at least partially compensate their inferior diplomatic resources by the assistance of civil society actors. By re-introducing their claims in alternative forums, they can ensure that the overall complex is more likely to also address their concerns. In this perspective, the complexity of the institutional network may even enhance its 'deliberative capacity' (Kuyper, 2014: p. 18).

Finally, the proponents of regime complexity hardly deny that more powerful states have bigger chances to avoid enforcement procedures that directly run against their interests. However, they also assume that the likelihood of such a behavior is rather low. During their ongoing participation in a regime complex, states (and corporations) may undergo a process of social learning (Struett et al., 2013; Ruggie, 2014). The involvement with a broad range of alternative perspectives within the global public sphere leads to a redefinition of self-interests which makes non-compliance morally at least less acceptable (Abbott, 2014: pp. 86–7).

All in all, it seems fair to say that the literature on regime complexity duly recognizes the influence of relational power, but also assumes that the blunt use of pressure politics can be mitigated by the dynamics of institutionalized cooperation among state and non-state actors at the international level. By this, regime complexes are not understood as a panacea for all global problems. In the absence of a centralized global coordination authority, it is nevertheless expected that they serve at least as a second-best option for the definition of GPGs, which can be judged to be a 'democratic advance – however far we may remain from any ideal' (Dryzek, 2012: p. 115).

However, the problem-solving orientation of the regime complexity literature as well as its functionalist underpinnings (Cohen and Cutler, 2013) make it difficult to address the more fundamental caveat of structural power. This notion had already been introduced by Susan Strange in the 1980s as a caution against the positive assessment of cooperation within the regime literature (Strange, 1982). In her later writings, Strange further elaborates on this concept. She hereby departs from Robert A. Dahl's mono-directional understanding of power as the 'successful attempt by "A" to get "a" to do something he would not otherwise do' (Dahl, 1957: p. 204, quotation marks added). Instead of an intentional interaction of two actors with relatively different power resources (Dahl, 1957), Strange defines power as 'simply the ability of a person or group of persons so to affect outcomes that their preferences take precedence over the preferences of others' (Strange, 1996: p. 17).

The conceptual expansion makes it possible for Strange to portray power as an abstract potential irrespective of its concrete manifestation, which enables her to argue that power also covers 'the indirect effect of authority on the context or surrounding conditions' of international negotiations (Strange, 1988: p. 23). Her understanding is inspired by the idea that actors observe each other and anticipate the potentials, attitudes, and possible courses of action of other fellow actors (Strange, 1996: p. 30). In her understanding, structural power hereby determines the 'rules of the game' and predefines the negotiable policy space (Verbeek, 2000a). That is why it is not necessary that power is directly and intentionally exerted to change the behavior of others. The mere expectation that the exertion of power might be possible suffices to channel the course of negotiations into a particular direction. Thus, international negotiations are inevitably characterized by a subliminal dominance of those actors who 'shape and determine the structures . . . within which other states, their political institutions, their economic enterprises and (not least) their scientists and other professional people have to operate' (Strange, 1988: pp. 24–5). These dynamics can only become visible if researchers do not exclusively focus on the actual outcome of trans- and international negotiations but remain sensitive to potentially unarticulated claims (Strange, 1982: p. 480).

Strange's understanding of power is in line with the literature on regulatory competition, which argues that states and corporations formulate their preferences in the light of those of the most important markets (Genschel and Plümper, 1997). Asymmetric interdependence, so it is argued, improves the bargaining position of those actors which have less to lose from withdrawal and an eventual failure of cooperation (Newman and Posner, 2010: p. 590). To influence the more dependent actors, there is no necessity for powerful actors to explicitly refer to their 'exit power' (Oberthür and Rabitz, 2014: p. 43). As long as the opportunity costs of non-cooperation outweigh the negative consequences of an agreement, weaker actors can be expected to adapt their preferences ex ante to those of the more powerful negotiation partners (Hirschman, 1969: p. 24), because they anticipate potentially negative repercussions of non-cooperation and therefore avoid obviously unrealistic alternatives (Wiener, 2001: pp. 467–8).

Although both Strange's conceptualization of structural power and the literature on regulatory competition remain essentially state-centric (Cowles, 2003: p. 103), their critique can easily be transferred to the horizontally and vertically integrated institutionalization in regime complexes. There is no reason to believe that the dynamics of mutual anticipations and ex ante adaptations should be exclusively limited to state actors (Verbeek, 2000b). Actually, Strange already admits that 'social groups, enterprises and organizations' are affected by structural power imbalances

(Strange, 1988: p. 24). From this observation, it is only one step further to conceptualize non-state actors as potential agents. Against this backdrop, it can be assumed that structural power has a significant impact on the (1) definition, (2) production, and (3) implementation of GPGs in regime complexes.

1. Most notably for non-state actors, the literature assumes that their potential to influence the course of a regime complex depends on the capability to provide 'usable knowledge' (Haas, 2004). If this holds true, they can be expected to make their claims palatable for structurally powerful, but recalcitrant negotiation partners. As they anticipate potentially damaging connotations, inferior actors will refrain from demands which might lower their influence chances. This form of self-censoring, however, already narrows the 'deliberative capacity' (Kuyper, 2014) of regime complexes. Instead, it can be assumed that '"constructive ambiguities" are sought to accommodate the widest possible range of positions' (Stevenson and Dryzek, 2012: p. 8).
2. When devising specific policy instruments and the degree of their bindingness, decision-makers can be assumed to reflect upon the acceptance of specific regulations among the relevant stakeholders. Implicitly, structurally dominant actors determine the 'range of options . . ., thus making it less easy to make some choices while making it more easy to make others' (Strange, 1988: p. 31). The common desire to advance in a particular issue creates a 'joint decision-trap', in which suboptimal outcomes take precedence over the risk of inconclusiveness (Scharpf, 1988: p. 271). All negotiators can plausibly be assumed to opt for policy alternatives which are acceptable for the structurally dominant actors (even if they are absent) and to acquiesce to negative externalities for those actors whose dissent will not negatively affect the feasibility of the chosen approach. The complexity of the negotiation structure makes this strategy even more attractive, because it helps to disguise co-responsibility in the case of later protests (Scharpf, 1988: p. 270).
3. As already described, many scholars perceive the (initially) low threshold of compliance obligations as one of the crucial success factors for the initial participation in regime complexes. If this holds true, it can be assumed that the selective compliance of structurally dominant states will be carefully observed or even anticipated by less powerful states and their domestic constituencies. They thus can be expected to refrain from implementation options which might be normatively desirable but create a competitive disadvantage vis-à-vis those states whose implementation course is more compatible with the preferences

of the structurally dominant states ('Delaware effect', see Genschel and Plümper, 1997: p. 640).

Against this background, it becomes highly questionable whether regime complexes necessarily stimulate the creation of GPGs. If structural power is taken into account, the deliberative character of the negotiations becomes rather debatable, and it seems that internationally institutionalized cooperation is more likely to produce globalized 'club goods' whose utility is limited to an elitist group of structurally dominant actors.[2] By this, regime complexes can be assumed to 'exclude hidden agendas and . . . leave unheard or unheeded complaints, whether they come from the underprivileged, the disfranchised or the unborn, about the way the system works' (Strange, 1982: p. 480).

4. CONTRACTION DESPITE COMPLEXITY: THE IMPACT OF STRUCTURAL POWER

To illustrate the impact of structural power, the chapter re-examines the RCB.[3] For the argument of the chapter, the RCB can be regarded as a least likely case (Odell, 2001: pp. 165–6), because it is frequently deemed to be the most advanced example of internationally institutionalized cooperation, whose complexity facilitates an outstandingly high participation of non-state actors (Morin and Orsini, 2011; Miller, 2007: pp. 341–2). If already the RCB is characterized by structural power imbalances and exploitative tendencies, it can be assumed that less institutionalized and inclusive regime complexes will display the same mechanisms to an even greater extent.

In essence, the RCB provides globally applicable rules and regulations to manage transnational transactions of genetic resources and hereto related traditional knowledge (GRTK). While the most valuable resources are held by indigenous and local communities in the provider states of the Global South,[4] their utilization predominantly takes place in the laboratories of life sciences and agricultural corporations in industrialized countries. The RCB defines the sustainable use of the world's biodiversity as a GPG whose preservation should be ensured by economic incentives. Alternative perspectives, which are rooted in the customary rights of indigenous communities, are by and large sidelined. The particular definitional scope of the public good can be explained by structurally unequal power relations during the recursively interwoven processes of problem definition, policy production, and implementation within the historical development of this regime complex.

4.1 The Foundation of the RCB in the 1980s and Early 1990s

The foundation of the RCB originates in the 1980s, when biotechnological research was spurred by a decision of the US Supreme Court to grant patents on biological material. Since then, governments in developing countries claimed financial compensation for the use of their biological resources (Raustiala and Victor, 2004: p. 289). They gained support from transnational environmental organizations who hoped for a more sustainable use of natural resources if their conservation became financially rewarded. This idea corresponded well with the major conclusions of the Brundtland Report (World Commission on Environment and Development, 1987), in which the World Commission on Environment and Development (WCED) recommended a holistic approach to reconcile economic, developmental, social, and environmental policies on a global scale. The UN Environment and Development secretariat pressured strongly for a globally binding agreement. It enjoyed the technical, personal, and financial support of the Business Council for Sustainable Development (BCSD), which was intensively involved with the pre-negotiations for the 1992 Earth Summit in Rio de Janeiro (Doran, 1993). Indigenous communities, on the other hand, were not directly admitted to participate at these meetings and the concluding summit. Although they organized parallel conference sessions, they did not have the financial means to ensure the participation of indigenous actors beyond the Latin American context. Moreover, a meaningful participation appeared hardly possible because they were not acquainted with the formal procedures and diplomatic conventions of international negotiations (Wold, 1993).

Pressured by transnational non-governmental organizations (NGOs), international organizations, and developing countries, industrialized countries nevertheless conceded that the exchange of GRTK should be subjected to an international regime, although in a rather narrow and unspecific sense (Bastos, 2009: pp. 23–38). In the Convention on Biodiversity (CBD) (United Nations, 1992b), they agreed on the principle that biological resources fall under the sovereign rights of the states of origin (Götting, 2004; Liebig et al., 2002: p. 12). Any extraction becomes subject to 'fair and equitable access and benefit sharing' (ABS) among bioprospecting organizations and state authorities (CBD, Article 8). However, the Convention remains ambiguous with regard to the rights of the indigenous groups and local communities. Most notably, their claims for a self-determined use and disclosure were swept under the rug because they were at odds with the sovereignty perceptions of their national governments. At the same time, their demands for non-disclosure rights were at least tacitly rejected by the dominant environmental NGOs from industrialized countries (Price, 1994), because they collided with the prevailing concept of 'liberal environmentalism', which relies on market-based incentives for the sustainable use of natural resources (Zelli et al., 2013).

Spurred by these transnational environmental groups and the 'biodiplomacy' of developing countries, the principles of the CBD nevertheless spilled over to the negotiations within adjacent fields (Dutfield, 2001). Most notably, the negotiations on seed varieties gained new momentum (Rosendal, 2006). After protracted negotiations in the Food and Agriculture Organization (FAO), the International Treaty on Plant Genetic Resources for Food and Agriculture (2002) (ITPGRFA) (Food and Agriculture Organization, 2011) adopted the concepts of state sovereignty on biological material (Dutfield, 2001: pp. 263–6). Its lengthy negotiation phase, however, already indicates that industrialized countries still remained very reluctant to subscribe to potentially costly commitments. The US, for example, signed both the CBD and the ITPGRFA but has never become a party to these treaties. Its reluctance reflects the concerns of major transnational companies, which were afraid of additional costs for their bio-explorations in the Global South (Carr, 2008).

At the same time, however, the corporate sector fought for a stricter protection of its own innovations in developing and emerging countries. Lobbied by a broad range of industries, the US Trade Representative pushed for the global adoption of rigorous intellectual property standards to prevent 'piracy' in the developing world. US companies convinced their European counterparts to support this move (Drahos and Braithwaite, 2002: pp. 121–6). Together, the US and the European Union bypassed the World Intellectual Property Organization (WIPO). Although this organization had already been concerned with the negotiations on patents, copyrights, and other protective measures for intangible goods since the 1960s, the largest trade powers added intellectual property issues to the negotiation package of the General Agreement on Trade and Tariffs (GATT) Uruguay round in order to subsume them under the jurisdiction of the newly founded World Trade Organization (WTO) (see Sell, 2010).

Attracted by the (never fully realized) promise of a facilitated access to the US and European agricultural and textile markets (Cottier and Panizzon, 2004), developing countries ultimately subscribed to the WTO Agreement on Trade-related Aspects of Intellectual Property Rights (TRIPS). The agreement significantly limits their possibilities to reproduce the inventions from industrialized countries, but remains quite vague with regard to the protection of GRTK (Raustiala and Victor, 2004: pp. 290–91). While inventions based on GRTK are subjected to patent protection, the underlying resources do not enjoy any comparable kind of intellectual property protection. In the late 1990s, developing countries strongly criticized the unfairness of the WTO agreement. Supported by prominent activists like Vandana Shiva and vociferous civil society groups, they contrasted their own severe obligations to the rampant 'bio-piracy' in their own countries (Dutfield, 2001: pp. 235–6).

4.2 The Consolidation of the RCB in the Late 1990s and Early 2000s

The international debate did not remain without consequences, especially after the disaster of the WTO meeting in Seattle (Dutfield, 2001). Most notably, the WIPO perceived the debate on biodiversity as an opportunity to put itself back into play and initiated several fact-finding missions in cooperation with the CBD. It successfully proposed the establishment of the Intergovernmental Committee on Intellectual Property and Genetic Resources, Traditional Knowledge and Folklore (Straus and Klunker, 2007). The initiatives of the WIPO secretariat coincided with an increased attention of developing and emerging countries to the potential role of this forum. Led by Brazil and supported by developmentally oriented NGOs, southern countries formed the 'Group of Friends of Development', which vociferously claimed for a recalibration of the international intellectual property architecture to make it more compatible with the needs of the Southern periphery (May, 2006).

In operational terms, the WIPO focused on an amendment to the international patent classification system, which made it possible for patent offices in industrialized countries to recognize documented GRTK during the examination of patent applications (Dutfield, 2001: pp. 268–9). Provider countries like India actively supported this reform because it facilitated the economic exploitation of indigenous resources. But even industrialized countries which had not ratified the CBD felt under pressure to contribute, because they were aware that a reputation as 'bio-pirate' would endanger the position of their corporations in the provider states of GRTK (Carr, 2008). Most notably, the US has concluded an agreement with Indian authorities to consider the Indian Traditional Knowledge Digital Library (TKDL) as a source for patent examinations (Narula, 2014). The consequences for Indian Adivasis, however, remain completely neglected. Due to rising economic and conservationist utility of GRTK, bio-explorations have massively increased on the Indian soil, and the extraction of indigenous resources against their own will is one of the reasons for the many violent contestations in the Indian tribal belt (Drahos, 2014: pp. 159–62).

WIPO officials as well as the bureaucrats in related international organizations know from their interactions with indigenous actors that the interests of governments from developing countries may not necessarily coincide with the needs of their domestic groups (Interview 091; Interview 317). However, they do not support the claims of indigenous communities, because they anticipate that their demands would provoke the resistance of governments from industrialized and developing countries alike (Interview 115). Moreover, indigenous representatives' claims for a right not to disclose their knowledge collide with the interest of the WIPO to advance its role in international intellectual property regulations (Interview 202). The organization even tries to prevent the publication of its own reports, which might undermine its preference for a compromise between industrialized and developing countries to the detriment of indigenous communities (Tobin, 2014b: p. 167).

Most notably, WIPO diplomats try to circumvent the debate on a legally binding connection between international patent law and the provisions of the CBD, as it is demanded by Brazil and other Latin American countries. Although such an amendment would be technically feasible and even enjoys the support of some industrialized countries like Norway and Switzerland (Oberthür and Pożarowska, 2013: p. 112; Hufty et al., 2014), WIPO diplomats anticipate that mandatory compliance controls in the context of patent examinations, as they are demanded by countries like Brazil, would eventually deter diplomats from most industrialized countries and prevent particularly the US from further cooperation (Eimer and Schüren, 2013). The lack of these controls, however, undermines the protection of undocumented GRTK, because it is not possible to challenge patent applications for 'pirated' resources in foreign jurisdictions without any written evidence of the resources (Interview 044). At the same time, it stimulates governments in developing countries to document the GRTK of their indigenous peoples even against their will in order to attract investments from transnational life science corporations and to avoid competitive disadvantages for their own companies on the global market (Interview 449).

Since indigenous groups have recognized that their participation at the WIPO discussion rounds rather obscure the lack of any meaningful involvement (Interview 202), they draw on their comparably stronger position within the United Nations (UN) human rights system in order to make themselves heard (Helfer, 2003; Engle, 2010: pp. 67–8). Against the fierce resistance not only from industrialized countries (Corntassel, 2008), they have achieved that the UN Declaration on the Rights of Indigenous Peoples (2007) (United Nations, 2007) explicitly confers on them 'the right to maintain, control, protect and develop their cultural heritage, traditional knowledge and traditional cultural expressions' (Article 31(1)).

Although not legally binding, the UN declaration served as a reference point during the negotiations on the Nagoya Protocol of 2010

(United Nations, 2010), which aimed to concretize the repartition of benefits as prescribed by the CBD. Despite their massive involvement with the Nagoya negotiations, transnational environmental groups generally refrained from supporting indigenous claims. Instead, they decided to ally with industrialized countries in order to get through with their preferences for market-based environmental policies (Witter et al., 2015). In the end, the Nagoya Protocol mirrors the interests and norms of governments, life science companies, and the leading transnational environmental groups. Against the objections of indigenous groups and some emerging countries, it only stipulates that governments 'shall . . . take into consideration indigenous and local communities' customary laws' (Nagoya Protocol, Article 12), which remains far below the standards of the UN Declaration on Indigenous Rights (Drahos, 2014: pp. 80–85).

4.3 Current Development Trends of the RCB

At least for the moment, the Nagoya Protocol can be perceived as the most important cornerstone of the RCB (Oberthür and Pożarowska, 2013), because it loosely connects the UN human rights, the CBD/FAO biodiversity, and the WTO/WIPO intellectual property regimes. The lack of bindingness, however, makes it prone to selective implementation patterns. The European Union, for example, has decided not to consider indigenous rights as a part of its responsibility, and a binding nexus between patent examinations and the observation of indigenous customs seems to be out of reach for the time being (Tobin, 2014a). Against this background, emerging countries like Brazil have already initiated reforms to weaken their own protective measures for indigenous groups, because they are afraid that these regulations might negatively affect their competitive position vis-à-vis other provider states of GRTK (Interview 431; Interview 434). Other Latin American states are likely to follow this course, because they compete on the same international market as Brazil (Interview 433). The ongoing reforms in Brazil already indicate that the increased competition among the provider countries are likely to further undermine the rights of indigenous and local communities in the entire Global South, because the Nagoya Protocol has increased the economic attention towards GRTK both in developing and industrialized countries.

Moreover, the coalescence of environmental and economic regimes to the detriment of the human rights dimension seems to spill over into the climate protection regimes such as the UN Framework Convention for Climate Change (UNFCCC) (United Nations, 1992a). The use of GRTK becomes increasingly important in the context of Reducing Emissions from Deforestation and Forest Degradation (REDD) initiatives, which are orchestrated by the UNFCCC, the UN-REDD, and the World Bank (Thompson et al., 2011). In essence, REDD+ initiatives are based on the sustainable use of GRTK in the Global South in exchange for financial compensations from the side of carbon dioxide emitting companies. Indigenous communities are often negatively affected, because their informal and customary rights are threatened by the increased commodification of formerly neglected resources (Ciplet, 2014: pp. 83–7; Sobrevila, 2008: pp. 29–42). In many cases, the initiation of REDD+ programs has already led to their forceful eviction (Griffiths, 2006; Interview 450).

Despite these shortcomings, REDD+ initiatives enjoy the broad support of the involved international organizations, environmental NGOs, transnational companies, and governments of developing countries, because they connect environmental goals to the economic interests of corporations and national governments (Ciplet, 2014). In the context of international negotiations, the protests of indigenous actors are not completely ignored. However, their representatives suffer from a 'participation paradox': if they want to contribute to the negotiations, they must acquaint themselves with considerable legal and political expertise, which in turn makes other actors doubt their ability to speak on behalf of their communities (Brugnach et al., 2014). In the end, indigenous voices are only accepted if they support the prevailing technocratic discourse (Wallbott, 2014). By that, however, they have to give up their core demand of self-determination on the use of GRTK. Additionally, the already initiated REDD initiatives have led to local contestations which make it often practically impossible for indigenous representatives to devote their already scarce means to (most probably) fruitless discussions (Interview 303).

While it is certainly impossible to predict the future, it seems fair to say that the RCB is currently subject to two secular trends. On the one hand, its subject matter is significantly broadened by the merger with climate protection regimes. On the other hand, however, the expanded regime complex is very likely to further distance itself from indigenous and human rights regimes. At least from the perspective of the negatively affected societal groups, this shift will be experienced as a further move from liberal environmentalism towards environmental authoritarianism, which significantly increases the club good character of the global regulatory framework.

5. CONCLUSION

The empirical evidence of the last section suggests that regime complexity does not necessarily lead to more comprehensive policy solutions. While it confirms liberal assumptions that internationally institutionalized cooperation weakens the impact of relational power, it also corroborates the critical caveat that regime complexes are shaped by and even reinforce the already existing structural power imbalances.

At least in the empirical example, the coordinative efforts of international organizations and transnational actors make it more difficult for powerful states to exert direct and intentional pressure on weaker countries. As expected in the liberal literature, inter-organizational cooperation and transnational pressure prevents them from relying on blunt pressure politics. Their ability to shift negotiations to more favorable forums can at least be counterbalanced by the regime-shifting of weaker states, if they are supported by civil society groups and the self-interests of international bureaucracies. Moreover, the analysis of the RCB illustrates that the communication within regime complexes and the consultations within additional forums make it possible for all participants to acquaint themselves with alternative perspectives, although it seems that social learning mainly takes place among public officials in international organizations and (already to a more limited degree) representatives of transnational civil society groups.

But social learning does not necessarily provoke a re-prioritization of normative values. This already hints at the importance of mutual expectations on policy preferences, as argued in the critical literature. International bureaucrats and transnational civil society actors know that they have to accommodate the framing of their demands and the presentation of policy options to the interests of structurally dominant states and the interests of their corporations. Without any direct pressure, they chose a wording that is acceptable to this audience, which implies that they sort out those regulatory alternatives which appear practically infeasible in the light of the dominant power structures.

As Theodor W. Adorno famously stated, 'there is no true life within a false life' (Adorno, 1951: p. 59). Norm entrepreneurs are well aware that they have to refrain from certain ambitions if they want to realize anything at all. In the end, this may imply that they are willing to sacrifice certain values (for example, human rights) for the sake of progress in other fields (for example, environmental protection) even if they are aware of the devastating consequences for structurally excluded actors. This certainly limits the democratic aspirations which are at least implicitly associated with the emergence of internationally institutionalized means of coordination. The 'global agora' bears many similarities to a stockholders' meeting in which the mutual anticipation of negotiation powers determines the agenda, whereas potentially deviant discourses are structurally excluded from the outset. The same mechanisms are at play in the implementation of regime complexes. Weaker states observe and anticipate the selective compliance of the more powerful ones and adapt their own policy choices to these preferences in order to avoid competitive disadvantages, even if this leads to normatively undesirable results. The regulatory 'race to the bottom' weakens already marginalized interests and thereby reinforces the pre-existing power imbalances both between and within states, which further limits the available policy space for the future.

Eventually, regime complexes do not emerge out of a deliberative discourse but reconcile the interests of powerful states and their corporations with the well-intended middle-class concerns as expressed by civil society organizations mainly from industrialized countries. Their compromises, however, may lead to the dispossession of those actors whose consent is not needed for a commonly agreed solution. All in all, it seems that regime complexes do not produce GPGs, at least if the needs, values, and interests of marginalized actors are taken into account. Instead, they yield globalized club goods and expropriate those who are structurally excluded from their definition, production, and implementation.

Against this background, it seems that the literature on regime complexity should significantly broaden its research agenda. The prevailing focus on the status quo of existing regime complexes tends to obscure parts of the dynamics of their formation, because it disguises the underlying power structures. That is why 'non-decisions' (Bachrach and Baratz, 1962), 'non-regimes' (Strange, 1982), and contractive tendencies within regime complexes and other forms of global commons would deserve far more attention in order to understand the conditions under which the creation of globalized club goods effectively leads to the production of GPGs. If we attempt to explain comprehensiveness, we must learn more about its absence.

NOTES

* The research for this article was supported by the Fritz-Thyssen Foundation (Az. 50.15.0.023PO, July–August 2015) and the Deutsche Forschungsgemeinschaft (Project D 7, SFB 700 Governance in Areas of Limited Statehood, 2010–14). Two preliminary versions of this chapter have been presented at the International Public Policy Conference in Milan (T06PO5 Policy implementation, 1–4 July 2015) and at the International conference on Global Commons, Global Public Goods and Global Democracy in Leuven (22 and 23 February 2016). I am grateful for the comments of the participants of these conferences. Moreover, I would like to thank Kolar Aparna, Herman de Jonge, Joan van Heijster, Alex Lehr, Bertjan Verbeek, and Angela Wigger (Radboud University Nijmegen) as well as Kristin Rosendal (Fridtjof Nansen Institute, Norway), Martin Deleixhe, and Amandine Orsini (Université Saint-Louis, Bruxelles) for their critical remarks.

1. In the literature, the avoidance of negative externalities is understood as a special form of

a public good, because it prevents public harm to the benefit of mankind at large (Kaul et al., 1999: pp. 5–6).

2. In the literature, club goods are defined as 'impure public goods ... which possess partially rival benefits that can be excluded' (Sandler, 1999: p. 23).
3. The analysis is based on a reinterpretation of the secondary literature as well as on 136 interviews with state officials and diplomats from industrialized as well as developing and emerging countries, bureaucrats from international organizations, and societal actors (business, civil society, scientists), which were conducted in Geneva, Berlin, Brussels, Brazil, and India between 2007 and 2015. Most notably, the empirical material also includes conversations with indigenous actors and representatives of local communities which are directly affected by the policies of the regime complex without being represented in its decision-making procedures.
4. Most particularly in the context of this book, it would be tempting to characterize indigenous customary rules on GRTK as commons. Due to the variety of local practices, however, this would be an oversimplification. Property rights structures within indigenous groups are very complex and often defy the definitions of 'Western' scholars (Drahos, 2014). Having said this, it is fair to say that all indigenous spokespersons insist on the right of self-determination with regard to their resources (see also Cogolati and Wouters, Chapter 12 in this volume).

REFERENCES

Abbott, K. W. (2014) Strengthening the Transnational Regime Complex for Climate Change. *Transnational Environmental Law*, **3** (1), 57–88.

Abbott, K. W. and Snidal, D. (2010) International Regulation without International Government: Improving IO Performance through Orchestration. *The Review of International Organizations*, **5** (3), 315–44.

Adorno, T. W. (1951) *Minima Moralia: Reflexionen aus dem beschädigten Leben*. Frankfurt, Suhrkamp.

Alter, K. J. and Meunier, S. (2006) Nested and Overlapping Regimes in the Transatlantic Banana Trade Dispute. *Journal of European Public Policy*, **13** (3), 362–82.

Bachrach, P. and Baratz, M. S. (1962) Two Faces of Power. *The American Political Science Review*, **56** (4), 947–52.

Barnett, M. N. and Finnemore, M. (1999) The Politics, Power, and Pathologies of International Organizations. *International Organization*, **53** (4), 699–732.

Bastos, R. Z. (2009) Rivalités géopolitiques sur la biodiversité, l'enjeu de régulation de l'accès aux ressources génétiques au Brésil. Doctoral thesis, Paris.

Beck, U. (1986) *Risikogesellschaft: Auf dem Weg in eine andere Moderne*. Frankfurt, Suhrkamp.

Bernstein, S. (2000) Ideas, Social Structure and the Compromise of Liberal Environmentalism. *European Journal of International Relations*, **6** (4), 464–512.

Betts, A. (2009) Institutional Proliferation and the Global Refugee Regime. *Perspectives on Politics*, **7** (1), 53–8.

Brugnach, M., Craps, M. and Dewulf, A. (2014) Including Indigenous Peoples in Climate Change Mitigation: Addressing Issues of Scale, Knowledge and Power. *Climatic Change*, (2014), 1–14.

Carr, J. (2008) Agreements that Divide: TRIPS vs. CBD and Proposals for Mandatory Disclosure of Source and Origin of Genetic Resources in Patent Applications. *Journal of Transnational Law and Policy*, **18**, 131–54.

Castells, M. (2008) The New Public Sphere: Global Civil Society, Communication Networks, and Global Governance. *The ANNALS of the American Academy of Political and Social Science*, **616** (1), 78–93.

Chayes, A. and Chayes, A. H. (1993) On Compliance. *International Organization*, **42** (2), 175–205.

Ciplet, D. (2014) Contesting Climate Injustice: Transnational Advocacy Network Struggles for Rights in UN Climate Politics. *Global Environmental Politics*, **14** (4), 75–97.

Coase, R. H. (1960) The Problem of Social Cost. *Journal of Law and Economics*, **3**, 1–44.

Cohen, E. S. and Cutler, C. (2013) Law, Contestation and Power in the Global Political Economy: An Introduction. *Oñati Socio-Legal Series*, **3** (4), 611–21.

Corntassel, J. (2008) Toward Sustainable Self-determination: Rethinking the Contemporary Indigenous-rights Discourse. *Alternatives: Global, Local, Political*, **33** (1), 105–32.

Cottier, T. and Panizzon, M. (2004) Legal Perspectives on Traditional Knowledge: The Case for Intellectual Property Protection. *Journal of International Economic Law*, **7** (2), 371–400.

Cowles, M. (2003) Non-state Actors and False Dichotomies: Reviewing IR/IPE Approaches to European Integration. *Journal of European Public Policy*, **10** (1), 102–20.

Dahl, R. A. (1957) The Concept of Power. *Behavioral Science*, **2** (3), 201–15.

Doran, P. (1993) The Earth Summit (UNCED): Ecology as Spectacle. *Global Society: Journal of Interdisciplinary International Relations*, **7** (1), 55–65.

Drahos, P. (2014) *Intellectual Property, Indigenous People and their Knowledge*. Cambridge, Cambridge University Press.

Drahos, P. and Braithwaite, J. (2002) *Information Feudalism*. London, Earthscan.

Drezner, D. W. (2005) Globalization, Harmonization, and Competition: The Different Pathways to Policy Convergence. *Journal of European Public Policy*, **12** (5), 841–59.

Drezner, D. W. (2009) The Power and Peril of International Regime Complexity. *Perspectives on Politics*, **7**, 65–70.

Dryzek, J. S. (2012) Global Civil Society: The Progress of Post Westphalian Politics. *Annual Review of Political Science*, **15**, 101–19.

Dutfield, G. (2001) TRIPS-related Aspects of Traditional Knowledge. *Case Western Reserve Journal of International Law*, **33**, 233–75.

Eimer, T. R. and Schüren, V. (2013) Convenient Stalemates: Why International Patent Law Negotiations Continue Despite Deadlock. *New Political Economy*, **18** (4), 533–54.

Engle, K. (2010) *The Elusive Promise of Indigenous Development*. Durham, Duke University Press.

Food and Agriculture Organization. (2011) International Treaty on Plant Genetic Resources for Food and Agriculture. Madrid, 3 November 2011. United Nations Treaty Series, 2400 (303).

Genschel, P. and Plümper, T. (1997) Regulatory Competition and International Cooperation. *Journal of European Public Policy*, **4** (4), 626–42.

Gilpin, R. (2001) *Global Political Economy: Understanding the International Economic Order*. Princeton, Princeton University Press.

Götting, H.-P. (2004) Biodiversität und Patentrecht. *GRURInt*, **9**, 731–6.

Grieco, J. M. (1988) Realist Theory and the Problem of International Cooperation:

Analysis with an Amended Prisoner's Dilemma Model. *The Journal of Politics*, **50** (3), 600–624.
Griffiths, T. (2006) *The Global Environment Facility and its Local Benefits Study: A Critique*. Cape Town, Forest Peoples Programme.
Haas, P. M. (1992) Introduction: Epistemic Communities and International Policy Coordination. *International Organization*, **46** (1), 1–35.
Haas, P. M. (2004) When Does Power Listen To Truth? A Constructivist Approach to the Policy Process. *Journal of European Public Policy*, **11** (4), 569–92.
Held, D. (2003) From Executive to Cosmopolitan Multilateralism. In: Held, D. and Koenig-Archibugi, M. (eds) *Taming Globalization: Frontiers of Governance*. Oxford, Polity Press, pp. 160–86.
Helfer, L. R. (2003) Human Rights and Intellectual Property: Conflict or Coexistence? *Minnesota Intellectual Property Review*, **5** (1), 47–61.
Helfer, L. R. (2004) Regime Shifting: The TRIPS Agreement and New Dynamics of International Intellectual Property Lawmaking. *The Yale Journal of International Law*, **29** (1), 1–83.
Hirschman, A. O. (1969) *National Power and the Structure of Foreign Trade*. Oakland, University of California Press.
Hufty, M., Schulz, T. and Tschopp, M. (2014) The Role of Switzerland in the Nagoya Protocol Negotiations. In: Oberthür, S. and Rosendal, G. K. (eds) *Access to and Benefit-sharing after the Nagoya Protocol*. London, Routledge, pp. 96–112.
Interview 044: Brazilian diplomat, 31 July 2007, Geneva.
Interview 091: Official of the World Intellectual Property Organization (WIPO), 15 July 2010, Geneva.
Interview 115: Official of the United Nations Conference on Trade and Development, 16 September 2010, Geneva.
Interview 202: Representative of an indigenous community, 18 August 2011, Brasília.
Interview 303: Adivasi representative, 18 February 2012, Maheshmunda, Jharkand, India.
Interview 317: Representative of the United Nations Development Program, 27 February 2012, New Delhi.
Interview 431: Representative of a Brazilian civil society organization, 23 July 2015, Brasília.
Interview 433: Representative if the Brazilian pharmaceutical industry, 28 July 2015, Brasília.
Interview 434: Representative of the Brazilian public prosecution department, 28 July 2015, Brasília.
Interview 449: Representative of the Law Society of Matto Grosso (Brazil), 10 August 2015, Campo Grande.
Interview 450: Representative of the Brazilian rubber tappers movement, 12 August 2015, Manaus.
Katzenstein, P. J. (1978) Introduction: Domestic and International Forces and Strategies of Foreign Economic Policy. In: Katzenstein, P. J. (ed.) *Between Power and Plenty: Foreign Economic Policies of Advanced Industrial States*. Madison, The University of Wisconsin Press, pp. 3–22.
Kaul, I., Grunberg, I. and Stern, M. A. (1999) Defining Public Goods. In: Kaul, I., Grunberg, I. and Stern, M. A. (eds) *Global Public Goods: International Cooperation in the 21st Century*. Oxford, Oxford University Press, pp. 1–19.

Keck, M. E. and Sikkink, K. (1998) *Activists Beyond Borders: Advocacy Networks in International Politics*. Ithaca, Cornell University Press.
Keeley, J. F. (1990) Toward a Foucauldian Analysis of International Regimes. *International Organization*, **44** (1), 83–105.
Kennedy, S. (2007), Transnational Political Alliances. An Exploration with Evidence from China. *Business and Society*, **46** (2), 174–200.
Keohane O. R. and Victor, D. G. (2011) The Regime Complex for Climate Change. *Perspectives on Politics*, **9** (1), 7–23.
Keohane, R. O., Macedo, S. and Moravcsik, A. (2009) Democracy-enhancing Multilateralism. *International Organization*, **63**, 1–31.
Kersbergen, K. and Verbeek, B. (2007) The Politics of International Norms: Subsidiarity and the Imperfect Competence Regime of the European Union. *European Journal of International Relations*, **13** (2), 217–38.
Krasner, S. D. (1983) Structural Causes and Regime Consequences: Regimes as Intervening Variables. In: Krasner, S. D. (ed.) *International Regimes*. Ithaca, Cornell University Press, pp. 1–22.
Kuyper, J. W. (2014) Global Democratization and International Regime Complexity. *European Journal of International Relations*, **20** (3), 620–46.
Levy, M. A., Young, O. R. and Zürn, M. (1995) The Study of International Regimes. *European Journal of International Relations*, **1** (3), 267–330.
Liebig, K., Alker, D., Chih, K., Horn, D., Illi, H. and Wolf, J. (2002) Governing Biodiversity. Access to Genetic Resources and Approaches to Obtaining Benefits from their Use: The Case of the Philippines, GDI Working Papers 5, 87.
Martin, L. L. and Simmons, B. A. (1998) Theory and Empirical Studies of International Institutions. *International Organization*, **52** (4), 729–57.
May, C. (2006) The World Intellectual Property Organization. *New Political Economy*, **11** (3), 435–45.
Miller, C. A. (2007) Democratization, International Knowledge Institutions, and Global Governance. *Governance*, **20** (2), 325–57.
Morin, J.-F. and Orsini, A. (2011) Linking Regime Complexity to Policy Coherency: The Case of Genetic Resources. GR:EEN Working Paper Series No. 15.
Morin, J.-F. and Orsini, A. (2013) Regime Complexity and Policy Coherency: Introducing a Co-adjustments Model. *Global Governance*, **19** (1), 41–51.
Morin, J.-F. and Orsini, A. (2014) Policy Coherency and Regime Complexes: The Case of Genetic Resources. *Review of International Studies*, **40** (2), 303–24.
Nanz, P. and Steffek, J. (2004) Global Governance, Participation and the Public Sphere. *Government and Opposition*, **39** (2), 314–35.
Narula, M. (2014) Impact of Indian Patent Law on Traditional Knowledge. *International Journal of Advanced Research in Management and Social Sciences*, **3** (6), 40–58.
Newman, A. and Posner, E. (2010) International Interdependence and Regulatory Power: Authority, Mobility, and Markets. *European Journal of International Relations*, **17** (4), 589–610.
Oberthür, S. and Pożarowska, J. (2013) Managing Institutional Complexity and Fragmentation: The Nagoya Protocol and the Global Governance of Genetic Resources. *Global Environmental Politics*, **13** (3), 100–118.
Oberthür, S. and Rabitz, F. (2014) On the EU's Performance and Leadership in Global Environmental Governance: The Case of the Nagoya Protocol. *Journal of European Public Policy*, **21** (1), 39–57.

Odell, J. S. (2001) Case Study Methods in International Political Economy. *International Studies Perspectives*, **2** (2), 161–76.
Olson, M. (1968) *Die Logik des kollektiven Handelns: Kollektivgüter und die Theorie der Gruppen*. Tübingen, Mohr Siebeck.
Orsini, A., Morin, J.-F. and Young, O. R. (2013) Regime Complexes: A Buzz, a Boom, or a Boost for Global Governance? *Global Governance*, **19** (1), 27–39.
Ostrom, E. (1999) Beyond Markets and States: Polycentric Governance of Complex Economic Systems. [Online] Available from: https://www.nobelprize.org/nobel_prizes/economic-sciences/laureates/2009/ostrom-lecture.html (accessed 11 June 2017).
Price, M. (1994) Ecopolitics and Environmental Nongovernmental Organizations in Latin America. *Geographical Review*, **84** (1), 42–58.
Putnam, R. D. (1973) The Political Attitudes of Senior Civil Servants in Western Europe: A Preliminary Report. *British Journal of Political Science*, **3** (3), 257–90.
Raustiala, K. and Victor, D. G. (2004) The Regime Complex for Plant Genetic Resources. *International Organization*, **58** (2), 277–309.
Rosenau, J. N. (1997) *Along the Domestic Frontier: Exploring Governance in a Turbulent World*. Cambridge, Cambridge University Press.
Rosendal, G. K. (2006) Balancing Access and Benefit Sharing and Legal Protection of Innovations from Bioprospecting: Impacts on Conservation of Biodiversity. *The Journal of Environmental Development*, **15** (4), 428–47.
Ruggie, J. (2014) Global Governance and 'New Governance Theory': Lessons from Business and Human Rights. *Global Governance*, **20** (1), 5–17.
Sandler, T. (1999) Intergenerational Public Goods: Strategies, Efficiency and Institutions. In: Kaul, I., Grunberg, I. and Stern, M. A. (eds) *Global Public Goods: International Cooperation in the 21st Century*. Oxford, Oxford University Press, pp. 20–50.
Scharpf, F. W. (1988) The Joint Decision Trap: Lessons from German Federalism and European Integration. *Public Administration*, **66** (2), 239–78.
Scharpf, F. W. (1993) Coordination in Hierarchies and Networks. In: Scharpf, F. W. (ed.) *Games in Hierarchies and Networks: Analytical and Empirical Approaches to the Study of Governance Institutions*. Frankfurt, Campus, pp. 125–66.
Sell, S. (2000) Structures, Agents and Institutions. In: Higgott, R. A., Underhill, G. R. D. and Bieler, A. (eds) *Non-state Actors and Authority in the Global System*. London: Routledge, pp. 74–90.
Sell, S. K. (2010) Cat and Mouse: Forum Shifting in the Battle over Intellectual Property Enforcement, paper presented at Transnational Copyright: Organization, Mobilisation and Law, Lake Como, Italy.
Sobrevila, C. (2008) *The Role of Indigenous Peoples in Biodiversity Conservation: The Natural but Often Forgotten Partners*. Washington, The World Bank.
Stein, A. A. (1982) Coordination and Collaboration: Regimes in an Anarchic World. *International Organization*, **36** (2), 299–324.
Stevenson, H. and Dryzek, J. S. (2012) The Discursive Democratisation of Global Climate Governance. *Environmental Politics*, **21** (2), 189–210.
Stone, D. (2008) Global Public Policy, Transnational Policy Communities, and their Networks. *The Policy Studies Journal*, **36** (1), 19–38.
Strange, S. (1982) Cave! Hic dragones: A Critique of Regime Analysis. *International Organization*, **36** (2), 479–96.
Strange, S. (1988) *States and Markets*. London, Pinter Publishers.

Strange, S. (1996) *The Retreat of the State: The Diffusion of Power in the World Economy*. Cambridge, Cambridge University Press.

Straus, J. and Klunker, N. S. (2007) Harmonisierung des internationalen Patentrechts. *GRURInt*, **56** (2), 91–104.

Struett, M. J., Nance, M. T. and Armstrong, D. (2013) Navigating the Maritime Piracy Regime Complex. *Global Governance*, **19** (1), 93–104.

Terhalle, M. (2016) Transnational Actors and Great Powers during Order Transition. *International Studies Perspectives*, **17** (3), 287–306.

Thompson, M. C., Baruah, M. and Carr, E. R. (2011) Seeing REDD+ as a Project of Environmental Governance by Environmental Sciences. *Environmental Science Policy*, **14** (2), 100–110.

Tobin, B. M. (2014a) Biopiracy by Law: European Union Draft Law Threatens Indigenous Peoples' Rights over Their Traditional Knowledge and Genetic Resources. *European Intellectual Property Review*, **36** (2), 124–36.

Tobin, B. M. (2014b) *Indigenous Peoples, Customary Law and Human Rights – Why Living Law Matters*. London and New York, Earthscan Routledge.

United Nations (1992b) Convention on Biological Diversity. Rio de Janeiro, 5 June 1992. United Nations Treaty Series, 1760 (79).

United Nations (1992a) United Nations Framework Convention on Climate Change. New York, 4 June 1992. United Nations Treaty Series, 1771 (107).

United Nations (2007) Declaration on the Rights of Indigenous Peoples. GA Res. 61/295. 13 September 2007, UN Doc. A/61/53.

United Nations (2010) Nagoya Protocol on Access to Genetic Resources and the Fair and Equitable Sharing of Benefits Arising from their Utilization to the Convention on Biological Diversity. Nagoya, 29 October 2010, UN Doc UNEP/CBD/COP/DEC/X/1.

Verbeek, B. (2000a) Criticizing US Method and Thought in International Relations: Why a Trans-Atlantic Divide Narrows IR's Research Subject. In: Lawton, T. C., Rosenau, J. N. and Verdun, A. C. (eds) *Strange Power: Shaping the Parameters of International Relations and International Political Economy*. Aldershot, Ashgate, pp. 139–57.

Verbeek, B. (2000b) Susan Strange als wegbereider van de Internationale Politieke Economie. *Vrede en Veiligheid*, **2**, 211–27.

Wallbott, L. (2014) Indigenous Peoples in UN Redd+ Negotiations: 'Importing Power' and Lobbying for Rights through Discursive Interplay Management. *Ecology and Society*, **19** (1), 21–35.

Wiener, J. (2001) Globalization and Disciplinary Neoliberal Governance. *Constellations*, **8** (4), 461–79.

Witter, R., Suiseeya, K. R. M., Gruby, R. L., Hitchner, S., Maclin, E. M., Bourque, M. and Brosius, J. P. (2015) Moments of Influence in Global Environmental Governance. *Environmental Politics*, **24** (6), 894–912.

Wold, C. (1993) An Earth Parliament for Indigenous Peoples: Investigating Alternative World Governance. *Colorado Journal of International Environmental Law and Policy*, **4**, 197–215.

World Commission on Environment and Development (WCED) (1987) *Our Common Future*. Oxford, Oxford University Press.

Young, O. R. (1999) Regime Effectiveness: Taking Stock. In: Young O. R. (ed.) *The Effectiveness of International Environmental Regimes: Causal Connections and Behavioral Mechanisms*. Cambridge, MIT Press, pp. 249–80.

Zelli, F., Gupta, A. and van Asselt, H. (2013) Institutional Interactions at the Crossroads of Trade and Environment: The Dominance of Liberal Environmentalism? *Global Governance: A Review of Multilateralism and International Organizations*, **19** (1), 105–18.

9. Knowledge commons and global governance of academic publishing

Maarja Beerkens

1. INTRODUCTION

The issue of open access to scientific research has become a prominent policy topic over the last decade in Europe, in the United States (US) and in many Western and non-Western countries. Although countries attempt to address the issue within their national boundaries, it is increasingly clear that scientific publishing is a global industry and regulating it within national borders can have, at most, only a limited success. We can observe increasing international coordination emerging in the field. In 2011, the United Nations Educational, Scientific and Cultural Organization (UNESCO) adopted a strategy for promoting open access in the world (UNESCO, 2011). A decade earlier, in 2004, the science and technology ministers of the Organisation for Economic Co-operation and Development (OECD) countries agreed on the Declaration of Access to Research Data from Public Funding (OECD, 2007). The European Commission (EC) issued a 'soft law' instrument on the issue, the 'Commission recommendation of 17.7.2012 on access to and preservation of scientific information' (European Commission, 2012). Despite all the initiatives, however, the transition towards open access is often judged as disappointingly slow (for example, JISC, 2016).

The strive for open access has become a 'typical' global governance challenge with hundreds of actors involved, different entangled narratives and norms, and various policy solutions competing for attention. The terms 'public good' and 'commons' come up often in the discussions on knowledge and research, sometimes in a neutral sense, often as a normative statement, and occasionally as a 'battle cry' (Hess and Ostrom, 2007: p. 14) to justify a desired course of action. The phrasing matters, though, as it determines not only the definition of the problem but also the menu of possible solutions. While the 'public good' angle tends to focus on the right balance between sharing knowledge and protecting it via intellectual property rights, a framework of 'commons' inspires to seek out an alternative, more inclusive and community-based governance system for academic knowledge. The aim of this chapter is twofold. We will examine the use of the concepts 'public good' and the 'commons' in addressing the issue of restricted access to knowledge. Secondly, we will analyse the challenge for open access as a collective action dilemma on the global arena, and we will evaluate the potential for replacing the current market-based structure of academic publishing with a self-governing system organized by a global (academic) community, as increasingly proposed within academia.

2. THE ISSUE OF OPEN ACCESS

Proponents of open access aim to reach a situation where academic knowledge is freely accessible to all people. Currently, access to academic publications is highly restricted. Most scholarly journals are owned by commercial publishing corporations, such as Elsevier, Taylor and Francis, or Wiley. Publications in these journals are available only after paying a fee for subscription or for a specific article, and these fees are prohibitively high for individual users and increasingly burdensome to institutional subscribers. This has created a paradoxical situation where academic research to a large extent is paid for by taxpayers, yet taxpayers have no access to the results that they have paid for. Furthermore, research results are an outcome of a long 'production chain' where a university (or another research organization), researcher, funder and publisher all play a part. Yet the last investor in the chain, the publisher, claims the property rights to this work even though its own investment relative to full costs of the entire research process tend to be very small (Willinsky, 2005). While the current publishing model has been serving the academic community and the society for many years, technological developments around academic publishing, as well as substantial changes within the publishing industry have made the model now highly questionable.

Several developments contribute to the current controversy. Most importantly, new technology has changed the nature of academic publishing. Journals are now distributed primarily online, not on paper, which considerably reduces publishing costs (that is, printing and distribution costs). Considering that authoring an article and peer review are usually a voluntary contribution to the journal, actual costs of a published article are quite low. This, however, conflicts with increasing subscription fees that libraries face, so that even the best endowed libraries struggle with paying the fees and are forced to cut subscriptions (Suber, 2012). Technological change is not the only reason for dissatisfaction with the current system. Thornton and Ocasio's (1999) rigorous historical study of the higher education publishing industry demonstrates how the industry itself has changed, particularly from the 1980s onwards. What used to be a craft industry characterized by relatively small, often family based firms, and based on editorial professionalism, grew rapidly into a corporate structure characterized by a strong orientation towards profit and towards growth by acquisitions. Academic publishing has indeed become a highly profitable business. Profits of major publishers reach up to 30 per cent, exceeding those in most other sectors (Suber, 2012). Such profit margins, along with increasing costs for subscribers, have created a feeling that something is not quite right in how the market of academic publishing performs.

Arguments for open access are diverse, representing different values and emphases: societal and scientific impact, (global) equality, distributional fairness, and economic efficiency, among others (for example, Finch, 2012; Swan, 2012). Restricted access to research can limit quality and speed of scientific progress. Developing countries are particularly sensitive to the high price barrier, which reduces not only the potential use of research results but also limits their ability to contribute to science (Swan, 2012). Furthermore, high subscription fees limit access to research particularly for societal groups outside of academia, including small and medium size enterprises, which seriously inhibits the societal impact of research. There is also a distributional fairness argument. As mentioned above, much of the academic research is funded by taxpayers, yet it is not accessible to them. Moreover, for some advocacy groups, 'openness' is a value of its own. Access to information, including scientific information, is about freedom and empowerment of people and it should not be restricted by commercial interests (see Open Knowledge Foundation, 2018; World Summit on Information Society, 2003). Last but not least, open access has become an issue of economic efficiency. The current coordination mechanism – that is, the market mechanism – seems to be failing. Increasing prices and high profit margins point to insufficient competition in the sector. An intervention may be needed, thus, to solve a market failure in this sector.

Over the past decade, many countries have made considerable steps towards open access. Some countries have even set specific targets, such as transition to full open access by 2024 in the Netherlands. There are, however, different trajectories towards the open access goal. The biggest divide is between the 'green' and the 'gold' route to open access, as originally presented by the Budapest declaration on open access (Budapest Open Access Initiative, 2002). 'Green' open access means that researchers make their published work open in designated repositories offered by universities or other research organizations, usually after a limited embargo period imposed by the publisher. This model has spread widely in recent years and a great many universities require their staff to submit their published work into the repository. Many research foundations (including the Horizon 2020 programme of the EC (European Commission, 2013)) require that work funded by their grant be made openly accessible *at least* through repositories.

'Golden' open access on the other hand requires that an article within a scholarly journal is publicly available free of charge in the journal itself. Usually this means that the author pays to the publisher the 'article processing charge' (APC), to compensate the lost income to the publisher. Some journals have switched entirely to the APC-based model. Numerous open access journals have been created in recent years all over the world, both of excellent and of dubious quality. The new unsettled market has created a need for some 'consumer protection' against predatory journals, such as the Directory of Open Access Journals (DOAJ). Next to fully open access journals, many traditional journals have switched to a 'hybrid mode', offering to their authors an opportunity to make their article openly accessible for a fee. This option seems attractive because it promises open access without asking authors to change their publishing preferences, but it has created much controversy due to the issue of 'double dipping'. In this model, the publisher benefits from the APC but the publisher does not lower their subscription price to the universities contributing the charge, so publishers get paid twice and universities (or funders) need to pay twice. Most recently, a 'diamond' open access model has been introduced whereby a journal is openly accessible and no APCs are imposed on authors, and the costs related to publishing are carried by a scholarly society, a fund or an institution.

Different countries lean towards different models of open access. In the last few years, the United Kingdom (UK) and the Netherlands have become the forerunners in the area and both are committed to the 'gold' open access. Both countries attempt to influence the entire academic publishing industry and bring down the publishing costs through transparent pricing. Some other countries have chosen the 'green route' and promote the use of repositories. Denmark, for example, is committed to this option because it sees itself as too small to be able to change the current commercial system (Adviesraad voor Wetenschap, Technologie en Innovatie, 2016). The most ambitious plan that is being promoted by some advocates of open access attempts to restructure entirely the current academic publishing industry. Instead of paying subscription fees to commercial publishers, libraries all over the world would pool their resources and use these funds to operate open access journals themselves, at an efficient cost level (see Schimmer et al., 2015). This is an intriguing idea that requires considerable coordination and cooperation activities at the international level.

Awareness about open access is spreading, policy options for addressing the issue are crystallizing, and a need for coordinated action on the global scale is becoming clearer. There is also increasing 'bottom-up' pressure to change the system. Within a few years more than 16,000 academics all over the world have joined the boycott against the biggest publisher, Elsevier.[1] Private donor money has supported initiatives to circumvent commercial publishers in academic publishing, such as Andrew W. Mellon Foundation's support to Open Humanities Library. Before zooming in to the governance challenges at the national and international level, the next section will first analyse the concepts of 'public goods' and 'commons', as relevant to the open access issue.

3. ACADEMIC KNOWLEDGE AS A 'PUBLIC GOOD' AND A 'COMMONS'

Knowledge has been presented as a 'public good' and a 'commons' both in conceptual discussions and in policy practice (Kaul et al., 2003; Stiglitz, 1999; Hess and Ostrom, 2007). The argument extends from a strictly economic definition of the terms to a more philosophical interpretation. According to welfare economics, a 'public good' is a good that is non-subtractable and non-excludable: individuals cannot be technically excluded from the good when the good is available, and using the good by one individual does not reduce its availability to others. Knowledge in the purest sense fulfils these two criteria. For example, once a theorem is made public, anyone can benefit from it; no one can be excluded from using it and its value will not decline with additional users (Stiglitz, 1999: p. 308). Public goods, from an economic perspective, tend to face the problem of being under-provided. The problems of relying on free market alone to create scientific knowledge can indeed be observed. No country leaves the production of scientific knowledge entirely to unregulated markets. In order to prevent under-production, states have created copyright rules, licencing and patenting opportunities, all of which are meant to remedy the non-excludability problem. Establishing property rights gives incentives for the private sector to supply knowledge. Even more importantly, governments step in also by directly paying for scientific knowledge, particularly in fundamental, non-applied sciences. Basic research in the world is, to a large extent, funded by government funds, and to a lesser extent also by private donations.

Furthermore, scientific research can be seen as a global and intergenerational public good. Its benefit extends beyond the borders of single countries and a present generation (Sandler, 1999). Since knowledge is a global public good (GPG), we might wonder why it is in the interest of one country to spend money on research when its benefits extend to other countries. Nation states invest a lot into their science systems, either out of responsibility, national identity, pride, solidarity or other norms. Science is usually respected and valued in its own right; it is a 'public good' not because it is non-excludable and subtractable, but because it is valued by the public beyond its instrumental, individual benefits (Deneulin and Townsend, 2007). Or perhaps the effect of knowledge production is contained within national borders after all, in order to justify the investments. Countries nowadays pay close attention to their Research and Development investments, which are believed to lead to economic growth, more jobs and higher income at the country level (see, for example, Europe 2020 (European Commission, 2010)). Although there are constant calls for more money for science, there is no clear indication of public under-investment in science. On the global scale, there may be inequality in science because knowledge relevant to developing countries (for example, in health research) may be underfunded (Bučar, 2012).

Joseph Stiglitz (1999), among others, sees the private vs. public provision of knowledge as an important dilemma. On the one hand, we can encourage private provision through stronger intellectual property rights. On the other hand, restricting access to knowledge may slow the pace of subsequent research and innovation. He particularly calls for ensuring widespread access to knowledge and avoiding exclusive rights to knowledge. Concerns over increasing privatization and enclosure of science have also encouraged thinking about knowledge as a 'public good' more broadly. Because of its accumulative nature, knowledge can be considered an 'intergenerational public good' (Sandler, 1999). The current pool of knowledge builds strongly on the investment of past generations, and the future knowledge is directly affected by our efforts now to maintain and advance the knowledge pool. This gives a greater responsibility for sustaining the knowledge pool, and it illustrates positive externalities of knowledge beyond its immediate benefits. The interdependency in knowledge production and its use leads to the idea of knowledge as 'a commons'.

In the classic article of Garrett Hardin (1968), a 'commons' refers to goods that are non-excludable but subtractable and, therefore, subject to the problem of overuse and depletion. Knowledge, strictly speaking, is the opposite of the 'commons' – it is excludable but non-subtractable. While in principle access to knowledge may be non-excludable, in practice access is restricted by subscription fees to published research. More importantly, it is a non-subtractable good and therefore not subject to the depletion problem. On the contrary, restricting access to the good by high price barriers causes welfare loss. Allowing free access to current non-users (for example, small and medium enterprises, researchers in poorer countries and institutions) would considerably increase social benefit with negligible added costs. Instead of the tragedy of commons related to knowledge commons, Heller (1998) argues that what we are faced with is a 'tragedy of anticommons', as we may be underusing scarce scientific resources because of excessive intellectual property rights.

It is important to distinguish between the notions of 'commons' as a 'common pool resource' and as a 'legal regime' where the 'commons' refers to commonly owned resources. Hess and Ostrom (2007) in their seminal book *Understanding Knowledge as a Commons*, link the intellectual history behind 'knowledge commons' to two different traditions. One, as also presented in Heller (1998), stems from the concern that information and knowledge are less and less 'commonly shared' because of increasing private property rights in the area. Another intellectual stream links the notion of 'commons' to its historical meaning, referring to 'shared spaces that allow for free speech and the democratic process, most notably the New England town commons' (p. 13). This other narrative emphasizes the inclusive nature of the world of science, where everybody is welcome to contribute, based on merit and the norms of science and collaboration for the benefit of all are valued.

As we will see below, the concepts of 'public good' and the 'commons' both appear in the policy documents on open access, especially in the early stages of the movement. The 'public good' framework has been helpful in questioning the right balance between market and hierarchy as a coordination instrument in this field. The 'commons' framework, however, can better explain the normative change related to academic knowledge as a shared resource and it drives an active search for an alternative, self-organizing mechanism by the community itself, beyond states and markets. Alongside these concepts, however, there is a 'competing' problem definition that drives action for open access, which needs to be discussed first. The market may be an inefficient coordination mechanism for academic publishing not because of the 'public' or 'common' nature of academic knowledge, but because the academic publishing industry has evolved, over the last few decades, into an oligopolistic market.

4. ACADEMIC KNOWLEDGE AND THE OLIGOPOLISTIC PUBLISHING MARKET

Most academic research is distributed by commercial publishers. From a theoretical perspective, market is an efficient coordination mechanism, assuming a fierce competition between different producers that pushes prices down close to the actual costs of producing the product. However, such a competition does not seem to be the case in the academic publishing industry. Although the industry consists of multiple publishers, the sector has been concentrating increasingly over recent years. The five biggest corporations – RELX Group (including Elsevier), Informa (including Taylor and Francis, Routledge), Springer Nature (including Springer, Palgrave Macmillan), Wiley-Blackwell, and Sage – publish the majority of all scientific articles. It has been reported that the total market share of the top five publishers has increased from 20 per cent in 1973 to 50 per cent in 2006 (Larivière et al., 2015) and the market has been concentrating rapidly since then. In the last few decades, several large-scale mergers have taken place within the sector. Some of the mergers have been subject to an investigation by competition authorities. The Office of Fair Trade (OFT) in the UK investigated the merger between Reed Elsevier and Harcourt in 2001. The OFT cleared the specific merger but the report pointed out that the publishing sector demonstrates some unusual characteristics and the sector as a whole needs to be investigated by a competition authority (UK Competition Commission, 2001). A follow-up investigation expressed a hope that the market will correct itself via new technology, but it warned that the sector should remain under scrutiny (Office of Fair Trade, 2002).

Market concentration within the sector seems to be pushing prices upwards, as expected. Between 1988 and 1998 Elsevier's journal prices more than tripled, after a merger with Pergamon Press (Nicholson, 2000). Non-competitive pricing is evidenced also in the fact that profit margins within the publishing industry exceed those in most other industries (Björk and Solomon, 2014). The price competition is limited also by other unique characteristics of the sector. Academic libraries are the main subscribers to scholarly journals. Libraries negotiate not over individual journals but over package deals, so called 'Big Deals'. Transparency is further reduced by non-disclosure agreements imposed by publishers, so libraries or consortia of libraries are not allowed to publicize the results of the negotiations. Since academic journals tend to be unique and not easily substitutable with another journal in the field, the competition between journals, in any case, is limited. When a publisher holds a significant share of the academic publishing market, like in the case of Elsevier, its market position is very strong, as libraries cannot easily opt out from the deal. Only very recently the restrictions to such information are starting to crumble. In 2016, universities in the Netherlands were obliged to publicize the amount of money they spend on buying books and journals, making use of the Dutch Public Access to Information Act ('Wet Openbaarheid Bestuur' in Dutch).

The lack of transparent pricing also extends to APCs in hybrid journals. Björk and Solomon (2014) show that the APCs in hybrid journals are almost twice as high as in journals that started off as open access journals. Many advocates see a transparent and competitive price mechanism as the primary goal of the open access initiative. In this line of reasoning, the key problem in academic publishing is not a market-based system per se, but the lack of a competitive market due to information scarcity and limited competition between providers.

In sum, there seems to be a lack of competition in the academic publishing market and a few publishers have taken an oligopolistic position. Economic theory suggests a few options for governments to address an oligopoly problem. Antitrust law offers ways to control anti-competitive behaviour among providers and, if necessary, intervene in the market structure, by regulating mergers and acquisitions. There is also a possibility for a stronger action: governments may conclude that, due to the nature of the market, commercial provision is not at all the optimal production mechanism. In these cases the state can take over the provision, increase competition by cutting the production chain into pieces, or delegate the provision to not-for-profit providers, who are more likely to provide the service at a fee closer to the true costs, due to the 'no profit' clause. Private donors and public funders have now indeed started to support open access journals, both on not-for-profit and for-profit but cost-transparent publishing platforms. A third route is to increase the market power of the other side, that is to say, of academic libraries and university associations. Due to increasing costs and budget constraints, libraries undeniably have had to become a more united force in negotiations with publishers (Maskell, 2008).

These struggles have led to two scenarios for achieving 'gold' open access. According to one scenario, open access will be based on article processing fees. Publishing an article is seen as the final stage in the research process and its costs should be thus included in the (public) research budget. Many funders have indeed started to include funds for open access in their research budgets (for example, Horizon 2020 in Europe, Research Councils in the UK). Here the challenge is that non-competitive fees should not feed the profits of the commercial publishing industry. An alternative route that is receiving increasing attention is much more ambitious, attempting to turn around the current model of the publishing industry. According to this model, libraries all over the world should use their budgets collectively, not to pay subscription fees (and high profits) to private publishers, but to fund open access journals (Schimmer et al., 2015). This would mean dropping the market as the main coordination mechanism, and relying on a self-regulating academic community organized around the management of a universal resource.

While possible solutions to address the problems are being actively discussed and are slowly starting to crystallize, the key problem emerging in practice is the difficulty of collective action at the global level. The publishing industry is transnational in its nature and so is science. The UK, for example, has recognized from the very beginning of the process that achieving open access can only be done in cooperation with other countries (Research Council UK, 2005) and recently it has been criticized for the costs it is facing for acting first and relatively alone. Regardless of whether we define open access as an issue of the commons, of a public good, or of an oligopolistic market, the solution requires international collective action. The challenge of international cooperation will be discussed in the next section.

5. COLLECTIVE ACTION AND GLOBAL GOVERNANCE

International collective action problems take a variety of forms. As expressed by cooperation theorists, different issues and issue domains have different strategic structures (for example, Barrett, 2007; Martin, 1992; Krasner, 1991; Oye, 1986; Peinhardt and Sandler, 2015). Specifying the nature of the issue domain is important not only for a clearer understanding of the problem, but also to advise on an optimal institutional structure for solving the problem. The open access challenge is not a highly controversial issue domain with strongly conflicting interests between countries. Open access is primarily a 'coordination game', where the key challenge is to coordinate activities between different actors to achieve a shared solution. It is less important what kind of approach to open access will be chosen, as long as there is some internationally coordinated action, since no country alone can sufficiently pressure the transnational publishing industry, change the academic labour market incentives, or provide competing infrastructure. Open access, however, is not a 'pure' coordination game where everybody would be better off even with some cooperation. It can be seen as a 'threshold game'. The positive effects from cooperating are attained only if a critical level of joint effort is achieved. In threshold coordination games, countries and actors want assurance that others cooperate as well to make their efforts worthwhile. Some stronger actors – the UK and the Netherlands – have made strong steps towards open access alone, partially with the goal to lead by example and thereby achieve the necessary threshold.

On the other hand, as Fearon (1998) points out, the focus on strategic structure may be heuristically helpful, but it can also misrepresent the problem of international cooperation in real life, 'as state leaders typically face it'. There are always many possible ways to arrange a specific domain, even when interests are not strongly conflicting, and therefore a coordination process always includes bargaining to decide which policy option to choose among different possibilities. According to Schelling's (1960) seminal argument, in games with multiple equilibria there is often a focal point, that is, one equilibrium often is more salient than the other(s) because of some property which all the players recognize. What makes an equilibrium salient is often the labelling. A relationship between the label and the common experience or common culture of the players matters for the establishment of a focal point. Cultural context can offer clues that make coordination more likely. The concepts 'public goods', 'commons' but also 'market efficiency' are potentially effective labels that can contribute to the shared understanding for reaching an equilibrium.

Furthermore, international cooperation does not take place in a vacuum but within an existing international regime (Fearon, 1998). The European Higher Education Area has created an effective forum, strengthened by shared institutions such as the European Research Council. We can indeed observe that European countries are most actively involved in international coordination for open access, even though the focal point has not yet fully crystallized. Another manner in which existing linkages contribute to finding the focal point concerns transnational networks. Global governance refers to the fact that much of the 'negotiation' and 'coordination' between countries does not happen at the political level through national level actors and via national diplomacy, but through increasingly well-organized networks of public agencies and organizations (for example, Slaughter, 2004; Raustiala, 2002). The network of European research agencies, research libraries and international university networks have played an active role in the transition towards open access.

Within the 10 or 15 years that the open access issue has been on the political agenda, the governance landscape has developed into a complex web of actors and interests, typical to any global issue. National governments, international organizations, non-state actors, private providers, and networks of stakeholders, play a key role in this development (see OECD, 2015). Libraries, research funders, and various advocacy groups are particularly active in this arena, both at the national level as well as via professional associations at the European and international level. In recent years we also witnessed the entrance of major international organizations, such as UNESCO.

Next to intergovernmental and governmental activities, the sector is much influenced by bottom-up societal initiatives. The boycott of academics against Elsevier in 2015 brought much visibility to the issue. Now more than 16,000 academics have 'declared publicly that [they] will not support any Elsevier journal unless they radically change how they operate' (see note 1 above). The boycott has had a snow-ball effect as journal editors (that is, academics) had to face the fact that some peers refuse to review for their journals, which led them to question the policies of the publisher. The publisher Taylor and Francis saw the entire editorial board of one of its journals resign in protest against the inflexible business practices of the publisher (New, 2013). The publishing industry is also strongly engaged in the discussions. It has been known to lobby vigorously against open access, for example supporting the US Research Works Act, which arguably has set back the current progress in open access (Poynder, 2013).

The challenge of open access is, thus, multi-faceted. It is an issue of global collective action, but it is also an issue of finding the 'focal point'. There are different views on what the problem is and what an appropriate solution could look like. The role of the notions 'public good' and 'commons' in this search for the 'focal point' will be discussed next. First, we will examine the developments towards open access in the early 2000s, with an eye towards the concepts of 'public good' and a 'commons', and thereafter we will look at the policy frameworks in two leading open access countries, the Netherlands and the UK.

6. OPEN ACCESS POLICIES

6.1 Early Developments towards Open Access

The late 1980s and 1990s brought a major technological change. Various digital platforms started to emerge that enabled researchers to share their work quickly and effectively, such as arXiv in natural sciences. By the late 1990s some of the platforms had become the key medium for sharing research within a discipline, and many new repositories were created. New technology, thus, seemed to promise a major change in the distribution of academic knowledge, but also in how to collaborate in earlier stages of the research process. The key policy statement towards open access came in 2002 with the Budapest Open Access Initiative (BOAI), with a declaration that was signed by an eclectic mix of people from library associations, societal organizations of internal nature, a publisher, and universities. The declaration pointed to two aspects. It made clear that new technology, the Internet, has the potential to make research universally accessible for the first time in history. Secondly, it articulated clearly the value of universal access and pointed to knowledge as a shared activity:

> Removing access barriers to [academic] literature will accelerate research, enrich education, share the learning of the rich with the poor and the poor with the rich, make this literature as useful as it can be, and lay the foundation for uniting humanity in *a common intellectual conversation and quest for knowledge*. (Budapest Open Access Initiative, 2002, emphasis added)

The declaration also refers to the concept 'public good' in its very first sentence:

> An old tradition and a new technology have converged to make possible an unprecedented *public good*. The old tradition is the willingness of scientists and scholars to publish the fruits of their research in scholarly journals without payment, for the sake of inquiry and knowledge. The new technology is the internet. The *public good* they make possible is the world-wide electronic distribution of the peer-reviewed journal literature and completely free and unrestricted access to it by all scientists, scholars, teachers, students, and other curious minds. (Ibid., emphasis added)

The Budapest declaration was followed by the Berlin Declaration of Open Access in 2003. The document articulates clearly the goal that knowledge (including data and cultural heritage) should be accessible and usable free of charge and without restrictions, and that all knowledge is digitally archived in public or not-for-profit platforms that adhere to open access ideals. The declaration does not define academic knowledge explicitly either as a 'public good' or 'a commons' but it does emphasize the globally shared nature of academic knowledge:

> For the first time ever, the Internet now offers the chance to constitute *a global and interactive representation of human knowledge*, including cultural heritage and the guarantee of worldwide access. (Berlin Declaration, 2003, emphasis added)

The declaration sets specific expectations to different types of organizations that can make the change happen: it encourages research funders to demand open access, it reminds to the academic community that career and promotion concerns should not hinder open access, and it advocates for further development of open access infrastructure. The number of signatories, which has been constantly and exponentially increasing since 2003, now includes many national research funding bodies in various countries, as well as universities and other scientific and cultural institutions. The early 2000s also saw several other declarations, such as the ECHO Charter about cultural heritage and the Bethesda Statement on Open Access Publishing of the biomedical community in the US.

Next to the declarations, several countries have taken concrete steps towards open access. The UK and the Netherlands are at the moment at the forefront of policy making in this area.

6.2 Open Access in the UK

The UK was probably the first in Europe to notice that there is a problem with the academic publishing industry. The essence of the problem was seen as a distorted market due to insufficient competition in the publishing sector that should be addressed by competition authorities. The first concrete steps towards open access came not from the government, but from the Wellcome Trust, a charitable foundation that gives financial support to a considerable amount of health research. In 2005, the organization adopted a policy that demanded open access to all research that was funded by the organization. A few years later, the governmental funding body, the Research Councils UK (RCUK) issued a 'Position statement on open access to research outputs' (Research Councils UK, 2005), which stated that publicly funded research should be publicly available, and that RCUK supports the creation of repositories to make research more easily accessible. In 2008, RCUK commissioned a study to examine the effects of open access, considering national and international trends in this area, exploring its impact on quality and efficiency of scholarly outputs, on publishing models, and the issue of institutional repositories. In response to the study results, RCUK took further steps towards open access. As a grant holder, the research councils require researchers to deposit research papers in a repository within an agreed time period, and the RCUK funds could be used to cover open access publishing fees.

In 2012 the highly influential, and controversial, 'Finch report' was published by the Working Group on Expanding Access to Published Research Findings (Finch, 2012). The government accepted the recommendations of the report, which would define the open access trajectory in the UK for the years to come. Most importantly, the report presented the 'gold' open access as the only viable option for the future. The implementation of the recommendations meant considerable additional funding (c. £10 million) from the RCUK as a block grant to universities and eligible research organizations to cover the cost associated with the 'gold' open access policy. In its argumentation, the Finch report is primarily framed from the perspective of market inefficiency. It expresses the hope that open access publishing will bring greater transparency on the costs and prices of publishing and dissemination, and thereby create a competitive market where universities and funders are able to use their power as purchasers to push down the prices. Thus, the UK defines the issue implicitly as a problem of imperfect competition, not an issue of a public good or a commons.

The Finch report of 2012 and its implementation plan were received with much criticism from various actors. The House of Lords Science and Technology Committee launched an inquiry into the policy, which pointed to a lack of clarity and insufficient guidance (House of Commons Science and Technology Committee, 2004). The House of Commons Business, Innovation and Skills Select Committee had announced its own inquiry, which also raised some concerns over the policy. The major controversy over the Finch report, however, is related to the disagreement on whether the policy plan indeed takes the country closer to its ultimate long-term goal. The report made a choice for the 'gold' open access but the policy also includes the option of repositories and allows embargo periods of up to 24 months. According to its critics, the extension of the embargo period is detrimental to the open access progress, as several publishers have been reported to extend their embargo periods as a result of the policy (Poynder, 2013). Another issue concerns the funds designated for covering APCs. Critics argue that additional RCUK funds are used to negotiate bulk deals with publishers for lower fees, but as a result the policy fails to achieve the most important aim in the transition, that is, to make the costs and prices for publishing open access transparent and competitive (ibid.).

Despite the ongoing debate, the UK is on a path towards open access, and towards Open Science more broadly. Open access requirements are not only linked to research supported by the research councils but they are also part of the regular research assessment of universities. The Research Excellence Framework collects evidence about all research conducted within universities in the UK. According to the new policy, authors' final peer-reviewed manuscripts must have been deposited in an institutional or subject repository, in order to be counted in the assessment. Deposited material should be searchable, and free to read and download for anyone with an Internet connection. Furthermore, research submitted for publication from 2013 onwards and funded by one of the research councils must be freely accessible online to everyone and everywhere, with a licence that permits copying, distribution and reuse. The Wellcome Trust also remains active in the field. The foundation now sets the standard by requiring that research, produced as a result of its funding and for which an open access fee is paid, must be licensed with a Creative Commons CC-BY, which means that copyright for this work may not be signed off to the publisher.

The UK is, thus, moving forward with its ambition towards open access. We can also see a slight shift in the policy rationale. In the early years, the discourse focused mainly on market inefficiency, but the recent efforts focus primarily on making knowledge openly accessible to the public. Academic knowledge can be recognized in this discussion as 'a commons', but of a unique kind. The trend setters in the policy wish to protect property rights, but those of the author, not the publisher, and at the same time demand that 'the property' is put into a shared use. Although the actions in the UK are contained within its own borders, the country has had a strong influence on policies in other countries, and an important role in advancing discussions in the international arena.

6.3 Open Access in the European Union and UNESCO

The EC started its activities in the area of open access relatively early. Through its Framework Programmes (FP) the EC distributes considerable research funding. An open access policy was first piloted in the FP7 (2007–2013), according to which research had to be openly published either through the 'green' or 'gold' route. The requirement for open access was also consistent with the overall purpose of the programme. The FP funding was never meant to support scientific progress but to serve the economic and societal needs of the union at large. Making results available outside of the academic community, thus, served the overall purpose of the programme. The pilot was preceded by a thorough study of the EC (European Commission, 2006) on the functioning of the academic publishing market and on the availability of infrastructure for open access publishing.

In 2012, the EC issued a Recommendation that encourages all European Union (EU) member states to make publicly funded research results freely available, in order to improve scientific knowledge and to strengthen the knowledge-based economy of the member states (European Commission, 2012). In order to support this transition, the national research councils, under the umbrella of Science Europe, unanimously adopted a set of Common Principles on the Transition to Open Access to Research Publications in April 2013. The EU Recommendation avoids taking a position between the 'green' and the 'gold' route to open access, and it is not being enforced or monitored. However, the initiative has a considerable effect by raising awareness, sharing experiences and building a commitment.

UNESCO entered the field in the second decade of the 2000s. In 2011, the General Conference adopted the strategy for promoting open access to scientific information and research (UNESCO, 2011). On the basis of the strategy document, the rationale for open access is defined particularly as instrumental, but it is explicitly linked to the original, constitutional purpose of UNESCO to protect common human heritage:

> Maintain, increase and diffuse knowledge: By assuring the conservation and protection of the world's inheritance of books, works of art and monuments of history and science . . . By initiating methods of international cooperation calculated to give the people of all countries access to the printed and published materials produced by any of them. (UNESCO, 2011: p. 6)

The strategy is, however, rather soft in its goals. It aims to provide upstream policy advice and build partnerships, strengthen capacity to adopt open access, and inform the global open access debate. The Executive Board saw UNESCO's strengths in this area particularly as a 'standards setting agency' and 'convening power' (UNESCO, 2011).

The UNESCO takes, thus, a facilitating role (Swan, 2012), and it does not attempt to shape the future policy in the field. UNESCO's constituency is also broad and heterogeneous, and the immediate concerns of less developed countries may be rather different from those of major research producers.

6.4 Open Access in the Netherlands

The Netherlands was influenced by the developments in the UK and in the EU and it has by now become one of the leaders in the transition towards open access. A major impetus for progress in this area was the letter from the State Secretary for Education, Science and Culture to the Parliament in 2013. The letter expresses a clear preference for the 'gold route' of open access and it sets specific targets for the country. According to the plan, full open access should be reached by 2024, and within five years 60 per cent of all articles should be available in open access journals (Rijksoverheid, 2013).

The letter had several important effects. Not only did it set the goal and the ambition for the coming years, it also encouraged tougher negotiations with major publishers. Of symbolic significance, the largest scientific publisher Elsevier is based in the Netherlands, which makes the Netherlands a particularly appropriate country to address the sticky issues with commercial publishers. As a result, the Netherlands Association of Universities (VSNU) started to hold serious negotiations with the main publishers to push the opportunities for open access and to deal with the problem or 'double dipping'. VSNU also represented the interests of universities in the negotiations with publishers in previous years. The level of negotiations, however, changed with the new policy. While in the past deals with publishers were negotiated via the VSNU by representatives of academic libraries, in the latest instance the university presidents sat on the other side of the negotiation table. The negotiations were not easy. Most notably, in 2015 the entire Dutch higher education sector was on the verge of being cut off from all Elsevier journals because the parties could not reach a satisfactory agreement.

Transition towards open access is now pushed by the Netherlands Organization for Scientific Research (NWO), the main body for distributing public funding to research. Researchers with NWO funding must ensure that their work is openly available from the moment of publication, either through the 'gold' or 'green' route. The NWO covers the costs for open access publishing, but as a promoter of full open access it no longer pays for APCs in hybrid journals. The NWO also supports infrastructure development for open access. It has supported repositories and the development of platforms for open access journals.

Unlike in the UK, however, the requirements of open access do not extend to the entire academic community in the Netherlands. One university has adopted an open access policy on its own initiative. The Technical University of Eindhoven requests that all published research is deposited in the university repository, while respecting the embargo periods set by the publisher. Nevertheless, the UK and the Netherlands are quite similar in their preferences, activities and the narrative. More so than the UK, the Netherlands focuses on the distributional equity argument. The key rationale for open access is the view that research funded by taxpayers' money should be available to the taxpayers.

The letter of 2013, furthermore, pointed to the fact that open access cannot be achieved by the efforts of one country alone and that the Netherlands should also promote open access in the international arena. This promise was also realized, as open access was one of the priority fields when the Netherlands held the presidency of the EU in 2016.

6.5 Non-State Initiatives and a Search for Alternative Coordination Mechanisms

While state policies increasingly seek ways to indirectly change the current private publishing system, some non-state initiatives have taken a much clearer stance against the current system. The Open Library of Humanities is a remarkable initiative that demonstrates the possibility for a (semi-) self-governing model for academic publishing. The platform operates open access journals without author processing charges, hosting both newly established open access journals as well as former subscription journals

(Eve and Edwards, 2015). While in the beginning the initiative was supported by the financial endowment of the Andrew W. Mellon Foundation, the initiative is now self-sustaining by small, voluntary contributions from more than 200 universities (mostly libraries) across the world. It is important to note that the distribution and technical platform for publishing a journal can still be in private hands, but this is a service contract which allows a relatively easy change of a provider if needed; the journal titles however are not privatized. It is a remarkable initiative because it proves that a voluntary collaboration at an international level is indeed possible; and it also reminds us that the 'commons' is not a singular concept (see Hess and Ostrom, 2003).

Such a new self-governing model based on voluntary collective action has now been proposed for the academic publishing sector as a whole. A group within the Max Planck Society, one of the key societal partners in the open access discussions, is promoting a model whereby academic publishing would become an internationally collaborative activity. The group demonstrates that the subscription fees that university libraries in the world currently pay to commercial publishers would be sufficient to pay for the fully open access publishing system (Schimmer et al., 2015). This initiative, thus, calls for a system whereby (public) money that governments and universities now pay to private publishers for subscription fees and APCs, would instead be pooled and used for sustaining an open access publishing system. Academic publishing would thereby be organized by academic communities themselves, with funding from the academic community via universities and libraries. This would mean a global self-organizing collective action effort to sustain the model.

7. CONCLUSION: OPEN ACCESS, COMMONS AND DEMOCRATIC VALUES

The issue of open access has gone through a rapid development over the past decade. A series of international declarations has contributed to awareness about the problem, strengthened the belief in the worthiness of the goal, and increased political support for the issue. Equally important, there has been much progress in creating infrastructure, such as designing repositories, establishing open access journals, and creating new platforms for such journals. There is, however, no shared view and clear framework yet on what the problem is and especially what an appropriate response would be. The notions of 'commons' and 'public goods' are both explicitly and implicitly part of the discussions. As presented above, we can observe a slight shift in how academic knowledge is perceived. The view that academic knowledge is a shared resource and citizens should be able to benefit from it, is not only promoted by certain activists and advocacy groups, but is increasingly endorsed by mainstream policies.

From the 1970s and 1980s onwards, research was increasingly seen as an important element in national innovation systems serving primarily the economic benefit and competitiveness of a country. Patents, licences, copyrights and other means to restrict access to knowledge were seen as vital incentives to boost innovation and to ensure long-term economic benefits. As such, they often became a goal of their own and a measure of quality. Recently, however, there appears to have been a shift in the approach to science policy more generally (Beerkens, 2016). The origins of open access go back to online platforms, where researchers could freely share their work, collaborate, but also test and criticize for the benefit of science. The orientation towards openness, collaborative action, and a shared nature of the 'knowledge resource' is now formalized in the 'Open Science' agenda, as presented by the EC and in many countries (for example, Nielsen, 2012).

'Open Science' is an alternative, powerful view on how to conduct and disseminate research. Instead of focusing on publishing research results to the academic community at the end of the research cycle, the 'Open Science' approach encourages data sharing and collaboration in research also at earlier phases of the research process, recognizing that science is a cumulative and, thereby, collaborative exercise. The idea of inclusiveness and collaboration goes beyond the borders of the academic community. Not only does open access allow society as a whole to use research, it also welcomes the contribution of citizens as research collaborators. The success of crowd-sourced Galaxy Zoo in astronomy or Wikipedia, has pointed to the potential of open and collaborative research spaces (Madison, 2014). The Netherlands took a step further and invited various experts, societal groups and citizens in general to contribute to the National Research Agenda of the country, thus inviting citizens to decide what questions science should be trying to answer. This view on science emphasizes its open, collaborative, and shared nature both within the academic community as well as in society more broadly, locally and globally.

Another development that draws attention to the public nature of academic knowledge is the growing concern over intellectual, cultural and information goods more broadly. Increasing enclosure of global information commons is becoming a major issue (see Boyle, 2003). Extensive restrictions via copyrights and patents not only restrict further development of the 'resource pool', they underestimate the extent to which current innovation and creations stand on the shoulders of past achievements (Boyle, 1997). Leaving some resources to commons may be a more effective solution than active government involvement in creating private property rights, and thereby creating a 'tragedy of anticommons' (Heller, 1998). Furthermore, similar discussions about other information and cultural goods bring to mind the effect of technological advancements on effective governance structures. The developments in information technology in the last few decades, most importantly, have separated the 'media' and the 'message', showing that what is really valuable to protect is the content itself (for example, music, film, knowledge, software) apart from the medium it is stored on. This also nuances the discussion on the 'commons'. Information and knowledge goods are part of a communication system of different layers: physical layer (hardware), code layer (software), and the content (product itself) (Benkler, 2000; Lessig, 2001). All these layers can either be governed as commons or not, independently from each other.

The framework of the commons in the case of open access has become stronger over time because of an interaction between normative views on academic knowledge as a commons, and the feasibility of new governance mechanisms inspired by self-organizing approaches beyond markets and hierarchies. As documented in public policy literature, the plane of problems and the plane of solutions in any policy sector tend to float around independently of each other, and a major change is likely to occur when a collision of the two creates a *window of opportunity* (for example, Kingdon, 1995). From a normative perspective, knowledge and informational fields can be conceptualized as a form of *environment* we live in, which alerts us to environmental values such as sustainability and stewardship to maintain the environment (Boyle, 1997). Recent developments in open access, furthermore, demonstrate that alternative coordination mechanisms are not only technically possible, but also that collective action dilemmas may be overcome. Bottom-up initiatives to share academic knowledge with peers, circumventing markets and hierarchies, have evolved into advanced coordination systems, where academic journals have started to return from the private domain to the (academic) communal domain. Recent developments in this case also increase optimism about self-regulatory governance at the global level. Voluntary cooperation between various non-governmental actors makes open access a remarkable example of adaptive governance of commons on a global scale.

NOTE

1. See 'The Cost of Knowledge' initiative: http://thecostofknowledge.com/ (accessed 6 July 2018).

REFERENCES

Adviesraad voor Wetenschap, Technologie en Innovatie (2016) *Durven delen: Op weg naar een toegankelijke Wetenschap.* Den Haag, AWTI. [Online] Available from: http://www.awti.nl/documenten/adviezen/2016/01/20/durven-delen (accessed 24 June 2016).

Barrett, S. (2007) *Why Cooperate? The Incentive to Supply Global Public Goods.* Oxford, Oxford University Press.

Beerkens, M. (2016) Higher Education and Its Stakeholders: Protecting 'the Commons'? Keynote speech presented at the European Society of Higher Education (EAIR) conference. Birmingham, 1 September 2016.

Benkler, Y. (2000) From Consumers to Users: Shifting the Deeper Structures. *Federal Communications Law Journal*, **52**, 561–79.

Berlin Declaration (2003) The Berlin Declaration on Open Access to Knowledge in the Sciences and Humanities of 22 October 2003. [Online] Available from: https://openaccess.mpg.de/Berlin-Declaration (accessed 24 June 2016).

Björk, B.-C. and Solomon, D. (2014) Developing an Effective Market for Open Access APCs. Final Report to a consortium of research funders. [Online] Available from: https://wellcome.ac.uk/sites/default/files/developing-effective-market-for-open-access-article-processing-charges-mar14.pdf (accessed 24 June 2016).

Budapest Open Access Initiative (2002) The Original BOAI Declaration. [Online] Available from: http://www.budapestopenaccessinitiative.org/read (accessed 6 June 2016).

Boyle, J. (1997) A Politics of Intellectual Property: Environmentalism for the Net? *Duke Law Journal*, **47**, 87–116.

Boyle, J. (2003) The Second Enclosure Movement and the Construction of the Public Domain. *Law and Contemporary Problems*, **66** (1/2), 33–74.

Bučar, M. (2012) Research Cooperation for Development: A Case with Much Room for Improvement. In: Gänzle, S., Grimm, S. and Makhan, D. (eds) *The European Union and Global Development: An 'Enlightened Superpower' in the Making?* London, Palgrave Macmillan, pp. 136–52.

Deneulin, S. and Townsend, N. (2007) Public Goods, Global Public Goods and the Common Good. *International Journal of Social Economics*, **34** (1/2), 19–36.

European Commission (2006) Study on the Economic and Technical Evolution of the Scientific Publication Markets in Europe. [Online] Available from: http://cordis.europa.eu/publication/rcn/200618784_en.html (accessed 6 June 2016).

European Commission (2010) *Europe 2020: A Strategy for Smart, Sustainable and Inclusive Growth.* Brussels, European Commission.

European Commission (2012) Commission Recommendation of 17.7.2012 on Access to and Preservation of Scientific Information. Brussels, C(2012) 4890 final.

European Commission (2013) Horizon 2020: Guidelines on Open Access to Scientific Publications and Research in Horizon 2020. [Online] Available from: http://ec.europa.eu/research/participants/data/ref/h2020/grants_manual/hi/oa_pilot/h2020-hi-oa-pilot-guide_en.pdf (accessed 6 June 2016).

Eve, M. P. and Edwards, C. (2015) Opening the Open Library of Humanities. *Open Library of Humanities*, **1** (1), 1–4.

Fearon, J. D. (1998) Bargaining, Enforcement and International Cooperation. *International Organization*, **52**, 269–305.

Finch, J. (2012) Accessibility, Sustainability, Excellence: How to Expand Access to Research Publications. Report of the Working Group on Expanding Access to Published Research Findings. [Online] Available from: https://www.acu.ac.uk/research-information-network/finch-report-final (accessed 24 June 2016).

Hardin, G. (1968) The Tragedy of the Commons. *Science*, **162** (3859), 1243–8.

Heller, M. A. (1998) The Tragedy of the Anticommons: Property in the Transition from Marx to Markets. *Harvard Law Review*, **111** (3), 621–88.

Hess, C. and Ostrom, E. (2003) Ideas, Artifacts, and Facilities: Information as a Common-pool Resource. *Law and Contemporary Problems*, **66** (1/2), 111–46.

Hess, C. and Ostrom, E. (2007) Introduction: An Overview of the Knowledge Commons. In: Hess, C. and Ostrom, E. (eds) *Understanding Knowledge as a Commons: From Theory to Practice*. Cambridge, Massachusetts Institute of Technology, pp. 3–26.

House of Commons Science and Technology Committee (2004) Scientific Publications: Free for all? Tenth Report of Session 2003–04. Volume I: Report. [Online] Available from: http://www.publications.parliament.uk/pa/cm200304/cmselect/cmsctech/399/399.pdf (accessed 6 May 2016).

JISC (2016) Academic Journal Markets, their Limitations, and the Consequences for a Transition to Open Access: A Thought Piece. [Online] Available from: https://www.jisc.ac.uk/reports/academic-journal-markets-limitations-consequences-for-transition-to-open-access (accessed 6 June 2016).

Kaul, I., Conceição, P., Le Goulven, K. and Mendoza, R. U. (eds) (2003) *Providing Global Public Goods: Managing Globalization*. New York, Oxford University Press.

Kingdon, J. (1995) *Agendas, Alternatives, and Public Politics*. 2nd edn, New York, Harper Collins.

Krasner, S. D. (1991) Global Communications and National Power: Life on the Pareto Frontier. *World Politics*, **43**, 336–66.

Larivière, V., Haustein, S. and Mongeon, P. (2015) The Oligopoly of Academic Publishers in the Digital Era. *PLOS ONE, June 10*. [Online] Available from: https://doi.org/10.1371/journal.pone.0127502 (accessed 17 July 2018).

Lessig, L. (2001) *The Future of Ideas: The Fate of the Commons in a Connected World*. New York, Vintage Books.

Madison, M. J. (2014) Commons at the Intersection of Peer Production, Citizen Science, and Big Data: Galaxy Zoo. In: Frischmann, B. M., Madison, M. J. and Strandburg, K. J. (eds) *Governing Knowledge Commons*. Oxford, Oxford University Press.

Martin, L. M. (1992) Interests, Power and Multilateralism. *International Organization*, **46** (4), 765–92.

Maskell, C. (2008) Consortia: Anti-competitive or in the Public Good? *Library Hi Tech*, **26** (2), 164–83.

Nielsen, M. (2012) *Reinventing Discovery: The New Era of Networked Science*. Princeton, Princeton University Press.

New, J. (2013) Journal's Editorial Board Resigns in Protest of Publisher's Policy toward Authors. *The Chronicle of Higher Education*, 26 March.

Nicholson, D. (2000) A Game of Monopoly. *The Scientist*, 8 November. [Online] Available from: https://www.the-scientist.com/news-analysis/a-game-of-monopoly-55382 (accessed 17 July 2018).

Office of Fair Trade (2002) The Market for Scientific, Technical and Medical Journals: A Statement by the OFT. September 2002, OFT396.

Open Knowledge International (2018) *Open Knowledge International: About Our Mission*. Available from: https://okfn.org/about/ (accessed 17 July 2018).

Organisation for Economic Co-operation and Development (OECD) (2007) *OECD Principles and Guidelines for Access to Research Data from Public Funding*. Paris, OECD.

Organisation for Economic Co-operation and Development (OECD) (2015) *Making Open Science a Reality*. Paris, OECD.

Oye, K. (ed.) (1986) *Cooperation under Anarchy*. Princeton, Princeton University Press.

Peinhardt, C. and Sandler, T. (2015) *Transnational Cooperation: An Issue-based Approach*. Oxford, Oxford University Press.

Poynder, R. (2013). The UK's Open Access Policy: Controversy Continues, Richard Poynder blog. [Online] Available from: http://poynder.blogspot.co.uk/2013/05/the-uks-open-access-policy-controversy.html (accessed 28 May 2016).

Raustiala, K. (2002) The Architecture of International Cooperation: Transgovernmental Networks and the Future of International Law. *Virginia Journal of International Law*, **43**, 2–58.

Research Councils UK (2005) RCUK Position Statement on Access to Research Outputs. [Online] Available from: http://www.rcuk.ac.uk/documents/documents/2005statement-pdf/ (accessed 24 April 2017).

Rijksoverheid (2013) Kamerbrief: Open Access van Publicaties. 15 November 2013, Den Haag. [Online] Available from: https://www.rijksoverheid.nl/documenten/kamerstukken/2013/11/15/kamerbrief-over-open-access-van-publicaties (accessed 6 May 2016).

Sandler, T. (1999) Intergenerational Public Goods: Strategies, Efficiency and Institutions. In: Kaul, I., Grunberg, I. and Stern, M. A. (eds) *Global Public Goods: International Cooperation in the 21st century*. Oxford, Oxford University Press, pp. 20–50.

Schelling, T. (1960) *The Strategy of Conflict*. Cambridge, Harvard University Press.

Schimmer, R., Geschuhnand, K. K. and Vogler, A. (2015) Disrupting the Subscription Journals' Business Model for the Necessary Large-scale Transformation to Open Access. A Max Planck Digital Library Open Access Policy White Paper. [Online] Available from: http://pubman.mpdl.mpg.de/pubman/faces/viewItemOverviewPage.jsp?itemId=escidoc:2148961 (accessed 24 April 2017).

Slaughter, A.-M. (2004) *A New World Order*. Princeton, Princeton University Press.

Stiglitz, J. E. (1999) Knowledge as a Global Public Good. In: Kaul, I., Grunberg, I., Stern, M. A. (eds) *Global Public Goods: International Cooperation in the 21st century*. Oxford, Oxford University Press, pp. 308–25.

Suber, P. (2012) *Open Access*. Cambridge, MIT Press.

Thornton, P. H. and Ocasio, W. (1999) Institutional Logics and the Historical Contingency of Power in Organizations: Executive Succession in the Higher Education Publishing Industry, 1958–1990. *American Journal of Sociology*, **105** (3), 801–43.

UK Competition Commission (2001) Reed Elsevier plc and Harcourt General, Inc.; A Report on the Proposed Merger. Cm. 5184, 5 July 2001.

UNESCO (2011) Decisions Adopted by the Executive Board at its 187th Session. [Online] Available from: http://unesdoc.unesco.org/images/0021/002144/214466E.pdf (accessed 24 June 2016).

Swan, A. (2012) Policy Guidelines for the Development and Promotion of Open Access. Paris, UNESCO. [Online] Available from: http://unesdoc.unesco.org/images/0021/002158/215863e.pdf (accessed 24 June 2016).
Willinsky, J. (2005) The Unacknowledged Convergence of Open Source, Open Access, and Open Science. *First Monday*, **10** (8). [Online] Available from: http://firstmonday.org/article/view/1265/1185 (accessed 14 December 2017).
World Summit on Information Society (2003) Geneva Declaration of Principles. WSIS–03/GENEVA/DOC/0004. [Online] Available from: http://www.itu.int/net/wsis/documents/doc_multi.asp?lang=en&id=1161|0 (accessed 12 June 2016).

PART III

Legal Perspectives

10. The ecology of international law: towards an international legal system in tune with nature and community?

Ugo Mattei*

1. INTRODUCTION

The idea behind this critical chapter about the ecology of international law emerged in the context of a public lecture which I was invited to give at the University of Leuven, Faculty of Law, on 4 May 2017. The co-editors, Samuel Cogolati and Jan Wouters, invited me to reflect upon a paradigm shift in international legal theory from the materialistic and extractive mentality of the Industrial Age to a new vision of the world as governed by a network of generative ecological principles. The title of the lecture and of this chapter, is inspired by my last books written with Fritjof Capra, *The Ecology of Law: Towards a System in Tune with Nature and Community* (2015) and Alessandra Quarta, *The Turning Point in Private Law: Ecology, Technology and the Commons* (2018). This chapter also echoes previous works, among which a book written with Laura Nader, *Plunder: When the Rule of Law is Illegal* (2008), and an article with Luigi Russi entitled 'The Evil Technology Hypothesis: A Deep Ecological Reading of International Law' (2012). These pieces together advance a quite provocative thesis that locates itself in a line of analysis aimed at the radical critique of some of the fundamental assumptions of the modern conception of the rule of law. This chapter builds upon them, and aims to think about international law in a more holistic and ecological perspective than what is common in the dominant Anglo-American professional legal setting.

In this chapter, as it is already clear from the title, I will attempt to answer the question as to whether international law can be 'ecological' – that is, in tune with both nature and community. My hypothesis is that it cannot. Instead, international law might be its own greatest problem, promoting a silent ethos of exploitation of the 'other' by reducing empathy and facilitating extraction; this I call the 'evil technology hypothesis'. The benefit of looking at international law in this way lies in the whole new horizon of questions it opens up, specifically about the scales of our economic system, of our civilization, and of our fundamental dependency on a model of extraction transforming the commons into capital.

This being the plan, Section 2 will provide some context against the background of which our main object of inquiry – international law – should be examined. Section 3 will then succinctly explore the current 'radical' debate on international law, focusing in particular on Martti Koskenniemi's 'indeterminacy thesis' and Anthony Anghie's depiction of international law as a technology. The tone of Section 4 marks an abrupt shift from the previous section, as it explores radical ecological literature in order to provide a general illustration of the idea that technology might contribute to an inherently 'evil' and detached order in which the environment and those around us are objectified and made easier to exploit. Section 5 discusses the application of the 'evil technology hypothesis' to the realm of international law specifically and shows how international law was instrumental in transforming commons into capital.

2. INTERNATIONAL LAW IN CONTEXT

Nothing less than our planet Earth concerns us in this chapter, since our object of inquiry is international law. The basic starting point for my contribution is that because we, humans, have only one planet, our ecological footprint should be equal to one planet – that is, we should consume only a fraction of our common wealth, enabling anyone else in the world to do the same, while maintaining conditions suitable to sustain and reproduce life (Capra and Mattei, 2015). The ecological footprint is basically the rate of sustainability of a given organization. This means that the ecological footprint of the Earth should be one planet. The current ecological footprint of our planet, however, is 1.5, which means that we would need 1.5 planets to sustain our global standard of living.

If you are optimistic, you may think that 1.5 planets is not too bad. Yet, if we disaggregate the number, we realize that the ecological footprint of, for example, the Bay Area (the region surrounding the San Francisco estuary in the State of California) where the best technologies and businesses are all represented, is six. This realization becomes worrisome when we consider that developing countries take the way of life of this region as a model of 'development'. Indeed, were everyone in the world to live like those in San Francisco, then we would need six planets to survive. It would be like consuming six times the same amount of a given capital every year.

Consequently, the question arises: if the United States and Western Europe consume so much, why is the total footprint still limited to 1.5 planets? In fact, the footprint is 1.5 only because many people in the Global South live far below the standard of one planet, due to material poverty. There are places in the world where the ecological footprint only represents 0.1, 0.2, 0.3, . . . and which do not consume any fair share of the whole planet. The West, however, consumes much more than its fair share. So, if the vision is planet Earth as a whole, as it should be under international law, then we have to start drawing some connections: the fact that the planet is still functioning (even if it is in decline), is because a large portion of the world's population remains very poor. Moreover, some people are under-developed because other people are over-developed.

International organizations, such as the United Nations (UN), the World Bank or the International Monetary Fund all have 'development' plans. The idea that the Global South is under-developed is a platitude. Yet, we never talk about *over*-development. In fact, you could argue that if your ecological footprint is six, you are over-developed – you are exploiting far more of the common wealth than you should in order to preserve everyone's fair share of the planet. Our admiration for people who over-consume is in fact quite astonishing. This reasoning conjures up the image of a person invited to a buffet where food is freely accessible, and rather than sharing the buffet with others, rushes in an attempt to maximize the amount of calories that can be stored at the expense of others, efficiently consuming the largest possible amount of food in the least possible time. Imagine that this person would state that he is simply maximizing his calorie intake, that efficiency is an important value of social organization, that he is not over-developed and that it is the others' problem if they are not efficient enough. He would argue that the others are the ones to blame because they are not fast enough, not big enough to behave in such a way. Normally, everybody would be outraged in such circumstances.

Yet, that is an accurate metaphor for what is going on globally today. A tiny minority of individuals organize themselves in political organizations – mostly, states – and try to consume as much as possible of the common-pool that is the Earth. The more states consume, the better they perform in terms of their gross domestic product. In other words, in the dominant rankings, the virtuous ones are the ones who behave exactly like the person in our example. This peculiar ideology around consumption habits, around extraction, around the contribution to the possible sustainability of the common-pool of resources which is our living planet, is the problem: the world is upside down. We accuse the losers of being social profiteers, we call them 'under-developed', we call them 'poor', we de-humanise them, we deny them political agency and we think that we can resolve their problems by filling up their bellies after we have filled ours obscenely. However, this idea of development is at odds with the very principle of *sustainability* of the planet. Global warming is just one of the – probably, most visible – consequences of the law of nature, which is the law of reproducibility of life itself on the planet.

We now turn to this very narrow body of knowledge which is called 'international law' and which only makes sense if understood in the broader geopolitical context in which it is deployed and entrenched (Monateri, 2018: p. 4). Indeed, talking about international law *per se*, as much as talking about law in general, does not make much sense. Such abstract reasoning does not allow us to understand much about its nature. If we want to understand something about international law – as well as about law in general – we have to look at it in context.

For that purpose, we first need a good ecological understanding of international law, which means placing the object under observation within the community of relationships in which it actually functions. In this sense, the ecology of international law would be composed of the whole of connections that make it a living part of a much more complex organism – which is the political, economic and geographical context. In a way, this means adopting a systemic approach to international law. This approach is not only interested in international law within its own box, but intends to also think beyond its confines, by studying it in its relationships and in its life, in a more complex manner. This is one first important meaning of an ecology of international law.

Now, let us try to see international law in practice: how it functions, how it works, what kind of losers and winners it produces, what kind of effects it has on sustainability, and whether it is part of the solution or the problem. Perhaps, if we look at international law within its own context, and we consider its impact on the overall social organization, it may be more part of the problem than of the solution. We cannot assume that it is inherently 'good'. This is something that a critical thinker must always be aware of: nothing is beyond questioning. The more you find people who become true believers of lovely ideas (for example, international human rights), the more a concept attracts consensus, the more it is worth questioning because usually this is where ideology hides. Usually, international law is a trendy thing to do in law school; but you need to understand what you are talking about.

So how do we actually understand whether a concept is ecologically desirable or not? What do we mean by ecologically desirable? Here we put another question on the table – that is, how we determine whether some sort of concept or some sort of institution is actually ecologically desirable or not. This notion is normative in nature. Indeed, according to the traditional understanding in social sciences, there are two ways to look at reality: on the one hand, descriptive/analytical claims ('how can I describe international law in a way that is thick enough to make sense and become an interesting topic of analysis?'), and on the other hand, normative claims ('what do we mean by ecologically desirable?'). The question we put forward in this chapter is nothing less than this: do we want international law or not? Is international law a good thing to begin with?

Some centuries ago, Voltaire (1694–1778), wrote an entry entitled 'law' in the *Encyclopédie*, which said that if you wanted good laws, you should throw away all old laws and define new ones. Essentially, in his view, the only way to have good laws in a context of radical critique of the *Ancien Régime*, is to discard all the old and existing laws and to start afresh. We could possibly argue something similar in international law. We could argue that international law is – at least in part – responsible for the state of the world that we described above. International law is arguably deeply part of the extractive system that today dominates the world.

International law is indeed a very important part of the global order today, and therefore it might share some responsibility for today's state of affairs – after all, the law is the way in which a community gives to itself a shared resolve and the way we manage such things as a *global* community is through international law. For example, if we realize that global warming is taking place, we may decide that we want to come down with a good international agreement to handle global warming. In fact, the 21st Conference of the Parties (COP) of the Framework Convention on Climate Change in Paris was an attempt to confront the issue through international law (United Nations, 2015). If the way we act globally is through international law, and if global efforts tend to be poor, one argument could be that international law is dysfunctional and that we should declare international bankruptcy. So, as was done by Voltaire with the laws of the *Ancien Régime*, we could say today that all international law instruments such as the UN Charter or other international human rights instruments are just words and good intentions. Institutionally, international law could be declared to be broke and we should then get rid of it.

To sum up, that is the first question which I will address in this chapter: are there good reasons to believe that international law could or should be thrown away? The second question, which is more interesting, is inspired by the second part of Voltaire's statement: can we do better? Is it still worth trying to draft new international laws and deploy conventions? Or should we avoid replacing it with a different kind of international law because any kind of international law is simply part of the problem and not of the solution?

3. INDETERMINACY AND LAW AS TECHNOLOGY

3.1 Koskenniemi's Indeterminacy Thesis

Summarizing the arguments of other scholars in one's own work is always a daunting task, as there is always the risk of over-simplifying, taking out of context, or simply misrepresenting views that are made in a certain argumentative flow which cannot be reproduced in its entirety. With that caveat in mind, this section endeavours to summarize Koskenniemi's argument about the 'indeterminacy' of international law, which he famously articulated in his book entitled *From Apology to Utopia* (2005).

First of all, Koskenniemi's indeterminacy thesis is not simply the observation that language is so open-ended that anything may mean both everything and nothing (2005: p. 595). Instead, Koskenniemi observes that the uncertainty of the political project behind international law has moulded international law into a soft framework in which competing political positions are able to find their way through in legal argumentation. International law appears as an industry of de-politicization. Koskenniemi puts this very clearly in the following passage, which is worth quoting in its entirety:

> [E]ven where there is no semantic ambivalence whatsoever, international law remains indeterminate because it is based on contradictory premises and seeks to regulate a future in regard to which even single actors' preferences remain unsettled. To say this is not to say much more than that *international law emerges from a political process whose participants have contradictory priorities and rarely know with clarity how such priorities should be turned into directives to deal with an uncertain future*. Hence they agree to supplement rules with exceptions, have recourse to broadly defined standards and apply rules in the context of other rules and larger principles. Even where there is little or no semantic ambiguity about an expression in a rule – say, about 'armed attack' in Article 51 of the UN Charter – that expression cannot quite have the normative force we would like it to have. It cannot because it is also threatening – what about an imminent attack? The same reason that justifies the rule about self-defence also justifies setting aside its wording if this is needed by the very rationale of the rule – the need to protect the state. And *because no rule is more important than the reason for which it is enacted, even the most unambiguous rule is infected by the disagreements that concern how that reason should be understood and how it ranks*

> *with competing ones*: what is it, in fact, that is necessary to 'protect the state' and how does that reason link with competing ones such as those of 'peaceful settlement'? *It follows that it is possible to defend any course of action – including deviation from a clear rule – by professionally impeccable legal arguments that look from rules to their underlying reasons, make choices between several rules as well as rules and exceptions, and interpret rules in the context of evaluative standards*. (2005: pp. 590–91, emphasis added)

Koskenniemi's position, however, is further complicated by the fact that he does not impute a naïve neutrality to international legal discourse. He recognizes, instead, the presence of a structural bias that systematically favours certain outcomes (ibid.: p. 607). As Susan Marks puts it: 'things can be, and quite frequently are, contingent without being random, accidental, or arbitrary' (Marks, 2009: p. 2). For Koskenniemi, however, structural bias does not seem to be grounded in the medium of international law itself, but rather, in the presence of 'a professional consensus or a mainstream answer to any particular problem' (2005: pp. 590–91). Accordingly, legal professionals can direct the discourse to their ends, precisely because of international law's indeterminacy. This Koskenniemi seems to state quite clearly in the following passage:

> [N]othing of our ability to challenge the bias is grounded in the law itself. The choice will be just that – a 'choice' that is 'grounded' in nothing grander than a history of how we came to have the preferences that we have and what we know of the world and our relationship to it. 'Theory' may be needed to create awareness of the origin and consequences of our choices – perhaps a theory of 'justice' or of economic efficiency – but those theories do not fully justify our choices. A 'gap' will remain between all such languages and what it is that we choose, whether the bias, or its contrary. The existence of this 'gap' is not insignificant for professional practice. If the practice is not determined by an anterior structure or vocabulary, then it cannot be reduced to an automatic production of such a structure or vocabulary either. The decision is made, and its consequences are thus attributable not to some impersonal logic or structure but *to ourselves*. (Ibid.: p. 615)

To restate the point, Koskenniemi appears to articulate a political 'malleability' of international legal discourse, which is smuggled in at the rupture between international law's formality and the fluidity of political concern. This means that international law is not, in and of itself, the problem. Rather, the problem is the inability of international lawyers to reclaim what is theirs, namely the ability to engage with the political side of international law. While international law is in practice 'steered' by an invisible consensus hidden under the cloak of professionalism, by removing that cloak thanks to a renewed political awareness, international law could become something different and thereby serve different ends from those it currently privileges. If only critical approaches to international law would become the mainstream, then it would become apparent that international law is a source of power. It is still possible in Koskenniemi's framework to bring about a kind of international law system that could take into account the reality of power imbalances, and that would therefore be desirable. So while Koskenniemi's critique of international law is very harsh, he admits that international law can somehow be good if people are politically conscious.

3.2 Anghie and Law as Technology

Anthony Anghie comes from a different starting point. Namely, he sees the very development of international law as inextricably tied to imperialist practices. In his view, international law, itself a product of colonization and therefore a deeply Western and European-centric enterprise, has been part of a narrative to persuade the oppressed that colonial violence is in their own interest. International law served to create the conditions of global exploitation and colonization. For Anghie, in particular, a crucial role is played by the idea of 'sovereignty', which:

> expels the non-European world from its realm, and then proceeds to legitimise the imperialism that resulted in the incorporation of the non-European world into the system of international law. The process of transforming the non-European world is completed through decolonisation, which enables the non-European state to emerge as a sovereign and equal member of the global community. (2006: p. 741)

The function of international law, in Anghie's view, is to convince those who are on the receiving end that it might actually be good for them to be plundered. It is what Antonio Gramsci called 'the hegemony' – the persuasion of those who are suffering from oppression that oppression in fact benefits them. Today, it is possible to find international law professors and lawyers in the Global South who have completely internalized this sense of guilt of being poor – even if blaming the victim may seem cruel and inappropriate (Mattei and Nader, 2008).

However, despite recognizing that '[t]his exclusion, and the imperialism which it furthers, constitute in part the primordial and essential identity of international law' (Anghie, 2004: p. 315), Anghie still appears to be sympathetic to the idea that international law could be changed from within to serve 'nobler' ends (ibid.: p. 318), thereby placing him closer to Koskenniemi than his starting point may suggest. For the purpose of this chapter, however, Anghie's work is particularly interesting for it crucially likens international law to a technology:

> The nineteenth century was the age of science, during which industry was applied for the betterment and progress of human society. We see here the suggestion that international law is not merely a science but a technology. As a technology, it could help realize the Victorian ideals of progress, optimism, and liberalism, which, when applied specifically to the non-European world, meant the civilizing of the benighted native peoples. (Anghie, 1999: p. 64)

The definition of technology that Anghie seems to presuppose here is that of *a means to facilitate ends the positive value of which is assumed.* In his view, international law has been depoliticized to the point of becoming a neutral technology. So, for instance, in Anghie's reconstruction of the colonial formation of international law, the latter is presented as a tool that was adopted to pursue the 'obviously' good objective of civilizing non-Western peoples through trade (1999: p. 64). International law developed in the late eighteenth–early nineteenth century when rules of laws were provided by the most civilized and advanced nations of the world in order to move in the direction of civilization.

Later, the International Court of Justice (ICJ) was established to litigate issues that should not be resolved by violence on the international plane. The League of Nations was weak and was unable to guarantee international legality, but international law was still considered to be a good idea, and we then tried to establish new rules of international law. In that regard, Article 38(1) of the ICJ Statute (United Nations, 1946), which provides the sources of international law, is of interest:

> The Court, whose function is to decide in accordance with international law such disputes as are submitted to it, shall apply:
>
> International conventions, whether general or particular, establishing rules expressly recognized by the contesting states;
>
> International custom, as evidence of a general practice accepted as law;
>
> The general principles of law *recognized by civilized nations*;
>
> . . . (emphasis added)

In other words, if the domestic law of the state is recognized by all of the civilized nations or most of them, it then becomes a general principle binding on every state in the world. In that sense, international law is nothing more than a technique to reach civilization. It is a technology; a means to an end.

What the law-as-technology language hid, of course, was the fact that the obvious goodness of the civilizing mission was not so obvious after all, and actually based on a value-laden differential construction of the 'other' (Anghie, 2004: p. 4). This shows that, in Anghie's and Koskenniemi's perspective, the problem with law's technological character appears simply to be that it directs the focus away from the political agenda. It follows that, by reawakening its political soul, international law could still be used to promote more 'worthwhile' ends (according to the international lawyer's own value judgements). International law can still be reformed. Once we realize that international law is not neutral, once we realize that international law is a technology, once we understand and apologize for the brutality of our past, maybe then we can create a kind of international law that is desirable again. The end, therefore, justifies the means (i.e., using international law to deliver a desired outcome).

4. THE EVIL TECHNOLOGY HYPOTHESIS

Much of the mythology of the neutrality of international human rights remains. The idea that there are certain kinds of universal ideas that actually are *per se* good to share and to spread is still very much alive among international lawyers and lawyers in general – and in policy-making discussions. There is still quite a heavy professionalized ideology that is hidden behind the question of desirability itself. Therefore, the argument I seek to make here goes one step further than Anghie's thesis. I assume as a starting point that the international legal project incrementally turned into the global framework of imperial law (Mattei, 2003), by excluding global resource redistributions other than those maintaining the bottom line. As an incrementally expanding 'reactive' institutional setting, international law has seized the historical opportunity produced by the demise of the Soviet model (Mamyluk and Mattei, 2011) to develop a strong global alliance with corporate power. This alliance has transformed international law into a disorder-spreading technology (Keizer et al., 2008), thus producing a global institutional scenario that progressively transfers common resources in corporate control by legitimizing plunder (Mattei and Nader, 2008). In particular, I contend here that such global transformation does not even require conscious political agency at this point. Indeed, the very interposition of a technology in the pursuit of a particular interest increases the distance between oneself and the 'other', and this invariably works to enable the expansion of unsustainable and exploitative relationships with the human and other-than-human inhabitants of the planet, even under the best of intentions. This, in other words, is the 'evil technology hypothesis'.

For instance, the London School of Economics and Political Science (LSE), which hosted a conference entitled 'Towards a Radical International Law' in May 2011, built a majestic New Academic Building (NAB). The seven-something-storey building radiated newness and modernity. The perfect building, one would say, to embody the ethos of excellence of the contemporary university. And yet, natural light was distinctively lacking. Small, encased windows and a see-through ceiling were not nearly enough to provide sufficient illumination, requiring the backup of copious artificial lighting. Additionally, stairs were apparently available only up to the first two floors, leaving elevators as the preferred means of transport to reach any higher floors. What kind of person might the architects who designed the building have had in mind as they set out to draw the plans? Clearly, the person must have been someone oblivious to the difference between natural and artificial light. Additionally, that person must also have been someone who values the minimization of 'body usage' to reach the classroom, bodies being simply brain vessels.

So, technology (lights and elevators) in the building crucially made it possible for people to hold or develop an ethos of separateness from nature, as well as one's body. And not even to question its awkwardness: all of the conference participants were, in fact, bathing in artificial light and taking those elevators, without even noticing the kind of detachment from their bodies and the world around them that the infrastructure was silently promoting. The mind did not need to be transported by the body, but by elevators. And, thus, there is a disconnect between mind and body. The subject is objectively separated from nature. This disconnection between human and nature, and human body and human mind, is symbolized in the NAB. Most banks today are similar. The urban life is also dramatically disconnected from the light of Gaia. The fact that more than half of the world's population is urbanized makes technology indispensable in order to channel resources to sustain these territories. We get addicted to technologies.

The dis-empathizing potential inherent in the use of technology – of any technology – is also nicely illustrated through a hypothetical example offered by radical ecologist Ran Prieur in his book *Civilization Will Eat Itself* (2001). Prieur suggests imagining a group of super-intelligent monkeys that learn to use spears. Spears make it easier for monkeys to kill, as opposed to using their bare hands (Prieur, 2001: pp. 27–8):

> So spear-using monkeys would kill in more ordinary circumstances, and more often. They would learn that spear-killing could get them better land, and better food, and better mates.
>
> They would get used to pleasures they could get only through spear-killing. Worse, they would lose the skills they needed to live without spears. Now, to give up their habit of making and using spears would be so painful that it would be impossible if you had the self-discipline of a monkey.
>
> Now, if you have the awareness of a monkey, you will experience your spear-killing societal pattern as an uncompromisable necessity, and you will viciously attack anything that threatens it. But what threatens it is the expansion of your own empathy. If you – or other monkeys – start feeling as close to a monkey at the end of a 30-foot spear throw as you used to feel to a monkey right in front of you, if it starts to get as hard for monkeys to kill with spears as it used to

> be to kill with bare hands, then you fear that the spear-killing technology will become emotionally unsustainable, and your civilization will collapse, and you will lose your economic advantages, and you and your friends and family will suffer and maybe die.
>
> So you viciously attack the expansion of your own empathy, and the empathy of others. Monkeys learn and teach others to stick a boundary between 'self' and 'other', to sustain fear and hatred indefinitely, to greet the unfamiliar with mistrust and discomfort and hostility, not curiosity and excitement and acceptance. And here, I say, is where the monkeys become what we call evil: when dependence on a harmful behavior leads them to inhibit their love.

This is where technology can bring about evil outcomes. While in Prieur's example the focus is solely on the empathy between 'monkeys', it is submitted that the example could well be extended – at least from the perspective of 'deep ecology' – beyond the feeling of empathy between beings of the same species. Deep ecology is the 'branch' of ecology that focuses not just on 'conservation' for anthropocentric survival concerns, but on re-defining the basic paradigm of the relation between humans and nature (Holder and Lee, 2007: pp. 48–50). It posits an underlying kinship between human and other-than-human beings, which has been explained, for instance, through a *panpsychist* understanding of the world that regards consciousness as a property inherent in all matter. In this framework, human consciousness simply becomes a property emerging out of the complex interaction of consciousness already present in matter. Adopting such a perspective, it becomes possible to argue that a basic empathy between human and other-than-human beings is at the root of life on the planet, so that something meaningful is also lost whenever the other-than-human world is objectified and made subservient to human needs.

Returning to the 'evil technology hypothesis', once technology enables 'a disconnection and contraction of consciousness, a forced channelling of wider energies to serve narrower interests' (Prieur, 2001: p. 10), a growth mechanism is set in motion whereby those narrower interests (such as the reproduction of a particular community), after being 'privileged' through technology, find room to expand and take a life of their own:

> You start doing it because it gives your pinched-off perspective (your side, your cause, your 'self', your status, your money) some advantage, and then you get yourself drawn into doing it more and bigger, and you forget how to get along without it, and you use it to build and maintain ways of being that you don't know how to build and maintain without it. (Ibid.: pp. 10–11)

Here, then, is the essence of the 'evil technology hypothesis': technology enables specialized care of certain narrow interests, which are consequently abstracted from the environment they originate from – and are symbiotically embedded in – to begin with. This separation facilitates the subordination of the same environment to such narrower interests, igniting positive feedback loops that reinforce their expansion. In relation to human communities, in particular, the use of technologies can be seen as the spark that, by positing 'man' in antithesis to the 'environment', sets off the exploitation of the latter by the former, igniting the growth of unsustainable human communities that are out of sync with the landbase they dwell on and require secure inflows of energy to sustain themselves. Most importantly, as a community takes the path of technology, it grows increasingly unaccustomed to living without technology, looking down on non-technological ways of living as being somewhat backwards, and re-defining its own standard of living as the 'correct' one (Prieur, 2001: pp. 30–31).

5. THE ECOLOGY OF INTERNATIONAL LAW

If we can assume that technology is introducing a certain kind of disconnection, is taking away empathy, is creating some sort of a dramatic separation within the world of the subject–object, we get an idea of how to build an ecology of international law – that is to say, to look at international law from the point of view of sustainability and resilience.

The technology of international law – the means to an end that is desirable *per se* – is actually in the making of modernity. Modernity produced a very broad and significant transformation of legal systems that were based on 'commons' institutions, into individual systems. Tremendous economic resources were needed to establish the centralized institutional settings that would usher in what economic historian Karl Polanyi called the 'great transformation' at the dawn of modernity (1944). The 'primitive' accumulation of capital, necessary for the jump-start of any early capitalist social organization, was generated not only by enclosures and the transformation of the biological time of communal life into the quantifiable, alienated time of factory work, but also by seeking resources from abroad (Mattei and Nader, 2008).

There was in the pre-modern era, in the *Ancien Régime*, a large abundance of commons – both physical and social. Capital was still very scarce at that time. Every peasant could, for example, enjoy the products of forests. Commons were also social institutions. Village economies were based on use value, and not exchange value. Families were commons. A lot of enterprises were run as commons: the guilds of notaries, painters and so on. People were not living by themselves, but as part of an organized structure where they would be living their whole lives.

The early political territorial powers required almost unlimited capital to complete the centralization of state authority. The legal constructions of modernity were therefore carried out by denying legal dignity to previous (commons-based) legal institutions. Jurists mixed together the doctrine of private property and public sovereignty, manipulating materials of Roman times. They made the assumption that all things – especially lands – that were not already deemed private property could be occupied. Ownership and sovereignty became the two organizational principles of legal modernity, structuring the individual-centred vision of law that is still with us today.

Rationalist natural law was, thus, instrumental in constructing the conditions for plunder. The early acts of incorporation, which created a legal personhood as a rational expansion of physical personhood, gave corporations limited liability and the right to bear arms in order to guarantee their own survival (Mattei and Quarta, 2018). This legal artefact led to tremendous colonial expansion and exploitation. Roman law, rationalized by the natural-law school, provided the language and the rituals to justify the oppression. The fundamental vision – given great prestige by writers such as Nicolò Machiavelli, Jean Bodin, and Thomas Hobbes – was that, in secular matters of sovereignty, might makes right (Capra and Mattei, 2015: pp. 74–6; Monateri, 2018).

International law as we know it today was created by Hugo Grotius (de Groot) (1583–1645), a Protestant Dutch lawyer and politician who founded what is known as the northern school of natural law, which was based on a Cartesian vision of rational natural laws. For most of his life, Grotius worked as a hired gun serving the interests of the Dutch East India Company, the first global corporation. He demonstrated a staggering capacity to deduct, from objective and universal principles of reason, legal solutions that favoured his powerful corporate clients yet remained acceptable to 'civilized' sovereign nations (Meiksins Wood, 2012). Of special importance was Grotius' ability to offer legal advantages to private corporations over states. For instance, in his book *Mare Liberum* (The Free Sea), he argued in favour of the East India Company's right to attack and plunder a Portuguese ship. Grotius argued that Portugal's claim of exclusivity on certain routes on the high seas was against the natural openness of this 'global common', thus justifying the attack as actually protecting the rational order. Thus the discipline of international law was born in an act of corporate plunder, paradoxically justified by a brilliant jurist deploying the Roman legal concept of the high seas as a natural common (*res communis omnium*). The Peace of Westphalia (1648) finally simplified the international legal order around a system of nation-states, fiercely independent from one another. These European states were owners of their territories, just as the ancient Roman paterfamilias had been the owner of his land (Capra and Mattei, 2015: pp. 63–4).

This is very important to understand the current situation, because today we are in a way discounting the consequences of the construction of a legal landscape that gives privileged status to certain kinds of institutions, as well as to the unlimited accumulation of wealth. The corporation was born together with international law. That was again a way to transform commons into capital, one of the tools in order to transform use value into exchange value. You create a corporate charter to give incentives to people who want to invest money to put them in a very safe position knowing that if things go badly, they will only lose that part of capital.

We were very successful in this enterprise. As humankind, we were so successful in the process of transforming commons into capital that today we do not have commons anymore but huge amounts of capital. In essence, international law was responsible for shaping the legal landscape that made this transformation of commons into capital possible. By producing the same kind of capitalist landscape as private law, international law was able to transform all commons into capital. Today, every single commons is suffering, and the capital is over-abundant – that became clear during the 2008 economic crisis.

The problem is that the conditions upon which we determine and review these legal institutions have completely changed. Now we have too much capital and too little commons. And yet, we still have the same fundamental international legal structure in place. International legal institutions still work in transforming more commons into capital. International law has not produced any fundamental rethinking of the discipline. Since its foundation by Hugo Grotius, international law has remained based on individualized Cartesian building blocks – legal persons in competition with each other within a mechanistic, depoliticized vision of law – rather than being interpreted as a genuine global network of relationships where actual power ratios between and within communities make it impossible to distinguish law from politics (Capra and Mattei, 2015: pp. 117–18).

The only commons that are left are social commons like friendship, which themselves are becoming capital. Nowadays, friendship is marketed on Facebook, Twitter and so on. Your personality becomes a commodity. What counts for these companies is the amount of knowledge they have about you, so that they can sell it to third parties for advertisement or control purposes. We are again in a moment of massive transformation.

In this state of affairs, the changes we need are radical. We need institutions that try to serve opposite purposes to what the legal institutions in force are doing today. This is what the ecology of international law is about: what kind of institutions do we need for sustainability? Are there fundamental laws of nature and reproduction of life on the planet that should not be conflated with the human law that we deploy in organizing our society? My point is that the laws of nature are based upon principles that are plainly ignored by human law. There is a big gap between what the needs of reproduction on the planet are (systemic thinking) and the way we look at our own laws (individual-centred and based on a pattern of extraction). International law is itself an extractive setting in need of progressive regeneration and conversion, because while we think globally, we act locally, where physical and cultural resistance can happen (Capra and Mattei, 2015: p. 156). International law, however, organizes the extractive machine *par excellence* – the centralized state, with the fiction of formal equality between states and with a pattern of commutative justice without the holistic distributive justice to which we actually need to resort.

If you look at early international legal scholars like Francisco de Vitoria (1492–1546), there was still a concern for distributive justice. Mostly active at the University of Salamanca, the Spanish scholastics were the first jurists in the Western legal tradition to attempt an ambitious synthesis of Roman law with the ideas of Aristotle and Thomas Aquinas, much as Aquinas had earlier worked to fuse Aristotle's ideas with Christian ideology (Gordley, 1990). Their highly organized system of natural law was designed to explain human laws within a holistic theory of God and nature, a grand vision that included a synthesis between the Aristotelian concepts of distributive and commutative justice. In Aristotle, distributive justice, which concerns the just distribution of goods in society, pertains to the whole, whereas commutative justice, concerned with the fulfilment of contractual obligations between individuals, pertains to the parts (Gordley, 2013).

The scholastic concern with distributive justice and, thus, the organic well-being of society continued to view the human as part of a holistic community. The humanistic spirit of the time, however, injected into this vision an unprecedented degree of concern with the rational individual as an 'atom' of society, capable of finding its way within itself and not simply as a member of all-pervasive collectivity. Sixteenth-century social and legal studies, developing in academic settings, could no longer resist the movement towards examining society as an algebraic sum of its component parts. Moving from the scholastic thinkers of Salamanca to Leiden with Hugo Grotius, natural law was reduced to a system of relationships between distinct sovereigns (physical or moral persons; the latter is a legal term for something like a state or a corporation) governed by a common law based on reason. Distributive justice was lost and only commutative justice remained in later international law writings (Capra and Mattei, 2015: pp. 62–3).

Now, if we look at the relationships between states through the lens of commutative justice, then you might accept the status quo and not care at all that some countries like Burkina Faso have an ecological footprint of 0.10 while others like the United States consume six planets. The only sort of justice international law cares about is justice 'in exchange'. Grotius also laid the foundations of modern international law by asserting that the relationship between sovereigns either can be voluntary (by treaty) or can be governed by principles of 'just war' waged by a legitimate sovereign, a notion he inherited from the Spanish scholastics (Capra and Mattei, 2015: p. 63).

6. CONCLUSION

This chapter has sought to provide a radical ecological reading of international law by articulating the 'evil technology hypothesis'. For this purpose, Section 2 started with the basic assumption that because we, humans, have only one planet, our ecological footprint should be equal to one planet. This is the criterion against which the sustainability of our actions on the international plane should be determined. Section 3 introduced Martti Koskenniemi's indeterminacy thesis, whereby the uncertain political grounds of the liberal project behind international law have made the latter prone to become an instrument that is able to justify even radically opposing outcomes, depending on the political motivations a certain international lawyer may decide to pursue in each particular case. This has been followed by a brief foray into Anghie's theory about the colonial genesis of international law and, most importantly, his depiction of international law as a technology, i.e., as a means to pursue ends, around which the value judgements are assumed to be uncontroversial. This section restated, as the starting point for our further argument, the idea of international law as incrementally transformed by corporate interests into imperial law, a reactive institutional setting which effectively precludes the possibility of distribution in favour of weaker actors.

Section 4 then investigated the possibility that technology in general – far from being a form that can accommodate different uses – is actually 'evil' in itself, in that it privileges certain modes of relation to the human and other-than-human world that systematically favours objectification of the 'other' and an ethos of domination over people and the planet. Secondly, the ability of technology to channel energies into narrow pursuits has been regarded as one possible factor behind the unsustainable growth of civilization, understood as a pattern of human living that (based as it is on elevation of the reproductive interest of a certain human community above the possibility for other human and other-than-human communities equally to renew themselves) is incapable of being supported by the land base and requires trade and extraction of resources.

These insights, articulated in ecological literature, have then been translated in the field of international law in Section 5. It has been said that international law is at odds with the way nature is actually organized. Nature is organized around commons and open patterns – not conservation of power or extraction. The kind of rules that we should look for are therefore generative rules – rules that allow life to reproduce according to its own processes and give subjectivity not just to humans (especially human individuals), but larger living communities that include humans and non-humans. International law has to open up and understand that its functioning can only become resilient if it is capable of allowing the natural process of life to reproduce itself.

This is why there is a more radical, fundamental critique of international law – because international law operates on too large a scale. Sustainability works only on a localized basis. The small scale of legal institutions is extremely important, because legal and political institutions serve the commons only when they are very close to the context from which they emerge. The moment these institutions become abstract artefacts, professionalized notions of law that remain in the domain of the 'transcendent', is when the solution becomes the problem. This is why I consider international law to be beyond repair.

NOTE

* This chapter benefited from the comments and reviews of Samuel Cogolati and Nils Vanstappen.

REFERENCES

Anghie, A. (1999) Finding the Peripheries: Sovereignty and Colonialism in Nineteenth-century International Law. *Harvard Journal of International Law*, **40** (1), 1–80.

Anghie, A. (2004) *Imperialism, Sovereignty and the Making of International Law*. Cambridge, Cambridge University Press.

Anghie, A. (2006) The Evolution of International Law: Colonial and Postcolonial Realities. *Third World Quarterly*, **27** (5), 739–53.

Capra F. and Mattei, U. (2015) *The Ecology of Law: Toward a Legal System in Tune with Nature and Community*. Oakland, Berrett-Koehler Publishers.

Gordley, J. (1990) *The Philosophical Origins of Modern Contract Doctrine*. Oxford, Oxford University Press.

Gordley, J. (2013) *The Jurists: A Critical History*. Oxford, Oxford University Press.
Holder, J. and Lee, M. (2007) *Environmental Protection, Law and Policy*. 2nd edn, Cambridge, Cambridge University Press.
Keizer, K., Lindberg, S. and Steg, L. (2008) The Spreading of Disorder. *Science*, **322** (5908), 1681–5.
Koskenniemi, M. (2005) *From Apology to Utopia: The Structure of International Legal Argument*. Cambridge, Cambridge University Press.
Mamyluk, N. and Mattei, U. (2011) Comparative International Law. *Brooklyn Journal of International Law*, **36** (2), 385–452.
Marks, S. (2009) False Contingency. *Current Legal Problems*, **62** (1), 1–21.
Mattei, U. (2003) A Theory of Imperial Law: A Study on U.S. Hegemony and the Latin Resistance. *Indiana Journal of Global Legal Studies*, **10** (1), 383–448.
Mattei, U. and Nader, L. (2008) *Plunder: When the Rule of Law is Illegal*. Malden, MA, Blackwell Publishing.
Mattei, U. and Russi, L. (2012) The Evil Technology Hypothesis: A Deep Ecological Reading of International Law. *Cardozo Law Review de Novo*, 2012, 263–77.
Mattei, U. and Quarta, A. (2018) *The Turning Point in Private Law: Ecology, Technology and the Commons*. Cheltenham, UK and Northampton, MA, USA, Edward Elgar.
Meiksins Wood, E. (2012) *Liberty and Property: A Social History of Western Political Thought from the Renaissance to Enlightenment*. London and New York, Verso.
Monateri, P.G. (2018) *Dominus Mundi: Political Sublime and the World Order*. Oxford, Hart Publishing.
Polanyi, K. (1944) *The Great Transformation*. New York, Farrar and Rinehart.
Prieur, R. (2001) Civilization Will Eat Itself: The Anarchist Library. Available from: http://theanarchistlibrary.org/library/ran-prieur-civilization-will-eat-itself (accessed 16 November 2017).
United Nations (1946) Statute of the International Court of Justice. San Francisco, 18 April 1946, United Nations Treaty Series, 33 (933).
United Nations (2015) The Paris Agreement. Paris, 12 December 2015, UN Doc. FCCC/CP/2015/L.9.

11. From eroding to enabling the commons: the dual movement in international law

Olivier De Schutter

1. INTRODUCTION

The history of international law is deeply entangled with that of the commons as a way of governing resources and of organizing community life. The inaugural moment of the discipline was in the successive attempts by Francisco de Vitoria and Hugo Grotius to recruit natural law to justify Spain's conquest of the 'New World' and, later, the expansion of the Dutch East India Company and the West India Company. The idea that the territories to be 'civilized' and converted to Christianism were functioning as a 'commons', in which land was neither subject to property rights nor controlled by a political sovereign deserving to be called a 'state' (since the control over a territory was seen as a defining characteristic of state sovereignty), was central to this project. Despite his humanitarian credentials, Vitoria was the first author to propose an elaborate defence of Spanish penetration of the New World by asserting that:

> it was permissible from the beginning of the world (when everything was in common) for any one to set forth and travel wheresoever he would. Now this was not to be taken away by the division of property, for it was never the intention of peoples to destroy by that division the reciprocity and common user which prevailed among men, and indeed, in the days of Noah, it would have been inhuman to do so. (Vitoria, 1917 [1532]: p. 151, cited by Anghie, 2005: p. 20)

In other terms, the lands which the Spanish conquistadores sought to control were considered 'available', because they were neither exploited by private owners nor subject to state control, and thus had retained their original status as 'common' to all mankind.

During this primitive phase, the notion of 'commons' and the theory of property rights were used instrumentally, either to justify the occupation of land or the travel along routes that were considered to belong to no one in particular (and not to be subject of sovereign control), or to support the idea that the non-Western peoples were less civilized (since property rights were a mark of the more advanced societies) and that colonization thus held the promise of 'development' and should be seen as benefiting them. These ideas were developed at greater length in the major work of Hugo Grotius, *De jure belli ac pacis*, which he published in three volumes in 1625. Grotius borrowed from Vitoria the idea that there exists a natural right to travel across the Earth and the right to wage just war when this is denied. But he also presented the shift from the 'commons' to property rights as inherent in the process of development:

> God gave to mankind in general, dominion over all the creatures of the Earth, from the first creation of the world; a grant which was renewed upon the restoration of the world after the deluge. All things . . . formed a common stock for all mankind, as the inheritors of one general patrimony. From hence it happened, that every man seized to his own use or consumption whatever he met with; a general exercise of a right, which supplied the place of private property. So that to deprive any one of what he had thus seized, became an act of injustice. [This state of affairs however] could not subsist but in the greatest simplicity of manners, and under the mutual forbearance and good-will of mankind. An example of a community of goods, arising from extreme simplicity of manners, may be seen in some nations of America, who for many ages have subsisted in this manner without inconvenience . . . [A 'community of lands for pasture' continued even after the destruction of the tower of Babel and the subsequent 'dispersion of mankind, who took possession of different parts of the earth'.] For the great extent of land was sufficient for the use of all occupants, as yet but few in number, without their incommoding each other . . . it was deemed unlawful to fix a land mark on the plain, or to apportion it out in stated limits. But as men increased in numbers and their flocks in the same proportion, they could no longer with convenience enjoy the use of lands in common, and it became necessary to divide them into allotments for each family. (Grotius, 1925 [1625]: Book II, chapter II)

In Grotius' view, property rights over land are therefore established as population increases and as it becomes necessary to clarify the boundaries of what belongs to each, in order to make the progress of civilization (and the division of labour) possible. This understanding of civilization and of the original role of the state (which is to protect the boundaries of private property) was commonplace at the time: it would be reiterated (indeed, almost literally reproduced) in chapter V of John Locke's *Second Treatise on Civil Government*, first published in 1690. But Grotius was anxious to reconcile his defence of property rights with the need to favour the expansion of the great trading companies (the Dutch East India Company in particular, which was for a time his paymaster (Borschberg, 1999; van

Ittersum, 2010)). His solution was to state that the reasoning according to which property rights are a mark of civilizational progress does not apply to the seas, since:

> Notwithstanding the statements above made, it must be admitted that some things are impossible to be reduced to a state of property, of which the sea affords us an instance both in its general extent, and in its principal branches . . . For the magnitude of the sea is such, as to be sufficient for the use of all nations, to allow them without inconvenience and prejudice to each other the right of fishing, sailing, or any other advantage which that element affords . . . The same appellation of common may be given to the sand of the shore, which being incapable of cultivation, is left free to yield its inexhaustable supplies for the use of all. There is a natural reason also, which renders the sea, considered in the view already taken, incapable of being made property: because occupancy can never subsist, but in things that can be confined to certain permanent bounds. (Grotius, 1925 [1625]: Book II, chapter II)

Moreover, Grotius added, 'among Theologians also it is a received opinion, that if in urgent distress, any one shall take from another what is absolutely necessary for the preservation of his own life, the act shall not be deemed a theft' (Book II, chapter VI); and 'another right [is also generally acknowledged], which is that of making use of the property of another, where such use is attended with no prejudice to the owner' (Book II, chapter XI). This justifies the right to travel, even through areas that are effectively occupied by a sovereign people, for the purpose of trade: '[i]t is upon the same foundation of common right, that a free passage, through countries, rivers, or over any part of the sea, which belongs to some particular people, ought to be allowed to those, who require it for the necessary occasions of life; whether those occasions be in quest of settlements, after being driven from their own country, or to trade with a remote nation, or to recover by just war their lost possessions' (Book II, chapter XIII).

It would be a mistake to see these views as idiosyncratic. Grotius was a highly influential author, read and discussed by the political elites of the period, and he was not merely expressing ideas of his own: he was describing with great clarity what was the received understanding of the times. Nor should they be dismissed as mere historical relic: in fact, though the wording may have changed and a process of euphemization taken place, they have remained very much central to international law to this day. This is obvious, perhaps unsurprisingly, when one considers the arguments for the establishment of the mandates system under the supervision of the League of Nations. The Covenant of the League of Nations described the exercise by the colonial powers of their 'tutelage' of peoples still 'not yet able to stand by themselves' as 'a sacred trust of civilisation', to be exercised under the supervision of a Permanent Mandates Commission of the League. Article 22 of the Covenant emphasizes the duty of the colonial powers to extend to those peoples the benefits of civilization:

> To those colonies and territories which as a consequence of the late war have ceased to be under the sovereignty of the States which formerly governed them and which are inhabited by peoples not yet able to stand by themselves under the strenuous conditions of the modern world, there should be applied the principle that the well-being and development of such peoples form a sacred trust of civilisation and that securities for the performance of this trust should be embodied in this Covenant.
>
> The best method of giving practical effect to this principle is that the tutelage of such peoples should be entrusted to advanced nations who by reason of their resources, their experience or their geographical position can best undertake this responsibility, and who are willing to accept it, and that this tutelage should be exercised by them as Mandatories on behalf of the League.

At the time when the Permanent Mandates Commission started to exercise its functions, Frederick Lugard, a former employee of the British East Africa Company and of the Royal Niger Company, and former Governor of Nigeria for the British Government, was at the apex of his prestige as a theorist of colonial rule. He published *The Dual Mandate in British Tropical Africa* in 1922, just as he joined the Permanent Mandates Commission as a representative of the United Kingdom. The major question the colonial powers were confronted with was how to reconcile the 'duty' to ensure economic development of the territories under control with that of 'securing the welfare of the natives': 'The problem', Lugard wrote in a report to the Permanent Mandates Commission on 'Economic Development of Mandated Territories in Its Relation to the Well-being of the Natives', 'is how these two duties should be reconciled without, on the one hand, subordinating policy to a purely utilitarian outlook or, on the other hand, adopting a standpoint too exclusively philanthropic' (PMC, *Seventh Session*: p. 197, cited by Anghie, 2005: p. 159).

There was a convenient way to address this problem, however. It was to recast the interests of the 'natives' as residing not in the preservation of their existing social relationships (which were communitarian, centred around the tribe, rather than individualistic) or in that of their relationships to nature (which was a potentially huge, but largely untapped, source of wealth), but in exploitation itself: not only should 'their raw materials and foodstuffs – without which civilization cannot exist . . . be developed alike in the interests of the natives and of the world at large' (Lugard, 1922: p. 60), but in addition the natives should be co-opted, as providers of cheap labour, into the capitalist system, in order to allow them to 'escape the confines of their communities' (Anghie, 2005: p. 162). Exploitation of both labour and land, perhaps, benefited colonial powers and 'the world at large', since it allowed the creation of wealth and extended the division of labour to the territories under mandate; but it also brought progress to the natives themselves, who would gradually become 'liberated *homini oeconomici*' – freed from the obstacles that formerly blocked their economic progress, and freed *thanks to very fact that they were being exploited.* The disruption of communal social relationships and the shift to an exploitative relationship to nature, in that view, was not the price to pay for economic development to proceed: they were the definition of progress itself, and were to be treated as benefits, not harms.

In the following section of this chapter I shall try to illustrate that the idea of development, in its contemporary versions, remains heavily indebted to this view of 'progress'. In this perspective, the process of individualization – the shift from *Gemeinschaft* to *Gesellschaft*, to borrow from the F. Tönnies' terminology (Tönnies, 2001 [1887]) – is an indicator that a polity is arriving at maturity; and the process of privatization – the gradual erosion of common-property regimes – is equated with modernity and with the promise of greater economic efficiency. Section 3 argues, however, that doubts have emerged concerning both the inevitability of this movement, and its desirability: starting in the late 2000s, a counter-movement has emerged, in search of an alternative. The rolling out of titling schemes, understood as certification of property rights leading to the commodification of land, was the main battlefield on which these two tendencies clashed. Section 4 then assesses the contribution to the most recent developments of international human rights law to protecting the commons, and enabling common-property regimes to resist the general trend towards commodification. Section 5 argues that this counter-movement in international law will be successful if it can strike the right balance between recognizing such regimes and enabling them to function, on the one hand, and on the other, providing them with the 'constitutional framework' – the ground rules – required to ensure that they are both legitimate and equipped to sustainably use the resources on which the community depends. A brief conclusion is offered.

2. THE MOVEMENT TOWARDS PROPERTY RIGHTS

The defence of colonial expansion as a process of civilization may sound exotic; in fact, the similarities are striking with the current period. In the 1950s and 1960s, 'developmentalism' was premised on the idea that development went through stages, from 'backward' and predominantly agrarian societies to societies in which the accumulation of capital would allow a transition of large parts of the population to the manufacturing and services sectors: though authors such as W. Arthur Lewis (1954) and Walt W. Rostow (1960) provide different versions, they shared this dominant narrative. In that ideological context, poor countries were expected to first identify their comparative advantage (which was predominantly in the exploitation of their natural resources and of cheap labour), in order to be able, later, to 'climb up' the ladder of development. Western capital was to facilitate this, first by encouraging the industrialization of agricultural production (thus allowing the emergence of an agricultural sector competitive on global markets), and then by financing the secondary and tertiary sectors of the economy. In low-income countries, however (a category defined by the World Bank that largely overlaps with the least-developed countries listed by the United Nations (UN) Economic and Social Council[1]), only the first part of this script was followed. Agriculture was increasingly channelled towards export markets after the 1960s, thus perpetuating the international division of labour that these countries inherited from the colonial period. In many of these countries, agriculture came to be understood as an extractive enterprise: it was seen as a means to ensure a steady flow of cheap raw commodities to industrialized countries, and it was developed with that purpose in mind, despite the highly problematic impacts – from the agronomic and the environmental point of view – of monocultures, typical of export-led agriculture.

The substitution of a Western conception of property rights to the commons has been an integral component of this programme. Of course, one major difference between the immediate post-colonial era and the current period is that we now have developed a greater awareness about the accelerated depletion of natural resources; indeed, on an increasingly crowded planet where a growing part of the population entertains the prospect of attaining the lifestyle of those living in the affluent West, fears about scarcity have suddenly re-emerged – triggered, for instance, by the global food price crisis of 2007–2008. Yet, paradoxically perhaps, far from leading us to slow down the process of natural resources exploitation and the push towards economic efficiency by deepening the international division of labour, we are seeking to speed up both, in the name of overcoming these very threats. Perhaps now, more than ever in human history, the exploitation of natural resources through means that are as rational and as efficient as possible is described as an urgent task, reminiscent of the 'sacred trust of civilisation' at the heart of the Mandates system of the interwar period, in order to be able to quench the thirst for more, despite the limitations imposed by a finite planet. The strong push towards the formalization of property rights over land, as a means to encourage economic growth and to create an investment-friendly climate, is largely perceived as an essential tool in this regard.

In that perspective, the 'commons' – the communal ownership of pastures, fishing grounds or forests, allowing all community members to enjoy access to shared natural resources – are perceived not as an essential safeguard against extreme deprivation for those who are landless or land-poor, but instead as an obstacle to development. Development, in turn, is understood as the maximization of wealth creation, *inter alia* by favouring the exploitation of natural resources, which – precisely because we are facing the threat of scarcity – should be turned into economic assets, tradeable if possible, in order to ensure that they will benefit the most efficient users. The prescription is clear: to strengthen private property rights wherever possible, and where this cannot be done, to ensure that natural resources are used rationally by establishing strong state control.

It is against this background that we can understand the insistence on the rolling out of titling schemes as a development tool, to favour the globalization of the Western conception of property rights. The promoters of such schemes see them as presenting a number of advantages. First, the security of tenure favoured through titling should encourage individual landowners to make the necessary investments in their land, thus improving their living conditions and, in rural areas, enhancing the productivity of the cultivated plot: the occupants, it is supposed, will not invest in their land unless they are certain to be protected from the risk of losing it. One major argument in favour of this view was put forward by the Peruvian economist Hernando de Soto, whose Institute for Liberty and Democracy (ILD) took a leading role in developing a major titling programme in Peru after 1998: in *The Mystery of Capital*, in which he attributes the lack of growth in developing countries to undeveloped property regimes (de Soto, 2000), de Soto forcefully argues that titling of their property allows the owners to mortgage their land, and thus to obtain access to credit, allowing them to make such investments. In what he calls the 'capitalisation process', 'dead (physical) assets' – 'where assets cannot be readily turned into capital, cannot be traded outside narrow local circles where people know and trust each other, cannot be used as collateral for a loan, and cannot be used as a share against an investment' – are turned into live capital, which can be mobilized for investment (de Soto, 2000: p. 6).

Perhaps unsurprisingly, de Soto's views found a warm reception within the World Bank, which, during the previous decade, had been assisting with the large-scale and rapid privatization of the formerly socialist economies of Central and Eastern Europe. Indeed, already in 1993, the World Bank had presented a paper entitled 'Housing: Enabling Markets to Work', in which – while it warned against costly titling programmes – it underscored the importance of 'systems of property registration and titling and workable systems of foreclosure and eviction', as these were considered 'necessary to ensure the collateral security of mortgage loans' (Mayo and Angel, 1993: p. 46). The emphasis in that report was more on ensuring security of tenure than on titling as one means of achieving it, but it did include a strong recommendation for the removal of any restrictions on the emergence of a market in property rights over land (Mayo and Angel, 1993: p. 117; and see Feder and Feeny, 1991). Ten years later, and after de Soto's contribution to the debate, the World Bank referred in the following terms to a study by the McKinsey Global Institute on the conditions of growth in India:

> With fewer assets in the formal sector, more entrepreneurs are excluded from using property as a collateral, and less credit is allocated. The possibility of getting loans is the only reason to take on the daunting task of registering in some countries . . . But when it is too difficult, few bother. Entrepreneurs will invest less if their property rights are less secure. Inefficient registration is associated with lower rates of private investment. And it leads to lower productivity, since it is harder for property to be transferred from less to more productive uses. The result is slower growth. One study estimates that restrictive land market regulations cost 1.3% of annual economic growth in India. (World Bank, 2004a: p. 40; see also World Bank, 2004b: p. 78)

According to this first argument in favour of titling schemes, thus, registered property can be used as collateral to obtain credit; but it can also be seen as a signalling device that provides information about the trustworthiness of the borrower: research in Indonesia illustrates this by relating titling to the practice of local banks, who tend to see titling of property as proof that the household will be able to repay the loan, independently of the use of the property as collateral (Castañeda Dower and Potamites, 2012).

Second, the clarification of property rights should encourage the emergence of efficient land markets: lowering transaction costs, it is supposed, will result in the land going to the most productive user, thus maximizing the productivity of land as an economic asset (Feder and Noronha, 1987). The World Bank notes, thus, that 'secure and unambiguous property rights . . . allow markets to transfer land to more productive uses and users' (World Bank, 2007: p. 138). The intellectual roots of this argument can be found in the work of Ronald H. Coase, according to which if transaction costs are low enough (and, ideally, reduced to zero), the freedom of transactions will result in solutions that are most economically efficient (Coase, 1960). The basic reasoning is simple enough: buyers of property will pay the price they considers reasonable, taking into consideration the streams of income that are expected to flow from making productive use of the assets acquired; therefore, if such assets are transferred to the highest bidder, as an efficiently functioning market for property rights should allow, they should ultimately be captured by the economic actors who can use them most productively, thus contributing to general economic growth.

Third, the clarification of property rights and the development of markets for land rights should attract foreign investors. This is why the *Doing Business* rankings of the World Bank, which use a series of indicators to measure the quality of the 'investment climate' of the countries surveyed, include among their criteria the time and cost of transferring a property title from one seller to the buyer – from the moment the buyer has a copy of the seller's title to the moment when the transfer is opposable to third parties, so that the property can be resold or used as collateral when approaching a bank (Chavez Sanchez et al., 2014). The easier it is to register property rights, the faster and cheaper the procedures are for transferring property rights, and the more investors will be willing to enter the country concerned and thus, it is hoped, to contribute to its development (although the automaticity of this relationship has, of course, been questioned: see De Schutter et al., 2012).

Fourth, the formalization of property rights over land allows public authorities to increase their tax revenues, and where necessary to deliver certain public services that depend on fees being paid by the users. As de Soto remarks, once they are formally registered, assets provide 'an accountable address for the collection of debts and taxes' as well as 'the basis for a creation of reliable and universal public utilities' (de Soto, 2000: p. 6). The two arguments are combined where public services are provided against the payment of users' fees: only where users have registered property can they be taxed (preferably at a rate that will depend on the value of the property that they own) in order to finance the provision of water, telephone lines or electricity to the areas in which they live. For cash-strapped countries, struggling to provide basic infrastructure to their populations in large part due to their inability to collect taxes efficiently, this is not of minor significance.

These are apparently powerful arguments in favour of titling programmes, and they have indeed been highly influential since the 1990s. The enthusiasm for the expansion of a Western concept of property rights was, perhaps, fuelled by a more general trend towards market-based solutions, following the collapse of the state-led economies of the socialist camp. But it was also a failure of political imagination. It betrayed an inability to think beyond the market and the state, beyond private property rights and centrally controlled forms of management of natural resources. And, as a means to reduce poverty in developing countries, it appears in retrospect as extraordinarily naïve. Less than a decade after the push for titling schemes started, the conditions were right for a counter-movement to emerge.

3. THE COUNTER-MOVEMENT: DOUBTS ABOUT THE DIFFUSION OF WESTERN-STYLE PROPERTY RIGHTS

As more lessons were drawn from a series of titling programmes implemented in the developing world during the 1990s, a number of ambiguities gradually came to the surface. A turning point was the establishment, in 2005, of the Commission for the Legal Empowerment of the Poor (CLEP). Launched at the initiative of a range of governments from different regions, working together with the UN Development Programme (UNDP) and the UN Economic Commission for Europe (UNECE), the CLEP was established under the co-chairmanship of Hernando de Soto and Madeleine Albright. It was tasked with studying the relationship between 'informality' and poverty. The concept note presenting the initiative states:

> One of the staggering facts about poverty, which is not addressed explicitly in the MDGs, is that the vast majority of the world's poor live their daily lives in what is often referred to as the *informal* or *extralegal* sector, often excluded from the benefits of a legal order. [The work of Hernando de Soto shows that] legal exclusion, in the sense that the assets and transactions of the poor are not legally protected and recognised, produces and reproduces poverty throughout the developing world and in former communist societies. (Commission for the Legal Empowerment of the Poor, 2005: pp. 3–4)

The process of 'capitalization', through which 'dead capital' is brought to life, was central to the inquiry of the Commission. Indeed, to many, the CLEP was seen as an opportunity to validate the findings of Hernando de Soto and his conclusion that under-development had much to do with the failure to establish reliable systems for property rights through the registration of assets, especially immovable assets. It therefore came as a surprise to most that, when it presented its final report in June 2008, the CLEP felt compelled to note a number of problems associated with titling schemes. The CLEP referred to the risks associated with 'elite capture': '[i]n many countries', it noted, 'speculators pre-empt prospective titling programmes by buying up land from squatters at prices slightly higher than prevailing informal ones. Squatters benefit in the short term, but miss out on the main benefits of the titling programme, which accrue to the people with deeper pockets' (Commission for the Legal Empowerment of the Poor, 2008: p. 80, citing Platteau, 2000: p. 68; on the risks of elite capture, see also,

Firmin-Sellers and Sellers, 1999). The Commission also identified, as one of the failures of titling programmes as they had been implemented in the past, that these programmes tended to neglect the role of collective rights and of customary forms of tenure: such forms of tenure, the Commission conceded, could be highly legitimate and effective in guaranteeing security of tenure (Commission for the Legal Empowerment of the Poor, 2008: p. 52).

The CLEP concluded that the benefits of titling schemes may have been exaggerated in the past, and that it may be inappropriate to simply transplant the Western concept of property rights into the legal systems of developing countries, the legal traditions and needs of which may be markedly different:

> Promoting a truly inclusive property-rights system that incorporates measures to strengthen tenure security requires learning from the mixed experience with past individual titling programmes. To ensure protection and inclusion of the poorest, a broad range of policy measures should be considered. These include formal recognition, adequate representation, and integration of a variety of forms of land tenure such as customary rights, indigenous peoples' rights, group rights, and certificates. Success depends greatly upon comprehensively reforming the governance system surrounding property rights . . . These systems need to be accessible, affordable, transparent, and free from unnecessary complexity. Above all, the poor must be protected from arbitrary eviction by due process and full compensation. (Commission for the Legal Empowerment of the Poor, 2008: p. 65)

These statements are significant, both because the initial bias of the CLEP clearly was in favour of following de Soto in his optimistic views about the virtues of titling, and of course because – although not a member of the working group on property – he was the co-chair of the commission. But the conclusions of the CLEP were foreshadowed by a number of studies published in the interim, after the first large-scale titling programmes had been launched (Firmin-Sellers and Sellers, 1999; von Benda-Beckmann, 2003; Unruh, 2002). Indeed, the World Bank itself noted in 2006:

> most policy analysts now no longer simply assume that formalization in a given context necessarily increases tenure security, and leads to collateralized lending. The original assumptions have now become questions for empirical research. (Cited in Payne et al., 2007: p. 3)

The very terms of 'clarification' and 'formalization', which are used to refer to the improvements to the property rights regimes that titling should allow, increasingly came to appear as ambiguous and perhaps even misleading. The purpose of titling schemes is, ostensibly, to confirm existing use rights. But these use rights are often complex. It is not unusual for conflicting claims to exist over any piece of land. And there are various types of land users, not all of whom are 'dormant landowners' awaiting an opportunity to register the land they occupy.

Moreover, prior to the formalization of property rights through titling, tenure generally is regulated by custom. Customary forms of tenure are often highly legitimate and, as recognized by an influential report authored in 2003 by Klaus Deininger for the World Bank, they can ensure a high level of security of tenure (Deininger, 2003: p. 53; African Union et al., 2009: para. 3.1.3.). They can also deliver the same services as formalized property rights, including by favouring, in certain cases, efficiency-enhancing exchanges (Deininger, 2003: pp. 31–2) or by allowing for the emergence of rental markets, which can improve access to land particularly for land-scarce and labour-abundant households with little education (Deininger et al., 2008). Research has highlighted that, in fact, traditional (or customary) systems of tenure in many cases allow for the individualization of ownership, and that even where communal ownership subsists, such systems allow for cultivation and possession to remain with individual households (Feder and Noronha, 1987). The superimposition of titling on these pre-existing, customary forms of tenure may result in more conflicts rather than in more clarity, and in less security rather than in improved security (Toulmin and Quan, 2000).

In addition, and of more immediate relevance here, customary forms of property may provide security for those depending on the commons – such as pastoralists, artisanal fishers, or those with small herds – for whom classic property rights are generally not an appropriate solution. As a result, we find ourselves today in a paradoxical situation. On the one hand, we have witnessed in recent years an increased competition for land and other natural resources. In cities, this competition is encouraged by the gentrification of certain areas and the financialization of housing markets, both of which encourage speculation and price inflation. In rural areas, competition for arable land is the combined result of demographic growth, urbanization and the sprawl of urban areas, pressures resulting from large-scale development projects, and the reservation of land for tourism and other purposes. Land degradation due to unsustainable agronomic practices and climate change, together with a growing demand for agricultural commodities for food, bioenergy, fibre and feedstock, increase the tensions between industrial agriculture, conducted on a large scale and often for export commodities, and agriculture practised on a smaller scale to meet the needs of local communities, further encouraging speculation over land. Against this background, concerns have been expressed in particular about the impacts of 'land grabs', fuelled by fears about the volatility of agricultural prices and facilitated by weak governance of tenure and corruption in land administration (De Schutter, 2011a; 2011b). The rolling out of titling schemes is the generally preferred solution to the risks associated with land grabs: such schemes have been widely seen as the best way to protect otherwise disempowered land users from the fear of dispossession without compensation, whether by large private landowners or by the state.

On the other hand, however, such titling schemes may in fact fuel new forms of dispossession of their own. This may seem paradoxical, since one of the very purposes of clarifying property rights is precisely to provide security of tenure: to allow slum dwellers to be recognized as owners of their home in the informal settlement where they are staying, or to allow those operating small farms to be protected from eviction from the land which they cultivate. Yet, as noted above, the clarification of property rights has also been justified by the need to establish a market for land rights, allowing a more fluid transfer of property rights – a lowering of transaction costs increasing the liquidity of these markets.[2] These two objectives may in fact be contradictory, as becomes clear once we realize that the commodification of property rights can be a source of exclusion and increase insecurity of tenure. First, as already seen, the process of titling itself may be captured by the elites – in addition to the risk of 'pre-emptive speculation' noted by the CLEP, titling schemes may be manipulated or tainted by corruption; or the formalization of property may be too costly or complex for the poorest segment of the population to benefit. Second, once property has been formalized and land demarcated, taxes may be imposed, and more easily collected, by public authorities. This may present an opportunity to better finance public services, as also noted above. But it may also have exclusionary effects: it may occur that the poorest are not able to pay those taxes and are forced to sell off their land as a result. Third, whether to pay those taxes or to make the necessary investments in their houses or on their cultivated lands, the poor (who by definition have no capital of their own) will be tempted to mortgage their land in order to have access to credit. But even if this works – even if, that is, lenders are willing to provide loans – the risk is that the debts will accumulate, and that the land will finally be seized by the lender: the commodification of land, in such a case, will have made the loss of land possible, rather than protecting the land user from such a risk. Fourth, the rural poor may be tempted to sell off land in order to overcome temporary economic hardship such as a bad harvest or a fall in the 'farm gate prices' received for their crops. In its 2003 report on land rights, the World Bank clearly recognized that land markets could encourage such 'distress sales', thus potentially increasing insecurity of tenure, rather than reducing it (Deininger, 2003: pp. 96–8).

This risk of dispossession following the rolling out of titling schemes, it is worth noting, should not be seen as *failure* of the system, or as a problem that should be remedied in order for the system to proceed more smoothly. Instead, it is *inherent in the very process of commodification of property rights* that gives property its value. It has been written that, in de Soto's view, the problem of informal forms of tenure is not so much too little security of tenure, but instead *too much*: the problem of 'dead capital' is that it cannot be lost, because it cannot be sold or mortgaged (Mitchell, 2006: p. 7). Indeed, de Soto is explicit about this, noting that one of the benefits of formal property systems is that they make people 'accountable', encouraging people 'in advanced countries' to 'respect titles, honor contracts, and obey the law', because of 'the possibility of forfeiture' (de Soto, 2000: pp. 55–6). In other terms, the counterpart of the improved security of tenure that formalization of property allowed, was the insecurity resulting from the possibility of losing property – whether because the household finds itself unable to reimburse the lender after having mortgaged the land, because the level of taxes makes paying those taxes unaffordable and forces the family to leave, or (where rural farming households are concerned) because the household finds it impossible to expand its property following the speculation fuelled by the titling process, and thus cannot achieve the economies of scale required to be competitive on the markets.

These dangers associated with the generalization of tradeable property rights are increased in a context in which fears of scarcity favour speculation over land and other natural resources. Indeed, there emerges a vicious cycle in which scarcity of resources increases commercial pressures over land, leading to accelerated titling processes (ostensibly in order to protect land users from dispossession), which in turn encourages speculation due to the inflated prices of land, thus further worsening the risks of scarcity. The further markets for land rights develop, the more there is a risk that the price of land will increase as a result of speculation. Speculation means that capital that could be put to productive uses, for instance for creating employment, will be immobilized. Even if we hypothesise that the 'speculative' part of price-setting can be separated from the 'market' price, the price of land following titling will increase, by at least 25 per cent according to most studies available (Payne et al., 2007: pp. 15–16). In principle, that represents a benefit for those who can register their land. But things look quite different when examined in a dynamic perspective: the poorest households may in fact be tempted to sell their land either to overcome a temporary shock or to profit from the opportunity resulting from sudden increases in the price of land, only to discover that the prices of other parcels too have become unaffordable, as the increased price of titled land creates ripple effects making all land more expensive (Payne et al., 2007: p. 16).

The speculation on land that follows registration processes, leading to inflated prices for land, leads one to question not only the de Soto hypothesis according to which such processes should benefit the poor by allowing them to use their (until then 'dead') assets as capital, but also the Coase hypothesis, which anticipates that, as markets for land rights develop, land will go to the most 'productive' users. As we have seen, these two narratives to a certain extent contradict each other: whereas the latter emphasizes the benefits to the poor of the formalization of property rights, the former emphasizes property's contribution to economic growth when in the hands of the most efficient actors. Yet, remarkably, both these narratives fail to take into account the impacts that result from the highly unequal distribution of purchasing power in many of the societies where such formalization processes take place. One implication of speculation over land is that the poorest landowners will be priced out of land markets, and that even those who manage to register their property may soon lose it, as a result of incurring unsustainable debts or because they seek to benefit from the 'windfall' effect that follows. Another implication is that where land is transferred it does not necessarily go to the most productive user, thus leading to efficiency gains and improving average productivity; rather, it goes to those who have the strongest purchasing power. Indeed, as interest for agricultural land has been rising significantly in recent years, the risk of the poorest being priced out of increasingly speculative land markets is higher now even than in the past.

Titling is, therefore, not the silver bullet it sometimes has been imagined to be. It does not truly protect the rural poor against the risks of dispossession of land; nor does it ensure that land is used either most efficiently or more sustainably. The search for alternatives has now begun. Instead of the diffusion of the Western concept of individual property rights and the creation of a market for land rights, we might seek to strengthen the institutions on which customary forms of tenure currently rely, including in particular for the governance of common-pool resources (CPRs). Indeed, it is remarkable that an important share of the land on which the rural poor rely in the developing world is governed through customary forms of tenure (see generally, Dell'Angelo et al., 2017). This is the case especially in Africa where, according to some estimates, about 70 per cent of the land that is currently used is customary common property (Alden Wily, 2011a; 2011b; 2012). Since the commercial pressures on natural resources increase, threatening in particular the rural poor, but since we have become aware of the dangers entailed by the commodification of land through the creation of a market for land rights, it is in this direction, perhaps, that we should move. Could international law help?

4. REVIVING THE COMMONS: THE NEW FRONTIERS OF INTERNATIONAL HUMAN RIGHTS LAW

It is perhaps not by accident that the most recent advances of international human rights law seek to rehabilitate the idea that common-property regimes, established as customary forms of tenure, should be better protected. In part, this may be interpreted as an attempt to move beyond the dilemma discussed above: it would be unacceptable to leave current land users (and, more generally, communities depending on access to natural resources for their livelihoods) without a legal protection, since this would expose them to the risks of dispossession; but the extension of individual property rights through titling programmes presents its own lacunae, and may in fact legitimize and accelerate forms of dispossession of its own.

But the shift towards the recognition of common-property regimes has also been encouraged by considerations for the sustainability of the management of natural resources. At the height of the developmentalist ideology, the general view was that users of natural resources would behave as rational economic agents, eager to maximize their individual utility and driven by a short-term urge to increase their revenue: it was on this utilitarian anthropology that Garrett Hardin founded his pessimistic view about the viability of shared resources, what he famously referred to as the 'Tragedy of the Commons' (1968). Since the 1990s, however, a large number of studies have demonstrated that under certain conditions, local communities are capable of managing common resources, and might even do so in ways that are more sustainable and more effective than if such management were left either to individual owners following a process of privatization, or to the state. These communities, after all, are ideally positioned to design the governance system that is best suited to the local conditions. The rules they set will be perceived as highly legitimate by the members of the community. Since community members will have contributed to shaping the governance regime, they have a strong incentive in contributing to the enforcement of the rules. And to a large extent, as the rules are set with a view to improving the situation of the community as a whole rather than that of individual members, they may be designed in order to minimize negative externalities and to preserve the long-term viability of the resource, thus improving sustainability (Ostrom, 1990; Agrawal, 2001; Cox et al., 2010).

International human rights law is gradually recognizing the importance of strengthening common-property regimes based on customary forms of tenure. This occurs through a variety of channels. It can consist in reinterpreting existing rules of international law to provide for such a recognition. Perhaps the most obvious route through which common-property regimes can be recognized is through the right to property, as protected in particular under Article 5(d)(v) of the International Convention on the Elimination of All Forms of Racial Discrimination (United Nations, 1965) and under Article 21 of the American Convention on Human Rights (Organization of American States, 1969).[3] The right to property, indeed, is not limited to the right to *individual* property. According to the Committee on the Elimination of Racial Discrimination, it includes the 'rights of all indigenous communities to own, develop and control the lands which they traditionally occupy, including water and subsoil resources' (*Guyana (Concluding Observations of 4 April 2006)*, Committee on the Elimination of Racial Discrimination, CERD/C/GUY/14: para. 16). The Inter-American Court of Human Rights has been explicit in noting that property should not be understood in a restrictive sense but can be an attribute of the group or the community. In 2001, it noted in the Case of *Mayagna (Sumo) Awas Tingni Community v. Nicaragua* that 'indigenous communities might have a collective understanding of the concepts of property and possession, in the sense that ownership of the land "is not centered on an individual, but rather on the group and its community"' (*Case of the Mayagna (Sumo) Awas Tingni Community v. Nicaragua (Judgment of 31 August 2011)*, Inter-Am. Ct. H.R., (Ser. C) No. 79: para. 148).[4] The African Court on Human and Peoples' Rights similarly considers that 'although addressed in the part of the [African Charter on Human and Peoples' Rights] which enshrines the rights recognised for individuals, the right to property as guaranteed by Article 14 may also apply to groups or communities; in effect, the right can be individual or collective' (*African Commission on Human and Peoples' Rights v. Republic of Kenya (Judgment of 26 May 2017)*, Application No. 006/2012: para. 123).

Other norms of international human rights law are perhaps even more relevant to duties of states to ensure that common-property regimes are strengthened under their jurisdiction. The right to self-determination of peoples and, specifically, the right of all peoples to freely dispose of their natural wealth and resources, as stipulated under Article 1 of both 1966 Covenants implementing the Universal Declaration of Human Rights (United Nations, 1966a; 1966b), has been relied upon for that purpose.[5] In the case of *Apirana Mahuika et al. v. New Zealand*, for instance, the Human Rights Committee reads Article 1(2) of the International Covenant on Civil and Political Rights (ICCPR) as allowing an arrangement concerning the management of fishing resources, emphasizing that the Maori people 'were given access to a great percentage of the quota, and thus effective possession of fisheries was returned to them', and that the new control structure put in place ensures not only a role for the Maori in safeguarding their interests in fisheries but, in addition, their 'effective control' (*Apirana Mahuika et al. v. New Zealand (27 October 2000)* Hum. Rts. Comm., Communication No. 547/1993: para. 9.7). Similarly, in its interpretation of the rights of minorities under the Covenant, the Human Rights Committee observed that 'minorities shall not be denied the right, in community with the other members of their group, to enjoy their own culture[, which] may consist in a way of life which is closely associated with territory and use of its resources'. This, the Committee added, 'may particularly be true of members of indigenous communities constituting a minority' (Human Rights Committee, 1994: paras 1 and 3.2).

Of course, it will be easier to recognize collective ownership where indigenous groups are concerned, not only due to the specific relationship to land and territories of indigenous peoples,[6] but also because the boundaries of the community will presumably be easier to define. National courts have routinely held that, by virtue of traditional occupation and use, the ownership of natural resources is vested collectively in an indigenous peoples. Thus, the practice of the Supreme Court of Canada is to assess claims of 'aboriginal title' by focusing on:

> the occupation and use of the land as part of the aboriginal society's *traditional way of life*. In pragmatic terms, this means looking at the manner in which the society used the land *to live*, namely to establish villages, to work, to get to work, to hunt, to travel to hunting grounds, to fish, to get to fishing pools, to conduct religious rites, etc. (*Delgamuukw v. British Columbia (Judgment of 11 December 1997)*), 3 S.C.R. 1010: para. 194 (emphasis in the original) (La Forest, J, writing also on behalf of L'Heureux-Dubé, J)

Similarly, in the case of *Alexkor Ltd and the Republic of South Africa v. The Richtersveld Cmty. and Others*, the South African Constitutional Court expressed the view that

> the real character of the title that the Richtersveld Community possessed in the subject land was a right of communal ownership under indigenous law. The content of that right included the right to exclusive occupation and use of the subject land by members of the Community. The Community had the right to use its water, to use its land for grazing and hunting and to exploit its natural resources, above and beneath the surface. (*Alexkor Ltd and the Republic of South Africa v. The Richtersveld Cmty. and Others (Judgment of 14 October 2003)*: para. 62)

In the *Case of the Ogiek Community of the Mau Forest*, the African Court of Human and Peoples' Rights derived from Article 21 of the African Charter on Human and Peoples' Rights, which guarantees the right to self-determination, a number of rights of the Ogieks to their ancestral land, 'namely, the right to use (usus) and the right to enjoy the produce of the land (fructus), which presuppose the right of access to and occupation of the land'; it found the said provision to be violated 'since the Ogieks have been deprived of the right to enjoy and freely dispose of the abundance of food produced by their ancestral lands' (*African Commission on Human and Peoples' Rights v. Republic of Kenya (Judgment of 26 May 2017)*, Application No. 006/2012: para. 201).

However, this component of the right to self-determination should not benefit indigenous peoples alone, nor should it only benefit recognized 'minorities' with a distinct ethnic, religious or linguistic identity. The requirements applicable to indigenous peoples are now extended to at least certain traditional communities that entertain a similarly 'profound and all-encompassing relationship to their ancestral lands' centred on 'the community as a whole' rather than on the individual: this, the Inter-American Court of Human Rights noted in the *Case of the Moiwana Community v. Suriname*, applies for instance to the Maroon communities living in Suriname, which are not indigenous to the region, but are tribal communities of former African slaves that settled in Suriname in the seventeenth and eighteenth centuries (*Case of the Moiwana Community v. Suriname, Preliminary Objections, Merits, Reparations and Costs (Judgment of 15 June 2005)*, Inter-Am. Ct. H.R., (Ser. C) No. 124: paras 132–3). In the *Case of Saramaka People v. Suriname*, where is was faced with a challenge to the granting of logging and mining concessions within the traditional territory of a tribal community (consisting, as in the *Moiwana Community* case, of descendants of self-liberated African slaves), the Inter-American Court explicitly noted that its jurisprudence regarding indigenous peoples' right to property 'is also applicable to tribal peoples because both share distinct social, cultural, and economic characteristics, including a special relationship with their ancestral territories, that require special measures under international human rights law in order to guarantee their physical and cultural survival' (*Case of the Saramaka People v. Suriname (Judgment of 28 November 2007)*, Inter-Am. Ct. H.R., (Ser. C) No. 172: para. 86).

Perhaps even more telling than these interpretations of international human rights law by domestic, regional and international bodies, is the fact that recent instruments have explicitly referred to common-property regimes based on customary forms of tenure, with a view to ensuring that such regimes are protected from encroachment. Such regimes are spectacularly endorsed, for instance, in the Voluntary Guidelines on the Responsible Governance of Tenure of Land, Fisheries and Forests in the Context of National Food Security (VGGT), adopted in 2012 by the Committee on World Food Security (CFS) (Food and Agriculture Organization, 2012). These guidelines provide that states should 'ensure that policy, legal and organizational frameworks for tenure governance recognize and respect, in accordance with national laws, legitimate tenure rights including legitimate customary tenure rights that are not currently protected by law' (guideline 5.3). They specifically note:

> that there are publicly-owned land, fisheries and forests that are collectively used and managed (in some national contexts referred to as commons), States should, where applicable, recognize and protect such publicly-owned land, fisheries and forests and their related systems of collective use and management, including in processes of allocation by the State. (Guideline 8.3)

Though the terminology of 'voluntary guidelines' may seem quite modest, such endorsement is significant, considering both the role of the CFS in global governance and the process through which the guidelines were adopted. Initially established in 1974 following the first World Food Conference as an intergovernmental committee within the UN Food and Agriculture Organization (FAO), the CFS was reformed in 2009 in order to become 'the foremost inclusive international and intergovernmental platform for a broad range of committed stakeholders to work together in a coordinated manner and in support of country-led processes towards the elimination of hunger and ensuring food security and nutrition for all human beings' (Committee on World Food Security, 2009: para. 4). It has since then been operating as a highly visible intergovernmental forum, with a strong legitimacy due to the fact that it involves in its deliberations, in addition to the governments as full members, civil society organizations, representatives of the private sector and of philanthropic organizations, and the most important international agencies whose mandates relate to food security. In other terms, the CFS expresses the consensus across the international community as to how global food security should be addressed, and the documents it adopts – such as the 2012 VGGT – are the result of complex intergovernmental negotiations, with a view to achieving a consensus across all the member states of the FAO.

Two years after the adoption by the CFS of the VGGT, another intergovernmental committee of the FAO, the Committee on Fisheries (COFI), adopted the Voluntary Guidelines for Securing Sustainable Small-scale Fisheries in the Context of Food Security and Poverty Eradication (SSF Guidelines) (Food and Agriculture Organization, 2015). The guidelines are the outcome of a three-year-long participatory process conducted between 2010 and 2013, involving more than 4,000 representatives of governments, small-scale fishers, fish workers and their organizations, researchers, development partners and other relevant stakeholders from more than 120 countries in six regional and more than 20 civil society organization-led national consultative meetings. They provide that 'States, in accordance with their legislation, should ensure that small-scale fishers, fish workers *and their communities* have secure, equitable, and socially and culturally appropriate tenure rights to fishery resources (marine and inland) and small-scale fishing areas and adjacent land, with a special attention paid to women with respect to tenure rights' (guideline 5.3, emphasis added). Like the VGGT, which were an important source of inspiration for the SSF Guidelines, they encourage states to recognize forms of co-management of fisheries based on customary forms of tenure:

> Local norms and practices, as well as customary or otherwise preferential access to fishery resources and land by small-scale fishing communities including indigenous peoples and ethnic minorities, should be recognized, respected and protected in ways that are consistent with international human rights law. (Guideline 5.4)

Indeed, very much for the same reasons why the generalization of individual property rights through titling schemes has been challenged as regards land tenure, the attribution of fishing rights based on the allocation of quotas – in particular, with a view to avoiding overfishing – has been questioned in the organization of the fishing sector. For many years, the dominant view was that a clarification and strengthening of access rights, including by the use of transferable fishing quotas, would increase economic efficiency and avoid overfishing (see, for instance, World Bank, 2004b; or Cunningham et al., 2009). But another, opposite view has now emerged, according to which priority should go to poverty-reduction objectives and to improving access to fishing rights to the communities who need it most – and who could be best placed to manage the CPRs concerned and monitor catches at the local level. This alternative approach to the allocation of fishing rights emerged from the concern that individual transferable quota systems may lead to rent capture by certain actors in a privileged position, an outcome which is difficult to reconcile with poverty-reduction objectives, and which the Human Rights Committee found to be a potential source of discrimination in violation of Article 26 of the ICCPR (*Haraldsson and Sveinsson v. Iceland (24 October 2007)*, Hum. Rts. Comm., Communication No. 1306/2004)[7] – a conclusion mirrored in the famous *Kenneth George* Case presented to the South African courts (*Kenneth George and Others v. Minister of Environmental Affairs and Tourism*, South African High Court, Order 2007).[8]

The shift to co-management of fisheries vesting collective rights with fishing communities is also based on the broadly positive assessment made of the establishment of fishing zones (whether lakes or coastal areas in seas) reserving fishing in these areas to local communities, allowing them to manage access rights (Sharma, 2011). Indeed, one of the contributions that influenced the adoption of the 2014 SSF Guidelines (see Ratner et al., 2014) was a report presented in 2012 by the UN Special Rapporteur on the Right to Food which, explicitly addressing the negotiations that were then being launched on this new instrument, noted that 'top-down management strategies have proved unsuccessful for the small-scale sector', and that '[t]he active and meaningful participation by communities in the management of fisheries and the integration into decision-making of local or traditional knowledge of fish and marine habitats held by fishers is paramount' (United Nations General Assembly, 2012: para. 58). The report cited a 2011 study which, comparing 130 co-management schemes (covering 44 developed and developing countries), demonstrated how local communities have often been able to develop legitimate institutions of self-governance and established sustainable approaches to managing fishing intensity and ecosystems impacts, provided strong community leaders emerge and robust social capital exists to monitor compliance with individual or community quotas (Gutiérrez et al., 2011). Other studies highlighted that co-management schemes could be successful provided certain conditions are present (Townsend et al., 2008; Béné et al., 2009), including in particular an enabling institutional environment at national level (Nielsen et al., 2004; Lewins et al., 2014) and a tradition of cooperation within the community (Jamu et al., 2011). Building on this literature, the report continued:

> Failures in co-management are partly explained by the fact that communities have been involved only in the implementation of policy, rather than in setting objectives of policy and ensuring that policymaking and evaluation are based on local knowledge on fish and marine ecosystems. The failure to integrate fishing communities into the design of policies affecting them, the top-down creation of community-based organizations to carry out functions for the State and approaches that are excessively donor-driven or that are captured by elites have all disappointed expectations. The solution to these difficulties is not to abandon co-management, but to build it in a more participatory way, based on the needs of the fishing communities. This in turn will be successful only if the livelihoods of fishers are also better secured, taking into account that the environment in which they operate, and the markets on which they depend, are increasingly risky. Only by linking fisheries management to the broader improvement of the economic and social rights of fishers, in a multisectoral approach that acknowledges how fishing fits into the broader social and economic fabric, can progress be made towards robust and sustainable solutions. (United Nations General Assembly, 2012: para. 59 (references omitted))

Finally and most recently, the revival of the commons in international human rights law can be seen in the proposal for a Declaration on the rights of peasants and other people working in rural areas, initially submitted by Bolivia within the Human Rights Council, and strongly inspired by the *Via Campesina*, the transnational network of small-scale food producers (for background of this attempt, see Claeys, 2015; Golay, 2015). At the time of writing, the proposal was under negotiation within an Intergovernmental Working Group of the Council. Article 5(1) of the draft Declaration (in the latest available version: Human Rights Council, 2017) refers to the right of peasants and other people working in rural areas 'to have access to and to use the natural resources present in their communities that are required to enjoy adequate living conditions' and to their right 'to participate in the management of these resources and to enjoy the benefits of their development and conservation in their communities'. Under the heading 'Right to land and other natural resources', Article 17(1) provides that '[p]easants and other people living in rural areas have the right, *individually and collectively*, to the lands, water bodies, coastal seas, fisheries, pastures and forests that they need to achieve an adequate standard of living, to have a place to live in security, peace and dignity and to develop their cultures' (emphasis added); and in wording clearly inspired by the 2012 VGGT, Article 17(3) adds:

> States shall provide legal recognition for land tenure rights, including customary land tenure rights, not currently protected by law. All forms of tenure, including tenancy, must provide all persons with a degree of tenure security that guarantees legal protection against forced evictions. States shall recognize and protect the natural commons and their related systems of collective use and management.[9]

Thus, a counter-movement is emerging within international human rights law, as a reaction to the push towards privatization and enclosures, of which, literally for centuries, international law has been an instrument (see also, Bakker, 2007). A number of challenges emerge, however, as the counter-movement develops.

5. THE CHALLENGES OF THE COUNTER-MOVEMENT

The first challenge, undoubtedly, is how to reconcile the autonomy of local communities in the collective management of resources with the risks of exclusion of certain members of the community. Customary forms of tenure which support common-property regimes have been found in many cases to exclude certain marginalized members of the community, including in particular women. Thus, in line with the requirements of human rights law,[10] the VGGT provide (in guideline 9.2) that:

> Indigenous peoples and other communities with customary tenure systems that exercise self-governance of land, fisheries and forests should promote and provide equitable, secure and sustainable rights to those resources, with special attention to the provision of equitable access for women. Effective participation of all members, men, women and youth, in decisions regarding their tenure systems should be promoted through their local or traditional institutions, including in the case of collective tenure systems. Where necessary, communities should be assisted to increase the capacity of their members to participate fully in decision-making and governance of their tenure systems.

A clear choice was made, in the negotiation of the guidelines, to prioritize full compliance with international human rights law, including as regards the prohibition of discrimination against women, in situations of conflict with customary forms of tenure: 'Where constitutional or legal reforms strengthen the rights of women and place them in conflict with custom, all parties should cooperate to accommodate such changes in the customary tenure systems' (guideline 9.6). This was also the choice made in the preparation of the UN Declaration on the Rights of Indigenous Peoples (UNDRIP) (United Nations, 2007), Articles 21 and 22 of which call for special attention to the needs of indigenous women and the adoption of special measures to protect them against all forms of violence and discrimination. Indeed, this constitutional priority which the VGGT recognize to human rights over customary rules is affirmed more broadly, for the benefit of all 'vulnerable and marginalized members' of the communities affected, whose 'full and effective participation' states should ensure 'when developing policies and laws related to tenure systems of indigenous peoples and other communities with customary tenure systems' (guideline 9.7).

Similarly, the draft Declaration on the rights of peasants and other people working in the rural areas affirms the primacy of human rights, dedicating a specific provision to the rights of peasant women (Article 4), who are 'often denied tenure and ownership of land' (Preamble: para. 9) and who in particular will 'have equal access to, use of and control over land and natural resources, independently of their civil and marital status and of particular tenure systems, and equal or priority treatment in land and agrarian reform and in land resettlement schemes' (Article 4(2)(h); see also, as regards women's right to land, Article 17(2)).

More generally, the recent recognition that international law should facilitate the recognition of common-property regimes based on customary forms of tenure – and, thus, the governance of the 'commons' by local communities – raises the question of the 'constitutional framework' that should be established in order to strengthen the ability of these communities to manage resources, in order to ensure that the outcomes are beneficial to societies as a whole. Based on her case studies on the management of CPRs, Elinor Ostrom identified a set of 'design principles' for long-enduring CPR institutions (Ostrom, 1990: pp. 88–102). Some of these principles (including clearly defined boundaries both of the community members and of the resource itself, and congruence or adequate 'fit' between the local conditions and the rules concerning the appropriation of the resource and the support given to its maintenance) can be said to be more or less independent of any recognition by the state. Other principles relate to the substance of the (primary, or operational) rules that govern the use of the resource (these conditions relate to the monitoring of the rules, to the adoption of a system of graduated sanctions, and to the accessibility of low-cost conflict-resolution mechanisms). Yet other principles may be said to relate to the 'secondary' rules relating to how the primary rules are adopted ('Most individuals affected by the operational rules can participate in modifying the operational rules'), and to the recognition by the official governmental authorities of 'rights to organize' ('The rights of appropriators to devise their own institutions are not challenged by external governmental authorities').

Thus, some form of intervention of the governmental authorities is not only inevitable, but to a large extent desirable. The framework enabling the emergence and endurance of CPR management systems (with its institutional, regulatory and policy components) is not simply about allowing such systems to emerge or to exist. It is not just about not obstructing them. It can be conceived as an active form of intervention, required both in order to ensure that the management by the local community of the CPR is perceived as legitimate and in order to ensure that the primary rules will maximize the chances of the system that is established lasting. For instance, the system could benefit from a requirement that decision-making procedures within the community are fully inclusive; that the operational rules take into account certain requirements linked to sustainable use;[11] that monitoring of the rules by the community members and the system of sanctions comply with certain conditions related, for instance, to legal security and to proportionality, ensuring that the rules are not enforced in ways that will be perceived as arbitrary, at the risk of creating divisions within the community (Nielsen et al., 2004); or even, that the community members be recognized as having certain basic rights related to the guarantee of an adequate standard of living, since more secure, less vulnerable community members, are better equipped to take part in participatory management systems, and may feel greater freedom to experiment as a result of their improved material security (for an argument along these lines in the context of fisheries, see Allison et al., 2012). The establishment of this 'constitutional framework' should not be seen as a violation of the principle of self-governance, by the community itself, of the CPR; instead, it should be seen as an *enabling* framework – as facilitating self-governance, and as increasing the resilience of the system.

Internationally recognized human rights could provide a source of inspiration for the establishment of such a 'constitutional framework' in support of the institution and maintenance of common-property regimes. There is no trade-off between the autonomy of the community that sets its own rules, as regards the use of resources and the allocation of duties across the community members, and such a framework set by the governmental authorities. Provided the role of government is appropriately conceived – to enable and to support, rather than to obstruct and to micro-manage – the two can in fact be mutually supportive. Own-governance by the community will ensure that the rules that are set are perceived as highly legitimate by the community members, since they will have been involved in setting the rules,[12] and be fully congruent with the local conditions and motivations. This allows the central governmental authorities to rely on such mechanisms for the effective management of the resource. Conversely however, the establishment by these authorities of an appropriate 'constitutional framework', in addition to ensuring that the common-property regime is perceived as legitimate,[13] may ensure the appropriate functioning of the regime, in particular by ensuring that it will be fully participatory (not excluding any part of the community), that the operational rules comply with certain requirements of non-discrimination and proportionality, and by protecting the resource from depletion.

Though the principle of a complementarity between the human rights-based constitutional framework on the one hand, and the self-governance by the community on the other hand, may be easy enough to accept, a number of further questions are more controversial. A first question is whether the framework should prohibit the selling off, by the community, in accordance with its internal decision-making rules, of the resource which its members are co-managing and sharing. In the case of the *Ogieks*, citing Article 26(2) of the UNDRIP (which speaks of the right of indigenous peoples 'to own, use, develop and control the lands, territories and resources that they possess'), the African Court of Human and Peoples' Rights remarked:

> the rights that can be recognised for indigenous peoples/communities on their ancestral lands are variable and do not necessarily entail the right of ownership in its classical meaning, including the right to dispose thereof (*abusus*). Without excluding the right to property in the traditional sense, this provision places greater emphasis on the rights of possession, occupation, use/utilization of land. (*African Commission on Human and Peoples' Rights v. Republic of Kenya (Judgment of 26 May 2017)*, Application No. 006/2012: para. 127)

In other terms, while recognizing the rights of the Ogieks to use and occupy the Mau Forest, the Court was agnostic (and perhaps sceptic) as to whether they should also be allowed to cede it, for instance against a monetary compensation or promises of relocation, in the absence of a strong public purpose that might justify eviction. Indeed, it may be argued that the recognition of the right of local communities to set the rules concerning the definition of appropriation/use rights and allocating responsibilities or duties to contribute should not extend to the right to liquidate the resource held in common, whether by tolerating an unsustainable use or whether by auctioning it to the highest bidder.

Another question concerns the role that should be recognized to the traditional authorities. Involving traditional authorities (such as customary chiefs, in indigenous communities) may strengthen the legitimacy of the common-property regime and thus favour its resilience. However, it has been found that the legitimacy of leaders elected by the members, and thus more directly accountable to them, could be as strong, and perhaps even stronger (Hara et al., 2002). Moreover, recognizing traditional authorities as having a leading role will perpetuate received hierarchies, and may lead to elite capture (see, for instance, Sandford, 1983; Baland and Platteau, 1999; Bardhan, 2002). Indeed, in situations where the traditional authorities are perceived to profit from their privileged position, and to act against the interest of the community, the trust on which the common management of resources relies may collapse entirely. It has been argued, therefore, that the traditional authorities 'should support, but not control the co-management enforcement activities' (Wilson et al., 2010: p. 660), and that a potential role for governmental authorities could be to 'ensure transparency of punishments' and that enforcement of the rules by the community leaders does not lead to personal gain.

6. CONCLUSION

International law has its origins in the colonial project and in the attempt, by the founders of the discipline, to legitimize it. Its very aim has been to 'civilize', which for the most part of its four-century-long history meant: to look more like the 'advanced' Western nations. Not anymore. A countermovement has emerged from the human rights regime, one of international law's most rebellious and untame departments. Whether the countermovement will be sufficient to resist the trend towards privatization and commodification, against the background of the increased competition towards the appropriation of natural resources, remains an open question. Provided, however, the challenges facing the counter-movement are well understood, and provided the task of enabling the commons to survive the assault they have been subjected to is taken seriously, international law could provide the space needed to write a new chapter of this script. The endless confrontation of the state and the market, of the public and the private, could soon end; a new character, the community, may emerge; and it will then become clear that, to a large extent, the state and the market have been complicit in their attempt to keep it out of sight, condemning it to oblivion.

NOTES

1. The classification of countries as 'low-income', 'lower middle income', 'upper middle income' and 'high-income', is published on http://data.worldbank.org and is revised once a year on 1 July, at the start of the World Bank fiscal year. Such classification is made on the basis of the Gross National Income (GNI) per capita of each country, using a three-year average exchange rate to avoid the classification being influenced by short-term changes in currency values. The list of least-developed countries (LDCs) is decided upon by the United Nations Economic and Social Council and, ultimately, by the General Assembly, on the basis of recommendations made by the Committee for Development Policy, using a set of criteria including per capita GNI, a human assets index and an economic vulnerability index (see Committee for Development Policy and United Nations Department of Economic and Social Affairs, 2015).
2. The expansion from the former conception of 'security of tenure' to include the latter appears in a 1987 study by two authors from the World Bank, where they note that 'the ability of an occupant to undertake land transactions that would best suit his interests' should be considered part of 'security of tenure' (Feder and Noronha, 1987: p. 159).
3. Article 21 establishes, *inter alia*, that: '1. Everyone has the right to the use and enjoyment of his property. The law may subordinate such use and enjoyment to the interest of society. 2. No one shall be deprived of his property except upon payment of just compensation, for reasons of public utility or social interest, and in the cases and according to the forms established by law.'
4. See also *Case of the Sawhoyamaxa Indigenous Community v. Paraguay (Judgment of 29 March 2006)*, Inter-Am. Ct. H.R., (Ser. C) No. 146: para. 120.
5. The African Charter of Human and Peoples' Rights (African Union, 1981) has an equivalent norm in Article 21, which provides in particular that: 'All peoples shall freely dispose of their wealth and natural resources. This right shall be exercised in the exclusive interest of the people. In no case shall a people be deprived of it'. As noted by the African Commission on Human and Peoples' Rights, the origins of that provision 'may be traced to colonialism, during which the human and material resources of Africa were largely exploited for the benefit of outside powers, creating tragedy for Africans themselves, depriving them of their birthright and alienating them from the land. The aftermath of colonial exploitation has left Africa's precious resources and people still vulnerable to foreign misappropriation. [In adopting Article 21,] the drafters of the Charter obviously wanted to remind African governments of the continent's painful legacy and restore co-operative economic development to its traditional place at the heart of African Society' (*The Social and Economic Rights Action Center and the Center for Economic and Social Rights v. Nigeria*, African Commission on Human and Peoples' Rights, Comm. No. 155/96 (2001): para. 56). For a comment, see Nwobike, 2005.
6. International Labour Organization (ILO) Convention (No. 169) concerning Indigenous and Tribal Peoples in Independent Countries, which entered into force in 1991,

provides for a number of guarantees related to land. Although it has been poorly ratified, this is compensated, in part, by the adoption of the UN Declaration on the Rights of Indigenous Peoples (UNDRIP) by General Assembly Resolution 61/295 on 13 September 2007, which reflects the existing customary law on this issue (A/RES/61/295). The Declaration provides in Article 8(2)(b), that states should prohibit 'any action which has the aim or effect of dispossessing [indigenous peoples] of their lands, territories or resources', a requirement that replicates Article 18 of the ILO Convention (No. 169). It also prohibits any forcible removal of indigenous peoples from their lands or territories, imposing requirements of free, prior and informed consent, agreement on just and fair compensation and, where possible, the option of return, for relocations (Article 10). For detailed comments on the status of land in the Declaration, see Errico (2011; 2017).

7. The Human Rights Committee found that the system established by the Iceland Fisheries Management Act No. 38/1990, in which the quotas originally held 'can be sold or leased at market prices instead of reverting to the State for allocation to new quota holders in accordance with fair and equitable criteria', could result in discrimination in violation of Article 26 of the ICCPR.
8. The South African High Court ordered a revision of the Marine Living Resources Act and requiring the development of a new framework taking into account 'international and national legal obligations and policy directives to accommodate the socio-economic rights of [small-scale] fishers and to ensure equitable access to marine resources for those fishers'. This resulted in the adoption of a new Small-Scale Fisheries Policy in May 2012, which recognizes the importance of small-scale fisheries in contributing to food security and as serving as a critical safety net against poverty.
9. Article 21(3) of the 2017 draft Declaration uses a similar formula with respect to access to water: 'States shall respect, protect and ensure access to water, including in customary and community-based water management systems . . .'.
10. The Convention on the Elimination of All Forms of Discrimination against Women (CEDAW) (United Nations, 1979) has a specific provision on women in rural areas. Article 14(1) provides that 'States Parties shall take into account the particular problems faced by rural women and the significant roles which rural women play in the economic survival of their families, including their work in the non-monetized sectors of the economy, and shall take all appropriate measures to ensure the application of the provisions of the present Convention to women in rural areas'. Article 14(2) then sets out the implications, including a requirement that states parties ensure to women in rural areas 'to participate in all community activities' (f) and to 'equal treatment in land and agrarian reform as well as in land resettlement schemes' (g). The CEDAW Committee also adopted a General Statement on Rural Women (2011).
11. For instance, the VGGT provide that '[a]ll tenure rights are limited by the rights of others and by the measures taken by States necessary for public purposes' insofar as such measure aim to promote, for instance, 'general welfare including environmental protection' and are 'consistent with States' human rights obligations' (guideline 4.4). They continue: 'Tenure rights are also balanced by duties. All should respect the long-term protection and sustainable use of land, fisheries and forests'. For an illustration, though the VGGT are not referred to, see African Court of Human and Peoples' Rights, *African Commission on Human and Peoples' Rights v. Republic of Kenya (Judgment of 26 May 2017)*, Application No. 006/2012, paras 129–30 (noting that the Ogiek could not be expelled from the Mau Forest even in the name of the 'preservation of the natural ecosystem', since there has been no evidence provided 'to the effect that the Ogieks' continued presence in the area is the main cause for the depletion of natural environment in the area').
12. Conversely, the top-down imposition of operational rules would result in a 'crowding-out' effect, undermining the legitimacy of the rules in the eyes of the community members (Cardenas et al., 2000; Ostrom, 2005).
13. It is noteworthy that, in countries as different as Norway and Japan, fisheries

co-management systems that have been the most enduring were provided a legal foundation (Jentoft and Kristofferson, 1998; Ruddle, 1989).

REFERENCES

African Union (1981) African Charter on Human and Peoples' Rights. Nairobi, 27 June 1981. United Nations Treaty Series, 1520 (217).

African Union, African Development Bank and Economic Commission for Africa (2009) *Land Policy in Africa: A Framework to Strengthen Land Rights, Enhance Productivity and Secure Livelihoods*. Background Document. Addis Ababa, AUC-ECA-AfDB Consortium.

Agrawal, A. (2001). Common Property Institutions and Sustainable Governance of Resources. *World Development*, **29** (10), 1649–72.

Alden Wily, L. (2011a) 'The Law is to Blame': The Vulnerable Status of Common Property Rights in Sub-Saharan Africa. *Development and Change*, **42** (3), 733–57.

Alden Wily, L. (2011b) *The Tragedy of Public Lands: The Fate of the Commons Under Global Commercial Pressure*. Rome, The International Land Coalition.

Alden Wily, L. (2012) Looking Back to See Forward: The Legal Niceties of Land Theft in Land Rushes. *Journal of Peasant Studies*, **39** (3–4), 751–75.

Allison, E. H., Ratner, B. D., Åsgård, B., Willmann, R., Pomeroy, R. and Kurien, J. (2012) Rights-based Fisheries Governance: From Fishing Rights to Human Rights. *Fish and Fisheries*, **13** (1), 14–29.

Anghie, A. (2005) *Imperialism, Sovereignty and the Making of International Law*. New York, Cambridge University Press.

Bakker, K. (2007) The 'Commons' versus the 'Commodity': Alter-globalization, Anti-privatization and the Human Right to Water in the Global South. *Antipode*, **39** (3), 430–55.

Baland, J. M. and Platteau, J. P. (1999) The Ambiguous Impact of Inequality on Local Resource Management. *World Development*, **27** (5), 773–88.

Bardhan, P. (2002) Decentralization of Governance and Development. *Journal of Economic Perspectives*, **16** (4), 185–205.

Béné, C., Belal, E., Ousman Baba, M., Ovie, S., Raji, A., Malasha, I., Njaya, F., Na Andi, M., Russell, A. and Neiland, A. (2009) Power Struggle, Dispute and Alliance over Local Resources: Analyzing 'Democratic' Decentralization of Natural Resources through the Lenses of Africa Inland Fisheries. *World Development*, **37** (12), 1935–50.

Borschberg, P. (1999) Hugo Grotius, East India Trade and the King of Johor, *Journal of Southeast Asian Studies*, **30** (2), 225–48.

Cardenas, J. C., Stranlund, J. and Willis, C. (2000) Local Environmental Control and Institutional Crowding-out. *World Development*, **28** (10), 1719–33.

Castañeda Dower, P. and Potamites, E. (2012) *Signaling Credit-worthiness: Land Titles, Banking Practices and Formal Credit in Indonesia*. Centre for Economic and Financial Research, New Economic School, Working Paper Series No. 186 (Moscow: CEFIR/NES).

Chavez Sanchez, E., Diniz, L., Meunier, F. and Rakhimova, P. (2014) Registering Property. In: World Bank, *Doing Business 2014, Understanding Regulations for Small and Medium-sized Enterprises*. Washington, World Bank, pp. 86–9.

Claeys, P. (2015) Food Sovereignty and the Recognition of New Rights for

Peasants at the UN: A Critical Overview of La Via Campesina's Rights Claims over the Last 20 Years. *Globalizations*, **12** (4), 452–65.
Coase, R. H. (1960) The Problem of Social Cost. *Journal of Law and Economics*, **3**, 1–44.
Commission on Legal Empowerment of the Poor (2005) Poverty Reduction through Improved Asset Security, Formalisation of Property Rights and the Rule of Law. Concept Paper, 6 September 2005.
Commission on Legal Empowerment of the Poor (2008) *Making the Law Work for Everyone*. Vol. I, Report of the Commission on Legal Empowerment of the Poor. New York, Commission on Legal Empowerment of the Poor and UNDP.
Committee for Development Policy and United Nations Department of Economic and Social Affairs (2015) *Handbook on the Least Developed Country Category: Inclusion, Graduation and Special Support Measures*. [Online] Available from: https://www.un.org/development/desa/dpad/wp-content/uploads/sites/45/publication/2015cdphandbook.pdf (accessed 11 July 2018).
Committee on the Elimination of Discrimination against Women on Rural Women (2011) General Statement on Rural Women. Decision 50/VI Adopted on 19 October 2011 during the 50th Session. UN Doc. A/67/38. [Online] Available from: http://www.ohchr.org/documents/HRBodies/CEDAW/Statements/StatementRuralWomen.pdf (accessed 11 January 2017).
Committee on World Food Security (2009) Reform of the Committee on World Food Security. 14, 15 and 17 October 2009, UN Doc. CFS:2009/2Rev. 2. [Online] Available from: http://www.fao.org/tempref/docrep/fao/meeting/018/k7197e.pdf (accessed 11 January 2017).
Cox, M., Arnold, G. and Villamayor Tomás, S. (2010). A Review of Design Principles for Community-based Natural Resource Management. *Ecology and Society*, **15** (4), 38.
Cunningham, S., Neiland, A. E., Arbuckle, M. and Bostock, T. (2009) Wealth-based Fisheries Management: Using Fisheries Wealth to Orchestrate Sound Fisheries Policy in Practice. *Marine Resource Economics*, **24** (3), 271–87.
Dell'Angelo, J., D'Odorico, P., Rulli, M. C. and Marchand, P. (2017) The Tragedy of the Grabbed Commons: Coercion and Dispossession in the Global Land Rush. *World Development*, **92**, 1–12.
De Schutter, O. (2011a). How Not to Think of Land-grabbing: Three Critiques of Large-scale Investments in Farmland. *Journal of Peasant Studies*, **38** (2), 249–79.
De Schutter, O. (2011b). The Green Rush: The Global Race for Farmland and the Rights of Land Users. *Harvard International Law Journal*, **52** (2), 503–59.
De Schutter, O., Swinnen, J. and Wouters, J. (2012). Introduction: Foreign Direct Investment and Human Development. In: De Schutter, O., Swinnen, J. and Wouters, J. (eds) *Foreign Direct Investment and Human Development: The Law and Economics of International Investment Agreements*. London and New York, Routledge, pp. 1–24.
de Soto, H. (2000) *The Mystery of Capital: Why Capitalism Triumphs in the West and Fails Everywhere Else*. New York, Basic Books.
Deininger, K. (2003) *Land Policies for Growth and Poverty Reduction: A World Bank Policy Research Report*. Washington, DC, World Bank.
Deininger, K., Jin, S. and Nagarajan, H. K. (2008) Efficiency and Equity Impacts of Rural Land Rental Restrictions: Evidence from India. *European Economic Review*, **52** (5), 892–918.
Errico, S. (2011) The Controversial Issue of Natural Resources: Balancing States'

Sovereignty with Indigenous Peoples' Rights. In: Allen, S. and Xanthaki, A. (eds) *Reflections on the UN Declaration on the Rights of Indigenous Peoples*. London, Hart Publishing.

Errico, S. (2017) Control Over Natural Resources and Protection of the Environment of Indigenous Territories. In: Hohmann, J. and Weller, M. (eds) *The UN Declaration on the Rights of Indigenous Peoples: A Commentary*. Oxford, Oxford University Press.

Feder, G. and Feeny, D. (1991) Land Tenure and Property Rights: Theory and Implications for Development Policy. *The World Bank Economic Review*, **5** (1), 135–53.

Feder, G. and Noronha, R. (1987) Land Rights Systems and Agricultural Development in Sub-Saharan Africa. *World Bank Research Observer*, **2** (2), 143–69.

Firmin-Sellers, K. and Sellers, P. (1999) Expected Failures and Unexpected Successes of Land Titling in Africa. *World Development*, **27** (7), 1115–28.

Food and Agriculture Organization (2012) Voluntary Guidelines on the Responsible Governance of Tenure of Land, Fisheries and Forests in the Context of National Food Security. Committee on World Food Security. [Online] Available from: http://www.fao.org/docrep/016/i2801e/i2801e.pdf (accessed 11 January 2018).

Food and Agriculture Organization (2015) Voluntary Guidelines for Securing Sustainable Small-scale Fisheries in the Context of Food Security and Poverty Eradication. [Online] Available from: http://www.fao.org/3/a-i4356e.pdf (accessed 11 January 2018).

Golay, G. (2015) Negotiation of a United Nations Declaration on the Rights of Peasants and Other People Working in Rural Areas. Academy In-Brief No. 5. Geneva Academy of International Humanitarian Law and Human Rights. [Online] Available from: http://www.ohchr.org/Documents/HRBodies/HRCouncil/WGPleasants/Session2/ChristopheGolay.pdf (accessed 11 January 2018).

Grotius, H. (1925 [1625]) *De jure belli ac pacis libri tres*. Oxford, Clarendon Press.

Gutiérrez, N. L., Hilborn, R. and Defeo, O. (2011) Leadership, Social Capital and Incentives Promote Successful Fisheries. *Nature*, **470** (7334), 386–9.

Hara, M., Donda, S. and Njaya, F. J. (2002) Lessons from Malawi's Experience with Fisheries Co-management Initiative. In: Gehab, K. and Sarch, M.-T. (eds) *Africa's Inland Fisheries: The Management Challenge*. Kampala, Fountain Publishers, pp. 31–48.

Hardin, G. (1968) The Tragedy of the Commons. *Science*, **162** (3859), 1243–8.

Human Rights Committee (1994) General Comment No. 23: The Rights of Minorities (Art. 27). 4 August 1994, UN Doc. CCPR/C/21Rev.1/Add.5.

Human Rights Council (2017) Draft Declaration on the Rights of Peasants and Other People Working in Rural Areas Presented by the Chair-Rapporteur of the Working Group. Open-ended Intergovernmental Working Group on the Rights of Peasants and Other People Working in Rural Areas, Fourth Session, 15–19 May 2017. UN Doc. A/HRC/WG.15/4/2.

International Labour Organization (1989) Indigenous and Tribal Peoples Convention (No. 169). Geneva, 27 June 1989. United Nations Treaty Series, 1650 (383).

Jamu, D., Banda, M., Njaya, F. and Hecky, R. E. (2011) Challenges to Sustainable Management of the Lakes of Malawi. *Journal of Great Lakes Research*, **37** (1), 3–14.

Jentoft, S. and Kristofferson, T. (1998) Fishermen's Co-management: The Case of the Lofoten Fishery. *Human Organization*, **48** (4), 355–65.

Lewins, R., Béné, C., Baba, M. O., Belal, E., Donda, S., Lamine, A. M., Makadassou, A., Mamane Tahir Na, A., Neiland, A. E., Njaya, F., Ovie, S. and Raji, A. (2014) African Inland Fisheries: Experiences with Co-management and Policies of Decentralization. *Society and Natural Resources*, **27** (4), 405–20.

Lewis, A. W. (1954) Economic Development with Unlimited Supplies of Labour. *The Manchester School*, **22** (2), 139–91.

Locke, J. (1986 [1690]) *Second Treatise on Civil Government*. Amherst, Prometheus Books.

Lugard, F. D. (1922) *The Dual Mandate in British Tropical Africa*. London and Edinburgh, William Blackwood and Sons.

Mayo, S. K. and Angel, S. (1993) Housing: Enabling Markets to Work. World Bank Policy Paper No. 11820.

Mitchell, T. (2006) *The Properties of Markets: Informal Housing and Capitalism's Mystery*. Working Paper No. 2, Cultural, Political Economy Working Paper Series. Lancaster, Institute for Advanced Studies in Social and Management Sciences, Lancaster University.

Nielsen, J. R., Degnbol, P., Viswanathan, K. K., Ahmed, M., Hara, M. and Raja Abdullah, N. M. (2004) Fisheries Co-management: An Institutional Innovation? Lessons from South East Asia and Southern Africa. *Marine Policy*, **28** (2), 151–60.

Nwobike, C. (2005) The African Commission on Human and Peoples' Rights and the Demystification of Second and Third Generation Rights under the African Charter. *African Journal of Legal Studies*, **1** (2), 129–46.

Organization of American States (1969) American Convention on Human Rights. San José, 22 November 1969. United Nations Treaty Series, 1144 (123).

Ostrom, E. (1990) *Governing the Commons: The Evolution of Institutions for Collective Action*. New York, Cambridge University Press.

Ostrom, E. (2005) Policies that Crowd Out Reciprocity and Collective Action. In: Gintis, H., Bowles, S., Boyd, R. and Fehr, E. (eds) *Moral Sentiments and Material Interests: The Foundations of Cooperation in Economic Life*. Cambridge, MIT Press, pp. 253–75.

Payne, G., Durand-Lasserve, A. and Rakodi, C. (2007) Social and Economic Impacts of Land Titling Programmes in Urban and Peri-urban Areas: A Review of the Literature. Paper presented at the World Bank Urban Research Symposium, Washington, DC, 14–16 May 2007.

Platteau, J.-P. (2000) Does Africa Need Land Reform? In: Toulmin, C. and Quan, J. (eds) *Evolving Land Rights, Policy and Tenure in Africa*. London, DFID-IIED-NRI, pp. 51–74.

Ratner, B. D., Åsgård, B. and Allison, E. H. (2014) Fishing for Justice: Human Rights, Development, and Fisheries Sector Reform. *Global Environmental Change*, **27**, 120–30.

Rostow, W. W. (1960) *The Stages of Economic Growth: A Non-communist Manifesto*. Cambridge, Cambridge University Press.

Ruddle K. (1989) Solving the Common-property Dilemma: Village Fisheries Rights in Japanese Coastal Waters. In: Berkes, F. (ed.) *Common Property Resources: Ecology and Community-based Sustainable Development*. London, Belhaven Press, pp. 168–84.

Sandford, S. (1983) *Management of Pastoral Development in the Third World*. Chichester, John Wiley and Sons.

Sharma, C. (2011) Securing Economic, Social and Cultural Rights of Small-scale and Artisanal Fishworkers and Fishing Communities. *Journal of Maritime Studies*, **10** (2), 41–62.

Tönnies, D. (2001 [1887]) *Community and Civil Society*. Cambridge, Cambridge University Press.

Toulmin, C. and Quan, J. (eds) (2000) *Evolving Land Rights, Policy and Tenure in Africa*. London, DFID–IIED–NRI.

Townsend, R., Shotton, R. and Uchida, H. (eds) (2008) Case Studies in Fisheries Self-governance, FAO Fisheries Technical Paper No. 504. Food and Agriculture Organization, Rome.

United Nations (1965) International Convention on the Elimination of All Forms of Racial Discrimination. New York, 21 December 1965. United Nations Treaty Series, 660 (195).

United Nations (1966a) International Covenant on Civil and Political Rights. New York, 16 December 1966. United Nations Treaty Series, 999 (171).

United Nations (1966b) International Covenant on Economic, Social and Cultural Rights. New York, 16 December 1966. United Nations Treaty Series, 993 (4).

United Nations (1979) Convention on the Elimination of All Forms of Discrimination against Women. New York, 18 December 1979. United Nations Treaty Series, 1249 (13).

United Nations (2007) Declaration on the Rights of Indigenous Peoples. GA Res. 61/295. 13 September 2007, UN Doc. A/61/53.

United Nations General Assembly (2012) Interim Report of the Special Rapporteur on the Right to Food. 8 August 2012, UN Doc. A/67/268.

Unruh, J. (2002) Poverty and Property Rights in the Developing World: Not as Simple as We Would Like. *Land Use Policy*, **19** (4), 275–6.

van Ittersum, M. J. (2010) The Long Goodbye: Hugo Grotius' Justification of Dutch Expansion Overseas, 1615–1645. *History of European Ideas*, **36** (4), 386–411.

von Benda-Beckmann, F. (2003) Mysteries of Capital or Mystification of Legal Property? *European Journal of Anthropology*, **41**, 187–91.

Vitoria, F. (1917 [1532]) *De indis et de iure belli reflectiones*. Washington, DC, Carnegie Institution of Washington.

Wilson, D. C. K., Ahmed, M., Delaney, A., Donda, S., Kapasa, C. K., Malasha, I., Muyangali, K., Nyaja, F., Olesen, T., Poiosse, E. and Raakjær, J. (2010) Fisheries Co-management Institutions in Southern Africa: A Hierarchical Analysis of Perceptions of Effectiveness. *International Journal of the Commons*, **4** (2), 643–62.

World Bank (2004a) *Doing Business 2005: Removing Obstacles to Growth*. Washington, DC, World Bank.

World Bank (2004b) *World Development Report 2005: A Better Investment Climate for Everyone*. Washington, DC, World Bank.

World Bank (2007) *World Development Report 2008: Agriculture for Development*. Washington, DC, World Bank.

Cases

African Commission on Human and Peoples' Rights v. Republic of Kenya (Judgment of 26 May 2017), Application No. 006/2012.

Alexkor Ltd and the Republic of South Africa v. The Richtersveld Cmty. and Others (Judgment of 14 October 2003), South African Constitutional Court, (CCT19/03) ZACC 18; 2004 (5) SA 460 (CC); 2003 (12) BCLR 1301 (CC).
Apirana Mahuika et al. v. New Zealand (27 October 2000), Hum. Rts. Comm., Communication No. 547/1993, UN Doc. CCPR/C/70/D/547/1993.
Case of the Mayagna (Sumo) Awas Tingni Community v. Nicaragua (Judgment of 31 August 2011), Inter-Am. Ct. H.R., (Ser. C) No. 79.
Case of the Moiwana Community v. Suriname, Preliminary Objections, Merits, Reparations and Costs (Judgment of 15 June 2005), Inter-Am. Ct. H.R., (Ser. C) No. 124.
Case of the Saramaka People v. Suriname (Judgment of 28 November 2007), Inter-Am. Ct. H.R., (Ser. C) No. 172.
Case of the Sawhoyamaxa Indigenous Community v. Paraguay (Judgment of 29 March 2006), Inter-Am. Ct. H.R., (Ser. C) No. 146.
Delgamuukw v. British Columbia (Judgment of 11 December 1997), Supreme Court of Canada, 3 S.C.R. 1010.
Guyana (Concluding Observations of 4 April 2006), Committee on the Elimination of Racial Discrimination, CERD/C/GUY/14.
Haraldsson and Sveinsson v. Iceland (24 October 2007), Hum. Rts. Comm., Communication No. 1306/2004, CCPR/C/91/D/1306/2004.
Kenneth George and Others v. Minister of Environmental Affairs and Tourism, South African High Court, Order 2007.
The Social and Economic Rights Action Center and the Center for Economic and Social Rights v. Nigeria, African Commission on Human and Peoples' Rights, Comm. No. 155/96 (2001).

12. International law to save the commons

Samuel Cogolati and Jan Wouters*

1. INTRODUCTION

Commons are nowadays on everyone's lips. Since the landmark book *Governing the Commons* by Nobel Prize winner Elinor Ostrom (1990), the commons represent an alternative governance model to share resources among communities beyond the logics of market and state. New commons like cohousing initiatives, community gardening, community land trusts, and open-source media like Wikipedia, are burgeoning all across the world. Yet, it is too often overlooked that millions of people, mostly living in developing countries, have in fact been depending on commons such as forests, pastures, grazing lands and fisheries to meet their basic needs for far longer (see Oxfam et al., 2016). Because these commons are often left unrecognized, they face the threat of enclosure, which risks depriving small-scale farmers, pastoralists, forest-dwellers, artisanal fishers and indigenous peoples in the Global South, from their most basic access to food, land, and other essential resources. This trend extends beyond the so-called 'global land grab' (Alden Wily, 2012; Narula, 2013), and includes the commodification of many other natural resources in developing countries. Think of concessions for land mining in Peru or Colombia (Padilla, 2012) and the privatization of water cooperatives in Bolivia (De La Fuente, 2003; Sauvêtre, Chapter 5 in this volume), which disrupt the communal system of existence of local populations. This movement is led by state and private investors – both domestic and foreign – but it is also facilitated by the dominant vision of economic development based on private property and wealth maximization.

In the face of this dramatic 'new wave of "enclosing the commons"' (Harvey, 2003: p. 148), legal scholars are called upon to rethink the prevailing private property narrative and the central role of the sovereign state in the Western legal culture. The commons have already caused much ink to flow in the legal literature. At the domestic level, legal scholars have devised new legal tools like collective property regimes and public trust doctrines. Some authors have even attempted to reframe the commons as a legal concept of its own (Marella, 2017; Mattei and Quarta, 2017). The main challenge, it seems, is to halt the seemingly inexorable process of transformation of commons into capital. For that purpose, all legal disciplines, from legal theory, (intellectual) property law to constitutional and administrative law, have contributed to the current debates on the commons. However, surprisingly, very little has been said about the role that *international law* can play in the empowerment of communities in the self-management of their resources and in the resistance against dispossession – notably in the Global South. Whereas *global* commons like outer space or the high seas are subject to special treaty regimes between states and international legal principles such as the common heritage of mankind, it remains particularly unclear to what extent international law can require states to recognize the commons as a social institution and protect marginalized populations from enclosure.

This chapter asks the question as to whether international law can be part of the solution in saving the commons from commodification. Although the commons can take various forms around the world – like social movements (see Boonen, Chapter 4 in this volume) or knowledge (see Beerkens, Chapter 9 in this volume) – this chapter focuses on more traditional, ecological, subsistence commons such as forests, seeds, pastures, lands and water resources, on which communities depend for their survival throughout Latin America, Africa and Asia. This chapter is structured into three main parts. Section 2 shows that even though the Ostromian model originates from the development policy field (see Sauvêtre, Chapter 5 in this volume), the institution of the commons is still far from being fully recognized by the World Bank – the world's foremost development institution. Section 3 acknowledges that while international law has long recognized areas and resources beyond state jurisdiction (like the high seas, deep seabed, outer space, the Moon and other celestial bodies, as well as Antarctica) as *global* commons (Schrijver, 2016; see also Brunnée, Chapter 13 in this volume), it has given much less attention to the commons defined as bottom-up self-governance institutions. Section 4 finally explores the potentially instrumental role of international and regional human rights instruments in closing the gap of international legal protection for the institution of the commons (see Mattei, Chapter 10 in this volume). This chapter concludes that while the World Bank still mainly promotes privatization strategies, community rights are emerging under international law to recognize the alternative autonomous governance and social system of the commons.

2. COMMONS IN DEVELOPMENT POLICIES: THE CASE OF THE WORLD BANK

Since the landmark publication of *Governing the Commons* by Elinor Ostrom (1990), the commons have been embraced by social movements as a new governance model to rethink the traditional public-private and market-state divides and to prioritize the ecological and human needs of communities. As this book shows, the commons are now also a popular subject of academic inquiry, which serves to recast the traditional foundations of a wide array of disciplines such as political theory, sociology, economics and law. Likewise, the field of development cooperation is not immune to these debates. Non-governmental organizations (NGOs) like Oxfam, the International Land Coalition (ILC) and the Rights and Resources Initiative (RRI), have recently launched a global call for action to endorse Ostrom's assertion 'that communities should have better control of their customary lands rather than having them taken away' (Oxfam et al., 2016: p. 25). Yet, even if – as Pierre Sauvêtre convincingly demonstrates in Chapter 5 of this volume – the Ostromian concept of the commons originates from the development community, the fact remains that today the prevailing model of development favoured by industrialized countries and grounded in individual private poverty and wealth maximization represents a threat to the commons around the world. It therefore comes as no surprise that the developmentalist model is being fundamentally called into question by commons activists and scholars. Fritjof Capra and Ugo Mattei, for instance, vigorously denounce an 'idea of "development"' as 'fundamentally quantitative' and 'rooted in seventeenth-century notions of "improvement"', which fails to recognize 'that unrestrained extraction and exploitation of natural and human resources is at odds with the fundamental principles of ecology' (Capra and Mattei, 2015: p. 9). In the same vein, David Bollier proposes to 'abandon the whole mindset of "development" itself' and, instead, to start talking about 'human flourishing' (2016). Dirk Löhr suggests that '[i]f community interests in shared natural resources are to survive, a new development agenda will need to be advanced, and it will need to sail against the wind' (2012).

This critique should be taken seriously. Indeed, economists and lawyers have traditionally assumed that, without private property, rational self-interested individuals will have no incentive to protect their resources and accumulate wealth (Feder and Feeny, 1991; Fitzpatrick, 2006). This postulate finds its origin in the classic Coase theorem, which views private ownership as the best way to minimize externalities and ensure the best allocation of resources (Coase, 1960). This negative depiction of collective ownership was confirmed in the famous article 'The Tragedy of the

Commons' by American ecologist Garrett Hardin (1968). Hardin argued that commons would automatically be depleted because individuals are only guided by their self-interest to grab what they can before the others destroy the shared resource. Under this pessimistic approach, the commons are basically unregulated and therefore seen as no man's land. Customarily owned lands are considered unowned and unoccupied. This is why development policy-makers have rarely gone beyond the public-private and state-market dichotomies (Glinavos, 2010: p. 72) and have often considered local forms of communal ownership as 'archaic and in need of modernization via privatization and market integration' (Vaccaro et al., 2009: p. 523). Hernando de Soto famously wrote in *The Mystery of Capital* that whereas in developed countries like the United States, lands can be used for credit and sold in secondary markets, land in many developing countries is 'dead capital' (2001: p. 7). As a critical commentator noted, development strategies are based upon the idea that 'informal, collective forms of property rights should be converted into private property because such policies will help ease land conflicts, enhance the efficiency of the land markets, guarantee tenure security and assure access to loans' (Löhr, 2012).

This negative view of the commons is reflected in the development policies of the World Bank – the world's foremost development agency with near global membership. Since the 1970s, the institution is well known as a fierce defender of privatization strategies in what used to be called 'structural adjustment programmes' (SAPs), which coerce developing countries to convert untitled lands like the commons into private property on the markets.[1] In a 1975 land policy reform paper, the Bank went so far as to advocate the abandonment of 'backward' customary tenure arrangements and the subdivision of the commons into plots over which 'modern' freehold titles would be granted (World Bank, 1975; Deininger, 2003: p. 62). Enforcement of property rights became a desirable standard economic reform supported by the Bank, in what was termed the 'Washington consensus'. In the 1990s, the Bank further established this policy in helping post-Soviet states to make the transition from state to private ownership of lands and services. This strategy was aimed at facilitating the integration of developing and post-Soviet countries into the world economy and the global supply chains of agricultural commodities. The Bank's land and agricultural policies, prescribed as conditionalities, therefore were directed at securing land tenure and transferability of private property rights through 'free' land markets, at the expense of informal and customary institutions governing communal rights of use. Under this market-based approach, the role of the state was reduced to protecting and enforcing private rights to property, in order to create an enabling environment for economic growth.

The Bank has demonstrated more openness for the commons in a 2003 comprehensive report on its *Land Policies for Growth and Poverty Reduction* (Deininger, 2003). It acknowledges therein that '[f]orests and other common property resources contribute significantly to people's welfare, especially of the poor' (p. 66) and that 'in most situations simply introducing private property rights will be neither feasible nor cost-effective' (p. 68). However, even though the Bank recognizes customary rights, the institution of the commons as such is not regarded as an optimal solution. On the contrary, the 2003 report recommends formalizing customary rights to integrate them 'into more formal systems' (p. 63). Ultimately, individual ownership is still considered to be 'the arrangement that provides the greatest incentives for efficient resource use' (p. 28). The commons are said to be warranted primarily in situations with 'limited economic development' (p. 29). As a land expert commented on this report, '[w]hile it is significant that the Bank has recognized the need to respect customary rights, it nevertheless sees individualistic rights of ownership of land as those which represent the most "modern" form of landholding' (Fortin, 2005: p. 170).

The Bank's World Development Reports (WDRs) – the annual flagship publications with policy recommendations on various aspects of development – confirm this:

- In its 2005 WDR on *A Better Investment Climate for Everyone*, the Bank advocates enhancing the security of private property rights as a means to create a better investment climate and foster economic growth: '[t]he better protected these rights, the stronger the link between effort and reward and hence the greater the incentives to open new businesses, to invest more in existing ones, and simply to work harder' (World Bank, 2005: p. 79). It is striking how the WDR's vision of property echoes Hardin's 'Tragedy of the Commons' (1968). The WDR straightforwardly states that registered titles to lands encourage investment, improve access to loans and enhance environmental stewardship. In the absence of clear property rights, it is said that those in control of a natural resource will use it as much as possible, since 'they are not sure the resource will be theirs tomorrow' (World Bank, 2005: p. 81). While the 2005 WDR does not rule out the existence of 'community-wide agreements on the use of resources', it clearly assumes that, when natural resources are 'held collectively', individuals have fewer incentives to protect them against depletion (World Bank, 2005: p. 82, Box 4.4).
- The 2008 WDR on *Agriculture for Development* has brought some nuance to this individualistic vision of property. It warns that

while '[e]arlier interventions to improve tenure security focused almost exclusively on individual titling, . . . this can weaken or leave out communal, secondary, or women's rights' (World Bank, 2007: p. 139).

- The 2017 WDR on *Governance and the Law* (World Bank, 2017: p. 57) now refers to Ostrom's book *Governing the Commons*, but it fails to present the commons as an institution for collective action and simply restates, at an abstract level, the tragic fate of unregulated commons depicted earlier by Garrett Hardin (1968). The report repeats that '[c]onflict over the mismanagement and overuse of common pool (or open access) resources is ubiquitous' (p. 115, Box 4.3), but it omits to present successful and sustainable management processes of shared resources as a commons, as Ostrom did in her case studies (1990).

At this stage, the Bank has not adopted a comprehensive policy recognizing the commons as a governance system of its own. This is problematic. In most developing countries the commons are, in practice, already recognized by local populations as a fully fledged management mechanism of natural and other common-pool resources (CPRs), such as grazing lands, forests, water and fisheries. The commons may not only represent an 'effective' way – in the economic sense – to ensure the management of shared natural resources, but millions of small-scale farmers, pastoralists, forest-dwellers, artisanal fishers and indigenous peoples also depend on them for their livelihood. The process of 'modernization' promoted by the Bank, and based on a conception of individual private property imported from the West, is likely to fail in securing the rights of communities and preventing conflicts over land and other natural resources in the Global South (Fortin, 2005: p. 170). External development interventions in the form of individual land titling and privatization programmes, not only seem inappropriate where communal systems exist (Palacio, 2006: p.18), but they also may destroy the traditional and communal way of life of people in developing countries. In this regard, the Commission on Legal Empowerment of the Poor (CLEP)[2] pointed out the recurrent mistake of development actors, inspired by the 'tragedy of the commons', of transforming customary tenure and interests in commons, into private property rights, instead of registering these as the group-owned property of communities (2008: p. 83). Instead, the Commission recommends that '[t]he state should enhance the asset base of the poor by enabling community-based ownership' and that commons 'should be recognised and fully protected against arbitrary seizure' (p. 65). The former United Nations (UN) Special Rapporteur on the Right to Food, Olivier De Schutter, similarly observed in a report of 2010 that 'the formalization of property rights and the establishment of land registries may be the problem, not the solution: it may cause [herders, pastoralists and fisherfolk] to be fenced off from the resources on which they depend, making them victims of the vast enclosure movement that may result from titling' (United Nations General Assembly, 2010: para. 25). The Special Rapporteur has emphasized that 'while security of tenure is important and should be seen as crucial for the realization of the right to food, individual titling and the creating of a market for land rights may not be the most appropriate means to achieve it' (para. 10). In his view, users' rights should instead be supported based on customary forms of tenure. He cited the examples of Kenya, where pastoralists were excluded from some land titling programmes, and Tanzania, where herdsmen had been deprived access to so-called 'unused' common grazing areas (see also De Schutter, Chapter 11 in this volume). To sum up, recognition of the commons, under the development policies of institutions like the World Bank, is crucial for their survival and legitimacy.

3. CLOSING THE COMMONS GAP IN INTERNATIONAL LAW

It is clear from the above that the commons cannot survive in a policy and legal vacuum. In fact, if we go back to Ostrom's seminal book *Governing the Commons*, the 'minimal recognition of rights to organize' is one of the eight design principles proposed to characterize a robust and sustainable commons-based institution. Ostrom summarized this principle as follows: '[t]he rights of appropriators to devise their own institutions [should not be] challenged by external governmental authorities' (1990: p. 90). She indeed observed, on the basis of her case studies, that 'if external governmental officials presume that only they have the authority to set the rules, then it will be very difficult for local appropriators to sustain a rule-governed [common-pool resource] over the long run' (p. 101). This principle is well supported empirically: commoners should be able to enjoy a minimum level of self-determination in order to organize local and small-scale governance systems with *ad hoc* rules. Commons scholars regularly emphasize that this right to self-government needs to be respected by the state and public authorities as a matter of law. Burns H. Weston and David Bollier, for example, argue that the establishment of commons 'will require the clarity and stability of law' (Weston and Bollier, 2013: p. 26). In the same vein, Alden Wily states that '[o]nly legal recognition . . . is sufficient to afford real protection' (2012). The law has, therefore, an important role to play in securing the commoners' right to self-government.

This is why, over the last decade, Ostrom's work has sparked a new wave of academic interest among legal scholars for the institution of the commons. Autonomous and bottom-up commons undoubtedly recast the dichotomy between public and private ownership, between state sovereignty and private market, as major normative frameworks. The main challenge for legal scholars, it seems, is to protect the commons against state and corporate enclosure. For that purpose, legal scholars – from the fields of legal theory, (intellectual) property law to constitutional and administrative law – have engaged in revising the basic categories of private property and state sovereignty in a more inclusive way. To accommodate the commons they have also devised new legal tools, like collective property regimes, intellectual property regimes (for example, the 'Creative Commons License' that protects shared resources, the copyleft, or even the denial of intellectual property rights), cooperatives, community land trusts and public trust doctrines (for example, rivers, shorelines and parks protected by the state for future generations). As Ugo Mattei and Alessandra Quarta observe, 'legal scholars interested in commons can use the existing rules and fill them with a new "generative" meaning, or try completely new proposals, which however require . . . quite a mighty political force to be put in place' (Mattei and Quarta, 2017: p. 79). As Maria Rosaria Marella writes, commons mirror 'a subversive site in the legal order' (2017: p. 63). However, these legal innovations so far have only occurred at the domestic level. Surprisingly, very little has been said about the role that *international law* can play in the empowerment of local communities in the self-management of their resources and in the resistance against the dispossession of the commons – especially in the Global South. This is what we call the 'commons gap' in international law – the gap of adequate international legal recognition or protection for the social institution of the commons.

The 'commons gap' issue is not as simple or uncontroversial as it may sound. To start with, international legal scholars are most familiar with the concept of *global* commons, comprising areas beyond the jurisdiction of any state, and much less so with the 'commons', as defined in this book in terms of bottom-up institutions of self-government. Global commons *sensu stricto* depict under international law physical resources which lie outside of the control of any state – that is, beyond territories subject to the sovereign jurisdiction of a state. International law typically recognizes as global commons the high seas, the deep seabed, outer space, the Moon and other celestial bodies, as well as Antarctica. There is, however, a fundamental distinction to be made between the 'global commons' ('*biens communs mondiaux*') as vast physical resource-domains (which are, in fact, in dire need of a governance framework), and the 'commons' ('*communs*') as social systems (which are already managed by communities with clear rules of access and use). The issue is not just one of terminological confusion between commons to be found at the local or global levels; the legal challenges posed by commons or global commons are also radically different. First, no single state can in principle appropriate and, in that sense, exercise sovereignty over global commons. As the United Nations Environment Programme (UNEP) stresses, '[d]espite efforts by governments or individuals to establish property rights or other forms of control over most natural resources, the Global Commons have remained an exception' (UN Environment Programme, 2017). For instance, the international law principle of the 'common heritage of mankind', which governs global commons like the Moon (Article 11 of the Moon Treaty (United Nations, 1979) and the deep seabed (Articles 136, 137(1) and 311(6) of the UN Convention on the Law of the Sea (United Nations, 1982)), has not been applied to areas under national jurisdiction such as forests or lakes due to the 'fear of infringements on national sovereignty' (Schrijver, 2016: p. 1258). Most commons are, in contrast, to be found within the jurisdiction of states. Second, the international law concept of global commons takes us back to Grotius' doctrines of *res communis* (common ownership for everyone) and *mare liberum* (free sea for everyone) which regard natural resources as inexhaustible and open to exploitation by any member of the international community. The lack of co-operation between states and the unsustainable management of shared natural resources is admittedly what still characterizes most of the global commons under international law today. No need to say that this depiction of the global commons resembles more the discourse of Hardin's tragedy of the unregulated commons and may even foreshadow their enclosure either by states or private entities. The ideas of open access and free-for-all exploitation of the global commons that are so entrenched in international legal doctrine have very little to do with Ostrom's work on self-governing institutions with well-defined rules of access and use of CPRs. In other words, the notion of the commons as an institution of collective action, that is the subject of this book, sits uneasily in the context of classic international law doctrines on global commons.

Another reason for this uneasiness with the commons under international law is that commons activists and scholars mostly favour local strategies at the municipal level 'to serve the interest of the commons' (Mattei and Quarta, 2017: p. 79). They believe that the transformation of our legal system should come from below, from the affected communities in the first place, and they are often sceptical that international law as it stands can serve as an instrument of resistance against enclosure. Fritjof Capra and Ugo Mattei state the following in their book *The Ecology of Law* (2015: p. 159):

> A global, top-down, eco-friendly enforcement system at this point is impossible to conceive of. It would be ineffective because powerful policy makers and their allied corporate lawyers have global jurisdiction and are bound to uphold the existing system. Consequently, seeking the use of 'top-down' international law to protect the commons is like trying to employ a fox to protect a chicken house.

This critical view posits that international law is not controlled by communities of commoners, but by states for the benefit of capital. Since its origins in the age of colonial expansion, the discipline of international law is said to be structurally biased towards the appropriation of natural resources to allow wealth accumulation. So we could say that not only international law has failed to protect the commons as a social institution of its own, but worse, that it has lent legal force to legitimate their enclosure. At the root of the depletion of the commons would be an obsolete, mechanistic international legal system inherited from the Industrial Age. Following this radical argument, international law would not be part of the solution, but of the problem itself (see Mattei, Chapter 10 in this volume).

Admittedly, the dominant doctrines under international law make it difficult to foreground other governance systems than public power or private property to manage CPRs at the local level. Yet, nothing precludes international legal scholars from rethinking the traditional foundations and assumptions of international law, and from conceiving a shift from an extractive model of law to a more ecological legal order, which promotes and protects stewardship of shared resources by local communities. The work of commons scholars and activists cannot be unrelievedly pessimistic when it comes to international law. In the face of the wave of enclosure – in particular in the Global South – international legal scholarship can indeed reflect on tools and strategies under international law to recognize and protect the commons upon which so many communities depend for their survival. Instead of rejecting any kind of international law solution, this chapter suggests to bridge the commons gap in international law and empower communities as key actors of their development by resorting to human rights. If international law certainly played a role in the vast enclosure of the commons from the colonial era, it may very well now constructively serve as a tool to combat the dispossession of communities around the world. The purpose is not to dismantle the idea of the commons by conceiving it in terms of vague and universal human rights language, thereby denying the concrete local and social distinctiveness of every single commons. Rather, our objective is to demonstrate that, pursuant to current international law, communities are entitled as a matter of legal rights to satisfy collective needs through the self-management of commons (Festa, 2016: para. 51).

As such, this idea is not new or revolutionary. The commons and human rights have, arguably, an intertwined history at least since the thirteenth century. The Magna Carta of 1215 – which legal scholars identify as the origin of modern human rights – and the less known accompanying Charter of the Forest of 1217 – which dealt with economic survival – both restricted autocratic behaviour and recognized 'common rights in restoring subsistence usufructs (goods or usages required for well-being)' (Linebaugh, 2008: p. 8). The latter gave to commoners legal protection from 'intrusions by privatizers' (p. 7) in the form of rights of grazing, fishing in streams, and extracting timber from forests. Over the last decade, commons scholars and activists have more intensively explored the potential of human rights to catalyse today's bottom-up communities of commoners at the local level. Human rights are currently going through a resurgence in this field. Thus, in their book *Green Governance: Ecological Survival, Human Rights, and the Law of the Commons*, Burns Weston and David Bollier have suggested that 'commoners have the fundamental human right, sanctioned by national and international law, to establish and maintain commons to protect their vital ecosystem resources' (Weston and Bollier, 2013). They even proposed in the appendix of their book a so-called 'Universal Covenant Affirming a Human Right to Commons- and Rights-based Governance of Earth's Natural Wealth and Resources'. Femke Wijdekop drew upon this idea to make the case for 'introducing procedural environmental rights to establish, maintain, participate in, be informed about and seek redress for ecological commons' (2014: p. 1). Saki Bailey similarly presented human rights as a legal and institutional tool capable of protecting the interests and values of the commons:

> [E]ven if rights may not be the most promising legal institution for the protection of the commons . . . rights as a legal institution may still serve the commons and intergenerational justice as a very promising and powerful *moral claim* capable of gaining strong public support for the redistribution of resources and even catalysing the creation of moral communities that emphasise duties over entitlements. Also, as the experience of recent events in Europe shows more clearly, rights may also serve as a powerful *political strategy* for reclaiming and/or preventing the privatisation of such resources where legislative politics has failed. (2013: pp. 125–6, emphasis added)

Admittedly, the status and jurisdictional reach of such a human right to the commons remain, at this stage, particularly unclear and speculative under international law. In our view, however, the right of access, use and management of the commons cannot merely remain an abstract 'moral claim' or 'political strategy' *de lege feranda*. On the one hand, even if the commons may imply moral values of cooperation, mutual trust, reciprocity, and participation which stand in stark contrast to the competition and individualism of the market, the law cannot be called upon to protect only the most virtuous ones. Besides, it would be a factual mistake to say of a commons that it is inherently 'good' – a commons may for instance discriminate internally against women or strangers. On the other hand, without denying the immense value of the alternative political horizon which the commons today open up in international law and global governance more broadly, it would be a strategic error to reduce the right to the commons to a utopian political ideology. For the commons respond to empirical realities and represent first and foremost a source of food, culture, and spirituality for millions of human beings around the world. So if we want to make any sense of such a right to establish and maintain commons, it is important to be able to enforce such entitlement *de lege lata*. This is why a more concrete question arises at the end of this chapter: can international and regional human rights instruments play any role in closing the commons gap in international law? And if so, what kind of rights, sanctioned by positive international law, are likely to protect commons-based institutions which are under threat in the Global South?

4. TOWARDS AN INTERNATIONAL HUMAN RIGHT TO THE COMMONS?

4.1 Right to Natural Resources

It is worth resituating the commons in the constellation of existing international and regional human rights law. First of all, Article 1(2) of both 1966 International Covenants, enshrines the right of all peoples to freely dispose of their natural wealth and resources, and prohibits depriving any peoples of their own means of subsistence (United Nations, 1966a; 1966b). Yet, as we have seen earlier, the commons represent, in most rural areas of developing countries, primary means of subsistence. This right is a basic constituent of the right to self-determination of peoples. It is also laid down at the regional level as a stand-alone provision in Article 21 of the African Charter on Human and Peoples' Rights (AfCHPR), which specifies under para. 2 that '[i]n case of spoliation, the dispossessed people shall have the right to the lawful recovery of its property as well as to an adequate compensation' (African Union, 1981). The African Court on Human and People's Rights (AfCtHPR) recognized, in a much publicized judgment on 26 May 2017, that the Ogiek Peoples, one of the last forest-dwelling communities in Kenya, had a major role to play in protecting the Mau Forest as an area on which they depend for their livelihood (*African*

Commission on Human and Peoples' Rights v. Republic of Kenya (Judgment of 26 May 2017), Application No. 006/2012). By evicting the Ogieks from the Mau Forest and depriving them of their traditional food resources therein, the Kenyan government was found to have violated their right to natural resources (para. 200).

4.2 Right to Property

It should further be emphasized that, under current international law, the right to property should not be understood in a restrictive, Western, individualistic sense only, but can be vested collectively in a group or community. Article 5(d)(v) of the International Convention on the Elimination of All Forms of Racial Discrimination includes the right to own property 'in association with others' (United Nations, 1965). Similarly, at a regional level, the Inter-American Court of Human Rights (IACtHR) has interpreted the right to property under Article 21(1) of the American Convention on Human Rights (ACHR) (Organization of American States, 1969) in an evolutionary fashion, so as to include communal property of indigenous peoples (*Case of the Mayagna (Sumo) Awas Tingni Community v. Nicaragua (Judgment of 31 August 2011)*, Inter-Am. Ct. H.R., (Ser. C) No. 79, para. 148). The IACtHR has ruled that, for the purpose of recognizing the property of indigenous communities 'lacking real title', possession of the land by reason of customary practices should suffice (para. 151).[3]

In the African system, the African Court has also recently interpreted the right to property (AfCHPR, Article 14) in a broad sense and in the light of indigenous rights. Although the right as such was addressed in a part of the Charter devoted to individuals, the Court held that it could 'apply to groups or communities' and include 'the right to use (usus) and the right to enjoy the produce of the land (fructus)' (*African Commission on Human and Peoples' Rights v. Republic of Kenya (Judgment of 26 May 2017)*, Application No. 006/2012: paras 123 and 201). That is not too surprising: the African Commission already promoted a broad understanding of the right to property as including 'rights guaranteed by traditional custom and law to access to, and use of, land and other natural resources held under communal ownership' (African Commission on Human and Peoples' Rights, 2010: para. 54). The African Commission not only recognized homes and lands as being protected from forced eviction, but also 'common property resources that were occupied or depended upon' (para. 1). Where indigenous communities like the Ogiek or other groups lack a formal title to land, the recognition of their informal collective rights of use may prove an effective strategy to counter large-scale land grabbing activities and commons dispossession in developing countries (Marella, 2017: p. 78). However, in our view, the right to (communal) property does not encompass the full spectrum of the meaning of the commons in shaping the identity, way of life and culture of local communities, and could be prone to an instrumentalist understanding of land and natural resources as commodities. The challenge remains to give full recognition to the commons as a social institution of its own in the use and management of natural resources.

4.3 Rights of Indigenous Peoples

As alluded to above, next to the rights to natural resources and property, the rights of indigenous peoples may also help protect local communities in the Global South against the enclosure of the commons. The UN Declaration on the Rights of Indigenous Peoples (UNDRIP) (United Nations, 2007) explicitly states in its preamble that it is concerned with the dispossession of indigenous lands, territories and resources preventing communities from exercising their right to development in accordance with their own needs and interests. Indigenous peoples have the right to autonomy or self-government in matters relating to their internal and local affairs (Article 4), to maintain and strengthen their own distinct decision-making institutions (Articles 5 and 18), and to be secure in the enjoyment of their own means of subsistence and development (Article 20). The traditional lands and shared resources of indigenous communities should therefore be protected against enclosures (Article 26). As the African Court held in the Ogiek case, '[w]ithout excluding the right to property in the traditional sense, [Article 26] places greater emphasis on the rights of possession, occupation, use/utilisation of land' (*African Commission on Human and Peoples' Rights v. Republic of Kenya (Judgment of 26 May 2017)*, Application No. 006/2012: para. 127). Article 26(3) indeed requires states to give legal recognition to lands, territories and resources 'with due respect to the customs, traditions and land tenure systems of the indigenous peoples concerned'.

While it is true that the UNDRIP is, as other United Nations General Assembly (UNGA) resolutions, not a legally binding instrument, it has been influential in the interpretation of treaty provisions such as the right to land in the African Charter. Moreover, as the UN Special Rapporteur on the rights of Indigenous peoples has argued (United Nations General Assembly, 2008: para. 41) and as the IACtHR has previously determined (*Case of the Mayagna (Sumo) Awas Tingni Community v. Nicaragua (Judgment of 31 August 2011)*, Inter-Am. Ct. H.R., (Ser. C) No. 79: para. 71), some provisions of UNDRIP can be said to reflect norms of customary international law. By contrast, the International Labour Organization's (ILO) Indigenous and Tribal Peoples Convention (No. 169) is legally binding upon states that have ratified it (International Labour Organization, 1989). It requires states parties to recognize the indigenous peoples' rights of ownership and possession over the lands which they traditionally occupy (Article 14), as well as the rights to participate in the use, management and conservation of natural resources (Article 15). Convention No. 169 has already been cited as a potential instrument for enforcing the use and exclusion rights – as defined by indigenous peoples themselves within their own collective systems of governance of natural resources (Bailey, 2013: p. 122). In the Inter-American system, Convention No. 169 served to resist against the enclosure of traditional indigenous lands. The U'Wa Nation, for example, successfully claimed before the Inter-American Commission on Human Rights (IACHR) that Colombia violated its right to land by developing oil drilling and mining projects on their sacred ancestral territory without prior consultation (*U'Wa Indigenous Community (Precautionary Measures)*, Inter-Am. Ct. H.R., Case No. 11.754).

4.4 Rights of Peasants

Even though the requirements for formal recognition as indigenous peoples have been interpreted broadly by regional human rights courts to include tribal people who also 'have a special relationship with their ancestral territories' (*Case of the Saramaka People v. Suriname (Judgment of 28 November 2007)*, Inter-Am. Ct. H.R., (Ser. C) No. 172: para. 86), the personal scope of indigenous rights remains limited. The former UN Special Rapporteur on the right to food recommended in a report in 2010 that, for the purpose of protecting 'access to fishing grounds, grazing grounds and water points for fisherfolk, herders and pastoralists, for whom the protection of commons is vital', '[t]he recognition of communal rights should extend beyond indigenous communities, at least to certain communities that entertain a similar relationship with the land, centred on the community rather than on the individual' (United Nations General Assembly, 2010: para. 40(c)). In that respect, the project of a UN Declaration of the Rights of Peasants now offers a window into the potential of generalizing this model of community rights for *all* people involved in small-scale food production, including all those who depend on commons for their livelihood – beyond the distinct identities, cultures and ways of life of indigenous and tribal peoples.

This new initiative follows a long-standing request of the international peasant movement, among which *La Via Campesina* (2016) and its

Indonesian affiliated group *Serikat Petani Indonesia*, who have denounced systematic human rights violations against peasants and other rural groups. Interestingly, one of the main factors triggering the international movement for peasants rights from Indonesia was the role that the World Bank played in attempting to revise the Indonesian Basic Agrarian Law. From a strategic point of view, international human rights action was deemed necessary by Indonesian farmers to fight against the Bank's intervention in the liberalization of land regulations in the country (Purwanto, 2013: p. 3). In this trend towards the recognition of rights of peasants and their fight for food sovereignty, peasant and farmer groups started framing their demands in terms of new rights to commons, as this excerpt from the 2011 Declaration of the European Forum for Food Sovereignty shows:

> Reclaiming the right to our Commons. We oppose and struggle against the commodification, financialisation and patenting of our commons, such as: land; farmers', traditional and reproducible seeds; livestock breeds and fish stocks; trees and forests; water; the atmosphere; and knowledge. Access to these should not be determined by markets and money. In using common resources, we must ensure the realisation of human rights and gender equality, and that society as a whole benefits. We also acknowledge our responsibility to use our Commons sustainably, while respecting the rights of mother earth. Our Commons should be managed through collective, democratic and community control. (Nyéléni Europe, 2011, quoted in Claeys, 2015: pp. 123–4)

Following civil society pressure, the UN Human Rights Council (2012) established in 2012 an open-ended intergovernmental working group with the mandate of negotiating a – non-binding – declaration, outlining the rights of peasants and other people working in rural areas. The UN Declaration articulates a number of – implicit and explicit – guarantees for the protection of the commons, particularly relevant in the context of development, including the right of peasants to control their natural resources, to enjoy the benefits of their development, 'the right to have access to and to use the natural resources present in their communities that are required to enjoy adequate living conditions', 'the right to participate in the management of those resources' (Article 5), and 'the right, individually and *collectively*, to the lands, water bodies, coastal seas, fisheries, pastures and forests that they need to achieve an adequate standard of living, to have a place to live in security, peace and dignity and to develop their cultures' (Article 17(1), emphasis added) (UN Human Rights Council, 2018a).

The development of a UN Declaration on the Rights of Peasants is particularly noteworthy for this chapter since it is arguably the first time that an international human rights document would expressly put forward a stand-alone obligation for states to recognize and protect the 'commons' as a governance model of its own. Article 17(3) of the Declaration indeed includes a collective dimension of the 'Right to land and other natural resources':

> States shall provide legal recognition for land tenure rights, including customary land tenure rights, not currently protected by law. All forms of tenure, including tenancy, must provide all persons with a degree of tenure security which guarantees legal protection against forced evictions. States shall recognize and protect the natural *commons* and their *related systems of collective use and management*. (UN Human Rights Council, 2018c) (emphasis added)[4]

The explanatory study on the rationale underlying the Draft Declaration prepared by the UN Office of the High Commissioner for Human Rights (OHCHR) provides that this formulation 'highlights the importance of providing tenure security, including through the protection of customary tenure rights and the protection of *commons*, over the land, fisheries, forests, water and other natural resources on which peasants and other people working in rural areas depend for their livelihood' (UN Human Rights Council, 2017: para. 240). This study defines the 'commons' by reference to the Oxford English dictionary as 'land or resources belonging to or affecting the whole of a community' (para. 240).

It is important to stress, however, that originally there was no specific reference to the term 'commons' in the very first draft presented by *La Via Campesina* and entitled 'Declaration of Rights of Peasants – Women and Men' (2008). It is only since 2016 and the proposal submitted by the Bolivian representative as chairperson-rapporteur of the working group that the Declaration includes a reference to the commons. The reason why the Declaration now includes this term is to use as much as possible so-called 'agreed language' – that is to say, formulations to be found in other international human rights instruments, as well as other relevant international policy platforms (Claeys, 2015: p. 127). The right to land in the current text is, indeed, largely inspired by the *Voluntary Guidelines on the Responsible Governance of Tenure of Land, Fisheries and Forests in the Context of National Food Security* (Tenure Guidelines) adopted in 2012 by the Committee on World Food Security (CFS) – an intergovernmental and highly inclusive platform which is today authoritative in the field of world food governance (see De Schutter, Chapter 11 in this volume: p. 249). These Tenure Guidelines are the result of several years of negotiations among UN agencies, states, civil society organizations like *La Via Campesina*, the private sector, and the then UN Special Rapporteur on the right to food, Olivier De Schutter. The Guidelines seek to protect the access to food of the rural poor by recognizing different – formal or informal – models of governance of shared natural resources at the local level, including the commons. Guideline 8.3 indeed provides as follows (Food and Agricultural Organization, 2012):

> [T]here are publicly-owned land, fisheries and forests that are collectively used and managed (in some national contexts referred to as *commons*), States should, where applicable, recognize and protect such publicly-owned land, fisheries and forests and their *related systems of collective use and management*, including in processes of allocation by the State. (Emphasis added)

In order to support the implementation of the Tenure Guidelines, the Food and Agriculture Organization (FAO) also prepared a series of technical guides, among which a publication entitled *Governing Tenure Rights to Commons* (Food and Agriculture Organization, 2016). This document defines the 'commons' as natural resources such as land, fisheries and forests, which are used and managed collectively by 'a group of people (often understood as "community")' (p. 57). Interestingly, like the Tenure Guidelines, this document extensively refers to international human rights treaties and declarations (p. 13). From the start, it states that '[s]ecure tenure rights to commons are crucial for women and men' and that '[t]he Guidelines represent a historic opportunity to guide governments and hold them accountable in assuming their duties and fulfilling their obligations to implement secure tenure for the legitimate holders of rights to commons' (p. v). As an expert of the working group on the UN declaration of peasant rights observed, the vision of the right to land promoted by the 2012 Tenure Guidelines is therefore 'very different' from 'the one that focuses on promoting individual property titles as the solution to secure land tenure' (Golay, 2013: p. 18).

Compared to the Tenure Guidelines, the UN Declaration on the Rights of Peasants represents a significant breakthrough in the process of recognizing the commons in international law. Indeed, the UN Declaration does not make the same mistake as the Tenure Guidelines of assimilating the commons to 'public' lands and resources. In the UN Declaration, the term 'commons' is preserved, but instead is recognized as a social institution of its own – separate from both public and private property. This also means that the proposed right to the commons is 'amongst the most controversial ones [particularly among Western states like the United States or Member States of the European Union], because of the collective nature of the rights claimed, because their indeterminate content departs from existing standards, and because of the challenges that their implementation would represent' (Claeys, 2015: p. 127).

After five years of work, the UN Human Rights Council has decided, during its 36th session in September 2017, that the open-ended intergovernmental working group would undergo its fifth and final round of negotiations from 9 to 13 April 2018 (United Nations General Assembly, 2017). Under strong pressure from the international peasant movement represented by *La Via Campesina* and NGOs – among which *Centre Europe – Tiers Monde* (CETIM) and *FIAN International* – the Declaration was finally adopted by the UN Human Rights Council during its 39th session on 28 September 2018 (United Nations General Assembly, 2018c). If subsequently approved by the UN General Assembly, and even if it falls under the category of 'soft law', the UN Declaration would represent an important step towards the international legal recognition of the commons, which peasants and other people working in rural areas have always used and managed in order to secure their livelihood.

5. CONCLUSION

The great contribution of American political economist Elinor Ostrom was to show that there are plenty of institutional arrangements which are formed by the communities themselves and which often prove more effective than the typical 'all-public' and 'all-private' solutions in safeguarding commonly shared resources. In particular, land and natural resources in the Global South are often governed as commons – that is to say that their use, access and management is socially defined and organized in a collective and autonomous way, aside from the state and the market. According to a recent report by Oxfam, ILC and RRI, 2.5 billion people, including 370 million indigenous people, rely on communal land and natural resources around the world, which represent approximately 50 per cent of the global land mass (Oxfam et al., 2016). However, although Ostrom's work was primarily addressed to the development community (see Sauvêtre, Chapter 5 in this volume), this collective model of bottom-up governance is still far from being generally accepted in the field. Instead, echoing Garrett Hardin's 'Tragedy of the Commons' (1968), development actors like the World Bank still seem to assume that commons should be commodified and privatized to secure land tenure and ensure their transferability in markets. Because so many commons are based on traditional usage and customary practice, and are still considered 'backward' by development institutions, these communal systems tend to be highly vulnerable to state and corporate enclosure in the Global South. To date, only one-fifth of the communal lands around the world would be legally recognized (Oxfam et al., 2016). This explains why local communities face the threat of being deprived from their most basic access to food, land and other essential resources.

Faced with this risk of enclosure in developing countries international law should provide tools and strategies to protect the commons. Admittedly, it remains difficult to foreground the notion of the commons in the international legal order, as it stands. The ideas of open access and free-for-all exploitation of the global commons that are so entrenched in the discipline of international law have very little to do with the self-governing practice of commoning according to *ad hoc* rules of access and use. Yet, it is possible to observe progressive developments in international and regional human rights instruments which recognize the commons as a social institution of its own. Even if its dominant conception probably remains statist and individualist in nature, as Ugo Mattei forcefully argues in this volume (see Chapter 10), international law may also be embraced 'from below' (Rajagopal, 2003) by civil society actors as a new guiding frame and weapon to save the commons in developing countries. International law may just represent yet another forum for contestation, but it is a new and significant one in the struggle for the commons. Not only traditional individual rights like the right to property have been interpreted by regional human rights courts in an evolutionary fashion to apply to groups and rights of use, but indigenous rights now also embrace a broader conception of the community rights of possession, occupation, use of land and other natural resources. These developments are likely to give legal recognition to commons-based institutions, with due respect to the autonomous rules of the communities concerned.

Most importantly, the project of a UN Declaration of the Rights of Peasants now puts forward, in its Article 17(3), a stand-alone obligation 'to recognise and protect the natural commons and their related systems of collective use and management'. Interestingly, this initiative did not come from above, but was driven by civil society groups representing the peasant movement around the globe. Agrarian activist groups, such as *Serikat Petani* in Indonesia, decided to engage in the creation of a *new* collective right to the commons at the *international* level to push for social change and resist their dispossession at the local level. Considering that peasants and rural workers represent 80 per cent of those suffering from hunger in the world today, the new attention given to the threats to this collective institution, through the UN Declaration, is a welcome development. It suggests, for the first time, the existence of a window of opportunity for a new international human right to the commons. In this way, international law is likely to offer a wider spectrum of legal strategies to assert the rights of communities to establish and protect commons against enclosure. It now remains to be seen if the final Declaration will effectively respond to the legitimate demands of the world's poorest and most marginalized commoners – small-scale farmers, pastoralists, forest-dwellers, artisanal fishers and indigenous peoples who depend on commons for their survival. The human right to the commons cannot remain an empty promise; additional protection is urgently needed for the commons under positive international law.

NOTES

* This chapter benefited from comments received at the Annual Graduate Law Conference 2017, 'Governing Our Commons: What Matters to Us Today', 13–14 May 2017, McGill University, Canada; the Symposium 'Why private property? Politics of property and its alternatives', 20–21 June 2017, Université libre de Bruxelles (ULB), Belgium; the ESIL 13th Annual Conference, Workshop 'Democracy and Participation *versus* Global Public Goods and Commons: Theoretical Challenges', 6 September 2017, Naples, Italy.

1. SAPs consists of loans to debt-strapped governments, conditioned upon the achievement of a number of policy reforms, among which privatization of government-held enterprises, liberalization of public services and greater efficiency of the free market. The term 'SAP' acquired such a negative connotation that it was abandoned by the institution in the 1990s.
2. The Commission on Legal Empowerment of the Poor (CLEP) is an independent working group established in 2005, hosted by UNDP and co-chaired by former US Secretary of State Madeleine Albright and Peruvian economist Hernando de Soto. The Commission published its final report in 2008 (see also, De Schutter, Chapter 11 in this volume: p. 240).
3. See also the reference to 'commons' as areas which are only used collectively by the community in the expert opinion of Rodolfo Stavenhagen Gruenbaum, anthropologist and sociologist: 'There are two concepts of collective land: the territory, generally, which the community considers common, although internally there are mechanisms to allocate temporary occupation and use by its members and which does not allow alienation to persons who are not members of the community; and the areas which are only used collectively, the "commons" which are not divided into plots. Almost all indigenous communities have a part used collectively as "commons", and then another part which can be divided and allocated to families or domestic units. Nevertheless, the concept of collective property remains, even if it is disputed by others, often the State itself, when there is no title. When there are problems, the need for property titles arises because the community risks losing everything. The history of Latin America has been one of almost constant dispossession of indigenous communities by external interests.'
4. Note, however, that the official French translation of the Declaration provides that 'Les états reconnaîtront et protégeront les *ressources naturelles communes* et les systèmes d'utilisation et de gestion collectives de ces ressources' (Human Rights Council, 2018b, emphasis added), which is not the same as 'natural commons' in English. The English term should indeed be translated in French as 'communs naturels'.

REFERENCES

African Commission on Human and Peoples' Rights (2010) Principles and Guidelines on the Implementation of Economic, Social and Cultural Rights in the African Charter on Human and Peoples' Rights, Adopted at the African Commission's 47th Ordinary Session held in Banjul, Gambia, from 12 to

26 May 2010. [Online] Available from: http://www.achpr.org/files/instruments/economic-social-cultural/achpr_instr_guide_draft_esc_rights_eng.pdf (accessed 20 November 2017).

African Union (1981) African Charter on Human and Peoples' Rights. Nairobi, 27 June 1981. United Nations Treaty Series, 1520 (217).

Alden Wily, L. (2012) The Global Land Grab: The New Enclosures. In: Bollier, D. and Helfrich, S. (eds) *The Wealth of the Commons: A World Beyond Market and State*. Amherst, Levellers Press.

Bailey, S. (2013) The Architecture of Commons Legal Institutions for Future Generations. In: Bailey, S., Farrell, G. and Mattei, U. (eds) *Protecting Future Generations through Commons*. Strasbourg, Council of Europe Publishing.

Bollier, D. (2016) Beyond Development: The Commons as a New/Old Paradigm of Human Flourishing. [Online] Available from: http://www.bollier.org/blog/beyond-development-commons-newold-paradigm-human-flourishing (accessed 20 November 2017).

Capra, F. and Mattei, U. (2015) *The Ecology of Law: Toward a Legal System in Tune with Nature and Community*. Oakland, Berrett-Koehler Publishers.

Claeys, P. (2015) The Right to Land and Territory: New Human Right and Collective Action Frame. *Revue interdisciplinaire d'études juridiques*, **75** (2), 115–37.

Coase, R. H. (1960) The Problem of Social Cost. *Journal of Law and Economics*, **3**, 1–44.

Commission on Legal Empowerment of the Poor (2008) *Making the Law Work for Everyone*. Vol. II, Working Group Reports. New York, Commission on Legal Empowerment of the Poor and UNDP.

Deininger, K. (2003) *Land Policies for Growth and Poverty Reduction: A World Bank Policy Research Report*. Washington, DC, World Bank.

de la Fuente, M. (2003) A Personal View: The Water War in Cochabamba, Bolivia: Privatization Triggers an Uprising. *Mountain Research and Development*, **23** (1), 98–100.

de Soto, H. (2001) *The Mystery of Capital: Why Capitalism Triumphs in the West and Fails Everywhere Else*. London, Black Swan.

Feder, G. and Feeny, D. (1991) Land Tenure and Property Rights: Theory and Implications for Development Policy. *The World Bank Economic Review*, **5** (1), 135–53.

Festa, D. (2016) Les communs urbains: L'invention du commun. *Tracées, Revue de Sciences humaines*, 2016 (16), 233–56.

Fitzpatrick, D. (2006) Evolution and Chaos in Property Rights Systems: The Third World Tragedy of Contested Access. *Yale Law Journal*, **115** (5), 996–1048.

Food and Agriculture Organization (2012) Voluntary Guidelines on the Responsible Governance of Tenure of Land, Fisheries and Forests in the Context of National Food Security. Committee on World Food Security. [Online] Available from: http://www.fao.org/docrep/016/i2801e/i2801e.pdf (accessed 11 January 2018).

Food and Agriculture Organization (2016) *Governing Tenure Rights to Commons: A Guide to Support the Implementation of the Voluntary Guidelines on the Responsible Governance of Tenure of Land, Fisheries and Forests in the Context of National Food Security*. Governance of Tenure Technical Guide No. 8. Rome, FAO.

Fortin, E. (2005) Reforming Land Rights: The World Bank and the Globalization of Agriculture. *Social and Legal Studies*, **14** (2), 147–77.

Glinavos, I. (2010) Transition or Development? Reassessing Priorities for Law Reform. *Progress in Development Studies*, **10** (1), 59–74.

Golay, C. (2013) Legal Reflections on the Rights of Peasants and Other People Working in Rural Areas. Background paper, Prepared for the First Session of the Working Group on the Rights of Peasants and Other People Working in Rural Areas, 15–19 July 2013. [Online] Available from: http://www.ohchr.org/Documents/HRBodies/HRCouncil/WGPleasants/Golay.pdf (accessed 20 November 2017).

Hardin, G. (1968) The Tragedy of the Commons. *Science*, **162** (3859), 1243–8.

Harvey, D. (2003) *The New Imperialism*. Oxford, Oxford University Press.

International Labour Organization (1989) Indigenous and Tribal Peoples Convention (No. 169). Geneva, 27 June 1989. United Nations Treaty Series, 1650 (383).

La Via Campesina (2008) Declaration of Rights of Peasants – Women and Men. [Online] Available from: https://viacampesina.net/downloads/PDF/EN-3.pdf (accessed 20 November 2017).

La Via Campesina (2016) Over 15 Years' Struggle for the Recognition Of Peasants in the International Human Rights System. [Online] Available from: https://viacampesina.org/en/index.php/main-issues-mainmenu-27/human-rights-mainmenu-40/peasants-right-resources/2123-over-15-years-struggle-for-the-recognition-of-peasants-in-the-international-human-rights-system (accessed 20 November 2017).

Linebaugh, P. (2008) *The Magna Carta Manifesto*. Berkeley, University of California Press.

Löhr, D. (2012) The Failure of Land Privatization: On the Need for New Development Policies. In: Bollier, D. and Helfrich, S. (eds) *The Wealth of the Commons: A World Beyond Market and State*. Amherst, Levellers Press.

Marella, M. R. (2017) The Commons as a Legal Concept. *Law and Critique*, **28** (1), 61–86.

Mattei, U. and Quarta, A. (2017) Théorie du Droit. Principles of Legal Commoning. *Revue juridique de l'environnement*, **42** (1), 67–81.

Narula, S. (2013) The Global Land Rush: Markets, Rights, and the Politics of Food. *Stanford Journal of International Law*, **49** (1), 101–75.

Nyéléni Europe (2011) Food Sovereignty in Europe Now! Nyeleni Europe 2011: European Forum for Food Sovereignty. 21 August 2011. [Online] Available from: http://www.nyelenieurope.net/sites/default/files/2016-06/NYELENI_Declaration_English.pdf (accessed 28 December 2017).

Organization of American States (1969) American Convention on Human Rights. San José, 22 November 1969. United Nations Treaty Series, 1144 (123).

Ostrom, E. (1990) *Governing the Commons: The Evolution of Institutions for Collective Action*. New York, Cambridge University Press.

Oxfam, International Land Coalition and Rights and Resources Initiative (2016) *Common Ground. Securing Land Rights and Safeguarding the Earth*. Oxford, Oxfam.

Padilla, C. (2012) Mining as a Threat to the Commons: The Case of South America. In: Bollier, D. and Helfrich, S. (eds) *The Wealth of the Commons: A World Beyond Market and State*. Amherst, Levellers Press.

Palacio, A. (2006) Legal Empowerment of the Poor: An Action Agenda for the World Bank. To the attention of the President of the World Bank. [Online]

Available from: http://siteresources.worldbank.org/INTLAWJUSTINST/Resources/LegalEmpowermentofthePoor.pdf (accessed 20 November 2017).

Purwanto, H. (2013) Local to Global: How Serikat Petano Indonesia Has Accelerated the Movement for Agrarian Reform. In: Saragih, H. (ed.) *La Via Campesina's Open Book: Celebrating 20 Years of Struggle and Hope*. Jakarta, La Via Campesina.

Rajagopal, B. (2003) *International Law from Below. Development, Social Movements and Third World Resistance*. New York, Cambridge University Press.

Schrijver, N. (2016) Managing the Global Commons: Common Good or Common Sink. *Third World Quarterly*, **37** (7), 1252–67.

UN Human Rights Council (2012) Promotion of the Human Rights of Peasants and Other People Working in Rural Areas. Res. 19/21. 24 September 2012, UN Doc. A/HRC/21/L.23.

UN Human Rights Council (2017) Normative Sources and Rationale Underlying the Draft Declaration on the Rights of Peasants and Other People Working in Rural Areas. Study by the Office of the United Nations High Commissioner for Human Rights. Open-ended Intergovernmental Working Group on the Rights of Peasants and Other People Working in Rural Areas, Fourth Session, 15–19 May 2017. UN Doc. A/HRC/WG.15/4/3.

UN Human Rights Council (2018a) Revised Draft United Nations Declaration on the Rights of Peasants and Other People Working in Rural Areas. Open-ended Intergovernmental Working Group on the Rights of Peasants and Other People Working in Rural Areas, Fifth session, 12 February 2018. UN Doc. A/HRC/WG.15/5/2.

UN Human Rights Council (2018b) Projet révisé de déclaration des Nations Unies sur les droits des paysans et des autres personnes travaillant dans les zones rurales. Open-ended Intergovernmental Working Group on the Rights of Peasants and Other People Working in Rural Areas, Fifth session, 12 February 2018. UN Doc. A/HRC/WG.15/5/2.

UN Human Rights Council (2018c) United Nations Declaration on the Rights of Peasants and Other People Working in Rural Areas. Thirty-ninth session. 28 September 2018. UN Doc. A/HRC/39/L.16.

United Nations (1965) International Convention on the Elimination of All Forms of Racial Discrimination. New York, 21 December 1965. United Nations Treaty Series, 660 (195).

United Nations (1966a) International Covenant on Civil and Political Rights. New York, 16 December 1966. United Nations Treaty Series, 999 (171).

United Nations (1966b) International Covenant on Economic, Social and Cultural Rights. New York, 16 December 1966. United Nations Treaty Series, 993 (4).

United Nations (1979) Agreement Governing the Activities of States on the Moon and Other Celestial Bodies. New York, 5 December 1979, United Nations Treaty Series, 1363 (3).

United Nations (1982) Convention on the Law of the Sea. Montego Bay, 10 December 1982, United Nations Treaty Series, 1833 (397).

United Nations (2007) Declaration on the Rights of Indigenous Peoples. GA Res. 61/295. 13 September 2007, UN Doc. A/61/53.

United Nations Environment Programme (2017) Global Commons. [Online] Available from: http://staging.unep.org/delc/GlobalCommons/tabid/54404/Default.aspx (accessed 20 November 2017).

United Nations General Assembly (2008) Report of the Special Rapporteur on the

Situation of Human Rights and Fundamental Freedoms of Indigenous People, S. James Anaya. 11 August 2008, UN Doc. A/HRC/9/9.
United Nations General Assembly (2010) Report of the Special Rapporteur on the Right to Food. 11 August 2010, UN Doc. A/65/281.
United Nations General Assembly (2017) Promotion and Protection of the Human Rights of Peasants and Other People Working in Rural Areas. Human Rights Council. 36th session. 25 September 2017, UN Doc. A/HRC/36/L.29.
Vaccaro, I., Zanotti, L. and Sepez, J. (2009) Commons and Markets: Opportunities for Development of Local Sustainability. *Environmental Politics*, **18** (4), 522–38.
Weston, B. H. and Bollier, D. (2013) *Green Governance: Ecological Survival, Human Rights, and the Law of the Commons*, Cambridge, Cambridge University Press.
Wijdekop, F. (2014) A Human Right to Commons- and Rights-based Ecological Governance: the Key to a Healthy and Clean Environment? [Online] Available from: http://earthlawyers.org/academic-papers/ (accessed 6 January 2018).
World Bank (1975) *Land Reform: Sector Policy Paper*. Washington, DC, World Bank.
World Bank (2005) Chapter 4: Stability and Security. In: *World Development Report 2005: A Better Investment Climate for Everyone*. Washington, DC/New York, World Bank/Oxford University Press.
World Bank (2007) Chapter 6: Supporting Smallholder Competitiveness through Institutional Innovations. In: *World Development Report 2008: Agriculture for Development*, Washington, DC, World Bank.
World Bank (2017) *World Development Report 2017: Governance and the Law*, Washington, DC, World Bank.

Cases

African Commission on Human and Peoples' Rights v. Republic of Kenya (Judgment of 26 May 2017), Application No. 006/2012.
Case of the Mayagna (Sumo) Awas Tingni Community v. Nicaragua (Judgment of 31 August 2011), Inter-Am. Ct. H.R., (Ser. C) No. 79.
Case of the Saramaka People v. Suriname (Judgment of 28 November 2007), Inter-Am. Ct. H.R., (Ser. C) No. 172.
U'Wa Indigenous Community (Precautionary Measures), Inter-Am. Ct. H.R., Case No. 11.754.

13. Procedure and substance in international environmental law and the protection of the global commons

Jutta Brunnée*

> We have entered an era . . . in which international law subserves not only the interests of individual States, but looks beyond them and their parochial concerns to the greater interests of humanity and planetary welfare . . . International environmental law will need to proceed beyond weighing . . . rights and obligations . . . within a closed compartment of individual State self-interest, unrelated to the global concerns of humanity as a whole.
>
> (*Gabčíkovo-Nagymaros Project* (*Hungary v. Slovakia*) (Separate Opinion of Judge Weeramantry) [1997] ICJ Rep 7: 118)

1. INTRODUCTION[1]

International law as traditionally conceived – public international law – was designed to govern the relations of sovereign states. Even in 2018, the structure and processes of international law remain anchored in these 'Westphalian' foundations. Since there is no single, central lawmaking authority that could legislate in the collective interest, international norms must emerge from inter-state interactions, deliberations and negotiations. Through their involvement in the international arena, other actors – individuals, non-governmental organizations (NGOs), business entities or international institutions – may help shape these norms. But, on the standard account, they become legally binding only when there is sufficient consensus among states to generate a rule of customary international law, or when states agree to be bound by a treaty.

According to some observers, this 'inter-national' law must, by definition, fail in realizing the common interests of humanity since it orders a 'world fit for governments' – an 'unsociety ruled by a collective of self-conceived sovereigns whose authority is derived neither from the totality of international society nor from the people but from the intermediating state-systems' (Allott, 1990: p. 249; see also Mattei, Chapter 10 in this volume). Most academic commentators, however, while noting the challenges inherent in the inter-state structure of international law, have tended also to find evidence that this structure is being adjusted and expanded to promote the 'greater interest of humanity'. Wolfgang Friedmann (1964) famously observed that an emerging international law of cooperation had begun to significantly modify the classical law of coexistence of states. Bruno Simma (1994) traced the shifts in international law from bilateralism to community interest. Ellen Hey posited the emergence of an 'international *public* law', through which 'common-interest normative patterns' are woven across the traditional 'inter-state normative patterns' (2003: p. 7).

International environmental law provides especially good terrain for assessing to what extent the law has evolved from a bilateral, consent-based legal system to one that reflects a multilateral approach to the collective protection of global commons. Questions about common goods, and hence obligations designed to further their protection, are at the heart of the field. Indeed, environmental global commons, such as the high seas, fisheries, the atmosphere or the global climate, also relate to 'classical' commons issues pertaining to tangible natural resources (see Cogolati and Wouters, Chapter 1 in this volume). However, to get at the attendant legal and conceptual issues, it is necessary to look beyond the global commons themselves and to the legal interests around the protection of which international law has grown. Since no state can lay a claim to the global commons as such, the key question is who owes legal obligations to protect the global commons, to whom, and under what circumstances states have a legal interest in global commons protection, or can invoke a collective legal interest. It is worth asking, then, whether contemporary international environmental law lives up to the yardstick set out by Judge Christopher Weeramantry some twenty years ago in his Separate Opinion in the *Gabčíkovo-Nagymaros* case. This chapter focuses on the procedural dimensions of international environmental law's evolution towards the protection of collective or community interests and, by extension, its capacity to protect global commons. Before delving into this topic, several interrelated definitional issues must be settled to delineate the scope of the inquiry.

An initial question concerns who is included in the 'community' or 'collective' in whose interests the global commons are to be protected. For the purposes of this chapter, I do not enter into the thorny debates about whether the often-invoked 'international community' actually exists in any meaningful sense,[2] and, if so, whether in legal terms it includes only states and, perhaps, the intergovernmental organizations through which they pursue collective goals,[3] or indeed humanity as a whole.[4] I use the terms 'community' or 'collective' simply as a shorthand for what this chapter is concerned with: instances in which international law addresses environment-related interests shared by a group of states or even all states and, generally speaking, by non-state actors (international institutions, NGOs, business entities and individuals) as well. It is also worth noting that non-state actors are not merely affected by environmental degradation or resource scarcity, but very often directly contribute to these phenomena (Brunnée and Hey, 2013). Indeed, one of the characteristics of international environmental concerns is the fact that they are caused primarily by non-state actor conduct. This feature highlights one of the challenges international environmental law must confront: in many respects, states are only the intermediaries – when they take on obligations to protect the global commons, the attendant task more often than not is to influence the conduct of non-state actors (Bodansky et al., 2007).

At the factual level, and here we return to the notion of 'global commons', community interests involve matters that require collective action, that is, environmental problems that cannot be solved unless several or even all states and other actors coordinate their actions. For example, it is impossible to combat global climate change effectively unless states, and non-state actors, cooperate to reduce greenhouse gas concentrations in the atmosphere. Similarly, ocean pollution or over-fishing generally can only be curbed if relevant actors work together, even if at times the cooperation of only one actor can make all the difference.[5] The flipside of the collective action imperative is that addressing the underlying concerns provides benefits shared by all. Such shared benefits accrue most obviously from dealing with global issues such as climate change. But the common benefit feature highlights that community interests in protection can also relate to certain resources, such as biological diversity or forests, located within the jurisdiction of individual states.

From a legal standpoint, such global commons issues and the attendant community interests involve situations in which no single state is in a position to demand a particular approach. For example, in community interest situations, states will typically find it difficult to prove significant harm to their territories, or to trace such harm back to the conduct of specific states. Therefore, a collective response is required not only for factual reasons, but also to avoid the legal constraints that individual states would face in attempting to defend a community interest by invoking the responsibility of another state under general international law, assuming they were willing to do so.[6] Furthermore, to protect areas or resources that lie beyond the jurisdiction of individual states, states must collaborate, for example on the basis of a treaty regime, because all states have access to the global commons but no state is legally entitled under general international law to impose a particular approach to their use or protection. With certain variations, the same applies to those resources within the jurisdiction of states from which collective benefits derive. Needless to say, if international law imposes constraints on states in dealing with community interests, it has traditionally made it virtually impossible for most non-state actors to do so.

Having delineated global commons issues and attendant community interests, it remains to be determined what counts as a 'procedural' matter in international environmental law. At first blush, this question seems straightforward. After all, international environmental lawyers routinely distinguish between 'substantive' and 'procedural' obligations.[7] Substantive rules set out standards that must be met through states' conduct, ranging from the general customary obligation not to cause serious transboundary environmental harm to specific emission or performance standards imposed by treaties. By contrast, procedural obligations include the duties to notify, warn, inform or consult states potentially affected by transboundary impacts, to undertake (transboundary) environmental impact assessments (EIA) and to monitor or report performance of treaty commitments as specified by the treaty.

However, drawing a neat conceptual distinction between substance and procedure is more difficult than it may first appear. The boundaries between the two are permeable and, indeed, substance and procedure tend to be in a symbiotic relationship. Substance typically frames the circumstances in which procedure operates, and the purposes that it is to serve. In turn, procedure has the potential to reinforce and develop, and to give concrete meaning and effect to, substance. International environmental law provides particularly vivid illustrations of this interplay, both in the rules of general international law and in the treaty-based regimes through which most community interest issues are addressed today.

I begin by exploring the close conceptual and practical connections between procedural and substantive obligations in international environmental law, focusing on efforts to flesh out the standard of due diligence that is at the core of the harm prevention obligation in customary law (Birnie et al., 2009). In turn, an Advisory Opinion of the International Tribunal for the Law of the Sea's (ITLOS) Seabed Chamber on *Responsibilities in the Area* suggests that the due diligence standard is a potential bridge between harm prevention and the duty to take precautionary measures, including to avert harm to the global commons (*Responsibilities and Obligations of States Sponsoring Persons and Entities with Respect to Activities in the Area (Advisory Opinion, Order of 1 February 11)*, ITLOS Reports, 2011). However, recent decisions of the International Court of Justice (ICJ) suggest that the specifics of the connections between procedure and substance may be less well settled than one may have assumed. Furthermore, while the procedural dimensions of the transboundary harm framework are being progressively refined in the context of inter-state disputes, their development in relation to community interests in the protection of the global commons is held back by the relative dearth of state practice and the uncertain status of relevant substantive obligations in general international law.

Against the backdrop of this assessment, the significance of treaty-based efforts to address community interests in the protection of global commons can be appreciated. Under the auspices of multilateral environmental agreements (MEAs),[8] international practice has been able to transcend the gaps and constraints of the customary law framework. I survey the rich array of procedural approaches to promoting and protecting community interests that has evolved in this setting, including lawmaking, implementation and oversight, and compliance and dispute settlement processes, as well as the range of ways in which non-state actors can be involved in these processes. I pay special attention to the global climate regime that has evolved under the umbrella of the UN Framework Convention on Climate Change (UNFCCC) (United Nations, 1992a), including through the Paris Agreement adopted in December 2015 (United Nations, 2015a). The climate regime is particularly well suited to highlighting the diversity and promise of procedural international environmental law.

I conclude by suggesting that, both under general international law and in the context of treaty-based regimes, the procedural dimensions of international environmental law hold the key to its ability to serve community interests in the protection of the global commons. As this chapter will illustrate, procedure can promote the protection of such collective interests in concrete ways. For example, procedural requirements can step into the breach when substantive requirements lack specificity or when states are reluctant to invoke them. In the context of treaty-based regimes, procedural elements play crucial roles when participants hold divergent positions, work towards shared understandings of community interests and collective action or work to develop, apply or revise substantive requirements. But the procedural aspects of international environmental law also are important in their own right. In all of its guises, procedure serves to enable, guide and at times even compel interaction between states and other international actors, including non-state actors. In so doing, robust procedural norms and practices contribute to the legitimacy and resilience of international law (Brunnée and Toope, 2010), a contribution that is particularly important in the context of efforts to advance community interests in global commons protection.

2. SUBSTANTIVE AND PROCEDURAL OBLIGATIONS IN CUSTOMARY INTERNATIONAL ENVIRONMENTAL LAW: THE DUTY TO PREVENT ENVIRONMENTAL HARM

International environmental law remains grounded in concepts meant to balance competing sovereign interests.[9] Under the foundational 'no harm' rule, states' rights to use their territories and resources are limited by the obligation to avoid significant transboundary harm, but neighbouring states must tolerate harm that remains below that threshold. States' duties to prevent transboundary harm caused by activities undertaken in their territories has since been affirmed and fleshed out through a series of MEAs and other international instruments, and several judicial decisions. According to Principle 21 of the 1972 Stockholm Declaration of the United Nations Conference on the Human Environment, states have 'the sovereign right to exploit their own resources pursuant to their own environmental policies, and the responsibility to ensure that activities within their jurisdiction or control do not cause damage to the environment of other States *or of areas beyond the limits of national jurisdiction*' (United Nations, 1972, emphasis added). The phrasing of Principle 21, affirmed in the 1992 Rio Declaration on Environment and Development (United Nations, 1992b), suggested that the harm prevention rule applies also to global commons, such as the high seas or the Earth's atmosphere.

The ICJ first confirmed in its 1996 Advisory Opinion on *Legality of the Threat or Use of Nuclear Weapons* that 'the general obligation of States to ensure that activities within their jurisdiction and control respect the environment of other States *or of areas beyond national control* is now part of the corpus of international law relating to the environment' ([1996] ICJ Rep 226: p. 242, emphasis added). The Court reiterated this conclusion in its 1997 decision in the *Gabčíkovo-Nagymaros* case ([1997] ICJ Rep 7: p. 41) and its 2010 judgment in *Pulp Mills on the River Uruguay (Argentina v. Uruguay)* ([2010] ICJ Rep 14: pp. 55–6), both of which revolved around inter-state impacts. In the *Pulp Mills* case, the ICJ elaborated on the procedural obligations that attach to the no harm rule, sketching out a framework upon which it built in its 2015 decisions in *Costa Rica v. Nicaragua/Nicaragua v. Costa Rica* (*Certain Activities carried out by Nicaragua in the Border Area (Costa Rica v. Nicaragua)* and *Construction of a Road in Costa Rica along the San Juan River (Nicaragua v. Costa Rica)* (Judgment) [2015] ICJ Rep 665), which also involved transboundary impacts. I first consider the Substance–Procedure framework that emerges from the case law on inter-state impacts and then explore its application to community obligations.

2.1 The Substance–Procedure Framework

In *Pulp Mills*, Argentina alleged that Uruguay had breached both substantive and procedural obligations under an agreement pertaining to the River Uruguay. In the course of its decision, the ICJ engaged at length with the relationship between procedural duties, including a new EIA requirement 'under general international law' (*Pulp Mills*: p. 83) and the substantive obligation to prevent significant transboundary harm under customary law (p. 49).

The ICJ emphasized that procedural obligations have a separate existence – they can be violated, for example, even when significant transboundary harm does not ultimately occur (p. 49). At the same time, the substantive obligation does not impose an absolute harm prevention duty (Birnie et al., 2009: pp. 147–50). Rather, it demands that states meet the requirements of due diligence in their efforts to prevent significant transboundary impacts (*Pulp Mills*: pp. 55–6). In satisfying these requirements, states must ensure 'not only the adoption of appropriate rules and measures, but also a certain level of vigilance in their enforcement and the exercise of administrative control applicable to public and private operators' (p. 79). Furthermore, due diligence requires appropriate procedural steps to avert transboundary impacts, such as conducting an EIA and notifying, informing or consulting potentially affected states (pp. 82–3). However, the ICJ did not hold that a failure to meet a procedural requirement necessarily implies a violation of the harm prevention duty, as Argentina had argued (p. 48). The Court's decision is ambiguous to the extent that its comments on this point focused on the interpretation of the treaty between the parties while, elsewhere in the judgment, it clearly connected procedural duties and due diligence (pp. 49, 82–3).

This ambiguity carried over to the Court's handling of the interconnected disputes regarding sovereignty over territory and various activities near a boundary river between Costa Rica and Nicaragua. In its decision on Costa Rica's complaint concerning Nicaraguan dredging, the ICJ observed that 'to fulfil its obligation to exercise due diligence in preventing significant transboundary harm, a State must . . . ascertain if there is a risk of significant transboundary harm, which would trigger the requirement to carry out an environmental impact assessment' (*Costa Rica v. Nicaragua*, pp. 706–7). The Court also held that, if the assessment confirms the risk, due diligence may require the state planning the activity 'to notify and consult in good faith with the potentially affected State' (p. 707). Then, however, the Court opined that, given the absence of the requisite risk, 'Nicaragua was not under an obligation to carry out an environmental impact assessment . . . [and so also] was not required to notify, or consult with, Costa Rica' (p. 708) regarding its plans. This conclusion might be explained by the Court's view that, on the facts of the *Costa Rica v. Nicaragua* case, none of the procedural or due diligence requirements had been triggered. But the Court's assessment of Nicaragua's complaint concerning Costa Rica's road building suggests there may be more to its approach.

In the *Nicaragua v. Costa Rica* case, the ICJ found that the road building plans did trigger the obligation to undertake an EIA, an obligation that Costa Rica had failed to discharge (pp. 720–23). The Court then concluded that there was no need to examine whether Costa Rica had a duty to notify or consult, since it had 'not complied with its obligation under general international law to perform an environmental impact assessment prior to the construction of the road' (p. 724). It is unclear whether the Court considered states' procedural duties to be strictly sequential, with notification and consultation being contingent upon a prior finding of risk through an EIA (pp. 706–7),[10] or whether it considered that the failure to conduct an EIA had already established a failure to act diligently. As in the *Pulp Mills* case, however, the ICJ concluded that, absent evidence of significant transboundary harm, there was no violation of the 'no harm' rule (pp. 731, 734, 736–7).

Strongly worded Separate Opinions on the Substance–Procedure question hint at just how much the Court wrestled with the relationship between the two. 'In the planning phase [of a project]', wrote Judge Donoghue in her Opinion, 'a failure to exercise due diligence to prevent significant transboundary harm can engage the responsibility of the State of origin even in the absence of material damage to potentially affected States' (*Costa Rica v. Nicaragua/Nicaragua v. Costa Rica* (Separate Opinion of Judge Donoghue) [2015] ICJ Rep 665: p. 3). In emphasizing the importance of due diligence throughout all phases of a given project, Judge Donoghue added forcefully that she did 'not find it useful to draw distinctions between "procedural" and "substantive" obligations, as the Court has done' (p. 3). It is important to note, however, that Judge Donoghue questioned whether the obligation to conduct an EIA had in fact emerged as an independent procedural obligation at customary law. Accordingly, she chose to read the Court's description of it as a 'general obligation' as referring to its grounding in due diligence requirements (p. 4).

Judge Dugard's Separate Opinion reached the opposite conclusion: the term 'general obligation' had to be understood as denoting 'a rule of customary international law requiring an environmental impact assessment to be carried out where there is a risk of transboundary harm' (*Costa Rica v. Nicaragua/Nicaragua v. Costa Rica* (Separate Opinon of Judge Dugard) [2015] ICJ Rep 665: p. 5).[11] He found that this duty was independent from the obligation to take diligent steps to prevent transboundary harm, as well as subject to a due diligence standard of its own, which served to determine its scope (p. 3). Judge Dugard shared Judge Donoghue's dissatisfaction with the Court's failure to distinguish between breaches of the harm prevention obligation and of the obligation not to cause transboundary harm. However, according to the judge, treating the due diligence obligation as the source of the EIA obligation risked allowing a state to argue in hindsight that, in the absence of proven harm at the time of the proceedings, 'no duty of due diligence arose at the time the project was planned' (p. 3). In Dugard's view, the ICJ adopted '[t]his backward looking approach' in its judgment (p. 3). Assessing the EIA obligation separately, he added, would help avoid the shortfalls of that approach, notably by clarifying that the threshold for triggering the obligation 'is not the high standard for determining whether significant transboundary harm has been caused but the lower standard of *risk* assessment' (emphasis original, p. 4).

All in all, it appears as if the ICJ distinguishes between the duty to take diligent steps to *prevent* significant transboundary harm, which it then deals with under the rubric of separate procedural obligations,[12] and the duty to take diligent steps not to *cause* harm, which it considers cannot be violated simply by a failure to act diligently. While the latter conclusion is clearly correct, it stands to reason that violations of procedural obligations do breach the harm prevention duty, even if no transboundary harm results from that breach.[13] At any rate, the Separate Opinions suggest that the Substance–Procedure framework of international environmental law, as well as the legal status of the EIA obligation, may be less settled than it might appear at first glance.

2.2 Substance, Procedure and the Global Commons

Notwithstanding the ambiguities highlighted by the recent ICJ case law, the Substance–Procedure framework revolving around the no harm rule could be a potentially powerful tool in protecting the global commons. Rather than having to prove, for example, that a given state's greenhouse gas emissions have caused or will cause specific harmful impacts, such as sea level rise, concerned states could focus on the preventive dimension of the no harm rule, holding the emitting state to its procedural duties. The emphasis would shift from a relatively amorphous 'negative' duty to avoid harm to a 'positive' duty to take concrete steps to protect the environment (French, 2018), including the substantive steps a state may have to take to meet its due diligence obligation once risks are revealed.[14] Furthermore, an initial finding of risk through an EIA would not only specify the triggers of the duties to notify and consult, but also reinforce the proposition that international law requires states 'not merely to notify what is known but to know what needs to be notified' (Birnie et al., 2009: p. 169).

The intervention of the Federated States of Micronesia in the environmental assessment of the plan to modernize a large coal-fired power plant in the Czech Republic, the Prunéřov II plant, provides a good illustration of the potential strengths of a procedural approach.[15] In a letter to the Czech Ministry of the Environment, Micronesia asserted that the project's environmental impacts could affect its territory and requested that a transboundary environmental impact assessment be undertaken in accordance with Czech law (Lopes, 2010). It further asserted that the planned modernizations failed to meet applicable best available technology (BAT) standards (Lefeber, 2012), an argument also advanced by several environmental organizations (Malkin, 2011). The Ministry ordered a third party assessment of the modernization project, which concluded that the project did not meet the BAT standards and that additional carbon dioxide would be emitted by Prunéřov II as a result. While the Ministry nonetheless approved the modernization, it asked the proponent power company to propose 'compensation measures' at its other power plants to offset the excess emissions (Lefeber, 2012: pp. 336–7).

Although the Prunéřov II episode involved a state arguing on its own behalf, it illustrates how procedural obligations might assist arguments based on community interests. While the Czech authorities did not acknowledge a legal obligation to offset the project's climate impact, or indeed the Micronesian request, it is perhaps no coincidence that the ICJ's *Pulp Mills* judgment was released around the same time as the Czech Ministry of the Environment made its decision ([2010] ICJ Rep 14). Micronesia's intervention highlights the potential 'bite' of the due diligence requirements that attach to the obligation to prevent harm, and the obligation to conduct assessments of transboundary impacts, even in the absence of clear evidence of present or future harm – indeed, the emissions of one power plant could hardly be said to cause sea level rise or other climate impacts.

But *could* a similar argument be deployed to protect the global commons? At first glance, the answer would seem to be 'yes'. After all, the applicability of the no harm rule to areas beyond national jurisdiction or control has been confirmed through international instruments and ICJ decisions and the no harm rule, in turn, entails procedural obligations. And yet, efforts to bring procedural obligations to bear in a global commons context will face two types of obstacles. An initial difficulty stems from the underlying substantive law, notably the question whether there exists any customary law on community interests to which procedural obligations could attach in the first place. Assuming the substantive foundation exists, a second difficulty concerns whether the procedural obligations that arise in the inter-state context are in fact equally applicable to community interests in the protection of a global commons.

Unfortunately, the substantive norms that would enable the procedural argument to be made, remain underdeveloped. To be sure, various concepts have emerged to express community concerns. The idea that certain environmental problems are the 'common concern' of humankind and that all states have 'common but differentiated responsibilities' to cooperate in addressing them has gained some currency (Brunnée, 2018). In addition, the precautionary principle and the notions of sustainable development and intergenerational equity have emerged to address the growing complexity and intergenerational dimensions of environmental degradation.[16] Each of these concepts has come to be reflected and, to varying degrees, fleshed out in the context of treaty regimes. But, it would be difficult to show that community concern norms have general effect as customary law.[17] Even in relation to the no harm rule, there is strikingly little direct practice on who would be entitled to invoke the rule in respect of harm to areas beyond national jurisdiction or control (Brunnée, 2018). Yes, states are obligated to prevent harm to the global commons; but is that obligation owed *erga omnes*, such that 'all States can be held to have a legal interest' in compliance with it (*Barcelona Traction, Light and Power Company, Ltd. (Belgium v. Spain)* (Judgment) [1970] ICJ Rep 3: para. 32)?[18]

For many commentators, the right of each state to invoke responsibility for violations is inherent in the very concept of obligations *erga omnes*.[19] This view finds support in the Advisory Opinion of the ITLOS Seabed Chamber on *Responsibilities in the Area* (p. 59). According to the Law of the Sea Convention (LOSC) (United Nations, 1982a), the 'Area and its resources are the common heritage of mankind' (Article 136). The Chamber, noting that the International Seabed Authority was tasked with acting on behalf of 'mankind as a whole', observed that each 'State Party may also be entitled to claim compensation [for harm to the Area] in light of the erga omnes character of the obligations relating to preservation of the environment of the high seas and the Area' (*Responsibilities in the Area*: p. 9). It supported this observation by referring to Article 48 of the International Law Commission's Draft Articles on Responsibility of States for Internationally Wrongful Acts (International Law Commission, 2001a), which envisage circumstances in which states other than those directly injured could invoke another state's responsibility for breaches of obligations owed *erga omnes*, or *erga omnes partes*.[20]

The ICJ has not pronounced itself on the *erga omnes* dimensions of the no harm rule. To be fair, the Court's recent case load has provided little opportunity to engage the issue, and the one earlier case that might have done so – the *Nuclear Tests* (*New Zealand v. France*) case ((Interim Measures) [1973] ICJ Rep 135) – did not reach the merits phase. In its application for interim measures against nuclear testing in the South Pacific, New Zealand invoked, *inter alia*, France's violation of the rights of all members of the international community to be free from nuclear fall-out and contamination of the high seas and atmosphere (p. 139).[21] But, given France's unilateral declaration that it would end testing, the ICJ never decided the merits of the case. Various separate or dissenting opinions showed the judges were divided on the standing issue. Some noted that while 'the existence of a so-called actio popularis in international law is a matter of controversy', it 'may be considered as capable of rational legal argument and a proper subject of litigation' (*Nuclear Tests (Australia v. France)* (Judgment) [1974] ICJ Rep 253: p. 370). For others, the applicant states had 'no legal title . . . to act as spokesman for the international community' (p. 390).

Some four decades later, the scope for cases invoking the harm prevention rule in relation to a global commons concern still seems limited, or at least states choose not to argue cases on that basis.[22] A case in point is Palau's 2011 attempt to mobilize support for an ICJ Advisory Opinion in the climate change context, which was limited to states' 'legal responsibility to ensure that any activities on their territory that emit greenhouse gases *do not harm other States*' (emphasis added, UN News Centre, 2011). Presumably, Palau's assessment was that a question focused on inter-state harm stood on stronger legal ground than one relating to harm to the global commons. In any case, pursuant to Article 96 of the UN Charter, the most likely path to an Advisory Opinion would be a request by the General Assembly, requiring the support of a majority of its members. While some states appeared supportive, others were concerned about interference with the negotiations under the auspices of the UNFCCC (UN Department of Public Information, 2012).

What, then, of the question whether, assuming the requisite substantive law foundation exists, the procedural obligations that attach to the no harm rule in an inter-state context apply equally to community obligations? It would seem only logical that this should be so.[23] Alas, here too the practice pertaining to customary international law is surprisingly thin and the ICJ, for its part, has been exceedingly cautious.

Although the Court had previously confirmed that states' duties to prevent environmental harm extend to the global commons, it chose in the *Costa Rica v. Nicaragua/Nicaragua v. Costa Rica* cases, to quote only those parts of its earlier articulation of the no harm rule that focus on inter-state transboundary harm. While this restraint might be explained by the inter-state nature of the disputes, that feature did not prevent the Court in the earlier *Gabčíkovo-Nagymaros* and *Pulp Mills* cases from restating the no harm rule in more expansive terms. It is quite possible, therefore, that the Court sought to limit the implications of its observations on procedural duties for situations involving community obligations. Such a narrow approach would be in line with the ILC's Harm Prevention articles (International Law Commission, 2001b), which focus only on transboundary harm, rather than environmental harm as such (Dupuy and Viñuales, 2015), and on which the Court appeared to rely.

A further aspect of its most recent decision concerning the no harm rule suggests reluctance on the part of the ICJ to apply procedural rules, and specifically the EIA obligation, to collective environmental interests. As pointed out by Judge Dugard in his Separate Opinion, the Court failed to give close consideration to the risks posed by Nicaragua's activities to wetlands located within Costa Rica, but protected under the Ramsar Convention (UNESCO, 1971) as of 'international importance'. The ICJ concluded, wrongly in Judge Dugard's view, that no EIA was required of Nicaragua given the absence of risk of significant transboundary harm. Aside from disagreeing with this conclusion on the facts (*Costa Rica v. Nicaragua/Nicaragua v. Costa Rica*, (Separate Opinion of Judge Dugard) [2015] ICJ Rep 665: pp. 10–13), and with the Court's failure to consider violations of the procedural obligations under the Ramsar Convention itself (pp. 14–16), Judge Dugard took the Court to task for failing to heed its own earlier assessment that the presence of a Ramsar-protected wetland 'heightens the risk of significant damage because it denotes that the receiving environment is particularly sensitive' (p. 13). In Dugard's view, the 'Court should have held that in a Ramsar-designated wetland there was a lower threshold of risk' (p. 12), triggering an obligation on the part of Nicaragua to consider the potential impact of its planned activities on the wetland in Costa Rica.

It is again the 2012 Advisory Opinion of the ITLOS Seabed Chamber in *Responsibilities in the Area* that brightens the otherwise rather bleak picture. Although the Opinion was concerned with deep seabed operations under the auspices of a treaty regime, it invoked due diligence requirements under general international law (p. 51). The Opinion, released in the year after the ICJ's *Pulp Mills* decision, built on that case in a number of ways. It highlighted the contextual nature of the due diligence standard, which the Chamber held may change over time and in view of the risks involved in a given activity (pp. 42, 43). The requirement of due diligence furthermore served as a bridge between the duty to prevent environmental harm and the proposition that, even in the absence of 'full scientific certainty', states must take precautionary measures to 'prevent environmental degradation' (Rio Declaration, 1992: Principle 15). The Chamber observed that, separate and apart from its status in the seabed regime and under customary law, 'the precautionary approach is also an integral part of the general obligation of due diligence' (p. 46).

According to the ITLOS Chamber, this obligation requires states 'to take all appropriate measures to prevent damage . . . [and] applies in situations where scientific evidence concerning the scope and potential negative impact of the activity in question is insufficient but where there are plausible indications of potential risks' (*Responsibilities in the Area*: p. 46). The Chamber concluded that a state 'would not meet its obligation of due diligence if it disregarded those risks' (p. 46). While this perspective seems sensible in many respects, it remains to be seen whether its sliding scale approach to prevention and precaution will be embraced by international practice.[24] Although the Chamber may well have spelled out what the ICJ merely alluded to in its *Gabčíkovo-Nagymaros* and *Pulp Mills* decisions,[25] the ICJ did not engage with the Chamber's Opinion in its discussion of the EIA obligation in *Costa Rica v. Nicaragua/Nicaragua v. Costa Rica.*[26] Either way, for present purposes, the most important implication of this 'sliding scale' approach to prevention and precaution is the increased importance that it accords to procedural obligations, including in particular EIA obligations (*Responsibilities in the Area*: p. 50).

3. INTERNATIONAL ENVIRONMENTAL REGIMES: INSTITUTIONALIZING COLLECTIVE INTERESTS

Notwithstanding the uncertainties surveyed above, the recognition of a duty to protect areas beyond national jurisdiction from environmental harm and the emergence of concepts such as common heritage, common concern, common but differentiated responsibilities, precaution or sustainable development have helped international law evolve to better reflect community interests. The impact of this substantive evolution, however, has been felt primarily in the development of treaty-based regimes, which have been relied upon to step into the conceptual gaps in general international law and to transcend the constraints that have kept its practice predominantly bilateral.

Such regimes have served to enshrine community interest concepts in relation to specific geographic areas or specific environmental concerns. For example, in endorsing the harm prevention rule, several agreements focus on impacts on global commons beyond national jurisdiction. The Vienna Convention for the Protection of the Ozone Layer (United Nations, 1985) and its Montreal Protocol (United Nations Environment

Programme, 1987) are two examples, the LOSC (1982) is another. The latter contains only environmental protection obligations pertaining to the high seas and, as already noted, it designates the deep seabed and its resources to be 'the common heritage of humankind' (Article 136). Furthermore, notwithstanding the fact that the status of the concept of common concern at customary law remains uncertain (International Law Commission, 2015), MEAs have designated particular issues, such as the loss of biological diversity and climate change, as common concerns of humankind.[27] Over time, such treaty practice could reinforce community interest concepts at general international law.[28] For the time being, however, their main impact has been to frame environmental regimes and help shape their evolution and implementation.

For example, the UNFCCC Preamble elaborates on the proposition that climate change is a common concern by acknowledging that its global nature 'calls for the widest possible cooperation by *all* countries . . . in accordance with their common but differentiated responsibilities and respective capabilities' (emphasis added). This common concern/responsibility framework provides the normative anchor for the climate regime and accounts for its global scope. The underlying understanding is reflected not only in the regime's universal membership, but also in the fact that its global approach has proven resilient even in the face of the challenges of collective decision-making. In short, there is a widely shared sense that an international legal response to climate change must involve states that are emitters of greenhouse gases as well states that contribute little to the problem, or stand to be victims of climate related harms. The differentiation dimension of the common responsibility frame has also been instrumental in guiding the evolution of the regime. Since the inception of the climate regime, parties have debated how responsibilities should be differentiated. Gradually, the regime's approach shifted from stark South-North differentiation, reflected in the Kyoto Protocol (United Nations, 1997), to the much more nuanced and dynamic differentiation that underpins the Paris Agreement.[29]

A key feature of community concern regimes is that they are not one-off contracts between states, but rather open-ended 'sets of implicit or explicit principles, norms, rules and decision-making procedures around which actors' expectations converge' (Krasner, 1982: p. 186).[30] The adoption of the underlying treaty thus marks not the endpoint of the international legal process but its beginning. MEAs typically establish treaty bodies for ongoing exchange and negotiation among parties, supported by treaty secretariats that provide an array of administrative services (Ulfstein, 2007). They enable long-term interaction among regime participants and help constitute the 'communities' that remain elusive in the customary law context but that are crucial to the legal enterprise of addressing common environmental concerns. In this institutionalization of community interests, procedural requirements play central roles in facilitating the evolution of the regime and the emergence of deeper substantive understandings.

As we have seen, in the customary law context, procedural obligations are tied closely to the harm prevention obligation and its due diligence requirements. MEAs also give pride of place to information exchange, consultation and environmental assessment duties, tailoring them to the features of the concern at hand. But in the context of MEAs a much more extensive set of procedural elements, including an array of lawmaking and standard setting processes, as well as compliance and dispute settlement processes, has taken hold. Furthermore, MEAs provide scope for non-state actors to benefit from or be involved in this range of procedural features. I consider each of these dimensions below.

3.1 Information Exchange and Scientific Assessment Processes

Notification, provision of information, assessment and consultation provide the necessary foundation for any effective effort to address a given concern, as well as for subsequent efforts to monitor the performance of both the regime and individual parties. All MEAs, therefore, require parties to cooperate in relation to research and scientific assessments and to report on their implementation of treaty requirements.[31] Typically, MEAs also enshrine detailed procedural requirements, such as guidelines on how to measure performance, or on what kind of information is to be reported in what manner. The Kyoto Protocol (1997) provides a good illustration (arts. 5, 7), as does the 2015 Paris Agreement, which places strong emphasis on 'monitoring, reporting and verification' (MRV) requirements (Article 13), even if some of the details remain to be developed by the parties (Article 13.13). The Paris Agreement's MRV regime, which is focused on individual parties' performance, will be complemented by a 'global stock-take', which is intended to assess 'collective progress towards achieving the purpose of [the] Agreement and its long-term goals' (Article 14). One important advantage of treaty-based procedural requirements is that their 'triggers', scope and content can be specified and nuanced far more than is possible under the general due diligence framework.

In addition to procedural requirements imposed on individual parties, many environmental regimes establish or collaborate with international scientific and other expert forums, providing a more cooperative setting for information exchange and scientific assessment than tends to be available in strictly inter-state contexts. For example, the UNFCCC established a permanent Subsidiary Body for Scientific and Technological

Advice (Article 9), but the regime also draws upon the expertise of the Intergovernmental Panel on Climate Change (IPCC), which operates under the auspices of the World Meteorological Organization and the United Nations Environment Programme (Birnie et al., 2009). Expert forums such as these are important in building consensus around the nature of community interests and the collective action that is required to address them. Their role in strengthening a regime's 'common-interest patterns' (Hey, 2003: p. 7) is an iterative one. Once decisions on the general thrust of collective action are taken, the expert bodies support the elaboration, refinement, or adjustment of regulatory strategies. In the climate regime, for example, the IPCC has been instrumental in bringing about acceptance of the need to keep global warming to 'well below 2° C' and to pursue efforts to limit it to 1.5° C above pre-industrial levels', and hence in concretizing, through the 2015 Paris Agreement (Article 2.1(a)), the parties' understanding of the UNFCCC regime's overarching objective to avert dangerous climate change (Article 2).[32]

3.2 Lawmaking Processes

At customary law, states' obligations to engage with other states concerning potential environmental impacts of their activities may require consultation, but do not extend to a duty to negotiate.[33] MEAs, it could be argued, do entail a duty for parties to engage in ongoing negotiations aimed at developing the regime as needed to meet its objective. In practice, in any case, MEAs do provide iterated, institutionalized opportunities for negotiation and lawmaking.

The lawmaking processes and further development of an MEA are usually in the hands of a plenary body, such as a Conference of the Parties (COP). The spectrum of opinions on the role of COPs is wide. Some commentators observed the emergence of issue-specific global legislatures (Palmer, 1992). Others have argued that COPs increasingly resemble international organizations (Churchill and Ulfstein, 2000). For yet others, a COP is a diplomatic conference (Boyle, 1991), albeit one that facilitates continuous processes and interlocking engagements between technical experts, policy-makers and lawyers. Be that as it may, COPs and their subsidiary bodies have come to be central venues for international standard setting activities around community interests.

Treaty-based lawmaking is of particular importance in this context because it settles the basic questions of who is entitled to set standards for the collective and on what terms. Community interest treaties enshrine the background assumption that standard setting is a collective enterprise, enabling all states to participate in shaping, and deciding upon, responses to the concern. MEAs also allow for the tailoring of lawmaking processes so as to strike a balance between the protection of state sovereignty through consent requirements and the need for timely collective action (Brunnée, 2002). To be sure, much regime development still occurs through ordinary consent-based processes. Hence, when an agreement is amended, or when an additional treaty, such as a protocol, is adopted, individual states are bound only when they consent to these instruments. But the 'edges of consent' have softened (Simma, 1994: p. 325). Under many agreements, especially when technical issues are involved, regulatory approaches can be adjusted with effect for all parties, except for those that explicitly opt out.[34] Perhaps more significantly, much regulatory detail is adopted through decisions of plenary bodies, without subsequent formal consent by individual states. In most cases, the resulting standards will not be legally binding, although they may well contain mandatory language. For example, under the UNFCCC and its Kyoto Protocol, provisions on central treaty matters, ranging from inventory and monitoring requirements to the protocol's mechanisms for trading of emission units or reduction credits, were adopted in this way (Brunnée, 2002). The Paris Agreement envisages a similar approach for the adoption of standards concerning key matters such as the communication of and accounting for parties' nationally determined contributions, and 'common modalities, procedures and guidelines' for monitoring and reviewing parties' commitments (Articles 4(8), 4(9), 4(13), and 13(13)).

As the slow evolution of the climate regime illustrates, even formally non-binding standards are subject to difficult negotiations (Brunnée and Toope, 2010; Bodansky et al., 2017). Nonetheless, on balance, soft regulatory processes allow speedier regime development and adjustment than processes that involve subsequent ratification by individual states. Equally important is that they facilitate agreement upon collective action and adoption of standards applicable to all parties – an important feature for efforts to address community interests (Barrett, 2016).

The 2015 climate negotiations in Paris highlighted an increasing willingness of states to combine a range of approaches to maximize the potential for and scope of collective standard setting. The Paris 'Outcome' consists of the Paris Agreement – a treaty – and a COP decision, which adopts the treaty text and supplements it in many key respects (Bodansky et al., 2017). The most experimental aspect of the Outcome is that, instead of enshrining binding emission reduction commitments, it relies on non-legally binding, 'nationally determined contributions' (NDCs) by parties. The Paris Agreement will obligate all parties to 'prepare, communicate and maintain successive' NDCs (Article 4.2), and will impose related procedural requirements, such as the ones related to performance assessment discussed above. But the NDCs themselves are 'housed' outside of the agreement – they are to be communicated to the UNFCCC Secretariat and will be published on the UNFCCC website (United Nations, 2015b: paras 13–14). As it turns out, this blend of lawmaking and standard setting approaches has shown more potential to achieve collective climate action than the binding emission reduction regime enshrined in the Kyoto Protocol.[35]

It is too soon to know whether or not this mixed approach will spread to other global commons issues. Climate change, after all, is the most complex of all community concerns, posing collective action challenges that do not necessarily find counterparts in other contexts. It is also not clear at this stage whether the example of the climate regime heralds the retreat from formal lawmaking processes that some observers have detected (Pauwelyn et al., 2014). However, at least in the climate context, the Paris Outcome signals a change in the role of formally binding treaty law, which now appears to be to enshrine the goals, principles and, not least, procedures that serve to anchor and support substantive commitments.[36]

3.3 Compliance and Dispute Settlement

Another key feature of community interest regimes is their approach to compliance and dispute settlement. As noted in the first part of this chapter, customary international law provides only limited options for invoking and compelling compliance with collective-interest norms. Furthermore, because community interests by definition raise polycentric issues, they do not easily lend themselves to traditional, bilateral dispute settlement.[37] At any rate, and further to the constraints highlighted in the discussion of the harm prevention obligation, options for judicial dispute settlement, for example by the ICJ, are generally constrained by the requirement that all parties must accept the Court's jurisdiction (United Nations, 1945: Article 36).

A different approach is taken under Part XV of the LOSC (1982). Any party to the convention can unilaterally bring environmental disputes, including disputes relating to the high seas, before the ITLOS, the ICJ or an arbitral tribunal (Articles 287–8). The relevant court or tribunal is empowered to prescribe provisional measures to forestall serious harm to the marine environment pending its final decision (Article 290). ITLOS has done so in a case concerning high seas resources: the dispute between Australia and New Zealand, on the one hand, and Japan, on the other, regarding the conservation and management of southern Bluefin tuna (*Southern Bluefin Tuna Cases (New Zealand v. Japan; Australia v. Japan), Provisional Measures (Separate Opinion of Judge Treves, Order of 27 August*

1999), ITLOS Reports 1999). Finally, where parties agree to bring a dispute before the ITLOS, 'entities other than States Parties can join the proceedings' (United Nations, 1982b: Article 20). It would appear, then, that the ITLOS Statute recognizes in at least a limited manner that the 'community' interested in the protection of the marine environment may also include private parties, NGOs or international organizations (Birnie et al., 2009).

However, the LOSC is not representative of global commons regimes. In MEAs, compulsory dispute settlement is rare (Birnie et al., 2009), partly because of states' reluctance to resort to it and partly because it may not satisfactorily address the community interests underlying the agreement. To be sure, sometimes enforcement action by individual states can serve to address a community interest. For example, in *Whaling in the Antarctic*, Australia (New Zealand intervening) brought an action against Japan, taking advantage of the fact that both states had accepted the jurisdiction of the ICJ under Article 36(2) of the ICJ Statute (United Nations, 1945). Australia argued that, as a party to the Whaling Convention (International Whaling Commission, 1946), it was acting in the common interest of all treaty parties in 'safeguarding for future generations the great natural resources represented by the whale stocks' (Preamble), not as an injured state.[38] Although Japan challenged the jurisdiction of the Court and countered the case on the merits, it did not question Australia's standing to bring the case (Fitzmaurice, 2015). More often than not, however, addressing the community concern animating a global commons regime requires the greatest possible degree of compliance by the widest possible range of parties, rather than finding that an individual party has breached its obligations. MEAs, therefore, have seen the emergence of procedures that assess parties' compliance with their treaty commitments and provide for a range of measures to facilitate or compel compliance.

Facilitation of compliance has been the primary objective of the majority of these compliance procedures. The procedure under the Montreal Protocol (United Nations Environment Programme, 1998) neatly encapsulates the facilitative approach, aimed, as it is, at 'securing an amicable solution . . . on the basis of respect for the provisions of the Protocol' (para. 8). This cooperative approach recognizes the fact that, in the context of ozone depletion, non-complying parties were most likely to be states with genuine capacity limitations. But the treaty setting also makes it possible to tailor the non-compliance regime to the underlying collective concern, and the needs of the parties involved. For example, under the Kyoto Protocol (1997) only developed countries and transition countries had emission reduction commitments (Article 3.1). Therefore, capacity building and financial assistance were less appropriate in promoting compliance. Moreover, the Kyoto Protocol regime had certain unique features, such as its emissions trading mechanisms, which necessitated a tougher approach to compliance. The Kyoto Protocol's compliance procedure, thus, explicitly declared its goals to 'facilitate, promote and *enforce* compliance' with the protocol (United Nations, 2002).[39] In turn, the Paris Agreement (2015), given its reliance on nationally determined, rather than internationally negotiated, emission reduction commitments returns to a 'mechanism to facilitate implementation . . . and promote compliance' (Article 15.1). It is to consist of a committee that is 'expert-based and facilitative in nature and function in a manner that is transparent, non-adversarial and non-punitive' and that is to be attentive to 'the respective national capabilities and circumstances of Parties' (Article 15.2).

MEA compliance procedures can generally be triggered by any state party, including by a state regarding its own performance. Yet there is also evidence of subtle movement towards a common-interest pattern. For example, under the Montreal Protocol procedure (United Nations Environment Programme, 1998), the treaty's Secretariat can and does trigger the procedure. The Kyoto Protocol procedure, by contrast, had an automatic trigger – whenever an expert review process revealed questions about a party's implementation of its commitments (United Nations, 2002).[40] While both procedures thus allow for a form of a collective-interest trigger, they remain anchored in inter-state foundations. The triggers for and other terms of the compliance mechanism for the Paris Agreement are to be adopted through a subsequent decision of the parties (Article 15.3).

3.4 Involvement of Non-State Actors: Broadening the 'Community'?

As noted in the introduction to this chapter, one of international environmental law's key features is the fact that most environmental concerns, including global commons issues, are caused by and affect actors other than states. Customary law's harm prevention framework, however, is focused almost entirely on states.[41] Even where it does contemplate community interests or protection of areas beyond national jurisdiction, the main puzzle has been whether and in what circumstances states could invoke attendant community obligations. International environmental agreements, once again, have provided the legal setting for a more inclusive approach to environmental concerns. Indeed, two agreements, the 1991 Espoo Convention on Transboundary Environmental Impact Assessment (UNECE, 1991) and the 1998 Aarhus Convention on Public Participation and Access to Justice (UNECE, 1998), provide significant avenues of public involvement, with the Aarhus Convention being entirely devoted to citizen access. However, both are concerned with transboundary environmental impacts rather than common environmental concerns.

In the latter context, the Paris Agreement offers the most comprehensive articulation yet of whose interests are engaged, albeit without granting non-state actors specific rights or status under the climate regime. Its Preamble opens by:

> *Acknowledging that* climate change is a common concern of humankind, Parties should, when taking action to address climate change, respect, promote and consider their respective obligations on human rights, the right to health, the rights of indigenous peoples, local communities, migrants, children, persons with disabilities and people in vulnerable situations and the right to development, as well as gender equality, empowerment of women and intergenerational equity. (Paris Agreement, 2015: Preamble; emphasis in the original)

While the Paris Agreement's explicit acknowledgement of a wide range of non-state stake-holders is nonetheless unusual, at a procedural level, MEAs have long been accessible to non-state actors, including international organizations, NGOs or business entities.

An important first dimension of accessibility concerns information about a regime's standard setting and performance monitoring activities. Although transparency through public availability of documents and data may seem ordinary today, it is worth noting that contemporary practice represents a significant departure from the previous practice of closed and strictly *inter partes* proceedings (Brunnée and Hey, 2013). The impact of shifting attitudes has been amplified by technology – treaty websites now enable non-state actors to access not only legal documents and meeting reports, but also scientific and technical information, including that compiled pursuant to parties' procedural obligations under the regime. Hence, although under the terms of most MEAs, the obligations as such are owed only to fellow treaty parties, in practical terms the beneficiaries are the diverse members of a much larger 'community'.

In addition to such 'remote' access to information about the practice of the regime and its parties, as well as to web-casts of plenary sessions, MEAs generally also provide direct access to meetings of the parties. Third states, intergovernmental organizations and NGOs can obtain observer status at COP meetings, distribute information or policy papers, meet with official delegations or report on negotiations.[42] In a formal sense, decision-making remains entirely in the hands of states, and key negotiating sessions will typically be restricted to state delegations. But non-state actors do have considerable opportunities to provide input into lawmaking processes or even help shape their outcomes (Brunnée and Hey, 2013).

Performance and compliance assessment is one area in which MEAs continue to restrict non-state involvement. Performance assessment under the Convention on International Trade in Endangered Species of Wild

Fauna and Flora (CITES) (International Union for Conservation of Nature, 1973) provides an unusual example, relying as it does on information provided by TRAFFIC, a non-governmental wildlife trade monitoring network.[43] The Kyoto Protocol's compliance procedure furnishes a more typical example (United Nations, 2002). It permitted NGOs to submit 'factual and technical information' relevant to the compliance review,[44] have access to meetings of the compliance bodies unless parties object,[45] and have access to the findings of the compliance body.[46] But NGOs were not to be able to trigger the procedure or make formal submissions. In this respect, the Paris Agreement follows suit. None of the three performance assessment processes (MRV, global stock-take, compliance mechanism) it establishes envisage direct non-state actor involvement. Thus, with respect to compliance, the 'international community' in the climate change regime remains primarily one of states. However, outside of the climate regime, NGOs have been increasingly active, compiling rigorous and widely respected performance assessments. While not concerned with compliance *per se*, these assessments did measure states' intended NDCs in the lead-up to the Paris Agreement against the yardstick of the climate regime's objective and taking into account the principle of common but differentiated responsibilities.[47] In this way, non-state actors have assumed a role that has been politically and, in the absence of formal emissions commitments under the Paris Agreement, legally difficult for the inter-state regime to take on.

4. CONCLUSION

The picture of the procedural aspects of international environmental law that emerges from this chapter is a mixed one, especially at customary law. The experience in the transboundary context suggests that procedural obligations have great potential to strengthen the preventive aspects of the harm prevention rule, as well as flesh out – or support, depending on one's reading of the ICJ case law – its due diligence standard. Procedural obligations can also serve useful purposes when states, or judges, are reluctant to entertain substantive arguments, or find it difficult to establish that environmental harm has been, or is being, caused by another state. Violations of procedural obligations are more easily established and, by holding states to their procedural duties, they can sometimes be prompted to correct harmful conduct, or at least to take more effective preventive measures going forward. Unfortunately, in relation to community interests, the operation of procedural rules is constrained by the dearth of international practice and the continued struggle with the substance of community obligations and the legal effects of *erga omnes* norms.

Treaty-based approaches have proven much better suited to addressing community interests in the protection of global commons, overcoming some of the constraints of general international law. Treaties serve to delineate global commons, recognize particular environmental issues as common concerns and establish long-term regimes that can adapt and grow as parties' understanding of the underlying problem and appropriate response action evolves. MEAs all have significant procedural elements and one of their advantages is precisely that they enable parties to tailor these elements to the features of the community interests at hand. In 2017, MEAs also routinely involve actors other than states, better reflecting the much broader international community contributing to and affected by most environmental concerns.

Overall, community interest regimes have proven to be both resilient and adaptable, in part because they place such strong emphasis on procedural elements and employ an increasingly diverse range of formal lawmaking and informal standard setting approaches. Has the price for this resilience been a relative absence of substance? It is difficult to provide a definite answer to this question, in part because, rather than merely camouflage the absence of substance, procedure serves its own, crucial functions. Precisely because agreement on substantive obligations, however desirable, cannot be pulled out of thin air but must be cultivated, procedural requirements play important facilitating and bridging roles. Successful community interest regimes, such as the Vienna Convention and its Montreal Protocol, underscore this point. What is more, some environmental concerns are so complex (number of actors, uncertainties, multi-dimensional, evolving nature of the problem) that it may not only be difficult but perhaps even *un*desirable to formally enshrine substantive obligations, not least because adapting them when needed would entail potentially time-consuming amendment processes. Hence, the Paris Agreement may well strike the right balance between procedure and substance in the global response to climate change.

Do the procedural aspects of international environmental law look beyond the interests of individual states and to the 'greater interests of humanity and planetary welfare' (*Gabčíkovo-Nagymaros* case, Separate Opinion of Judge Weeramantry)? The answer is a qualified 'yes'. Regardless of how important substantive rules may be in a given situation, strong procedural elements are indispensable to the law's capacity to serve community interests in the protection of global commons. As this chapter has illustrated, procedure can promote the protection of such community interests both directly and indirectly, by promoting, guiding and even compelling interaction.

NOTES

* This chapter is a slightly modified version of Brunnée (2018). It appears with the permission of Oxford University Press.
1. The first two paragraphs draw on Brunnée (2007).
2. See also Benvenisti (2013) positioning his trusteeship concept between statist and globalist approaches and emphasizing that it does not presuppose the existence of an 'international community' (pp. 300–301).
3. For a comprehensive analysis, see Paulus (2001).
4. See *Gabčíkovo-Nagymaros* case (Separate Opinion of Judge Weeramantry).
5. See here Japan's whaling practice, which was challenged by Australia in *Whaling in the Antarctic (Australia v. Japan: New Zealand Intervening)* (Judgment) [2014] ICJ Rep 226.
6. In *Whaling in the Antarctic (Australia v. Japan: New Zealand Intervening)* (Judgment) [2014] ICJ Rep 226 Australia and New Zealand, as parties to the International Convention for the Regulating of Whaling were able to act in the common interest of all treaty parties. See *Whaling in the Antarctic (Australia v. Japan: New Zealand Intervening)* ICJ Pleadings, CR/2013/18: p. 34: para. 20 (Boisson de Chazournes).
7. For a brief overview, see Dupuy and Viñuales (2015).
8. See generally Brunnée (2011) and Gehring (2007).
9. See *Island of Palmas (Netherlands v. United States of America)* (1928) 2 RIAA 829 holding that '[t]erritorial sovereignty . . . has as corollary a duty: the obligation to protect within the territory the rights of other States, in particular their right to integrity and inviolability . . .' (p. 839).
10. The ICJ's 'sequenced' approach mirrors that outlined by the International Law Commission (2001b: Articles 7–8). See also International Law Association (2014), Principles 7A, and 7B and commentary.
11. For the same reading, see *Responsibilities in the Area*, p. 51.
12. For a similar assessment, concerning the *Pulp Mills* case, see McIntyre (2010: p. 490).
13. See also *Pulp Mills*: p. 120; Birnie et al. (2009) noting that the no harm rule is 'an obligation to prevent or minimize as far as possible the risk of significant harm, not merely a basis for reparation after the event' (p. 143). And see *Southern Bluefin Tuna Cases (New Zealand v. Japan; Australia v. Japan), Provisional Measures (Separate Opinion of Judge Treves, Order of 27 August 1999)*, ITLOS Reports 1999, p. 2. But see also Knox (2002).
14. See *Pulp Mills*: pp. 77, 79–80 on adoption of appropriate rules and measures, vigilance in their enforcement, and exercise of administrative control over public and private operators.
15. Under Czech law, any state whose territory could suffer significant environmental impacts due to a project may participate in the EIA process. See Greenpeace (2010).
16. See, for example, Pedersen (2014); Lowe (2000).
17. For example, that is the conclusion of the ILC's Drafting Committee on the Protection of the Atmosphere with respect to the notion of 'common concern'. See International Law Commission (2015) noting that the committee opted instead to describe the protection of the atmosphere as a 'pressing concern of the international community as a whole' (p. 10).
18. But see also *Barcelona Traction, Light and Power Company, Ltd. (Belgium v. Spain)* (Judgment) [1970] ICJ Rep 3: p. 47 requiring a concrete treaty mechanism to provide standing.
19. For an overview see Brunnée (2018).
20. On the Draft Articles, see Brunnée (2005: pp. 33–5).
21. Australia, in a parallel case, did not frame its claim explicitly in terms of the rights of all members of the international community. It did, however, argue that the French tests would infringe the freedom of the high seas. See *Nuclear Tests* case, p. 103.
22. See the Prunéřov II episode, discussed above; and see Jacobs (2005).
23. See Birnie et al. (2009).

24. See, for example, International Law Association (2014), Principles 7A and 7B and Commentary.
25. In both decisions, the ICJ noted that 'in the field of environmental protection, vigilance and prevention are required on account of the often irreversible character of damage and of the limitations inherent in the very mechanism of reparation of this type of damage' (*Gabčíkovo-Nagymaros* case (Separate Opinion of Judge Weeramantry): p. 77; *Pulp Mills*: p. 66).
26. But see *Costa Rica v. Nicaragua/ Nicaragua v. Costa Rica* (Separate Opinon of Judge Dugard): p. 3.
27. See United Nations (1992a; 1992c).
28. One tangible effect of the treaty-based development of harm prevention duties and collective concern concepts is their translation from emerging *erga omnes* obligations into concrete obligations *erga omnes partes.* See Brunnée (2005: p. 43).
29. For in-depth analysis see Bodansky et al. (2017: pp. 219–28).
30. Krasner (1982) provides a still influential, general definition of regimes that is salient also in the context of community interests.
31. See, for example, Vienna Convention (1985), Article 3 (Research and Systematic Observation) and Article 5 (Transmission of Information).
32. See also Brunnée and Toope (2010: pp. 146–51), tracing the meandering path towards agreement on the temperature goal.
33. See range of procedural duties set out in International Law Commission (2001b).
34. See also van Aaken (2014), exploring the benefits of opt-out mechanisms and other treaty design features across issue areas.
35. Whereas the Kyoto Protocol subjected only a small number of parties accounting for a small share of global emission to reduction commitments, as of 4 February 2016, the Paris Outcome had generated NDCs representing 188 countries and accounting for close to 98.7 per cent of global carbon emissions. See World Resources Institute (n.d.).
36. This shift has been characterized by some as a move to 'orchestration' rather than regulation (Vihma and van Asselt, 2012: p. 7).
37. See *Gabčíkovo-Nagymaros* case (Separate Opinion of Judge Weeramantry), pointing to the additional problems that flow from the fact that the court's procedures, focused as they are upon disputes between specific state parties, are ill-suited to doing 'justice to rights and obligations of an *erga omnes* character' (p. 117). And see, generally, Fuller (1978).
38. *Whaling in the Antarctic (Australia v. Japan: New Zealand Intervening)* ICJ, Pleadings, CR/2013/18, p. 28: para. 19 (Burmester).
39. See para. 1 (emphasis added).
40. See para. VI.1.
41. Yet, states may be required to inform the public likely to be affected by a potential transboundary impact and provide equal access to administrative and judicial procedures.See International Law Commission (2001a), Articles 13 and 15.
42. On the challenges, see Brunnée and Hey (2013: pp. 35–6).
43. See also Reeve (2014: pp. 68–9).
44. See para. VIII.4.
45. Ibid., para. IX.2.
46. Ibid., para. VIII.7.
47. See, for example, World Resources Institute (n.d.) and CAT Consortium (2009).

REFERENCES

Allott, P. (1990) *Eunomia: New Order for a New World.* Oxford, Oxford University Press.

Barrett, S. (2016) Collective Action to Avoid Catastrophe: When Countries Succeed, When They Fail, and Why. *Global Policy*, **7** (1), 45–55.

Benvenisti, E. (2013) Sovereigns as Trustees of Humanity: On the Accountability of States to Foreign Stakeholders. *American Journal of International Law*, **107** (2), 295–333.

Birnie, P., Boyle, A. and Redgwell, C. (2009) *International Law and the Environment*, 3rd edn, Oxford, Oxford University Press.

Bodansky, D., Brunnée J. and Hey, E. (2007) International Environmental Law: Mapping the Field. In: Bodansky, D., Brunnée J. and Hey, E. (eds) *The Oxford Handbook of International Environmental Law*. Oxford, Oxford University Press, pp. 1–25.

Bodansky, D., Brunnée, J. and Rajamani, L. (2017) *International Climate Change Law*. Oxford, Oxford University Press.

Boyle, A. (1991) Saving the World? Implementation and Enforcement of International Environmental Law through International Institutions. *Journal of Environmental Law*, **3** (2), 229–45.

Brunnée, J. (2002) COPing with Consent: Lawmaking under Multilateral Environmental Agreements. *Leiden Journal of International Law*, **15** (1), 1–52.

Brunnée, J. (2005) International Legal Accountability through the Lens of the Law of State Responsibility. *Netherlands Yearbook of International Law*, **26**, 21–56.

Brunnée, J. (2007) Common Areas, Common Heritage and Common Concern. In: Bodansky, D., Brunnée J. and Hey, E. (eds) *The Oxford Handbook of International Environmental Law*. Oxford, Oxford University Press, pp. 550–73.

Brunnée, J. (2011) Multilateral Environmental Agreements. In: *Max-Planck Encyclopedia of Public International Law*. Oxford, Oxford University Press.

Brunnée, J. (2018) International Environmental Law and Community Interests: Procedural Aspects. In: Benvenisti, E. and Nolte, G. (eds) *Community Interests across International Law*. Oxford, Oxford University Press.

Brunnée, J. and Hey, E. (2013) Transparency and International Environmental Institutions. In: Bianchi, A. and Peters, A. (eds) *Transparency in International Law*. Cambridge, Cambridge University Press, pp. 23–48.

Brunnée, J. and Toope, S. (2010) *Legitimacy and Legality in International Law: An Interactional Account*. Cambridge, Cambridge University Press.

CAT Consortium (2009) *Climate Action Tracker*. [Online] Available from: http://climateactiontracker.org/ (accessed 19 February 2016).

Churchill, R. and Ulfstein, G. (2000) Autonomous Institutional Arrangements in Multilateral Environmental Agreements: A Little-noticed Phenomenon in International Law. *American Journal of International Law*, **94** (4), 623–59.

Dupuy, P. and Viñuales, J. (2015) *International Environmental Law*. Cambridge, Cambridge University Press.

Fitzmaurice, M. (2015) *Whaling and International Law*. Cambridge, Cambridge University Press.

French, D. (2018) Trail Smelter (United States of America/Canada) (1938 and 1941). In: Bjorge, E. and Miles, C. (eds) *Landmark Cases in Public International Law*. Oxford, Hart Publishing, pp. 159–88.

Friedmann, W. (1964) *The Changing Structure of International Law*. New York, Columbia University Press.

Fuller, L. (1978) Forms and Limits of Adjudication. *Harvard Law Review*, **92** (2), 353–409.

Gehring, T. (2007) Treaty-making and Evolution. In: Bodansky, D., Brunnée J. and

Hey, E. (eds) *The Oxford Handbook of International Environmental Law*. Oxford, Oxford University Press, pp. 467–97.
Greenpeace (2010) *Legal Steps Taken by the Federated States of Micronesia against the Pruněřov II Coal-fired Power Plant, Czech Republic.* [Online] Available from: http://www.greenpeace.org/international/Global/international/planet-2/report/2010/3/teia_fsm.pdf (accessed 9 February 2016).
Hey, E. (2003) *Teaching International Law: State-consent as Consent to a Process of Normative Development and Ensuing Problems*. The Hague, Kluwer Academic.
International Law Association (2014) *Legal Principles Relating to Climate Change*. [Online] Available from: http://www.ila-hq.org/en/committees/index.cfm/cid/1029 (accessed 17 November 2017).
International Law Commission (ILC) (2001a) Draft Articles on Responsibility of States for Internationally Wrongful Acts. *Yearbook of the International Law Commission*, **2** (2), 26.
International Law Commission (ILC) (2001b) International Liability for Injurious Consequences Arising out of Acts Not Prohibited by International Law (Prevention of Transboundary Harm from Hazardous Activities). *Yearbook of the International Law Commission*, **2** (2), 144.
International Law Commission (ILC) (2015) *Statement of the Chairman*. [Online] Available from: http://legal.un.org/docs/?path=../ilc/documentation/english/statements/2015_dc_chairman_statement_atmosphere.pdf&lang=EF (accessed 2 November 2015).
International Union for Conservation of Nature (1973) Convention on International Trade in Endangered Species of Wild Fauna and Flora. Washington, DC, 3 March 1973. United Nations Treaty Series, 993 (243).
International Whaling Commission (1946) International Convention for the Regulation of Whaling. Washington, DC, 2 December 1946. United Nations Treaty Series, 161 (72).
Jacobs, R. (2005) Treading Deep Waters: Substantive Law Issues in Tuvalu's Threat to Sue the United States in the International Court of Justice. *Pacific Rim Law and Policy Journal*, **14** (1), 103–28.
Knox, J. (2002) The Myth and Reality of Transboundary Environmental Impact Assessment. *American Journal of International Law*, **96** (2), 291–319.
Krasner, S. (1982) Structural Causes and Consequences: Regimes as Intervening Variables. *International Organization*, **36** (2), 185–205.
Lefeber, R. (2012) Climate Change and State Responsibility. In: Rayfuse, R. and Scott, S. (eds) *International Law in the Era of Climate Change*. Cheltenham, UK, and Northampton, MA, USA, Edward Elgar, pp. 321–49.
Lopes, P. (2010) FSM v, Czech: A New 'Standing' for Climate Change. *Climate Law Reporter*, **10** (2), 24. [Online] Available from: http://digitalcommons.wcl.american.edu/cgi/viewcontent.cgi?article=1029&context=sdlp (accessed 9 February 2016).
Lowe, V. (2000) Sustainable Development and Unsustainable Arguments. In: Boyle, A. and Freestone, D. (eds) *International Law and Sustainable Development*. Oxford, Oxford University Press, pp. 19–38.
Malkin, B. (24 May 2011) Micronesia Mounts Unprecedented Legal Challenge over Czech Power Station. *The Telegraph*. [Online] Available from: http://www.telegraph.co.uk/earth/environment/climatechange/8532796/Micronesia-mounts-unprecedented-legal-challenge-over-Czech-power-station.html (accessed 9 February 2016).

McIntyre, O. (2010) The Proceduralization and Growing Maturity of International Water Law: Case Concerning Pulp Mills on the River Uruguay (Argentina v Uruguay), International Court of Justice, 20 April 2010. *Journal of Environmental Law*, **22** (3), 475–97.

Palmer, G. (1992) New Ways to Make International Environmental Law. *American Journal of International Law*, **86** (2), 259–83.

Paulus, A. (2001) *Die Internationale Gemeinschaft im Völkerrecht.* Munich, Verlag C.H. Beck.

Pauwelyn, J., Wessel, R. and Wouters, J. (2014) When Structures Become Shackles: Stagnation and Dynamics in International Lawmaking. *European Journal of International Law*, **25** (3), 733–64.

Pedersen, O. (2014) From Abundance to Indeterminacy: The Precautionary Principle and Its Two Camps of Custom. *Transnational Environmental Law*, **3** (2), 323–39.

Reeve, R. (2014) *Policing International Trade in Endangered Species: The CITES Treaty and Compliance*. London, Routledge.

Simma, B. (1994) From Bilateralism to Community Interest in International Law. *Recueil des Cours de l'Academie de Droit International de la Haye*, 250, 217.

Ulfstein, G. (2007) Treaty Bodies. In: Bodansky, D., Brunnée J. and Hey, E. (eds) *The Oxford Handbook of International Environmental Law*. Oxford, Oxford University Press, pp. 877–89.

UN Department of Public Information (2012) Press Conference on Request for International Court of Justice Advisory Opinion on Climate Change. 3 February 2012. [Online] Available from: http://www.un.org/News/briefings/docs/2012/120203_ICJ.doc.htm (accessed 17 November 2017).

UN News Centre (2011) Palau seeks UN World Court Opinion on Damage Caused by Greenhouse Gases. [Online] Available from: http://www.un.org/apps/news/story.asp?NewsID=39710&Cr=pacific+island&Cr1#.UbtgAr5zYeg (accessed 17 November 2017).

UNESCO (1971) Convention on Wetlands of International Importance especially as Waterfront Habitat. Ramsar, 2 February 1971. United Nations Treaty Series, 1976 (245).

United Nations (1945) Statute of the International Court of Justice. San Francisco, 18 April 1946. United Nations Treaty Series, 33 (933).

United Nations (1972) Stockholm Declaration of the United Nations Conference on the Human Environment. Stockholm, 16 June 1972. International Legal Materials, 1416 (11).

United Nations (1982a) United Nations Convention on the Law of the Sea. Montego Bay, 10 December 1982. United Nations Treaty Series, 1833 (397).

United Nations (1982b) Statute of the International Tribunal for the Law of the Sea. Montego Bay, 10 December 1982. United Nations Treaty Series, 1833 (3).

United Nations (1985) Vienna Convention for the Protection of the Ozone Layer. Vienna, 22 March 1985. United Nations Treaty Series, 1513 (293).

United Nations (1992a) United Nations Framework Convention on Climate Change. New York, 4 June 1992. United Nations Treaty Series, 1771 (107).

United Nations (1992b) Rio Declaration on Environment and Development. Rio de Janeiro, 3–14 June 1992. International Legal Materials, 31 (874).

United Nations (1992c) Convention on Biological Diversity. Rio de Janeiro, 5 June 1992. United Nations Treaty Series, 1760 (79).

United Nations (1997) Kyoto Protocol to the United Nations Framework

Convention on Climate Change. Kyoto, 10 December 1997. International Legal Materials, 37 (22).

United Nations (2002) Decision 24/CP.7 of the Conference of the Parties to the United Nations Convention on Climate Change. Procedures and Mechanisms Relating to Compliance under the Kyoto Protocol. 21 January 2002, UN Doc. FCCC/CP/2001/13/Add.3.

United Nations (2015a) The Paris Agreement. Paris, 12 December 2015, UN Doc. FCCC/CP/2015/L.9.

United Nations (2015b) Decision 1/CP.21 of the Conference of the Parties to the United Nations Convention on Climate Change. Adoption of the Paris Agreement. 29 January 2016, UN Doc. FCCC/CP/2015/10/Add. 1.

United Nations Economic Commission for Europe (UNECE) (1991) Convention on Environmental Impact Assessment in a Transboundary Context. Espoo, 25 February 1991. United Nations Treaty Series, 1989 (309).

United Nations Economic Commission for Europe (UNECE) (1998) Aarhus Convention on Access to Information, Public Participation in Decision-making and Access to Justice in Environmental Matters. Aarhus, 25 June 1998. United Nations Treaty Series, 2161 (447).

United Nations Environment Programme (1987) Montreal Protocol on Substances that Deplete the Ozone Layer. Montreal, 14–16 September 1987. United Nations Treaty Series, 1522 (3).

United Nations Environment Programme (1998) Annex II: Non-compliance Procedure. *Report of the Tenth Meeting of the Parties to the Montreal protocol on Substances that Deplete the Ozone Layer.* Montreal, United Nations Environment Programme.

van Aaken, A. (2014) Behavioral Law and Economics. *Harvard International Law Journal*, **55** (2), 421–82.

Vihma, A. and van Asselt, H. (2012) Great Expectations: Understanding Why the UN Climate Talks Seem to Fail. Finnish Institute of International Affairs. Report Number 109. [Online] Available from: http://www.fiia.fi/en/publication/270/great_expectations/ (accessed 8 April 2016).

World Resources Institute (WRI) (n.d.) *Climate Data Explorer*. [Online] Available from: http://cait.wri.org/indc/ (accessed 17 November 2017).

Cases

Barcelona Traction, Light and Power Company, Ltd. (Belgium v. Spain) (Judgment) [1970] ICJ Rep 3.

Certain Activities carried out by Nicaragua in the Border Area (Costa Rica v. Nicaragua) and *Construction of a Road in Costa Rica along the San Juan River (Nicaragua v. Costa Rica)* (Judgment) [2015] ICJ Rep 665.

Gabčíkovo-Nagymaros Project (*Hungary v. Slovakia*) (Judgment) [1997] ICJ Rep 7.

Island of Palmas (Netherlands v. United States of America) (1928) 2 RIAA 829.

Legality of the Threat or Use of Nuclear Weapons (Advisory Opinion) [1996] ICJ Rep 226.

Nuclear Tests (Australia v. France) (Interim Measures) [1973] ICJ Rep 99.

Nuclear Tests (Australia v. France) (Judgment) [1974] ICJ Rep 253.

Nuclear Tests (*New Zealand v. France*) case (Interim Measures) [1973] ICJ Rep 135.

Pulp Mills on the River Uruguay (Argentina v. Uruguay) (Judgment) [2010] ICJ Rep 14.
Responsibilities and Obligations of States Sponsoring Persons and Entities with Respect to Activities in the Area (Advisory Opinion, Order of 1 February 2011), ITLOS Reports 2011, 10.
Southern Bluefin Tuna Cases (New Zealand v. Japan; Australia v. Japan), Provisional Measures (Separate Opinion of Judge Treves, Order of 27 August 1999), ITLOS Reports 1999.
Whaling in the Antarctic (Australia v. Japan: New Zealand Intervening) (Judgment) [2014] ICJ Rep 226.

14. Conclusion: is the governance of the commons a model for a new global governance?

Martin Deleixhe

1. BACKGROUND

The immediate aftermath of the end of the Cold War sparked a new cosmopolitan enthusiasm for common goods, such as the environment, public health or knowledge, to be governed cooperatively by a wide array of actors on the international scene. There was a palpable sense of urgency and a keen desire to seize this opportunity to design a worldwide institutional framework capable of managing sustainably the goods vital to the future of mankind. But beyond this minimalistic consensus, there was no further political agreement. How was this global governance to be designed? What goods should be subjected to it? Who should participate and how? The ambition of this book has been to tackle those questions in some detail and to explicate on a normative, institutional and legal level what shape a global governance of those crucial goods could adopt.

The editors of this volume offer a captivating overview as well as a detailed scrutiny of an innovative model of governance that, in their view, could beneficially be transposed to the global stage and implemented on a different scale by international actors. This model of governance is associated with the commons, a specific type of community-level self-organization. Popularized by the trail-blazing work of Elinor Ostrom in the field of political economy, this model of governance recently took a more explicitly political tone. As Cogolati and Wouters expose in their introduction to this volume (Chapter 1), commons exist only insofar as they are sustained through 'commoning' practices, that is horizontal and self-determined cooperative practices and norms that compel virtually all community members. The governance of the commons is thus in itself a highly peculiar model of governance, whose legitimacy relies strongly on its proto-democratic character (Deleixhe, 2018). For the co-participants to the commoning practices are also its co-deciders, thus providing the collective of the stakeholders with a decision-making process to determine their preferences in terms of collective policies.

I would like in the conclusion to this stimulating volume to argue that the political principle underlying the commons resonates with the emerging global governance and offers an innovative political model to reform and regulate international interactions. For commons are intrinsically associated with a polycentric logic of *governance*, involving all stakeholders in the definition of the practices to be adopted to manage them sustainably. To substantiate this claim, I will proceed in three steps. I will first emphasize that the commons should not be associated narrowly with a certain type of goods but rather deserve to be treated as a ground-breaking model of governance. I will then highlight that the type of governance provided by the principle of the common bears some striking similarities with the concept of global governance as it was introduced in the academic and political debate in the 1990s. Finally, to stress the originality and the added-value of the commons, I will contrast them with another contemporary model of governance advocated on the international stage, that is the model of global public goods (GPGs). I will stress that the latter reiterate a (slightly amended) logic of *government* on a different scale, including the recourse to a centralized authoritative power, whereas commons provide opportunities for a decentralized and proto-democratic global governance to arise.

2. THE COMMONS AS AN INNOVATIVE MODEL OF GOVERNANCE

The word 'commons' traditionally refers to resource domains available for joint use by community members. By extension, the term commons came to be used to refer to 'a resource to which no single decision-making holds exclusive title' (Wijkman, 1982: p. 512). Prior to the seminal work of Ostrom, it was widely admitted that their open access and the rivalrous nature of the goods they contained would lead to a collective action problem (Olson, 1965). As a result, only two distinct policies could be prescribed to ensure that long-term interests would prevail over immediate individual gains: either the invisible hand of the market or the Leviathan state (Ostrom, 1990: pp. 8–13). Elinor Ostrom convincingly showed that the pessimistic 'metaphoric model' of the prisoner dilemma was misleading. It rests on a mistaken construal of the commoners, which clearly does not tally with empirical facts. Through a careful scrutiny of numerous case studies in the Philippines, Switzerland, Japan and Spain, Ostrom argues that commons have existed and proven themselves sustainable over long periods of time (centuries in the case of the Andalusian irrigation system) (Ostrom, 1990: pp. 58–88). For commoners are social actors who communicate, observe social norms and judge their fellow members on the basis of their reputation (Ostrom, 1990: pp. 15–21). They understand that it is in their own best interest to build institutions that will create incentives for others to cooperate. Notably, they design monitoring and conflict-resolution mechanisms that foster mutual trust by preventing commoners from free-riding (Ostrom, 1990: p. 94). In sum, commoners have proven themselves capable of self-organization and autonomous government of the commons on which they depend for their subsistence (Ostrom, 1990: pp. 90–102).

Ostrom's originality lies partly in what we may call her constructivist/institutionalist turn. For she was the first author to clearly expose that commons were not just a pool of resources but depended on a coordinated governance. The collective institutions and social norms created by the community members are not just instrumental in sustaining the commons. In fact, they are *part of* the commons themselves. Commons are therefore not only a natural *thing* but also a *social construct*. Sauvêtre (Chapter 5 in this volume) makes forcefully this point. In his view, commons amount to the institutionalization of cooperative practices and can by no means be reduced to a resource domain to be managed. Hence his stark distinction between two politics of the commons in the Global South: *either* the affirmation of a social sovereignty *or* a developmentalist strategy to optimize the exploitation of resources without depleting them.

But Ostrom eventually appeared to shy away from her own conclusions. Instead of adhering to her rationale and considering that anything could become a commons *if it was governed as such*, Ostrom inconsistently argued that only certain goods, namely common-pool resources and the knowledge commons, should be collectively administered (Dardot and Laval, 2014: pp. 30–33). The 'reification of the commons' in Ostrom's work is condemned by critical commons scholars, such as Dardot and Laval. Firstly, it fails to explain why the initial movement of enclosures (that is the forced privatization of commons) had historically occurred (Dardot and Laval, 2014: pp. 30–33). If meadows and forests ceased to be governed as commons all over Europe in the sixteenth and seventeenth centuries, it was not because landlords suddenly realized that their naturally open layout could be altered to make them exclusive. Rather, it was due to a shift in the social relations between the gentry and the commoners (Meiksins Wood, 2002). Similarly, Susan Buck observes that open-access goods tend to be regarded as natural or global commons to be governed multilaterally (Antarctica, deep seabed, outer space and so on) only while there exists no technology that makes their exploitation profitable (Buck, 1998: p. 1).

Commons denote not a relation between a resource and a community, but a specific kind of relation between individuals who consider themselves to belong to a shared and constructed community. If no good is naturally common, it follows that goods must be instituted as commons; that is, they have to be *put in* common. Collective self-governance is not *part of* the commons, it is *constitutive* of the commons.

Cogolati and Wouters, following Dardot and Laval (see also the contribution of Dardot, Chapter 2 in this volume,), suggest calling this collaborative activity itself *the common* to radically distinguish it from its reified forms. The principle of the common invites us to 'introduce everywhere, in the most radical and most systematic fashion, the institutional form of self-government' (Dardot and Laval, 2014: p. 46). It contrasts radically with the two classical policy prescriptions, that is the recourse to market or to the state, in that it is not articulated as a property regime. It is not assumed that the political solution to the conundrum of having multiple owners making claims to a single pool of goods lies in clarifying the rightful owner (whether by distributing private property rights, turning the commons into a public good or even outlining what a common ownership of the good would potentially look like). For it struggles against any form of definite appropriation and intends to substitute the right of use for any claim to property. Hence only those that take an active part in the production of the commons are entitled to be co-participants in the decision-making process about its use. As a matter of fact, many social activists across the world united around the idea that 'the world was not for sale', that is, that not all goods were meant to be commodified, and that some areas of social life should remain governed through bottom-up initiatives, which would include resisting any top-down attempt to assign them a property regime.

Secondly, the common blurs the distinction between the social and the political. Empirical examples of commons, from region-wide irrigation systems to locally organized inshore fisheries and peer-to-peer data transfer, prove at once to be an efficient model of economic production – ensuring that a collective resource will not only be preserved but also proliferate in the long run for the greatest benefit of all – and to be instrumental in shaping self-governed communities. The *commoning* process creates autonomous social organizations that escape the classical dichotomy between private and public, and reshuffle the boundaries between the social and the political (Dardot and Laval, 2014: pp. 463–4). The radical demand of self-governance that underpins the principle of the common is as valid for small production schemes as it is at the level of the whole political community, where what is at stake is society's creation of itself (Castoriadis, 1999).

But commons are not only small, self-organized communities. Several of the resource domains on which mankind depends (the atmosphere, the high seas, Antarctica) are to be found on a global scale (Levin, 2006). And as things currently stand, they are in dire need of a governance framework (Clancy, 1998). Additionally, we can identify a new type of commons that, far from requiring to be used parsimoniously have on the contrary to be shared and used widely to prosper, such as the cultural or the knowledge commons (Frischmann et al., 2014). Along with new infrastructures of communication and innovative information technologies came the rise of decentralized, horizontal and egalitarian networks producing immaterial goods (Benkler, 2006). Here too open-access and non-rivalrous goods, though key tenets of the digital commons, are not a quintessential quality of the goods in question, for information can just as easily be turned into an exclusive commodity. The ownership regime of these goods can fall prey to IP regulation, copyrights and other patents generating financial rents out of a restrictive access to a piece of information (Boyle, 2008; Rifkin, 2000). What characterizes those ground-breaking cooperative practices is rather their governance regime, that is, their stubborn resistance to any form of centralizing authority (Galloway, 2004; Himanen, 2002) coupled with a rejection of the wage relationship typical of the labour market (Lessig, 2001). In her contribution to this volume, Beerkens (Chapter 9 in this volume) brings this peculiarity of the knowledge commons to the fore. In academic publishing, an oligopoly of commercial publishing corporations prevents the establishment of an open access to scientific knowledge and undermines the effort to replace this market-based distribution of knowledge by a self-governance of scientific knowledge by the academic community. At stake is an opposition between a restricted and monetized access to scientific knowledge and a universal scheme of knowledge exchange inside the scientific community.

Commons are therefore not only very diverse in nature but also potentially universal in scope. The self-organization that is quintessential to their model of governance can be found in large networks of actors. The efforts to coordinate action on the international scene to preserve or develop them have had some limited successes (for instance regarding the mitigation of climate change) but have otherwise remained at a very inchoate stage (Nordhaus, 1994). They nonetheless generated an exponentially growing literature on how to better design their principles of governance (Stern, 2011).

Any enthusiasm regarding the potentialities of the commons should thus be tampered by an important consideration, highlighting that scale is of the essence for those issues (Ostrom et al., 1999). The reason why small-scale commons have proven to be sustainable is because they relied on a community whose thick relationships allowed them to design self-governance schemes and curb anti-social behaviours. It remains to be seen whether the international community shares some of the features that are found at the local level and whether there is enough trust and reciprocity amongst its members to ensure a peaceful provision of global institutions designed to ensure compliance with its rules and social norms at an international level. Though it may appear a tall order, a substantial literature on global governance highlights some promising features of the post-Cold War international community.

3. A REAPPRAISAL OF THE NOTION OF GLOBAL GOVERNANCE

It has by now become a truism to say that global governance is a concept that has low informational value: '[Governance is] a ubiquitous "buzzword" which can mean anything or nothing' (Jessop, 1998: p. 30). Claiming that an activity belongs to the realm of governance tells us little about its actual processes and contents, the way in which the actors involved relate to each other, or the legal architecture framing its cooperation. As a consequence, the concept itself has often been criticized for the fuzziness of its boundaries. To some, it is now akin to an 'empty signifier' (Offe, 2009). In the words of Finkelstein: '"global governance" appears to be virtually anything' (1995: p. 368). But the concept remains, in spite of all criticism, widely used (Weiss, 2000).

The introduction of the concept of global governance in the scientific debate by James Rosenau did little to prevent its refraction into a myriad of related, but nonetheless different definitions. It pits governance against the older notion of government and, while admitting that both are concerned with the steering of human affairs, it comes to the conclusion that: 'Both refer to purposive behavior, to goal-oriented activities, to system of rules; but government suggests activities that are backed by formal authority . . . Governance . . . is a more encompassing phenomenon than government. It embraces governmental institutions but it also subsumes informal, non-governmental mechanisms' (Rosenau, 1992: p. 4). From this opposition between a centralized authority backed by coercive powers and a looser and more decentralized cooperation that involves a wide array of actors who willingly engage in a common network (see also the distinction which Christiaan Boonen draws in Chapter 4 of this volume between *power-over* and *power-with*), Rosenau draws the following principle: 'governance is a system of rule that works only if it is accepted by the majority (or, at least the most powerful of those it affects), whereas governments can function even in the face of widespread opposition to their policies' (Rosenau, 1992: p. 4). Since it relies on the consent of its participants, governance presupposes an element of *deliberate* cooperation. And when governance proves to be ineffective, the result is not *bad* governance but rather its absence, that is anarchy.

Since the world as a political system lacks an authoritative central power, all types of interactions that go beyond national boundaries could potentially be defined as global governance. But such an understanding runs the risk of watering down the concept and rendering it insignificant. In my view, it is therefore necessary to draw a few sharp distinctions if we want to isolate the peculiarity of governance (Risse, 2011). We need to resist the suggestion made by Rosenau that governance would encompass government. For the core state institutions, we should retain the term *government*. But on the other hand, governance implies a deliberate coordination overseen by multiple actors and is often embedded in institutional frameworks (that is, international organizations on the global stage), which sets it apart from the spontaneous interactions carried out by utility-maximizing actors in a free social space. In other words, market transactions and free social interactions should remain beyond the scope of governance. A last caveat should be added. Governance might be a cooperative activity, but this does not entail that it is friction-free. Imbalances of power remain one of its hallmarks (Barnett and Duvall, 2005), as well as an unequal distribution of its burdens and benefits (Strange, 1996). In this volume, Eimer (Chapter 8 in this volume) insists on this critical point. A well-orchestrated global governance may mitigate crude political pressures in asymmetrical relations of power. But in his view, it still fails to address the issue of *structural* power imbalances, that is power imbalances significant enough to be internalized by the relevant actors and to determine the negotiation context and outcomes, even in the absence of any threat or pressure. Boonen (Chapter 4 in this volume) goes one step further by indicating that any attempt to overcome this uneven distribution of power may generate violence, be it from dominant positions resisting any institutional evolution or from the actors trying to reverse the current status quo and this potential for violence cannot be ignored when thinking about the governance of the commons.

Furthermore, because of globalization and of the perceived democratic deficit in the functioning of international organizations, an additional development emerged that brought a new layer of complexity to the concept of global governance: a political discourse in support of global *democracy*. Now that the world was no longer divided into two political blocks relentlessly pitted against each other by their world views, global democracy was regarded not only as a desirable and idealistic horizon but also as a feasible prospect. Of course, opinions diverged wildly on whether the logics of democracy and global governance were mutually reinforcing or rather undermining each other. Likewise, views were split on whether there was any chance to ever bring democracy to function properly beyond its cradle: the nation state. The cosmopolitan enthusiasm that followed the fall of the Berlin wall would soon subside. But during approximatively a decade, the 1990s, it had become virtually impossible to relate global governance exclusively to a question of effectiveness. Global governance was expected to soon become robust enough to meet some democratic standards and prove its legitimacy.

And, for a while, global governance was indeed regarded as being positively correlated to democracy since it implied a shift away from the exclusive and sovereign authority of the states, resulting in a decentralization and horizontalization of decision-making. Many authors thus saw a bright future for a process of democratization expanding beyond the boundaries of the nation state (Habermas, 2001; Archibugi, 2004; Held, 2009). However, this belief in the democratizing force behind the shift toward governance seems lost in later articles. Soon, harsh critics, such as Mark Bevir and Chantal Mouffe, would describe the efforts to make global governance more inclusive as window-dressing and non-democratic in essence (Bevir, 2006). Others rather see a necessary trade-off between effectiveness and democracy (Scharpf, 1999). One would have to choose between a swift and efficient process of decision-making that may overlook some of the requirements of democracy and a democracy in the thick sense of the word that would inevitably prove to be slow and impractical at the international level.

What would nevertheless remain from those polemical exchanges is the fleeting vision of an international community that would no longer be satisfied with the mitigated chaos that so often characterizes its interactions and appears ripe to engage in a more self-conscious regulation of its practices.

4. THE MODEL OF GLOBAL PUBLIC GOODS

One example of such a model of self-governance on the global level was provided, with the support of the United Nations Development Programme (UNDP), by a group of renowned scholars who coined the term GPGs to express and frame the challenges urgently faced by the international community. Drawing a comparison with the literature on public goods at the level of the nation state, it was suggested that supreme international coordination was required to overcome the structural under provision of certain public goods on a global level. New governance instruments and methods were needed to bridge the gap between expectations and deliveries of public goods at the global level. The term has since then enjoyed a spectacular success and permeated much of the international policy discourse.

Academically, the concept of GPGs can be traced back to the pioneering work of Paul Samuelson grounded in neoclassical economics (1954). In his seminal article, Samuelson identifies the features that make a good public (that is its non-rivalry and non-excludability) and stresses that, if a good presents those traits, a free rider problem is likely to arise. For, if there is no way for the agent providing the good to exclude other agents from benefiting from it, how could he obtain some returns on its investment from it? The resulting situation is therefore a suboptimal one, in which the public good is not provided even though most of the agents desire it and would be willing to contribute (Sandler, 2001; Anand, 2004). The logical way out of this conundrum is that a legitimate third party with coercive means at its disposal must produce and distribute this public good. For only an authoritative entity can collect a financial contribution of all the beneficiaries. In a domestic economy, the most likely candidate to shoulder that responsibility is the sovereign state. Public goods are, in this sense, market failures that ought to be corrected by a state-like authority.

Attempts have been made by a network of researchers closely associated with the UNDP and led by Inge Kaul to transpose this rationale onto the global scene (Kaul et al., 1999; Kaul et al., 2003; Kaul and Conceiçao, 2006). If markets fail to provide public goods at the national level, there is no reason to assume that they would fare any better at the international level. But the situation is further complicated by a structural difference: there is no state-like entity to appeal to on the international stage (Kindleberger, 1986). No single actor is powerful or legitimate enough to compel other agents to contribute and cooperate. Therefore, it is up to a coalition of actors to step into the state's shoes and coordinate themselves through governance mechanisms and international law to ensure the provision of the public good in question (Schaffer, 2012).

But while both GPGs and commons came to refer to some implicit models of global governance, the similarities stop here. Although the two approaches touch on the issue of the shortcomings of collective action, include a global dimension, and overlap partly with regard to the goods to which they apply, they put an emphasis on different policy instruments, advocate distinct governance mechanisms and carry a different set of political, economic and legal implications. Crucially, they put forward contrasting views on the role of the state, multilateral organizations (in particular the United Nations) and international law in providing GPGs and preserving the global commons.

Contrast the respective assessments of the relation between the law of the commons and international law to provide GPGs offered by Groff and Karlsson-Vinkhuyzen (Chapter 7 in this volume), Mattei (Chapter 10 in this volume), De Schutter (Chapter 11 in this volume), Cogolati and Wouters (Chapter 12 in this volume), and Brunnée (Chapter 13 in this volume). While Groff and Karlsson-Vinkhuyzen (Chapter 7) see the international rule of law as *the* primordial GPG supporting and making possible the global governance of the commons, Mattei (Chapter 10) argues from a deep-ecological point of view that international law is part of the problem, and certainly not part of the solution, calling for a strict return to local, community-level governance. The four remaining scholars adopt a somewhat more nuanced position on this relationship. De Schutter (Chapter 11) looks at the historical dynamic of the relationship between commons and international law and concludes that, though this relationship started on the wrong foot since international law was tasked with the legitimation of exploitative practices in the colonial world, this historical injustice can be redressed by a practice of international law that puts human rights at its core. Cogolati and Wouters (Chapter 12) argue in the same vein that innovative legal instruments already provide juridical resources to protect and preserve commons in the Global South, such as the right to natural resources or some elements of the rights of indigenous peoples and peasants. Brunnée (Chapter 13) stresses that, in assessing the relation between international law and the governance of global commons, one should not only consider the content of the relevant legal instrument but also pay attention to the effects of its procedural requirements.

In contrast, while the governance of the commons cannot be dissociated from bottom-up management practices and relies on a decentralized decision-making process that turns the community of the stakeholders into masters of their own fates, the governance of public goods presupposes a high degree of centralization of the decision-making process and calls for the creation of a towering authority tasked with the monitoring of the compliance of all actors. This distinction is highlighted and further substantiated by several contributions to the book. Dardot (Chapter 2 in this volume) is keen to point out that, since the governance of the commons is rooted in local cooperative practices, the most appropriate institutional design to govern the commons is a non-centred federalism. Approaching the same issue from the viewpoint of political economy, Hagen and Crombez (Chapter 6 in this volume) reach a surprisingly similar conclusion. To be both efficient and legitimate, global governance of commons should not strive for the integration of its different international regimes into a single scheme but rather improve their interconnectedness and increase their overlap, thus creating a tightly-knit polycentric governance. This claim prompts Brando and De Schutter (Chapter 3 in this volume) to express their scepticism as to whether such a governance would still qualify as 'federal'. Since the emphasis is firmly laid on a decentralized distribution of the competences, would such a model not be better described as 'confederal'? And in this case, would it have the resources to promote shared rules across its subcomponents?

The parallel with the analytical distinction between governance and government is striking. Commons, just as governance, depend on a decentralized scheme of cooperation and cannot operate if the stakeholders do not consent to the social rules they must observe (or because they are nudged into adopting a social behaviour to enhance their reputation) whereas GPGs respond to a logic of government, since they require a strong and centralized authority (the United Nations is the usual suspect in the literature to fulfil this role) to escape the collective action dilemmas leading to their under-provision. Bearing this in mind, the governance of the commons seems to offer a more promising model for an effective and legitimate global governance than the governance of GPGs. Not that the latter cannot be effective, but its organizational mode is closer to an inchoate world-state than to a polycentric federalism.

REFERENCES

Anand, P. B. (2004) Financing the Provision of Global Public Goods, *The World Economy*, **27** (2), 215–37.

Archibugi, D. (2004) Cosmopolitan Democracy and its Critics, *European Journal of International Relations*, **10** (3), 437–73.

Barnett M. and Duvall, R. (eds) (2005) *Power in Global Governance*. Cambridge, Cambridge University Press.

Benkler, Y. (2006) *The Wealth of Networks: How Social Production Transforms Markets and Freedom*. New Haven, Yale University Press.

Bevir, M. (2006) Democratic Governance: Systems and Radical Perspectives. *Public Administration Review*, **66** (3), 426–36.

Boyle, J. (2008) *The Public Domain: Enclosing the Commons of the Mind*. New Haven, Yale University Press.

Buck, S., (1998) *The Global Commons: An Introduction*. Washington, DC, Island Press.

Castoriadis, C. (1999) *L'institution imaginaire de la société*. Paris, Seuil.

Clancy, E. A. (1998) The Tragedy of the Global Commons. *Indiana Journal of Global Legal Studies*, **5** (2), 601–19.

Dardot, P. and Laval, C. (2014) *Commun: Essai sur la révolution au XXIe siècle*. Paris, La Découverte.

Deleixhe, M. (2018) Conflicts in (the) Common(s)? Radical Democracy and the Governance of the Commons. *Thesis Eleven*, **144** (1), 59–79.
Finkelstein, L. S. (1995) What is Global Governance? *Global Governance*, **1** (3), 367–72.
Frischmann, B., Madison, M. and Strandburg, K. (eds) (2014) *Governing Knowledge Commons*. Oxford, Oxford University Press.
Galloway, A. (2004) *Protocol: How Control Exists after Decentralization.* Cambridge, MIT Press.
Habermas, J. (2001) *The Postnational Constellation: Political Essays*. Cambridge, Polity Press.
Held, D. (2009) Restructuring Global Governance: Cosmopolitanism, Democracy and the Global Order. *Millennium: Journal of International Studies*, **37** (3), 535–47.
Himanen, P. (2002) *The Hacker Ethic and the Spirit of the Information Age*. New York, Random House.
Jessop, B. (1998) The Rise of Governance and the Risk of Failure: The Case of Economic Development. *International Social Science Journal*, **50** (155), 29–45.
Kaul, I. and Conceiçao, P. (2006) *The New Public Finance: Responding to Global Challenges*. New York, Oxford University Press.
Kaul, I., Grunberg, I. and Stern, M. A. (eds) (1999) *Global Public Goods: International Cooperation in the 21st Century*. New York, Oxford University Press.
Kaul, I., Conceiçao, P., Le Goulven, K. and Mendoza, R. U. (2003) *Providing Global Public Goods: Managing Globalization*. New York, Oxford University Press.
Kindleberger, C. P. (1986) International Public Goods without International Government. *The American Economic Review*, **76** (1), 1–13.
Lessig, L. (2001) *The Future of Ideas: The Fate of the Commons in a Connected World*. New York, Random House.
Levin, S. (2006) Learning to Live in a Global Commons: Socioeconomic Challenges for a Sustainable Environment. *Ecological Research*, **21** (3), 328–33.
Meiksins Wood, E. (2002) *The Origin of Capitalism: A Longer View*. London, Verso.
Nordhaus, W. (1994) *Managing the Global Commons: The Economics of Climate Change.* Cambridge, MIT Press.
Offe, C. (2009) Governance: An 'Empty Signifier'? *Constellations*, **16** (4), 550–62.
Olson, M. (1965) *The Logic of Collective Action: Public Goods and the Theory of Groups*. Cambridge, Harvard University Press.
Ostrom, E. (1990) *Governing the Commons: The Evolution of Institutions for Collective Action*. Cambridge, Cambridge University Press.
Ostrom, E., Burger, J., Field, C. B., Norgaard, R. B. and Policansky, D. (1999) Revisiting the Commons: Local Lessons, Global Challenges. *Science*, **284** (5412), 278–82.
Risse, T. (ed.) (2011), *Governance without a State: Policies and Politics in Areas of Limited Statehood.* New York, Columbia University Press.
Rifkin, J. (2000) *The Age of Access: The New Culture of Hypercapitalism, Where all of Life is a Paid-for Experience*. New York, Tarcher/Putnam.
Rosenau, J. (1992) Governance, Order and Change in World Politics. In: Rosenau, J. N. and Czempiel, E.-O. (eds) *Governance without Government: Order and Change in World Politics*. Cambridge, Cambridge University Press, pp. 1–29.

Samuelson, P. (1954) The Pure Theory of Public Expenditure. *The Review of Economics and Statistics*, **36** (4), 387–9.

Sandler, T. (2001) *On Financing Global and International Public Goods*. Washington, DC, World Bank.

Schaffer, G. (2012) International Law and Global Public Goods in a Legal Pluralist World. *European Journal of International Law*, **23** (3), 669–93.

Scharpf, F. W. (1999) *Governing in Europe: Effective and Democratic?* Oxford, Oxford University Press.

Stern, P. C. (2011) Design Principles for Global Commons: Natural Resources and Emerging Technologies. *International Journal of the Commons*, **5** (2), 213–32.

Strange, S. (1996) *The Retreat of the State: The Diffusion of Power in World Economy*. Cambridge, Cambridge University Press.

Weiss, T. G. (2000) Governance, Good Governance, and Global Governance: Conceptual and Actual Challenges. *Third World Quarterly*, **21** (5), 795–814.

Wijkman, M. (1982) Managing the Global Commons. *International Organization*, **36** (3), 511–36.

Afterword

Tine De Moor

What this book adds to the currently thriving field of commons-studies is first and foremost its explicit recognition of various approaches to commons as objects of study and practices of governance. Until approximately 2005, the study of commons was based nearly exclusively on extensive empirical, analysis-based research, with many theoretical 'spin-offs' based on that research and often in line with Ostrom's fundamental work, and delivered by researchers from a very wide range of disciplines, from history, sociology and law to natural resource management and biodiversity students. Over the past decade we have, however, seen the emergence of a more normative approach to commons, which is closely knit to more ideological interpretations, and the implications thereof in practice. The latter builds on current citizens' movements but also revives older sentiments about collective ownership, management and use of resources. And confronts the world of commons-researchers with a need to consider more deeply so far at times neglected factors, such as power-relationships, fair distribution of goods, and the wider societal implications of the choice for a particular type of resource governance. Though a broader, multi-faceted approach should be applauded and demonstrates that the field of commons-studies is permeating all corners of academic research and even beyond, this book also reminds us that there is still a relatively wide gap between various approaches to commons as governance models, regardless of the disciplines those approaches are linked to. In fact, even though this book brings together various but still relatively close disciplines – all from social sciences (economists, political scientists and lawyers) and humanities (political philosophers) – they demonstrate that there is still ample ground for debate on how to perceive the commons and their implications.

The topic of global resource governance, central to this book, is probably the most difficult angle to bridge several sides of the debate, but at the same time also the most obvious one: what binds those interested in commons together is a fundamental belief in the capacities of self-governance and collective action by citizens with the purpose of solving current major societal problems. The 'gap' we still find today consists of two parts: on the one hand the normative approach is capable of delivering rather abstract scenarios as solutions to major societal problems, but lacks the empirical, systematic study of – so far relatively few – examples of supra-national governance regimes based on self-governance and collective action. On the other hand, the more analytic approach offers results based on systematic analysis of local commons, but has so far undertaken little effort to translate these into new governance models that could tackle the global resource crisis and other challenges that go with it. The overarching goal of this book matches the need to find out how to upscale what we know about commons, supported by empirical research often based on the study of very local, small-scale forms of commons, to a much higher, global resource level.

One of the first steps in achieving this ambitious goal, is to conquer the Tower of Babel and understand each other better, quite literally. This book shows us the wide variety of usage of the term 'commons', with rather different interpretations of the commoners a 1,000 years back, who referred to their collectively owned and managed grazing pastures, and those of political activists today. Juxtaposing the different meanings that are given today, as is exemplified throughout this book, makes it easier for all those interested in the commons to communicate among each other. But there is more. In times when effects of human behaviour on resources seem to be even larger than forecasted, in domains such as biodiversity, global warming and resource depletion, such a renewed attention to governance models is absolutely vital. In between the application of innovative and potentially problem-solving technologies – ranging from realistic tools such as electric cars to hacking-the-planet-ideas, such as moving to Mars – and an actual profound change in human behaviour stand institutions. The governance model that we as humans choose to govern our global resources, and with it its rules and norms that build the institutions, deserves much more attention from policy makers as it decides upon the potential success and failure of how and by whom our resources – depletable and renewable – are managed and distributed, regardless of the technologies at hand to aid us in our endeavours. Normative approaches to governance regimes remind us of the difficulties to reach consensus over the 'right' ways of using, dividing, managing and saving the resources we have together, on a global scale and the policies that should support the choices that are made.

The insights provided in this book based on research by 'commons-thinkers' will not just make it easier to connect to 'commons-analysts but also to the 'commons-doers', who are demanding a better understanding of what they are actually putting into practice on a daily basis. The ideas provided in this book are inspired by and thrive on the current renewed interest for commons as an alternative governance model, with many local new collectivities popping up across the developed world, whilst also generating renewed interest in the historical commons and commons currently still existing in developing countries. The next step is now to further enrich that essential interaction between science and society, with new ideas and new empirical evidence of commons as an alternative governance model.

Index